Praise for Dan Balz and C

"Dan Balz's *Collision 2012* is the best presiden[...] years. It is a great book, in part because it isn't a[...] about how people in the campaigns were thinking. It is unusual in that it gives proper place to the impact of thought on political outcomes."

—Peggy Noonan, *The Wall Street Journal*

"The behind-the-scenes reporting throughout—heck, the Christie chapter alone—makes the book a must-read. . . . It was a fascinating ride, which Balz captures vividly in this most worthy sequel to *The Battle for America 2008*."

—Al Kamen, *The Washington Post*

"This is more than a look back at the last presidential race. It is a close look into the campaign. I lived it every day, but I'm already learning a lot from Dan's deep reporting. It will go on my shelf as a bible of the great 2012 race."

—Jeff Zeleny, ABC News

"Coming from one of the most respected reporters in politics, Balz's account is perhaps the most highly anticipated of the 2012 campaign retrospective genre."

—*The Huffington Post*

"With a sharp eye for detail, crisp and often evocative prose, an understanding of politics and politicians, and the experience gained over decades as a thoughtful old-school journalist, Balz re-creates the rhythms of the grueling presidential year of 2012."

—*The Washington Times*

"This book explains how the Obama technical model will be standard operating procedure for both sides in 2016—and how in 2012, the Romney team never knew what hit it."

—Howell Raines, *The Washington Post*

"I could go on and on. Balz's new book, *Collision 2012*, is so full of anecdotes and revelations that it is hard to stop. But I will. . . . I think this is one of the best political books I have ever read, harkening back to the 'Making of the President' books in terms of its richness of detail and analysis."

—Roger Simon, *Politico*

"As the *Washington Post*'s chief correspondent, Dan Balz is one of a handful of old media lions who can still shape the conventional wisdom; as such his new campaign book *Collision 2012* is as close to an account-of-record as we're likely to get."

—Alex Halperin, *Salon*

PENGUIN BOOKS

COLLISION 2012

Dan Balz is the chief correspondent at *The Washington Post* and its former national editor, political editor, White House correspondent, and Southwest correspondent. He is the coauthor of two books, the *New York Times* bestseller *The Battle for America 2008* (written with Haynes Johnson) and *Storming the Gates*. He is a regular panelist on PBS's *Washington Week* and MSNBC's *The Daily Rundown*.

COLLISION 2012

The Future of Election Politics
in a Divided America

Dan Balz

PENGUIN BOOKS

PENGUIN BOOKS
Published by the Penguin Group
Penguin Group (USA) LLC
375 Hudson Street
New York, New York 10014

USA | Canada | UK | Ireland | Australia | New Zealand | India | South Africa | China
penguin.com
A Penguin Random House Company

First published by Viking Penguin, a member of Penguin Group (USA) LLC, 2013
This edition with a new afterword published by Penguin Books 2014

THE LIBRARY OF CONGRESS HAS CATALOGED THE HARDCOVER EDITION AS FOLLOWS:
Balz, Daniel J.
Collision 2012 : Obama vs. Romney and the future of elections in America / Dan Balz.
pages cm
"A James H. Silberman Book."
Includes bibliographical references and index.
ISBN 978-0-670-02594-7 (hc.)
ISBN 978-0-14-312568-6 (pbk.)
1. Presidents—United States—Election—2012.   2. Presidential candidates—United States.
3. Obama, Barack.   4. Romney, Mitt.   I. Title.
JK5262012 .B35 2013
324.973'0932—dc23
2013016957

Printed in the United States of America
1   3   5   7   9   10   8   6   4   2

In memory of
David S. Broder and Haynes Johnson,
good friends and great colleagues,
who set the standards
for all who follow

And again, to Nancy,
for love and friendship,
and for everything

There is a New America every morning when we wake up.
It is upon us whether we will it or not.

—Adlai E. Stevenson II

Contents

BOOK THREE: THE CHOICE

To the Reader

This book is a sequel to one I coauthored with Haynes Johnson about the 2008 election. That campaign was historic in many ways, and as I began this project it seemed unlikely that 2012 could deliver a story as rich or compelling as that one. As it turned out, 2012 *was* different from 2008 but in its own way just as compelling. The election of 2008 was the story of Barack Obama, the rise of what Johnson and I called "the most unlikely presidential prospect in all of American history." The election of 2012 was a sprawling story about a divided America, the unusual cast of characters who sought to lead the country, and the underlying forces that helped determine the outcome. It was not an uplifting campaign by any stretch of the imagination. At times the plain nuttiness of it all cried out for Hunter S. Thompson to chronicle it. But both as political theater and as a window into the struggle between where America has been and where it may be going, it was as engaging as it was instructive about the state of our politics.

This book is based on several hundred interviews that were done over a period of two years. The interviewees included candidates, strategists in and outside the campaigns, citizens, and scholars. Most of the interviews were done on the record, although some of those were embargoed until publication of the book. Others were done with the agreement that the interviewee not be identified. The book is also grounded in my daily reporting and writing for the *Washington Post* during the course of the campaign. A few passages in the book are drawn directly from that work with the *Post*'s permission.

In so many ways, Campaign 2012 was a departure from what had come before. The basic architecture wasn't that different. For example, the calendar hadn't changed much from years past and still dictated the pace of the action and the movement of the candidates. But candidates were operating in a new environment. More money was spent than ever before. Super PACs taking unlimited contributions became a force. Polls proliferated unlike in any previous campaign. Debates played a more central role than ever. Social media, led by Twitter and Facebook, changed the way campaigns and the media did business. For the candidates, maintaining control of their campaigns in the face of these fast-moving forces was even more of a challenge in 2012 than it had been in earlier elections.

Campaign 2012 was one in which the best of campaign tactics and strategies collided with the immutable forces that do as much to affect the outcome as anything candidates and their advisers may do or say. Economic cycles, demographic shifts, and the hardening of partisan lines shaped this campaign from start to finish. It was almost as if there were two campaigns playing out at once—the campaign on the surface that captured headlines and drove the commentary, and the subterranean campaign that was little seen but ever powerful.

Keeping track of all this tested the best of strategists, analysts, reporters, and political scientists. It was a campaign about big things but one often fought out in small ways. If 2008 was inspiring, 2012 was often negative and nasty—big stakes but not always a campaign to do them justice. By the time it ended, most Americans were ready to say good riddance. And yet from start to finish, it was an extraordinary story about a nation divided in search of its future.

COLLISION
2012

CONTRASTS

The President

December 6, 2011

The presidential campaign year is set to open in less than a month and President Obama has come to Osawatomie, Kansas. It has been a long year for the president—endless (and fruitless) budget battles with the Republicans in Congress, unexpected political setbacks that left him in a funk, and, worst of all, a stubborn economy that has not responded well to his policies. Unemployment stands at 8.6 percent. By numbers political strategists watch closely, he is as vulnerable as any president seeking reelection in two decades. His presidency, which began with themes of hope and change, is at risk.

He is no longer the bright and shining politician who captivated the nation four years earlier. The once aspirational candidate of 2008 is now scarred by his battles with a militant and hard-right Republican opposition that has decided to no longer play by the old rules. His presidency has left the country even more deeply polarized than it was under George W. Bush. Many voters recognize the obstacles that Republicans have put in his path, and yet they wonder why this president, who offered so much promise, has not found a way to make the system work. No one is quite sure who he is or what he really wants to fight for.

The president needs a fresh start and a sharper edge. He needs a new way to set the terms for the coming reelection campaign. He has come to Osawatomie because it was where a century earlier President Theodore Roosevelt delivered his famous "New Nationalism" speech. In this same small town, Roosevelt argued that a strong federal government was necessary to protect ordinary citizens from the destructive power of big corporations.

Obama carries with him the text of a speech that seeks to build on the foundation laid by that trust-busting Republican president. He wants to frame the choice for the 2012 election as one of the biggest in a generation, a collision between competing philosophies about the economy, the role of government, and the well-being of the struggling middle class. He talks about income inequality and says, "This is a make-or-break moment for the middle class and all those who are fighting to get into the middle class." Of the Republican approach he says this: "It doesn't work. It's never worked."

This Obama is different from the one the country has seen, the assertive progressive many of his followers have been looking for. He has set the terms of the campaign on populist themes, drawing the starkest of contrasts with the Republicans who have countered his every move for three years. He has found the ground on which to run. The day marks the real opening of what will be a high-stakes reelection campaign.

The Challenger

May 17, 2012

Mitt Romney is in Boca Raton, Florida. It has been a month since he freed himself—finally—from a long and destructive battle for the Republican nomination. The last of his rivals has been vanquished, the last in a string of candidates who rose unexpectedly, one after another, to challenge him for a nomination that seemed from the beginning almost within his grasp. In winning, he demonstrated that he understands many of the new rules of presidential politics, especially the importance and power of money. He has shown resilience and ruthlessness, qualities that any challenger to a sitting president will need.

But the primary campaign has left nagging questions about Romney. Inside his party there is still a noticeable lack of enthusiasm for the candidate. Obama, not their nominee, is the great unifier among Republicans. The former governor also is not very well known throughout the country, despite having run for the nomination in 2008 and having been in the public eye now for more than a year as he sought that prize for a second time. On the positive side of the ledger, he is seen as a devoted family man with a record of success in private business. On the negative side, he is seen as someone of such wealth and seeming privilege as to be a distant figure with whom voters cannot identify personally.

Romney is banking his hopes of becoming president on the pervasive disappointment that so many Americans feel about the economy. His campaign is grounded in this idea: that no matter how much people may like Barack Obama personally, they find him lacking as a leader. Romney has described the president as someone who doesn't understand how the economy works, whose policies are the antithesis of what is needed to get the engines of growth roaring again, and who is simply in over his head as a leader in a capital poisoned by partisanship. All that may be sound thinking, but only if the public warms up to him.

He has come to Boca Raton to the home of Marc Leder, a private equity manager with a flamboyant reputation. He has come to raise money, which he desperately needs to replenish his campaign after the long nomination battle. About 150 people have paid $50,000 apiece to join the candidate for the evening, and as is customary he takes questions from the audience. Someone points out that more and more people have been told that government will take care of them. How can Romney persuade them to take care of themselves?

Inexplicably, Romney takes aim at the 47 percent of the country he says will never vote for him, who are in Obama's column already. They act like victims, he says. They believe they are entitled to government assistance. As part of his rambling response, he says, "My job is not to worry about those people. I'll never convince them that they should take personal responsibility and care for their lives." In one answer, Romney manages to reinforce all the stereotypes he has been fighting to overcome and sets out a worldview that sounds like the opposite of his opponent's.

Of course, it's all off the record, or so he believes. Off to the side of the room, unbeknownst to the candidate or his advisers, a small video camera is recording Romney's words, a political time bomb waiting to explode.

The People

October 15, 2011

It is a bright autumn weekend in Denver. I am in Colorado to talk with people about the country and the candidates. Colorado seems an ideal place to stop as the campaign year approaches. It symbolizes the changing electoral map and the emergence of the Rocky Mountains as a pivotal region in the upcoming election. Barack Obama claimed his nomination in Denver in August 2008, and the voters repaid the favor by giving him a handsome victory that November. But three years into his presidency, Obama's grip on the state is anything but firm. Colorado also is a good place to examine the possibilities and liabilities of the Republican Party. In 2010, Republicans squandered opportunities to pick up a Senate seat and the governor's mansion because of fallout from candidates closely tied to the Tea Party. Finally, Colorado is a laboratory in which to examine close up the shifting demographics and changing cultural attitudes that are altering American politics in real time.

What I hear underscores the dissatisfaction that forms the backdrop of the political year ahead. People see and feel an economy that is still inflicting pain on them and their families and friends. Anger with politics is palpable. People see Washington as a swamp of bickering and gridlock. When I ask one couple— a retired pharmacist and a retired teacher—about Washington, it is as if a huge spigot has been opened wide. Their frustrations spew forth. Republicans and Democrats are going down separate roads that never intersect, the husband tells me. "And if there's a bridge between them," his wife says with evident disgust, "they'll burn it." A retired electrician warns that public patience is limited. "People are angry and frustrated and have no focal point," he says. "You think the Arab Spring can't happen here? Think again." Another man points to the Occupy Wall Street protests that are then popping up in many cities. "It's kind of like a volcanic gurgle," he says. "The mountain hasn't exploded, but it's rumbling."

Onetime supporters of the president recognize the size of the problems he inherited and the opposition he faces and sympathize. But they wonder if he can be reelected. Some aren't sure he deserves to win. One woman who had backed him has lost faith in his leadership. "I don't think he knows how to bring people together," she says. But the voters here are not yet impressed with what they see in the Republican Party. A few say Mitt Romney could be a presentable candidate. Beyond that there is little from which to choose. "That is one of the problems of the Republican Party," one woman tells me. "There is no one who is a strong leader who can gain support and bring things back together."

My day in Colorado helps frame the questions that are at the heart of the 2012 election:

- First, how much do frustrations with the slowly recovering economy threaten the president's reelection? This is the threshold issue of the campaign. Is the economy recovering just fast enough to save the president, or is the uneven pace deadly to his chances?

- Second, will the anger that is so evident manifest itself in some direct way? Will it strike against incumbents of both parties, or of just one party, as it had in 2006, 2008, and 2010? Will it give rise to a third-party candidate, like Ross Perot in 1992, who somehow harnesses those frustrations to affect the outcome?

- Third, how will perceptions of the candidates' personal traits affect the outcome? How much will character and personality override other issues?

- Fourth, will polarization outweigh almost everything else? Are voters so locked into their separate camps that other factors become secondary to the cause of advancing the interests of red or blue America?

- Finally, can or will the election resolve any of the fundamental issues before the country? Will Campaign 2012 do anything to improve the prospects for governing in 2013 and beyond?

BOOK ONE

THE PIVOT

CHAPTER I

On the Cusp of History

I t ended where it began. On the evening of November 5, 2012, twenty thousand people lined the streets of the East Village section of downtown Des Moines. The golden dome atop the Iowa Capitol building stood in the background, brilliantly illuminated against the black sky. From the Capitol to the Des Moines River, the streets were cordoned off and had been for days, awaiting the president's arrival. Behind the stage sat the old headquarters from the first campaign—a squat one-story building that was now a church. For many in the traveling party, including the president, it was still familiar ground. Some of them could recall exactly where people sat four years earlier as they made the final phone calls to supporters during the caucuses in 2008. They remembered too their nervousness as they awaited the returns from precincts across the state and their elation when he had finally won on that frigid January night. It had all happened so fast, and now, even more quickly, they were at the end. The verdict would come the next day from the voters.

The whole team was there: David Axelrod, David Plouffe, and Robert Gibbs, the trio of advisers who led the first campaign; speechwriter Jon Favreau and his 2008 writing partner Ben Rhodes, now deputy national security adviser. Friends Marty Nesbitt and Mike Ramos were along for the ride. So too was Valerie Jarrett, the president's White House confidante and one of his and the First Lady's closest friends. Reggie Love, the president's irrepressible body man who was now off on other pursuits, had come back too. Jen Psaki, who had logged almost every mile with Obama in 2008 and spent time in the White House, was back as traveling campaign spokeswoman. Jay Carney had seen the 2008 campaign from the outside as *Time*'s Washington bureau chief. Now he too was in the staff cabin on Air Force One as White House press secretary. Trip director Marvin Nicholson, who was also the president's golfing buddy, tried to keep the operation moving to schedule. It was like the end of a long-running television series in which all the characters from previous seasons had come back to make cameo appearances, Axelrod said. The whole family was back together one last time.

It was easy to forget how far Obama had come in such a short time, and how dramatic the ascent had been. He had been on the national stage barely eight years, beginning with that night in Boston in 2004 when as a little-known Illinois state senator he gave a keynote address that electrified the Democratic convention of John Kerry. Soon he became a vessel for the hopes and dreams of millions of Americans, who had rallied behind him as he began an improbable quest for the White House. That first election made history and brought almost two million people to the Washington Mall for his historic inauguration day. He came to office amid great expectations and facing enormous problems. His presidency had been rocky—his aides called it a roller-coaster ride, which was a charitable way to put it—as he dealt with the deepest recession since the Great Depression, battled a Republican Party unified in its opposition to almost everything he proposed, and suffered a historic midterm election defeat just two years after he stood in Chicago's Grant Park to claim the presidency. He was confident as he approached election day 2012—he was never one to lack for self-confidence about anything. But those around him could also sense the weight of the moment bearing down on him. He had told someone that he believed that everything—everything—about his presidency was on the line with this election: how he would be viewed by history, his legacy, his accomplishments, and the future of the country. He wasn't nervous so much as he was clear-eyed about the enormity of the moment and the consequences of defeat.

The final swing had begun on Sunday, November 4, when he left the White House for a flight to New Hampshire. Bill Clinton joined him. The president and former president, tense rivals during those 2008 primaries between Obama and Hillary Rodham Clinton, were now allies. They had campaigned together the night before in Virginia and were to do one last joint rally before splitting off in separate directions for the final day and a half of campaigning. On the half-hour ride from the Manchester airport to Concord, Plouffe and Axelrod joined them in the president's limousine. Clinton was delighted to be back in the state that had saved his candidacy during the primaries in 1992 and resurrected his wife's ultimately failed candidacy in 2008. "I love New Hampshire," he exclaimed. New Hampshire summoned different memories for Obama's team. They all remembered the pain of losing the primary there to Hillary Clinton when everyone believed Obama was a sure winner. Plouffe wouldn't say he exactly hated the state, so he said, "We like New Hampshire, but we like Iowa a little bit more." From New Hampshire, Obama had flown south to Florida and then back to the most contested of all the battlegrounds, Ohio, for an evening rally with Stevie Wonder at the University of Cincinnati. Hecklers interrupted him, one of them an anti-abortion demonstrator who gripped the railing of the balcony as police took him away. After the rally, the traveling press corps broke off from the presidential party and flew on to Madison, Wisconsin. But Obama had one more stop, a late-night rally in Aurora, Colorado. By the time he got to his hotel in Madison, it was after 3 a.m.

If Sunday was a grueling march across the country and back, Monday was a day of nostalgia and emotions, for the president and all those with him. Racing through the president's mind, Axelrod believed, was the improbable journey he had been on and the finality of knowing that whatever came the next day, this chapter was ending. On one flight during the day, Obama said to Axelrod, Plouffe, and Gibbs, Listen, I remember the night of [the 2008 primary in] New Hampshire, you three knocking on my door and pulling me out of dinner with my wife to tell me that we had lost. If you show up at my door tomorrow night, just remember I'm still going to be president for two more months. Everybody had a good laugh at that, and Axelrod said, "No problem, Mr. President, we already talked about this. If someone is knocking, it's going to be [campaign manager Jim] Messina."

Bruce Springsteen was also with him that day. On the trip from Madison to the president's second stop of the day in Columbus, Ohio, Springsteen rode on Air Force One. During the flight, the president placed a call to New Jersey's Chris Christie. The Republican governor and the Democratic president had bonded in the wake of Hurricane Sandy, the storm that had devastated parts of the East Coast a week earlier. Republicans were dismayed by what they saw as Christie's excessive praise for the president, given the closeness of the election. Christie was a huge fan of Springsteen, but it was an unrequited love. Obama decided to have some fun with his new friend the governor. Aboard Air Force One, Obama's companions thought Christie didn't recognize Springsteen's voice. Nonsense, Christie said later—he instantly knew who Obama had on the line. "[Obama] says to me, 'You know, in a crisis like we're going through, you know the only thing that's better than one guy from Jersey?' I said, 'No.' He goes, 'Two guys from Jersey.' Then I hear, 'Hey, Gov, we meet in the wildest places, don't we?' I said to him, 'Are you on Air Force One?' He said to me, 'It is unbelievable, it is unbelievable, yes, I'm on Air Force One,' and you could just tell that Springsteen was, like, beside himself happy that he was on Air Force One, just thrilled."

Before his rally in Columbus, Obama did a round of satellite television interviews into other battleground states, his eye cocked at times to a screen where he could see Springsteen and Jay-Z performing in the arena. After his speech, he and his team had dinner together and told stories. Before leaving Columbus, Obama stopped by one of the campaign offices to greet the volunteers. One of the field organizers asked for a photo with the president. "We're

gonna do pictures with everybody," Obama said, in a tone that suggested he
thought the staffer was thinking too much about himself. "You're a field organizer. You gotta be looking out for your volunteers." Then they were off to Iowa
for the last rally he would ever do as a candidate for office.

Air Force One landed at the Des Moines airport at 8:58 p.m., central time.
The First Lady's plane arrived moments later. As her aircraft taxied to a stop,
the president's motorcade pulled up alongside. Obama got out of his limousine
and waited at the bottom of the stairs to greet her. He had told her during the
final stretch that if he got a second term, he was determined to get out of Washington more. It was, he told her, good for his soul. Together they rode the short
distance into town and before going onstage toured the old campaign offices.
It was a cold night—forty degrees—but felt colder, and the president wore his
signature black jacket over a sweater. He seemed impervious to the night air. It
was the last time he would ask anyone to vote for him, and he was in no hurry.
He had prepared his riffs, including the story of his "Fired up, ready to go!"
call-and-response chant from 2008. His staff had invited Edith Childs, the
Greenwood County, South Carolina, councilwoman who had given birth to
"Fired up, ready to go!" to join him onstage for the last rally. No, she said, I have
too many doors to knock on in North Carolina to take time out for a trip to
Iowa. That's what this is all about, he told those on the flight. She didn't want
to ride on Air Force One. She didn't want to come to a rally. She's busy trying
to get out the vote in North Carolina. It reinforced for Obama everything he
believed his campaign should be about.

Springsteen played "No Surrender" and joked about Obama's musical aspirations. The president had crooned a couple of bars of Al Green's "Let's Stay Together" at a January 2012 fund-raiser, and the video quickly went viral. Then
Springsteen turned serious. He said he had spent his life measuring the distance
between the American dream and American reality. "Our vote tomorrow is the
one undeniable way we get to determine the distance in that equation," he said.
He introduced Michelle Obama, who spoke briefly about what was at stake, and
then it was the president's moment. "I've come back to Iowa one more time to
ask for your vote," he said. "I came back to ask you to help us finish what we've
started. Because this is where our movement for change began. Right here.
Right here." He mentioned the headquarters behind him. "This was where some
of the first young people who joined our campaign set up shop, willing to work
for little pay and less sleep because they believed that people who love their
country can change it. This was where so many of you who shared that belief
came to help. When the heat didn't work for the first week or so, some of you
brought hats and gloves for the staff. These poor kids, they weren't prepared.
When the walls inside were bare, one of you painted a mural to lift everybody's

spirits. When we had a steak fry to march to,[*] when we had a J-J Dinner [Jefferson-Jackson Dinner] to fire up"—the Iowans began to applaud at the memory of those touchstones of the first campaign—"you brought your neighbors and you made homemade signs. When we had calls to make, teachers and nurses showed up after work—already bone tired but staying anyway, late into the night." And then his voice grew huskier and there was a catch in his throat and his eyes began to glisten slightly. *Washington Post* photographer Nikki Kahn could see it and moved for a better angle. The famously cool president, the unflappable, no-drama politician, was overcome by the moment. He gently wiped the corner of his left eye. "And you welcomed me and Michelle into your homes. And you picked us up when we needed a lift. And your faces gave me new hope for this country's future, and your stories filled me with resolve to fight for you every single day I set foot in the Oval Office. You inspired us." A tear had rolled down his cheek and he wiped his eye again. "You took this campaign and you made it your own. And you organized yourselves, block by block, neighborhood by neighborhood, county by county, starting a movement that spread across the country"—the crowd began to applaud—"a movement made up of young and old, and rich and poor, and black and white, Latino, Asian, Native American, gay, straight, Democrats, Republicans, who believe we've got something to contribute, that we all deserve a shot at our own American dream." His voice was strong now, but his eyes gave away the emotions inside him and he wiped away a tear once more. "And when the cynics said we couldn't, we said, 'Yes we can!'" Deafening applause erupted on the streets of Des Moines.

When he finished speaking, it was after 10:30 p.m. and he was exhausted, but he lingered. He worked the rope line for another thirty minutes, back and forth three times by the count of one of his advisers, who remembered because it was so unusual. On the short flight back to Chicago, Obama called Jim Messina, the campaign manager, who was at headquarters. "I'm proud of what you built," he said, prompting Messina to break down. Messina thought the candidate sounded at peace. Air Force One was back in Chicago in less than an hour, and by 1 a.m. the president was at his home in Hyde Park, now to wait as he looked to election day rituals to pass the time. The first votes had already been recorded in New Hampshire: Tiny Dixville Notch's ten voters had split five-five. In nearby Hart's Location, Obama had won by twenty-three to just nine for Romney.

---

[*]Iowa senator Tom Harkin held an annual steak fry, which Obama and all the other 2008 presidential candidates attended in the fall of 2007. His supporters marched together into the field where the event was held.

———

Contrary to Obama's 2004 convention speech in Boston, there were two Americas that day, as there had been throughout Obama's presidency and back before that. Red and blue America lived in different worlds and saw events through separate prisms and got their information from separate sources. Though Obama and Mitt Romney were crisscrossing through the same states, they were cocooned in these separate compartments. If anything, the enthusiasm in Romney's world was even greater at that moment than in Obama's. Romney's schedule called for him to end his campaign in New Hampshire, the site of his announcement speech and the first big victory of the 2012 race. He was returning to friendly ground for his final rally, just as the president had for his. The two rivals were operating on the same clock. Moments after Obama landed in Des Moines on election eve, Romney's charter touched down in Manchester. At least twelve thousand people waited for him inside the Verizon Wireless Arena, packed together from the stadium floor to the upper-tier seats. They were wild with enthusiasm, giddy at the prospect of turning Obama into a one-term president. They got an extra energy shot from Kid Rock, whose song "Born Free" had become the Romney campaign anthem. Mitt and Ann Romney were supposed to wait in a holding room during Kid Rock's short set but insisted they wanted to see it like everyone else. They were taken to one of the suites and found a perch on a balcony from which to watch. The rapper-rocker put on a dazzling laser light show, which ended with him singing from atop a piano adorned with a bumper sticker that read, "Bad Ass." No one found anything incongruous about the juxtaposition of the bawdy musician and the strait-laced candidate.

The crowd was in a raucous mood as Romney walked onstage. He pointed with both arms to the other end of the arena to acknowledge Kid Rock. The deafening noise continued to crash over him. They chanted, "Mitt! Mitt!" After almost a minute of applause, he began to speak, but they wouldn't let him. He tried again, but it kept coming. He stepped away and laughed, throwing his head back. The ovation continued for another minute and the audience broke into chants of "USA! USA! USA!" He tried to yank the microphone loose, thinking he wasn't close enough to be heard. But it wasn't the microphone; it was the crowd that was drowning out almost everything he was saying. Finally, after almost three minutes of nonstop sound, the audience quieted enough for him to begin.

His last two days had begun Sunday morning in Des Moines, where the size and enthusiasm of the crowd caught him and the staff by surprise. On this morning the room was filled to overflowing, and as Romney worked the rope line, his traveling aide, Garrett Jackson, kept tugging on him. Gov, he said, we've got to go. The schedule was incredibly tight, and time lost would be difficult to make up. From there he was on to Ohio—always Ohio. Mike Leavitt, the former governor of Utah and former Health and Human Services secretary, was aboard that morning. Romney had put him in charge of transition planning. As the charter headed east from Des Moines, Romney slid into the seat next to Leavitt, and for the rest of the flight the two were in deep conversation about the new government that Romney hoped—believed—he would be putting in place starting in three days. Along the way that day, Katie Packer Gage, the deputy campaign manager, asked Romney how he felt: "He said, 'I'm excited,' and I said, 'Why, do you think we're going to win?' And he said, 'I don't know if we're going to win, but if we do win I'm excited because I know exactly what it's going to take to turn this thing around and I can't wait to get started.' He said, 'If we don't win I have a great life, I have a great family, I have a great wife, and I get to just spend more time with them, and I haven't had enough of that in the last year and so I'm excited for that. So whatever comes on Wednesday, I'm excited for the outcome.'"

Pennsylvania was a late addition to Romney's Sunday itinerary. His advisers saw something in the polls that made them think it was worth sending the candidate in for a rally outside of Philadelphia, which long had been a killing ground for Republican presidential candidates. By the time they arrived in Philadelphia, they were more than an hour behind schedule because of a fire at the airport. Romney hated to be late to anything. Once he was coming into New York from the airport for a meeting and got caught in Midtown traffic. He paid the driver, hopped out of the taxi, and with luggage in tow ran ten blocks in the summer heat to his meeting. Thirty thousand or more people were waiting for him when he finally arrived in Morrisville. It was a cold day—so cold, someone said, that you couldn't feel your feet after an hour standing on the grass. People had waited three, four, five hours for the candidate. But it was like this everywhere Romney was going in the final days. Big crowds at many stops and an outpouring of emotion and enthusiasm the candidate had never experienced. Then he was on to Virginia, arriving in Newport News at 9:30 p.m.—still way behind schedule. He had phoned in to the rally before leaving Philadelphia to tell them he was running late but would be there soon. The crowd cheered wildly simply at the sound of his voice. He ended the day just after 1 a.m. after a last flight to Orlando. He was on the move again seven and a half hours later.

Florida was a battleground state Romney had to win if he hoped to become president, and he was confident he would. Backstage before his morning rally in Orlando, he joked and laughed with Jeb Bush and others. At one point, the crowd interrupted and began to chant, "One more day! One more day!" He made eye contact with Garrett Jackson, who had been his constant companion on the road for three years and was standing in the buffer area. It was as if to say, "Can you believe it? One more day!" Next stop was Lynchburg, Virginia, and then he was on to northern Virginia, which was Obama territory. As the motorcade arrived at George Mason University, Romney's team could see streams of people walking to the event, so many that the fire marshal had to close the doors. Thousands were directed to an overflow area, and the Romneys spoke to them from a makeshift public address system after the main rally.

Then it was back to Ohio one last time for a rally at the Columbus airport. The advance team had commandeered a hangar in the general aviation area, and it too was packed when Romney's charter touched down at 6:38 p.m. The plan called for a dramatic entry, with the plane supposed to pull its nose inside the hangar just near the back of the stage. It took the pilot several tries to line it up properly, and then, as the plane stopped, the flight attendant could not make the door open. Romney was impatient to get out there—"champing at the bit," an aide recalled—as the flight crew struggled with the door. Finally it popped open and there was a huge roar from the crowd. Everyone had come for this one. The Marshall Tucker Band provided the warm-up act. Golf legend Jack Nicklaus, a native of Columbus, spoke. Governor John Kasich was there too, as was Senator Rob Portman, who had become one of the campaign's most valuable assets—a vice presidential finalist and the person who masterfully played President Obama in Romney's debate preparations. And then finally he was in New Hampshire to close his day as Obama was ending his. "This is where the campaign began," he said. "You got this campaign started a year and a half ago. Tomorrow your votes and your work here in New Hampshire will help me become the next president of the United States."

At 4 a.m. on election day, eighty members of the Obama team got a robo-call: Wake up! It's election morning! Polls in Virginia opened at 6 a.m. eastern time, 5 a.m. in Chicago. The campaign had set up its war room on the seventh floor of One Prudential Plaza, and it was open for business before sunup. Messina had briefed everyone the day before. Tomorrow will be the most amazing day of your life, but also the hardest, he told them. Whatever happens, we're ready. He gave three instructions: First, no panicking; if something goes wrong, fix it. Second, understand the goal for the day, which is to turn out every vote in every precinct in every battleground state. Everyone's job on election day is to help the field team. Third, he said, hydrate. It will be a long day. And no drinking tonight. Tuesday morning, Axelrod arrived in the war room after a round of television appearances. Can I say something? he asked Messina. This is the last campaign I'm ever going to work on, he told those assembled, and I just want to tell you that you're the best I've ever seen and I'm proud of each and every one of you. But as I look around, you all look terrified, and I want to tell you one thing that's going to make you feel better. If we lose, everybody is just going to blame Messina, and if we win, everyone wins, so come on! The room broke up with laughter.

Obama's team was supremely confident as the polls opened. Dan Wagner's analytics team had done its modeling, and it showed Obama winning between 50 and 51 percent of the popular vote. Of the battleground states, only North Carolina was pretty much gone. Joel Benenson's final polling matched the findings of the analytics team. Everybody had written down predictions. Plouffe said Obama would win 332 electoral votes that night.* Messina, ever cautious, predicted 291. Earlier, Messina had asked Wagner to remodel the battlegrounds. The Obama team could see the size of Romney's rallies and the enthusiasm of the crowds. Messina wanted Wagner to ratchet up their estimate of Republican turnout well above the campaign's projections. What happens if that happens? he wanted to know. On Sunday morning, Wagner came back with the answer. Even if the Republicans were five points above what Wagner's models were predicting for turnout, Obama would still win at least 270 electoral votes. Jim, he said to Messina, we're going to win.

In Boston, there was optimism tempered with concern. The campaign's final poll in Ohio, conducted Sunday night, showed Romney down two points. He had slipped there. In other places he was competitive but not over the hump. Neil Newhouse, the campaign's pollster, called the mood "cautiously optimistic." They knew that it was still uphill, as many analysts were predicting, but that Romney had a genuine chance to win. The reason was not just what they were seeing in their polls but also what they could see and feel on the ground. Enthusiasm among Republicans was incredibly strong. Hurricane Sandy a week earlier had set the campaign back, they believed, as Romney and running mate Paul Ryan were forced to the sidelines as the president carried out his responsibilities to help organize the cleanup and comfort the victims. Chris Christie's warm embrace of the president hadn't helped either, nor had Christie's decision not to attend a rally with Romney across the New Jersey border in Pennsylvania in those final days. But the feeling in Boston was that if they were a point or two down they could overcome that with a surge of votes on election day.

---

*Plouffe had long predicted a comfortable victory. He told me in June 2011 that he thought Obama would win more than 300 electoral votes, with a popular vote margin of two to three points.

———

Obama had voted two weeks earlier, so there was no ritual visit to mark his ballot that morning. Instead he visited a field office near his home to thank the volunteers and make calls. "Hi, is this Annie?" he asked. "This is Barack Obama. You know, the president." When he hung up the phone, he said, "She was very nice to me even though she initially didn't know who I was." He made brief remarks to the press pool and cameras. "I also want to say to Governor Romney, congratulations on a spirited campaign. I know that his supporters are just as engaged and just as enthusiastic and working just as hard today. We feel confident we've got the votes to win, that it's going to depend ultimately on whether those votes turn out." From there he was taken to the Fairmont Hotel for a round of satellite interviews to Iowa, Wisconsin, Ohio, Florida, Colorado, Nevada, and Washington, D.C., for voters in northern Virginia. Just after 1 p.m., he arrived at the Attack Athletics facility on West Harrison Street for his traditional election day basketball game. He was home for dinner before 6:30 p.m.

Romney began his day at his home in Belmont, Massachusetts, with several radio interviews. Ann, he said to his wife after he was done, it's trash day. The candidate didn't want to miss the trash pickup, and before he left the house that morning he started to clean out the refrigerator. This is bad, he would say as he pulled a jar from the refrigerator and tossed it in the trash bag. An aide watched, thinking, By the end of the day this man could be president-elect and he's worried about missing trash day. At 8:40 a.m., his motorcade arrived at the Beech Street Center, where he cast his ballot. Tagg Romney and his wife had just voted in another part of town, and as they were taking their children to school they noticed a traffic jam. He realized his father's motorcade was going to the Beech Street Center. He and his wife decided to go watch. They arrived just after his father had voted. Romney was getting into his car and looked over. Do you want to come along? Tagg had not spent a day on the road with his father during the entire general election. With his wife's assent, he and his eleven-year-old son, Joe, jumped in for the day's quick fly-around to Ohio and Pennsylvania. Romney felt good. On the plane, he and Bob White sat next to each other, and one of the other staffers took a photo of the two business partners with big smiles on their faces. White asked how Romney had slept. "I slept great," Romney replied. "I feel good. I feel like I've done everything we could do to put ourselves in a position to win."

Romney's first stop was Cleveland, where he joined up with Paul Ryan for a visit to a campaign office in Richmond Heights. "Thanks for your work," he said. "It's all coming together today." As he spoke, some of the campaign volunteers standing in the hallway began to sing "God Bless America." Romney whistled for everyone to come into the main room, where Ryan introduced him as "the next president of the United States." "We are about to change America," Romney said. "The country has been going in the wrong direction. We are going to steer it back onto a course that is going to help the American people have a brighter future." The crowd chanted, "Rom-ney! Rom-ney!" As Romney worked a makeshift rope line outside, an Obama supporter standing nearby shouted, "Four more years!" A Romney supporter turned to her as everyone was leaving and said, "You will be flushing Obama down the toilet."

Romney's plane landed at the Pittsburgh airport at 3 p.m. As the plane taxied to a stop, the traveling party looked out in amazement. On the edge of the airport, fenced off from where they were, was a parking garage. Hundreds and hundreds of people—maybe even a thousand or more—were standing in the garage cheering and applauding. They had heard that Romney was coming to Pittsburgh and spontaneously created a welcoming committee. Romney quickly exited the plane and with a swift step went over to the fence to thank them for coming out. He turned to the press pool accompanying him. "Well, that's when you know you're going to win," he said. He got into his car with his son and grandson and Garrett Jackson. Boxed pizza was on the seat. Romney was overcome with the emotion of the moment. He repeated what he had said to the press pool. It was the first time he had openly shown his confidence about the outcome. Tagg Romney too was moved by what he had witnessed. He had rarely seen such passion in the campaign. "That was the first moment where I let myself believe we're going to win," he said. He was hardly alone in that belief, though by most objective measures his father's chances were hardly good at that point.

Romney's charter left Pittsburgh about 4:20 p.m. and touched down at Logan Airport in Boston about 5:45 p.m. A cheer erupted from the staff and reporters to mark the charter's last flight. As the plane was landing, everyone aboard checked cell phones. Romney switched on his iPad. The first round of exit polls was now ricocheting across the blogosphere. The numbers were not good. In the staff van, the mood turned grim. Senior adviser Ron Kaufman spit out an expletive. "This is not going to end up where we want it to end up," he told the others. Romney was taken to the Westin Hotel, where he would have dinner with his family. He had talked with campaign manager Matt Rhoades and political director Rich Beeson. He knew what the numbers meant but tried not to show any emotion. Tagg's wife was excited when the group arrived at the hotel, but she could instantly sense something was wrong.

CHAPTER 2

Obama and Romney

Barack Obama and Mitt Romney shared little in common, save for love of family, degrees from Harvard Law School, and a mutual disrespect for the ideas and policies espoused by the other. They were both strivers but they came from different generations. Romney was part of the early stage of the baby boom and Obama the very end of that demographic bubble, though Obama seemed more a child of the counterculture sixties than did the straitlaced Romney. They grew up in circumstances that were worlds apart—Romney in privilege and comfort in the American heartland, Obama in far more modest circumstances on the island state of Hawaii and for a time in the exotic environs of Indonesia. Romney was raised in a traditional two-parent household, Obama by an often absent single mother and by grandparents who gave him love and shelter but only humble surroundings. In their early adult years, Obama was a searcher, in quest of his identity as the child of a white mother from Kansas and a black father from Kenya. Romney was a striver, the devoted son of a self-made man who had run a Detroit automobile company and was elected governor of Michigan three times. The biggest of all differences were the paths each followed into politics—Obama as a community organizer, and Romney through the world of business and private equity. Beyond their far different childhoods, if there was anything that shaped their distinctly different views of the world, it was this. Obama saw the world through the experiences of Chicago's South Side and the capacity of ordinary people to challenge established power. Romney saw things from the perspective of a venture capitalist and a business owner. When he talked about the economy, it was through the eyes of those who started and ran businesses, rarely through the eyes of the workers. It was no wonder they had such different solutions to the country's economic and other problems.

David Axelrod said he told Obama not long after the 2008 election that his Republican opponent in 2012 would be Mitt Romney. Yet as Obama was preparing to take the oath of office for the first time, Romney was thinking about everything but a second campaign. He came out of the 2008 experience disappointed that he had lost the nomination and dispirited over John McCain's defeat at the hands of Obama. A person who knew them well said of Mitt and Ann Romney, "They were done." After that campaign, according to the recollections of a friend, Ann had pulled aside a videographer from the staff. She wanted her views recorded for posterity. Get this on tape, she said. I will never let Mitt run again. We're done with this. It's too hard. But it was Axelrod who proved correct. Sometimes political strategists do see the road ahead more clearly than the politicians and their families.

The two protagonists met on the political battlefield of 2012 as representatives of the major political parties in the United States. But their campaign was also a clash between two individuals—one brainy, cool, and seemingly aloof, the other also brainy and with the energy and demeanor of a born salesman rather than a natural politician. But who were they really? Were they both just pragmatic technocrats who thrived on rational analysis, or were they actually closet ideologues coming at each other from opposite ends of the political spectrum? At the start of the campaign many Americans wondered whether they truly knew either man. David Maraniss, who authored a brilliant biography of Bill Clinton and another of Barack Obama that was published in the summer of 2012, wrote, "As Obama approached the fourth year of his presidency, many people considered him more of a mystery than when he was elected. This seemed especially true for those who supported him and wanted him to succeed but were frustrated at various points by his performance in office." For Romney, the 2008 campaign cast its own shadow of uncertainty. He was on the national stage for such a short time that most voters hardly took a measure of him. But for those who had, he was, if not exactly an enigmatic figure, then something of an unknown quantity, in large measure because of the contradictions in his own political profile. Was the Romney who had run and lost in 2008 the real Romney or a political poseur hesitant to reveal his true self to the people? Did he have convictions or simply ambitions? Answers to questions about each candidate became part of the calculus of the election.

If Americans wondered exactly who Barack Obama was, it was in part because he seemed to hold himself at bay as president. He almost always spoke, in formal and some informal settings, with the aid of a teleprompter, though he could be an effective extemporaneous speaker. An Obama friend once suggested to me that the teleprompter was a perfect metaphor for the president, a physical symbol of how he kept the world at arm's length. He was famous for not enjoying schmoozing with other members of Congress. He despised what he once called the "Kabuki dance" of Washington—the political posturing before serious work can begin. He was impatient with the petty niceties of the capital, as well as the incessant chatter of the cable and Twitter culture. Like all other politicians he took energy from crowds, but he was no Bill Clinton along a rope line. As a politician he seemed dependent on a very small number of people. He was not really the product of the Chicago political machine, though his Republican opponents always like to say he was. During his rise to power, and particularly his run for the White House, he was not identified with any particular constituency or group or faction in the party, whether organized labor or party centrists, though he took advantage of those drawn to him. His ties even to the institution of the Democratic Party were minimal. The enterprise he oversaw politically—whether known as Obama for America or Organizing for America—was first and foremost about the care and feeding and protection of Barack Obama. The *Washington Post*'s Scott Wilson, in an article headlined "Obama, the Loner President," wrote that Obama maintained "a political image unattached to the racial, ethnic and demographic interests that define constituencies and voting blocs." There is another way to put it, as someone did to one of the most senior officials in the Obama White House during the transition after the 2008 election. This person said of Obama, "This guy travels light."

Until after he was elected president and real biographies finally appeared, Obama had largely written his own story. What people knew about him pre-politics—particularly his youth—came almost entirely from Obama. Most of that was from the autobiographical book *Dreams from My Father*. An elegantly written memoir published before he was a public figure, it was largely, but not entirely, a work of nonfiction. His unusual upbringing fed right-wing conspiracies that he was Muslim, not Christian, and that he was born in Kenya or somewhere else, not in the United States. When Obama chose to tell the story of America, he invariably put himself in the middle of it. When John Kerry asked Obama to give the keynote address at the 2004 Democratic National Convention in Boston, his first instinct was that he would use his own story to deliver the message of unity that he wanted to give that night. *Dreams from My Father* is also a reminder that while he owed a debt to trailblazers before him, he was very much a singular character who made his own way. If he kept his distance from almost everyone, it was because he had learned to rely on himself. His mother may have been the single greatest influence on him, but he had found his own path and his own identity. Though he had a few close friends and he listened to a handful of trusted advisers, his greatest confidence was in himself. I once asked him what was the best advice he had received during the last months of 2006 when he was consulting with close friends and advisers about whether he should run for president. "Well," he replied, "I would have to say it was advice I gave to myself."

Obama also remained politically opaque to many people. Just how liberal was he? Was he the Barack Obama who as a candidate for the U.S. Senate opposed the Iraq War, or the Obama who in 2008 favored escalating the war in Afghanistan? Was he the president who bragged about ending two wars, or the president who ordered a dramatic increase in the use of unmanned aerial drones to hunt down and kill enemies? Was he the president who pushed for the biggest social program since the Great Society (the Affordable Care Act), or the president who made clear his ambivalence about a public option as part of his health care reform? Did his long period of reluctance to embrace same-sex marriage reflect a person genuinely wrestling with a difficult decision, or a politician afraid to say what he really believed? Was he someone willing to take on the toughest of fights for his agenda, or a president too willing to cave in to pressure from Republicans?

In his first campaign, he presented two faces to the country. The first was the Obama who sounded the call to turn the page on a poisonous chapter in its political history, to move beyond the old quarrels and transcend the politics of polarization. It was that Obama who struck such a chord, starting in 2004 and throughout his presidential campaign. Even Republicans were drawn to him, particularly in those flush days in early 2008. But he was also a candidate whose policy sympathies leaned distinctly toward liberalism, and his Senate voting record was among the most left-leaning in the chamber. He saw a role for government to attack and solve problems, though he managed to shade his proposals enough to leave room for different interpretations as to just where he stood ideologically. He could support a national health care bill but oppose an individual mandate, as he did in his first campaign. This was not an electoral pose. It was a trait evident in Obama much earlier. When the nuclear freeze movement arose while he was a student, he embraced nuclear nonproliferation and negotiations with the Soviets rather than the freeze. His first campaign for president was masterful for never having to square the circle between the aspirations of someone calling for a new politics and the one advocating ideas that might fit comfortably as part of the old liberal politics. In office, the questions persisted: Who was Obama? Was he the transcendent politician who talked about moving beyond red and blue America to find a new consensus, or was he actually a closet liberal with an agenda to extend government's reach at every opportunity? The most conservative of Republicans believed they knew the answer. They thought he was a socialist. Liberals, however, were far from sure he was even a real liberal.

One of the most thoughtful efforts to understand Obama's worldview and intellectual underpinnings as a new president was a work published in 2011 by Harvard historian James T. Kloppenberg entitled *Reading Obama: Dreams,*

Hope, and the American Political Tradition. Kloppenberg argued that Obama was difficult to decipher because people were trying to understand him through conventional lenses. "His approach to politics seems new only to those who lack his acquaintance with the venerable traditions of American democracy: respect for one's opponents and a willingness to compromise with them," he wrote. "His commitment to conciliation derives from his understanding that in a democracy all victories are incomplete. In his words, 'no law is ever final, no battle truly finished,' because any defeat can be redeemed and any triumph lost in the next vote. Building lasting support for policies and substantive changes is not the work of months or even years but decades." Kloppenberg went on to write that Obama was steeped in the history of America but that he did not draw on the same things many Democrats had drawn on in the past. Obama's thought process was a reflection of what Kloppenberg called "profound changes in American intellectual life" after Obama was born. "Obama's ideas and his approach to American politics have thrown political observers off balance," he wrote. "His books, his speeches and his political record make clear that he represents a hybrid of old and new, which explains why he puzzles so many contemporaries—supporters and critics alike—who see him through conventional and thus distorting lenses." Kloppenberg's analysis is based, as the title suggests, mostly on a careful reading of Obama's writings and on some of the known history of him before he became president. As such, it was insightful but incomplete. Like many other people who watched Obama's rise to the presidency, Kloppenberg was struck by the new leader's seeming commitment to negotiation, conciliation, and compromise. He wrote, "Obama's commitments to philosophical pragmatism and deliberative democracy—to building support slowly, gradually, through compromise and painstaking consensus building—represent a calculated risk as political strategy. It is a gamble he may lose. But it is not a sign of weakness, as his critics on the right and left allege. It shows instead that he understands not only the contingency of cultural values but also how the nation's political system was designed to work. Democracy means struggling with differences, then achieving provisional agreements that immediately spark new disagreements. . . . His predilection to conciliate whenever possible is grounded in his understanding of the history of American thought, culture and politics."

In December 2008, I interviewed President-elect Obama at his transition headquarters in Chicago. I noted that he had announced his candidacy on the grounds of the Old State Capitol in Springfield, Illinois, where Abraham Lincoln had given his famous "House Divided" speech, and would be following some of the same route Lincoln took as he made his way to Washington for his first inaugural. How did Lincoln inform his view of the presidency? I asked. Lincoln, he said, was his favorite president, though he did not want people to believe he was drawing an equivalency between himself and the sixteenth president. Then he offered a revealing window into his own thinking about leadership and power. "What I admire so deeply about Lincoln," he said, "number one, I think he's the quintessential American because he's self-made. The way Alexander Hamilton was self-made or so many of our great iconic Americans are, that sense that you don't accept limits, that you can shape your own destiny. That obviously has appeal to me given where I came from. That American spirit is one of the things that is most fundamental to me and I think he embodies that. But the second thing that I admire most in Lincoln is that there is just a deep-rooted honesty and empathy to the man that allowed him to always be able to see the other person's point of view and always sought to find that truth that is in the gap between you and me. Right? That the truth is out there somewhere and I don't fully possess it and you don't fully possess it and our job then is to listen and learn and imagine enough to be able to get to that truth. If you look at his presidency, he never lost that. Most of our other great presidents, there was that sense of working the angles and bending other people to their will—FDR being the classic example. And Lincoln just found a way to shape public opinion and shape people around him and lead them and guide them without tricking them or bullying them, but just through the force of what I just talked about—that way of helping to illuminate the truth. I just find that to be a very compelling style of leadership. It's not one that I've mastered, but I think that's when leadership is at its best."

Someone who worked in the Obama White House during the first term made a related observation about Obama and Lincoln, which went to the question of both Obama's ideology and his leadership style. He explained it this way: "His relationship with our left is no different than Lincoln's relationship with the radical Republicans who thought that Lincoln was too cautious, that he wasn't going for it in the Civil War, that he wasn't doing the things that he really needed to do to win the Civil War, that he wasn't moving fast enough on emancipation, that he was too cautious, that he was too this and too that. We look back in history and think of Lincoln as one of our great risk-taking, transformational presidents. But in the context of politics in his time he was seen as very much trying to stay in the middle."

Those who observed Obama from close in had other views about his ideology and leadership style. They said that whatever doubts the left might have about Obama, he was not a centrist in Bill Clinton's mold (although by now the two agreed on most issues). Obama saw no particular virtue in planting his flag in the middle or in finding compromises that somehow split the differences between left and right. Triangulation for triangulation's sake was not a strategy that interested him. He was, they believed, fundamentally progressive in his outlook, motivated most by social and economic justice, though more a cool rationalist than a bleeding heart. Obama himself resisted labels and character-izations. He objected when columnists suggested at different points in his presidency either that he was moving to the center or that he had found his inner populist. Obama saw consistency in his views and his approach.

If he had a weakness, some of those who watched him closely said, it was for smart people, the belief that if you could just get enough smart people in a room, they could figure out a solution to whatever the problem was and the public would accept it. Treasury Secretary Timothy Geithner, upon leaving the admin-istration, pointed to Vice President Joe Biden as one member of the administra-tion who saw the limits of that approach: "I loved watching you, in briefings with the economic team, often in disbelief, saying, 'Where did you people come from? And have you ever been exposed to the real world in any way?'" Demo-crats who knew both Obama and Clinton said Obama was less likely to change course simply because of the political risks involved. Compared with Clinton, however, he had less capacity to put himself in the minds of his opponents, to understand where they were coming from and why, or to channel their point of view as a way to figure out how to negotiate with them successfully.

What was harder to decipher was just how expansive his vision for govern-ment action was or should be—particularly if he was reelected—and how the battles of his first years in office had shaped or changed that vision. As he prepared for the reelection campaign, the other question was whether he had lost some of his ability to connect with the voters. Was the disappointment that registered in the polls something that could be overcome with a vigorous campaign, or had too many people simply given up on him?

Mitt Romney was unknown in a more ordinary way. Though he had run for president in 2008, he left few deep impressions on the public. He had a glit-tering record of success, a résumé that was enviable in both the public and private sectors, and a huge personal fortune. What he lacked was a clear po-litical identity. Was he a northeastern moderate, as he had appeared in his earliest incarnations as an office seeker? Was he a true conservative, as he had tried to present himself in his first campaign for the White House? Or was he a conservative of convenience, who saw changes in his own party and the constituencies he was trying to please and made the necessary adjustments, adapting in order to succeed?

If there was a single influence on his life, it was his father, George Romney. The father had been born in Mexico in a Mormon colony, the child of a family that had fled the United States and then, when George Romney was five, would flee Mexico and return to the United States under threat from revolutionaries. George Romney was a powerful personality and a driven man who in the postwar years had risen through the ranks of the automobile industry to become chairman and CEO of American Motors Corporation. In 1962, he ran for governor of Michigan, after first asking his family whether he should run as a Democrat or a Republican. At the 1964 Republican convention in San Francisco, he walked out in protest of Barry Goldwater's opposition to civil rights legislation. As the 1968 presidential campaign neared, he was considered a leading contender for the Republican nomination, but his candidacy proved to be short-lived, undone by a comment in which he said he had been "brainwashed" by the generals and others about the Vietnam War.

Mitt was the youngest child in the family, and he developed a special and close relationship with his father. Mitt Romney was at his father's side throughout his father's rise in politics. He accompanied his father on the campaign trail, offered advice to his father when he was governor, and ached over his demise as a presidential candidate. Their personalities were different. His father was headstrong and outspoken, sometimes to a fault. Mitt Romney was more cautious and careful—and reserved. In their revealing biography *The Real Romney,* Michael Kranish and Scott Helman wrote, "A wall. A shell. A mask. There are many names for it, but many who have known or worked with Romney say the same thing: he carries himself as a man apart, a man who sometimes seems to be looking not in your eyes but past them. . . . Even some of Romney's closest friends don't always recognize the man they see from afar. This is a vexing rap to those in his inner circle—his wife, his family and his closest confidants. They see a different Mitt Romney. . . . The man they know is warm. He's human. He's silly. He's funny, though sometimes his attempts at humor drift into corniness or just pure oddness. He's deeply generous with both his time and his money when people need a lift."

Mitt Romney began his life in a comfortable neighborhood in Detroit, but the family moved when he was six to Bloomfield Hills, a wealthy suburb. He attended the exclusive Cranbrook School, a private boys' school, beginning in seventh grade. He went on to Stanford University, where he avoided the antiwar demonstrations and experimentation with drugs that were characteristic of his generation. Later he spent two years as a Mormon missionary in France. In 1969, he married Ann Davies, who converted to the Mormon faith, and they began building a family of five rambunctious sons. He simultaneously took degrees from Harvard's law school and its business school. He joined Bain & Company, where he was an immediate star, and when the founder decided to form a new company, a private equity firm called Bain Capital, he recruited Romney to make it a success. The theory behind Bain Capital was that rather than simply offering consulting advice to troubled companies, the partners would also invest in them, sharing in the profits. Romney built his reputation as a shrewd technocrat who depended on careful analysis and deep number crunching to lead him to the right decisions. Every aspect of his life seemed grounded in dispassionate analysis. Kranish and Helman wrote that Romney once explained that "he preferred eating only the tops of muffins, so as to avoid the butter that melted and sank during baking." Bain proved to be a major success story, and Romney became fabulously wealthy along the way. By the time he ran for president a second time, his net worth was estimated at more than $200 million.

In 1994, Romney decided it was time to try the other part of the family business, politics, challenging Edward M. Kennedy for the Senate. Kennedy was an icon in the state but a senator who had not faced a serious opponent in his recent campaigns. The political climate was challenging for Kennedy, as it was for Democrats across the nation that fall. By early September, polls showed the race almost even. Romney, who had been a registered independent until 1993, was running as a moderate-to-liberal Republican. He was pro-choice on abortion, as was his mother, Lenore. He said at one point that he would do more than Kennedy to ensure rights for gay and lesbian Americans. He declined to endorse the Contract with America, the campaign manifesto put together by Newt Gingrich, who was leading the Republican effort to take control of the U.S. House. In the early fall, the Kennedy campaign launched a counterattack. Kennedy would turn Bain Capital into a negative on Romney's résumé. The campaign aired a series of ads featuring angry workers who portrayed Bain as a rapacious company that had forced layoffs and reduced wages at their firm. The ads had a devastating effect and drove Romney's poll numbers lower. The final blow came in their first debate, when a theatrical and sarcastic Kennedy demolished his Republican rival. It was in that debate that Kennedy charged that Romney was a clone of Ronald Reagan. "Look, I was an independent during the time of Reagan-Bush," Romney replied, running away from his party. "I'm not trying to return to Reagan-Bush."

In December 2011, the *Post*'s Philip Rucker and I interviewed Romney. We asked about that statement concerning Reagan and Bush and about his opposition to the Contract with America. "I applaud the fact that he was wise in crafting the Contract with America," he said of Gingrich. "I didn't think it was a very good political step. He was right; I was wrong. The Contract with America was a very effective political tool. I didn't think it would be. It certainly was. I was, after all, in my first political race, and I learned not only from the wisdom of that contract, but also the wisdom of Ted Kennedy, who beat me soundly. And I have learned since that time, and I can tell you that over the years, my admiration and respect for the policies of Ronald Reagan has grown deeper and deeper."

After the loss to Kennedy, Romney returned to Bain. His next call to national service came in 1999, when he was asked to rescue the 2002 Winter Olympics, which were to be held in Salt Lake City.* The Salt Lake Organizing Committee had been hit with scandal over bribery and corruption. The winter games were short of funds and in deep trouble. Both the leaders of Salt Lake City and the state of Utah, along with much of the population, were humiliated by the corruption that had infected the committee. Romney took on the challenge, and with the skills he had applied to failing companies at Bain he turned the games around. With that success, he again set his sights on political office, this time the governorship of Massachusetts.

Romney's gubernatorial campaign finally gave him the political victory that had eluded him eight years earlier in his challenge to Kennedy. He muscled aside a sitting Republican governor, won a subsequent primary, and defeated his Democratic rival to claim the office. He was sworn in as governor in January 2003. He had run as a businessman and an outsider who vowed that he would be a CEO governor. He brought the same style to government that he had practiced in business—sizing up problems, analyzing mounds of data, dissecting options, and finally settling on a course of action. Politically he was anything but a natural. Democrats in the state legislature found him standoffish and at times imperial in his approach. He inherited a sizable budget shortfall and moved swiftly to cut spending on a host of programs. But when spending cuts alone would not close the entire gap he turned to revenues, ending some loopholes and raising fees. He governed as a fiscal conservative, pressing a resistant legislature to cut taxes. But he was more successful in preventing any general tax increase than he was in enacting significant cuts. When he realized that Democrats would continue to block his agenda, he campaigned during the 2004 elections in an effort to boost Republican strength in the legislature. Instead, his party lost ground. His relations with the Democrats left the state polarized politically on most issues unless Democrats were motivated by self-interest to cooperate.

The one area where Romney found common ground with the Democrats was on comprehensive health care reform, which became his signature achievement as governor. The Massachusetts law required every citizen to

---

*Among those also under consideration for the job was Jon Huntsman Jr., a former diplomat, the son of one of Utah's richest and best-connected businessmen, and a future governor and rival to Romney.

purchase insurance—an individual mandate—or pay a penalty. Romney was initially skeptical about whether the state could in fact achieve universal coverage. Once he was convinced it was possible, he threw himself into the effort to design a program. He called in outside experts and applied the tools of a management consultant to the task. Democratic legislators expanded the measure beyond what Romney had recommended, but he proudly signed it into law, with his old rival Ted Kennedy at the ceremony. "My son said that having Senator Kennedy and me together like this on stage, behind the same piece of landmark legislation, will help slow global warming," Romney joked. "That's because Hell has frozen over." When it was Kennedy's turn to speak, he said, "My son said something too and that is when Kennedy and Romney support a piece of legislation, usually one of them hasn't read it." Pausing for laughter from the audience, he said, "That's not true today, is it governor?"

As governor, Romney underwent a transformation on social issues. He shifted on gay rights. He had never supported same-sex marriage and spoke out against the state's highest court when it approved it. He also backed away from his endorsement of a federal antidiscrimination statute and a more expansive position on whether openly gay soldiers should be allowed to serve in the military. He changed his position on abortion. When he ran for governor he said he was personally pro-life but would do nothing to limit a woman's right to choose. Later, as he was working on the issue of stem cell research and funding, he said he came out of the experience with a different view. He declared that he was staunchly pro-life. The bumpy transition came as Romney's ambitions shifted from Massachusetts to the presidency.

In February 2005, a group of reporters from the *Post* interviewed Romney at the National Governors Association meeting in Washington. He was already eyeing the race for president but had not yet publicly ruled out running for reelection as governor. I noted that his position as stated then—personally opposed to abortion but opposed to any changes in the law that would restrict a woman's right to obtain one—was almost identical to that of Senator John Kerry. But Kerry called himself pro-choice while Romney called himself pro-life. I asked him to explain the difference. "I can tell you what my position is," he said, "and it's in a very narrowly defined sphere, as candidate for governor and as governor of Massachusetts, what I said to people was that I personally did not favor abortion, that I am personally pro-life. However, as governor I would not change the laws of the commonwealth relating to abortion. Now, I don't try and put a bow around that and say, 'What does that mean you are—does that mean you're pro-life or pro-choice?' Because that whole package—meaning I'm personally pro-life but I won't change the laws, you could describe that as—well, I don't think you can describe it in one hyphenated word." My colleague Ruth Marcus then asked, "Do you support making abortion illegal? I'm not talking about what you would do as governor." Romney replied, "But that's the furthest I'm going to take you right now. I'm governor of Massachusetts, I'm running for governor of Massachusetts, and I'm telling you exactly what I will do as governor of Massachusetts, but I'm not going to tell you what I'd do as mayor of Boston or a congressman or any of those positions." Marcus pressed him again: "I just wanted to understand the thinking behind that status quo theory. If the majority of the state has a particular position, is that the position that you have?" she asked. Romney's concluding response was this: "I'm not going to enter into a philosophical 'where it comes from.' I'm just telling you . . . what it is." It was that kind of slippery language and evasiveness that gave rise to skepticism among conservatives that he was truly one of them.

By the end of his term as governor, Romney's approval ratings had fallen sharply into negative territory. He chose not to run for reelection, a race he likely would have lost. Instead he ran for president. The once moderate Romney perceived a vacuum on the right in a race where the two best-known candidates—John McCain and New York mayor Rudy Giuliani—were at odds with the party's conservative base. Romney tried to fill the space by emphasizing social issues rather than running on his strengths as a businessman and problem solver. In late 2006, as the race was just beginning, McCain's campaign pointed reporters to the tapes of the Kennedy-Romney debates and to other Romney statements from his first campaign. The flip-flop label stuck to him then and stayed with him throughout the campaign. He had some early successes in 2007—he won the Iowa Straw Poll in August of that year—but lost the Iowa caucuses to Mike Huckabee and the New Hampshire primary to McCain.

By February 2008 he was out of the race—a candidate who not only had proved to be an underachiever but whose political identity remained in question. Romney's response was to start working on a book in the late spring of 2008, a project he hoped would allow him to express his political philosophy and policy ideas more clearly than he had as a candidate. By the time Obama was getting ready to take the oath of office, Romney had retreated to the sidelines. He and Ann Romney, who had just been diagnosed with breast cancer, were at their home in La Jolla. "He was out in California, Ann was undergoing these treatments [for breast cancer], and he was working on his book," said Beth Myers, his gubernatorial chief of staff and 2008 campaign manager. "That's where his head was. He was listening to the waves at night. We were certainly not on the phone saying, 'Okay, we've got to get you to New Hampshire four times.'"

———

How these two politicians, so different in so many ways, dealt with the challenges of defining or redefining themselves and reconnecting with the voters helped to decide the outcome of the 2012 election. But as the campaign cycle began, that general election contest was still far in the future. It may have been predictable, as Axelrod said, that Obama and Romney would face each other, but before they could do that, they had other battles to fight and win.

CHAPTER 3

Under Siege

Barack Obama's road to reelection began inauspiciously. Just after 1 p.m. on November 3, 2010, the president stood impassively in the White House East Room. The day before, his party had absorbed the worst midterm election defeat in more than half a century. Democrats lost sixty-three seats in the House, the biggest midterm loss by a party since 1938. They lost six seats in the Senate—a number that easily could have been worse were it not for the deeply flawed GOP candidacies of Delaware's Christine O'Donnell (the wackiest of all the candidates, who ran an ad declaring she was not a witch), Nevada's Sharron Angle, and Colorado's Ken Buck. All three were products of the Tea Party movement that had shaken up the Republican Party before concentrating its anger on the president and his Democratic majorities in Congress. In the states, the wreckage was even greater as the conservative tidal wave swept aside years of Democratic advances. Republicans captured a majority of the governorships, and Democrats were lucky not to have lost more. Republicans picked up nearly seven hundred state legislative seats and now controlled legislatures in twenty-six states. In twenty-one states, Republicans held both the governor's mansion and the legislature. The reflexive rejection of Obama and his party was so powerful that in the days after, Democrats privately lamented that it could take a decade to recover in some states.

Obama met the press that afternoon for a familiar post-election ritual. In these circumstances, the embattled leader is expected to show humility and contrition, all to demonstrate that he has gotten the message of the voters. Other recent presidents had been there. Ronald Reagan had seen his party stumble in 1982 during the deep recession of that decade. Bill Clinton saw Democrats lose control of Congress in 1994 after forty years in power in the House. What Obama had experienced was as bad as that, if not worse. Two years after his historic victory he was asked to explain a historic defeat. He repeated shopworn lines from his campaign appearances that fall, while showing little emotion. He blamed the economy, not himself or his policies, for the public's frustrations. He had some grounds to do so. The unemployment rate stood at 9.6 percent, more than a point and a half higher than his economic advisers unadvisedly had said would be the ceiling if Congress enacted the president's $800 billion stimulus package in the spring of 2009. Whatever Obama had promised for restoring the economy had not come to pass. In all other ways, Obama resisted interpretations that suggested shortcomings on his part. Not the big health care initiative that had divided the country. Not the government spending that so many independents objected to. Not the distance that now existed between the country and a young leader whom so many Americans had embraced with such passion just two years earlier.

Only in the final moments did the stoic façade begin to crack. "I'm not recommending for every future president that they take a shellacking like I did last night," he said to laughter from reporters. "I'm sure there are easier ways to learn these lessons." Finally TV had its sound bite and the press its headline. He called the election part of a process of growth and evolution. "The relationship that I've had with the American people is one that built slowly, peaked at this incredible high, and then during the course of the last two years, as we've together gone through some very difficult times, has gotten rockier and tougher. And it's going to, I'm sure, have some more ups and downs during the course of me being in this office."

Two days after the election, he taped an interview for CBS's *60 Minutes*. Correspondent Steve Kroft pressed him repeatedly to explain the midterm results. "I think that there are times where we said, 'Let's just get it done,' instead of worrying about how we're getting it done. And I think that's a problem," he said. Later he explained, "In terms of setting the tone and how this town operates, we just didn't pay enough attention to some of the things that we had talked about. And, you know, I'm paying a political price for that." For supporters, Obama's performances were dismaying. "You can't govern if you can't tell the country where you are taking it," Frank Rich, once one of the president's most ardent advocates, wrote in the *New York Times*. "If he has such a plan, few, if any, Americans have any idea what it is."

Obama immediately set about to rebalance his presidency and his White House. Over a period of weeks, he invited a series of outsiders into the Oval Office for private conversations. After a few official photographs, it was just the president and his invited guest. No staff members were included; often they didn't know who was on his schedule. Obama sometimes brought a pad of paper and took careful notes in his precise handwriting. To at least one visitor he looked older—his hair was noticeably grayer than during the campaign—and thinner. Obama was drinking milkshakes to keep his weight up, one visitor said he was told. In these conversations, his visitors did not find Obama defensive.

"Friendly, not downbeat," said one. "Probing." But he was clearly concerned about his presidency and his White House. One visitor said, "He knew things were off the rails."

The group that came to see the president included Washington veterans of both parties. One was Tom Daschle, the former Senate majority leader and an early Obama supporter whose former staffers now played key roles in Obama's White House. Another was Leon Panetta, Obama's first CIA director, who later became defense secretary. Panetta's résumé included being Bill Clinton's White House chief of staff and budget director, and before that a respected House member. A third was David Gergen, who had advised presidents of both parties and was now stationed at Harvard, from where he dispensed political insights for CNN. The group also included John Podesta, another Clinton White House chief of staff; Kenneth Duberstein, who had served as Ronald Reagan's last chief of staff; Ken Mehlman, the former Republican National Committee chairman and a Harvard Law School classmate of the president's; and Matthew Dowd, a former senior political adviser to George W. Bush who later broke with Bush over Iraq.

Obama's visitors offered constructive criticism about how he had handled himself during his first two years. "I remember telling him I thought he had lost his narrative," one of the visitors recalled. "I didn't think that he knew what his presidency was really about and that—and everybody told him this— he wasn't nearly as inclusive as he needed to be in terms of even his own staff, cabinet, and supporters." This person told Obama, "I bet if I go down the street and talk to ten people about what your presidency is about I'll get probably ten different answers." Another visitor said, "I think he clearly got that his presidency had been defined by the worst of the congressional skirmishes . . . , that he was like the chief butcher in the sausage factory and that's all [people] knew about him."

Obama may not have been defensive, but he was not passive in these conversations or reticent to challenge his visitors. He knew which of his guests had been critical of his presidency or his leadership and made a point to let them know that he knew. He wondered aloud about whether other leaders had found moments of doubt when they had run into problems, implying that he had gone through those moments himself—an unusual admission from a politician who exuded a self-confidence that his opponents regarded as arrogance. But those who saw him in those days said he was not like Bill Clinton had been after his political battering in 1994. "Bill Clinton took it a lot more personally and Obama is much more philosophic, more detached, more willing to let it roll off," said one person who saw him.

Obama heard other criticism from his visitors. "I think the way I put it was the business community hates you," one said. "There was no mincing about that." Another guest said, "I told him there are cabinet members who told me that they hadn't talked to him personally in over six months and they felt excluded, they felt unused, they felt locked out in ways publicly that were very harmful to him in his effort to try to do something." Others told him he needed to improve relationships on Capitol Hill and that there was no one in the White House, including himself, who had shown any capacity or willingness to build bridges to those who might be on the other side. "You reach out only when you need something, not to build a relationship for relationship's sake," one person recalled telling the president. Obama acknowledged that the two sides "were just shouting at one another," but seemed reluctant to try to develop those relationships. When he was urged at several different points to reach out more directly and more personally in informal settings to incoming House Speaker John Boehner or to Senate minority leader Mitch McConnell, he almost blanched at the thought.

His visitors also reminded Obama that he had failed to change the culture of politics in Washington. "I said, 'This is not to relitigate, but if your goal was to bring the country together, you haven't fixed the means of governing, you've concentrated on the ends of governing,'" one person said. This person told Obama that the reason he had gotten so little political benefit from passing health care was that it was done in such a polarizing way. Obama responded that the White House had a communications problem. "I said, no, it wasn't really a communications problem. If you really want to fix this problem directly you've got to fix the problems of governing." This visitor had seen other White Houses. "It's hard not to get bubbled in in this office," he told the president. "You have to reach out. If you depend on the staff it will never happen." Obama said that's what he was doing by setting up these meetings.

Those private conversations were only part of the reorientation of Obama's presidency as he prepared for coming battles with congressional Republicans and began setting up the machinery for his reelection campaign. He focused his immediate attention on a lame-duck session of Congress, which included a long list of pressing business: what to do about expiring Bush era tax cuts, an arms treaty with the Russians that needed to be ratified, an unfulfilled promise to repeal the Pentagon's "Don't Ask, Don't Tell" ban on gays in the military. In a flurry of activity, he accomplished almost everything on his list. With Vice President Biden's help, he brokered a tax deal with Republicans. Congressional Democrats hated it. They thought he had caved on key features of the agreement. But Bill Clinton made the case that those Democrats were wrong and the president was right. When Obama signed the legislation, then—House Speaker Nancy Pelosi and Senate Democratic leader Harry Reid didn't show up, but Senate Republican leader Mitch McConnell, who had said defeating Obama in 2012 was the Republicans' highest priority, did. Repealing the Pentagon's ban on gays threatened the arms treaty ratification, but Obama got both through. When he signed the repeal of "Don't Ask, Don't Tell" at an emotional ceremony at the Department of the Interior, the audience chanted, "Yes we did! Yes we did!" Someone yelled out, "You rock, Mr. President." Joe Solmonese, then the executive director of the Human Rights Campaign, was backstage with the president. Obama gave Solmonese a hug and said to him, "You really got beaten up over this." Solmonese replied, "So did you." "Yeah," the president said, "but I get beaten up every day."

When Obama departed for Hawaii, where he would join his family for two weeks of Christmas vacation, one member of the traveling party said he was "as happy as I've ever seen him." In Hawaii, he lingered. No world events interrupted his time away. No terrorist put explosives in his underwear and tried to blow up an airplane, as had happened the year before. No natural disasters hit the continent. Obama was free to enjoy his family and friends on the islands where he grew up. As the date of his departure neared, he extended his stay another day. Whatever success he had wrung out of the lame-duck session, Obama knew the coming year would be far more challenging. "He knew he was stepping back into a new world," one adviser said.

Among those who traveled with the presidential party to Hawaii was Jim Messina, who was preparing to leave the White House to become campaign manager for Obama's reelection committee. Messina was tall, rangy, and intense. "My favorite political philosopher is Mike Tyson," he said. "Mike Tyson once said everyone has a plan until you punch them in the face. Then they don't have a plan anymore. [The Republicans] may have a plan to beat my guy. My job is to punch them in the face." Before joining the Obama team, Messina had worked for Senator Max Baucus, chairman of the Senate Finance Committee. Baucus was like a father to him. In the summer of 2008, when Plouffe was on the verge of leaving the Obama campaign because he was burned out, Messina was recruited to shoulder many of the day-to-day responsibilities of running the campaign. After the election, he was named White House deputy chief of staff and troubleshooter and was almost immediately slotted to become campaign manager for the reelection effort. In one of his early conversations with the president, Messina asked for a pledge that they not rerun the 2008 campaign. Obama looked puzzled. "You know we won that one," he deadpanned. Messina explained that in their bids for reelection, Jimmy Carter and George H. W. Bush had both tried to rerun their first campaigns. Clinton and George W. Bush threw the rulebook out and ran a different race. Obama accepted what Messina said but reiterated his insistence that he wanted to run a grassroots-based campaign for a second time. He did not want to lose that connection.

In Hawaii, Messina began to devour everything he could about past campaigns, reading books and other materials. His Christmas reading list included Karl Rove's *Courage and Consequence: My Life as a Conservative in the Fight*. He made sticky notes as he read and pasted them around the room. This is looking like a scene from Russell Crowe in the movie *A Beautiful Mind*, he thought. To make other notes, he used a whiteboard and a roll of butcher paper. "I went all the way back to the Johnson [campaign in 1964] and just kind of tried to find advice." The two most relevant campaigns were Reagan in 1984 and Bush in 2004, but of the two, 2004 offered the most compelling lessons and parallels. Messina was not alone in that conclusion. "The brilliance of the George Bush campaign in 2004 was they thought they were going to run on the strength of a triumphant war," David Axelrod said. "The war turned sour, everybody hated the war. They rotated the message and the message became, 'Here's a guy who had the courage to do an unpopular thing because he knew it was in the interests of the country.' And they turned it into a character point and against Kerry it was particularly effective."

From his study of past campaigns, Messina concluded that he had to use the coming year to get a few big things done. He presented a list of five objectives to the president. The first was to reconnect Obama to people. In December, Obama had met with Bill Clinton at the White House. Clinton said Obama likely would experience what he had experienced as he prepared for his 1996 reelection campaign. People don't know what you did, he said. You've got to go tell them what you did, and the campaign is the vehicle to do that. Messina's second goal was to rebuild the grassroots operation that had been so important in 2008. He and others knew there was much work to do here. Obama's 2008 supporters were disappointed, fatigued, or simply not engaged. Messina's plan was to begin with a listening tour, to go to the states and sit down with volunteers from 2008 and find out how they felt, what they wanted, and what it would take to reengage them. A third goal was to improve the campaign's use of technology. This surprised the president. His 2008 campaign had been lauded for technological innovation. No other campaign had done more with the emerging tools of social networking. But Messina was obsessed with how technology had changed in just four years. Smartphones were the symbol of that change—a platform for the delivery of messages and fund-raising appeals that didn't even exist in 2008. Facebook was now an even more powerful force for organizing. Messina toured Silicon Valley tech giants to tap their expertise. Google's Eric Schmidt became a key adviser on everything from how to manage a start-up, to the kind of computer platforms to set up, to the most efficient placement of online advertising. "Jim is extremely analytical, so what he wanted was a technology base and analytical base to make decisions," Schmidt told me. "For advertising, he would like to have a scientific basis for where you put the money, and so we worked at some length to try to understand what kind of marketing made sense."

The fourth goal was to build a financial operation that could equal or exceed the campaign's phenomenal fund-raising totals from 2008. Obama's first campaign raised $800 million, more than half of it from online donations. Messina told the president the campaign needed to reenergize the grassroots supporters before starting to ask them for money. In the meantime, he said, he hoped to build a national finance network that would make what George W. Bush had done with his Rangers and Pioneers look small in comparison. He said he planned to start traveling the country recruiting bundlers who would be expected to raise $350,000 by the end of 2011. In 2008, the campaign had two hundred bundlers at $250,000 each. Messina was looking for double the number, at the higher threshold. Lastly, Messina said the campaign had to be relevant in 2011 while the Republican presidential candidates were flooding Iowa and New Hampshire and South Carolina, attacking the president's record. He wanted to quickly establish a presence anywhere Obama would be under attack from the GOP candidates.

Unstated but obvious was the importance of continuing to find new voters. Obama had won in 2008 in part because he attracted new voters—young people, more African Americans and Latinos, women, especially single women and younger married women. Messina knew that would be even more important in 2012, given the likely drop-off in support for the president because of dissatisfaction with the economy. As he prepared to leave Washington for Chicago, he told me, "We've got to go expand the electorate even more in some ways than we did the last time."

Messina's departure from the White House was one of a series of personnel changes under way, aimed at fixing the deficiencies that by then had become glaring and at preparing for the reelection. Gone were two of the president's closest advisers. David Axelrod returned to Chicago to reprise his role as chief strategist of the campaign. Robert Gibbs, the White House press secretary, departed for a role as general surrogate and attacker of Republicans. To replace Rahm Emanuel, the first chief of staff, who was on his way to becoming mayor of Chicago, Obama brought in another Chicagoan, Bill Daley, the brother of outgoing mayor Richard M. Daley. To some people, that looked like substituting one Chicago pol for another. But Daley was not an Obama confidant and was not able to assemble a team of his own around him.

At the beginning of 2011, tragedy struck. On January 8, twenty-two-year-old Jared Lee Loughner opened fire outside a Safeway store in Tucson, Arizona, killing six people and wounding thirteen. Among the most gravely injured was his apparent main target, Gabrielle Giffords, a young and popular Democratic member of the House. On January 12, with the country convulsed by the tragedy, Obama participated in a service for the victims. The crowd that night was noisy and raucous, and the event took on many of the characteristics of a political rally rather than a solemn remembrance. Despite the atmosphere, Obama delivered one of the most effective speeches of his presidency. "At a time when our discourse has become so sharply polarized—at a time when we are far too eager to lay the blame for all that ails the world at the feet of those who happen to think differently than we do—it's important for us to pause for a moment and make sure that we're talking with each other in a way that heals, not in a way that wounds," he said. "What we cannot do is use this tragedy as one more occasion to turn on each other."

Obama's speech drew praise across the political spectrum. Conservatives who had led the political movement that dealt Obama's party such a terrible defeat in November gushed in their reactions. Two weeks later, on the eve of his State of the Union address, Obama's approval rating had again risen, to 54 percent, in the *Washington Post*/ABC News poll, the highest point in nine months. Far faster than Bill Clinton after his drubbing in 1994, Obama appeared to have rebounded and begun to right his presidency as he headed into the battles ahead.

Once the 112th Congress was sworn in, with Republican John Boehner installed as Speaker of the House and its big freshman class of Tea Party–inspired newcomers, Obama faced months of trench warfare over the budget, spending cuts, taxes, and the deficit—all the issues that had come into play during the midterm elections. With an eye on the coming campaign, Obama hoped he and Congress could reach agreements that would bolster the economy. His advisers believed there was no more effective reelection strategy than boosting growth and reducing unemployment. Anything they could do on either front would improve his shaky prospects for reelection.

In early February, House Republicans offered their first plan to cut the current-year budget. "Washington's spending spree is over," said Paul Ryan, the Wisconsin congressman who chaired the House Budget Committee.

Democrats in the House and Senate attacked the plan, but the White House held its fire. Administration officials worried that an all-out assault on the Republican measure could poison negotiations over a continuing resolution needed to fund the government for the rest of the year. Democrats were critical of the White House. Obama was playing a longer game, his advisers said, aimed at getting through an early fight to fund the government in a way that would help bring about a bigger deal later in the year when the debt ceiling needed raising. In the early months, many Democrats were trying to goad Republicans into shutting down the government in the spring, believing they and Obama could profit from a repeat of what had happened in 1995, when Republicans had forced a shutdown in negotiations with Bill Clinton and paid a political price. Obama was more worried about what a shutdown would do to economic confidence, given the economy's still fragile state. "I don't think any of us are anxious to test the proposition," said one of the president's closest advisers. "The best thing here would be to come to an agreement through the end of the fiscal year. Then you can move to the bigger act, which is, how are you going to deal with the rest of the budget?" White House officials were also hopeful that the fervor of the freshman Republicans in the House would ease as they were confronted by the consequences of trying to cut the budget too much and too quickly.

Instead, negotiations over the continuing resolution dragged on and on—through March and toward the April deadline. When the two sides finally reached agreement just before a midnight deadline that would have shut down the government, Obama sounded an optimistic note. "It's my sincere hope that we can continue to come together as we face the many difficult challenges that lie ahead, from creating jobs and growing our economy to educating our children and reducing our deficit," he said. "That's what the American people expect us to do. That's why they sent us here."

As the negotiations over the continuing resolution were concluding, Republicans put down their next marker in the budget wars: Paul Ryan's blueprint for shrinking the federal government and restructuring Medicare and Medicaid. It became an opening volley of the presidential campaign. Ryan was being urged to run for president in 2012 but was reluctant to do so. But he was a far bigger force within his party than were many of those seeking the presidency. His budget would become a central part of the presidential campaign debate. Ryan, who was in his seventh term in the House, came from Janesville, Wisconsin, a blue-collar town in the state's southern tier. The once vibrant city had seen its share of economic hardship and plant closings, including a General Motors factory. After graduation from Miami University in Ohio, Ryan considered graduate work at the University of Chicago in economics, but politics kept calling him. As a college student he worked in the office of Wisconsin senator Bob Kasten. After college he went to work at Empower America, a conservative think tank, where he wrote speeches for Jack Kemp, the former NFL quarterback and congressman from Buffalo and the party's 1996 vice presidential nominee, and for William Bennett, the sharp-tongued outspoken former secretary of education. Kemp was a father of supply-side economics. He was also a proponent of a brand of conservatism that believed in trying to revitalize urban America. He challenged his party to reach out to African Americans and Hispanics. Ryan adopted much of Kemp's worldview but came to believe that the growth in government spending and rising deficits—never great concerns to Kemp—had to be dealt with as well. He was a number cruncher in a world where such attention to detail was considered unusual. He became an expert on the budget and over time was rewarded by his colleagues, who looked to him to flesh out their vision of a smaller federal government. Ryan produced such a plan in 2010. Obama even praised it as "a serious proposal," though he disagreed with most of the specifics. With Republicans now in control of the House, Ryan offered an updated version of the plan, called "The Path to Prosperity."

Obama had earlier issued his fiscal 2012 budget, which everyone in both parties had ignored. Ryan's budget was the first serious deficit plan of the new Congress, but it was also politically toxic. He sought to reduce deficits by $4 trillion over ten years. He advocated deep cuts in domestic spending and in income tax rates for individuals and corporations. He proposed turning Medicaid into a block grant for the states. Most controversial was his recommendation that Medicare undergo dramatic restructuring. For those already retired or nearing retirement, he called for a continuation of the existing program. For younger workers, Ryan wanted the government to offer payments to individuals, who then would purchase insurance on the open market. Polls showed strong public opposition to the Medicare changes—or, for that matter, most changes to entitlement programs. Democrats saw the controversial budget as the vehicle that could help them win back the House in 2012.

On April 13, 2011, Obama went to George Washington University, where he outlined a plan of his own to cut the deficit by $4 trillion, the same target as Ryan's but over twelve years rather than ten. He called for a ratio of three dollars in spending cuts for each dollar in new revenues. Far more memorable than the specifics of the proposal was Obama's blistering political attack on Ryan and the Republicans. He called Ryan's blueprint a "deeply pessimistic" one that would lead to a "fundamentally different America" than the country had known for generations. "This vision is less about reducing the deficit than it is about changing the basic social compact in America," he said. "Ronald Reagan's own budget director said there's nothing 'serious' or 'courageous' about this plan. There's nothing serious about a plan that claims to reduce the deficit by spending a trillion dollars on tax cuts for millionaires and billionaires. And I don't think there's anything courageous about asking for sacrifice from those who can least afford it and don't have any clout on Capitol Hill. That's not a vision of the America I know." He said of the Medicare restructuring in Ryan's plan, "Put simply, it ends Medicare as we know it."

White House officials had decided it would be helpful to invite the leaders of Obama's fiscal commission, former Republican senator Alan Simpson and former Clinton White House chief of staff Erskine Bowles, to the speech. Then they decided to invite all members of the commission, even those who had voted against it. That included Ryan, who was given a front-row seat for what turned into a public whipping. When the newly installed Bill Daley walked into the auditorium, he immediately saw Ryan. "Holy shit!" he thought. One of the president's aides had told Ryan he would like the speech. Ryan said he expected a Clintonesque, politically triangulating speech by the president. "Then this torrent of demagoguery comes out," Ryan said. The congressman noticed a photographer with his telescopic lens trained directly on him. He sat poker-faced as Obama spoke, but inside he was seething. "It occurred to me, holy cow, this guy [Obama] is not a moderate. This guy is a real ideologue and he is already in hyper campaign mode," he said. When the speech ended, Ryan and several of his House colleagues left quickly. Ryan issued a curt statement calling the speech "excessively partisan, dramatically inaccurate, and hopelessly inadequate to address our fiscal crisis." The next day the president asked Simpson and Bowles to the White House. Simpson said that Bowles told the president, "I thought you were very harsh on the Republicans and on Ryan." Simpson said he told Obama that "it was like inviting the guy to his own hanging." He said it would have been better not to invite him or not to attack him. "Well, [Obama] didn't like that," Simpson said.

The first two rounds of the budget battle were now over, and instead of creating a climate for cooperation and bipartisanship, they had done the opposite. The president's speech had turned what was to have been a moment designed to set a tone for productive talks into another show of partisanship. Austan Goolsbee, who was chairman of the Council of Economic Advisers at the time, later concluded that the president's policy team had made a sizable error in judgment. They had assumed that with every small deal, they were making a grand bargain more possible. Instead, those small deals were leaving Tea Party activists more and more dissatisfied. "So that sets the stage for the debt ceiling, for it to blow up there, and unfortunately that's the worst possible place for it to blow up," he said.

———

Obama began the negotiations over the debt ceiling just after one of the crowning achievements of his presidency: the killing of Osama bin Laden on May 1. Obama had made the risky decision to launch the Navy SEAL team strike against the compound in Abbottabad, Pakistan, over the opposition of Defense Secretary Robert Gates and the strong reservations of Secretary of State Hillary Clinton and Vice President Joe Biden. The intelligence was no better than fifty-fifty that bin Laden was in the compound. "If you went in to get a search warrant on the evidence we had, no judge in Washington would have given you that search warrant," one senior administration official said a month after the raid.

A day after giving the order to go ahead with the raid and a day before it was carried out, Obama attended the annual White House Correspondents' Association Dinner, delivering his jokes with perfect timing. He showed none of the tension that gripped those few in the administration who knew about the president's order. Before the dinner, Axelrod had lunch with the president. A national security aide came in, and the president asked Axelrod to leave. As he waited outside the Oval Office, he overheard nearby chatter that the National Security Council team did not want Obama playing golf the next morning because of a possible meeting. He was curious about that. When he went back in to see Obama, they went over some of the jokes the president was considering for his speech that night. One involved Tim Pawlenty, the former Minnesota governor who was running for president. The joke went something like: Poor Tim Pawlenty, he had such potential as a candidate, except for the unfortunate middle name bin Laden. Obama said, "That's so hackneyed, why don't we take that out?" One of the president's speechwriters offered up an alternative. It was changed to "Hosni" rather than "bin Laden." Axelrod thought the new version was not as funny but thought, What the hell, it's his routine. He had no idea that Obama was planning something more permanent for bin Laden than eliminating him from his comedic routine.

The president's approval ratings spiked in the wake of the killing of bin Laden, though everyone around him knew the spike was temporary.

Vice President Biden led the opening round of bipartisan negotiations, which went on for weeks. At times there was a sense of optimism that the two sides could reach agreement, as they identified a series of specific spending cuts. But Republicans were divided and revenues were not a serious part of the discussions, as the administration was insisting. In late June, Eric Cantor, the House majority leader, who had close ties to the Tea Party freshman class, announced that he was pulling out. Obama had been largely invisible to that point, and the lack of progress generated new criticism of the president's lack of leadership. *New York Times* columnist David Brooks, to whom the White House paid considerable attention, wrote a column about management styles and how to get things done in an era of austerity. He compared Obama with New Jersey governor Chris Christie and Chicago mayor Rahm Emanuel, describing Christie as a "straight up the middle" leader and Emanuel as an insurgent. "Being led by Barack Obama is like being trumpeted into battle by Miles Davis," he wrote. "He makes you want to sit down and discern." It was time, he said, for the "former messiah" to become a manager. Two days later, Obama held a news conference and showed uncharacteristic flashes of anger. He said his daughters took a more responsible approach to their homework assignments than Congress was taking to the debt ceiling issue. "Malia and Sasha generally finish their homework a day ahead of time," he said. "They don't wait until the night before. They're not pulling all-nighters." Republicans in Congress, he said, "need to do their job." He noted the on-again, off-again congressional schedule. "You need to be here," he said. "I've been here. I've been doing Afghanistan and bin Laden and the Greek [debt] crisis. You stay here. Let's get it done."

The next day I sat down with one of Obama's senior White House advisers. He said Obama had come off the stage after the press conference and told his advisers that it "felt good just to speak the truth." The adviser said a lot of what Obama said was extemporaneous, but not entirely. "In our prep, we decided, 'Let's challenge Congress a little bit,'" he said. "'Let's sort of tell the truth,' like this whole notion of where's the president's leadership? I mean give me a break." Doesn't it bother him? I asked. "It doesn't bug him, he's bemused by it." That spring, an unnamed official in the administration had been quoted in the *New Yorker* as saying that on the uprising in Libya, the president was "leading from behind." The characterization triggered a torrent of uncomplimentary commentary, especially from the right, and seemed to capture a growing perception about Obama during his third year in office. The president's adviser said, "When you look at the fights he's taken on in terms of 'Don't Ask, Don't Tell,' health care, saving the auto industry, I think when this story is known about the deficit—however it ends up—I think people will at least acknowledge that there was some boldness there."

Obama liked John Boehner personally but saw the speaker as a Chamber of Commerce type, a country club Republican suddenly forced to try to tame the Tea Party tiger. He invited Boehner to play golf, and from that outing came a secret meeting between Obama and Boehner at the White House on June 22, which then led to the first serious negotiations over a grand bargain. Their private negotiations seemed to be making progress until some of the details began to leak. Cantor was alarmed at what he saw as Boehner's coming capitulation. The *Wall Street Journal* editorial page weighed in on Saturday, July 9, with a tough editorial warning the speaker not to cut the deal. "Mr. Boehner shouldn't bet his majority on Mr. Obama's promises," the editorial stated. That night, Boehner called the president, who was at Camp David. "I just can't do it right now," he said. That marked the beginning of weeks of turmoil in Washington, which were later re-created in meticulous detail in a series of books and articles. The two neared an agreement and then pulled back, eventually producing a miserable compromise that resolved none of the big issues and set the stage for what would be repeated confrontations over the next two years. The low point came when Obama could not get a call to the Speaker returned for twenty-four hours, which was followed by dueling press conferences assigning blame to the other side. It was a failure of leadership by any measure.

For Obama it brought a sudden end to his belief that he could somehow lead the Republicans and his own party to an agreement. From that moment forward, he would operate with a different calculus. "There was no hoping, dreaming, or encouraging for any alternative," Daley said. "[Obama] said, 'That's it. What are we going to do, sit here and keep getting pounded, trying to reach out? No. We're not going to do this anymore.' . . . When it got to the end of that week, when it finally got done, I think our whole attitude was, this thing's over and any dream of anything coming together—for anything—is over." Another official said, "The president is a person who likes to do big things, has a taste for the legacy project, over a series of school-uniform kind of things. I think in his mind was growing the desire of, okay, it's a new environment, but we can do a legacy project of long-run fiscal consolidation." When the talks collapsed, Obama "realized there are not going to be any legacy items for the next two years. There's just going to be a big fight over who's going to be the president."

In the aftermath of the debt ceiling collapse, Obama's inspiring rhetoric from the 2008 campaign about changing Washington seemed quaint, even naïve. Instead of bipartisanship there was polarization as deep as it had been in modern times. Instead of cooperation there was constant confrontation. Instead of civility there was rudeness. The political system appeared frozen and more resistant to compromise than ever. Republicans bore the principal responsibility. The party's strategy of opposing Obama at every turn created what some analysts called asymmetrical political warfare. But Obama was not blameless. Presidents are expected to solve problems and overcome political obstacles. Did Obama ever have a strategy to achieve that goal? Should he—could he—have built better relationships with congressional Republicans? Most important, would it have made any difference if he had done any of these things? He arrived in Washington with the hope of bringing the parties together through a guiding hand, not a whip. But his belief that he could guide opposing parties to a consensus and eventual compromise collided with the ingrained partisanship of Washington and a Republican Party that was playing by new rules. Almost every battle drove the two sides further apart.

There were few better illustrations of how the two sides had ended up at loggerheads than a story involving Newt Gingrich, the former House Speaker who had both fought with and compromised with former president Bill Clinton during the 1990s. Gingrich was at the Capitol with his wife, Callista, for Obama's swearing-in ceremony. He was impressed with Obama's rhetoric—the speech on election night in Grant Park and now what he said on inauguration day. He said he believed that the country was hungry for a diminishment of political conflict in Washington and truly wanted the nation's first African American president to succeed. "I told Callista leaving the Capitol after the inaugural, I said, 'If he follows through he will be Eisenhower and he will split the Republican Party,'" Gingrich said to me. Later that evening, Gingrich joined a dozen or so other Republicans, who were dispirited but determined to plot a comeback, for a dinner at the Caucus Room restaurant just off Pennsylvania Avenue. Robert Draper in his book *Do Not Ask What Good We Do* quoted Gingrich as he left the dinner saying, "You'll remember this as the day the seeds of 2012 were sown." When I later asked Gingrich how he reconciled his belief that the country wanted Obama to succeed and that the president was in a position to split the Republican Party with the plotting that went on at the dinner, his response encapsulated both the initial promise of the Obama presidency and the obstacles he would encounter in trying to fulfill it. "Our job was to design the optimum GOP strategy," Gingrich said. "Obama's job was to govern so our strategy would fail." David Axelrod scoffed at Gingrich's explanation. "If on inaugural night leaders of the Republican Party are meeting to talk about how they could thwart the president, it belies the notion that they are waiting patiently by their phones for a call from the president to see if they could work together," he said. "They had a strategy predicated on not working together."

Republicans complained that Obama never genuinely tried to reach out to them. Axelrod said, "We entered office at a time of maximum peril. We frankly didn't have the luxury of waiting for the logjam to break before we could act." The debt ceiling collapse brought back talk of Obama's failure to build relationships, something he had heard in the weeks after the midterm election. He made some preliminary efforts, hosting receptions for members of Congress during the first months of his presidency, inviting a bipartisan group to watch the Super Bowl, and meeting with committee leaders from both parties on issues such as education and financial regulatory reform. The role of schmoozing with Congress fell to the vice president. Tennessee senator Lamar Alexander said the president didn't seem interested in even trying to develop relationships. When I asked whether it was really worth trying, given the implacable opposition of congressional Republicans, he replied, "If just that causes you to stop, that just shows you don't know very much about what you're doing." Democrats said Obama didn't work very hard to develop relationships with them either. One senior senator described him as "aloof, cold." A senior House member said, "I find him a very warm person with a good sense of humor—a good guy to be with. But there is a sort of reserve that he has that does not encourage the sort of relationships beyond that crowd that he feels comfortable with. That's not his inclination on either the Democratic side or the Republican side, and I think it's hurt him."

The debt ceiling battle ended any illusions about Obama's power to change Washington, certainly for his first term. He was up against an implacable foe, opposition he had not bargained for. He had not found a way to break the gridlock in the face of that opposition. The aspirational candidate of 2008 who came to bind up the nation's wounds now faced a difficult and extremely partisan reelection campaign. His Democratic critics said he was foolish to have believed he could extract any concessions from the Republicans. Republicans saw in Obama a combination of ideology, ambition, vanity, and weakness. The final indignity after the talks collapsed was to see the government's credit rating downgraded because the political system was judged to be so dysfunctional. "I think there's no doubt that I underestimated the degree to which in this town politics trumps problem solving," he would later tell Charlie Rose on *CBS This Morning*. "Washington feels as broken as it did four years ago," Obama said. "And, if you asked me what is the one thing that has frustrated me most over the last four years, it's not the hard work, it's not the enormity of the decisions, it's not the pace. It is that I haven't been able to change the atmosphere here in Washington to reflect the decency and common sense of ordinary people—Democrats, Republicans, and independents—who I think just want to see their leadership solve problems. And there's enough blame to go around for that."

In the wake of the debt ceiling battle, Obama's reelection prospects appeared worse than ever.

CHAPTER 4

Message for the Middle Class

One of the hallmarks of Obama's 2012 campaign was its prodigious appetite for research and data. The trio at the top of the operation—Jim Messina and David Axelrod at the campaign and David Plouffe in the White House—were all enthusiastic consumers of research. Though different in their approach to politics—Axelrod operated intuitively; Plouffe's watchwords were "prove it"; Messina wanted to be able to measure everything—they all pushed the campaign team for more research, testing, analysis, and innovation. Everyone knew that the economy represented the president's biggest obstacle to reelection. Obama's top advisers wanted to make the 2012 election a choice and not a referendum on the president's economic stewardship. They doubted he could win a race on the latter. But to avoid the election becoming a referendum, they knew they had to do two things. First, they had to develop and refine a message that somehow leapfrogged the debate about the current state of the economy, which would always leave Obama on the defensive. And second, they had to disqualify their opponent—they assumed that would be Mitt Romney—from being seen as a credible alternative able to do for the economy what Obama had failed to do.

The first priority was to understand what had happened in 2010: Why had many of the people who had bought into the hope and change message from Obama's 2008 campaign decided just two years later that they were ready to burn down the house? Obama's team was eager to know what was really behind the shellacking. They decided to look for answers in a familiar place: Iowa. For Obama's team, Iowa was always the touchstone. Whenever the Obama team was in trouble, whenever they needed reassurance or understanding, or were merely curious about something, they thought first of Iowa. What do Iowans think? So in late 2010 they convened a focus group in Des Moines composed of independent voters who had supported Obama in 2008 and then backed the Republicans in 2010. One man in particular, who was in his fifties, caught the attention of the Obama advisers who were watching from Washington. One adviser summed up the grievances encapsulated in the man's response this way: "I can't send my kid to college next year. I can't do it because my house is underwater now and I was going to refinance it to pay for tuition. I don't think any parent knows how hard it is to tell your kid I can't send you to school. I haven't had a raise in five years. I'm paying more for health insurance and getting less. My 401(k) that was supposed to be the reward for doing everything the right way is gone. I am sick and tired of giving bailouts to the folks at the top and handouts to the folks at the bottom. I'm going to fire people [politicians] until my life gets better."

That was the beginning of what would become a massive research effort that went on from early 2011 into the late summer. As Obama engaged in politically debilitating hand-to-hand combat with congressional Republicans, his political advisers were quietly at work developing the framework for the reelection campaign message. The Obama team launched parallel efforts in early 2011 to probe more deeply the psyche of the country. "We began to understand that the real demand in the electorate was not just to recover from the recession," said Larry Grisolano, who oversaw media and message. "If we just got back to where we were in 2008, that was not a good place to be. They saw the long erosion of what it meant to be middle class in America."

Not long after David Plouffe had settled into his new role at the White House, he had a conversation with Joel Benenson, Obama's lead pollster in 2008, who was in the same role for 2012. They talked about the research operation for the coming two years, and Plouffe urged Benenson to think creatively about new ways to examine the electorate and the state of the country. Benenson described a project he had done for the Service Employees International Union after the 2004 election—what he called the "middle-aged, middle-income, middle America" study. They had mailed journals to a selected group of people and asked them to fill them out, describing their lives from a personal financial perspective. The more he explained it, the more Plouffe liked the idea. That conversation launched the campaign's ethnography project, which David Simas, the director of opinion research for the campaign, later described as "the best and most important research we did the entire campaign because of the insight it gave us into truly how people view the economy, not on a macro level but on a day-to-day level."

Benenson started the project in the spring of 2011. He recruited about 150 people who said they were willing to participate; in the end just over 100 actually did. The participants were all between the ages of thirty-five and sixty-five, with household incomes of $40,000 to $100,000. They were either white or Hispanic and lived in the suburbs of Columbus, Denver, or Orlando. They had little or no allegiance to either political party. They were either self-identified independents or weak partisans. While definitely planning to vote, they were undecided—they were open to both Obama and the eventual Republican nominee. Obama's campaign, which wanted what Benenson called a "totally nonpolitical deep dive into their lives and values," did not reveal that it was behind the research. The subjects were chosen because they were considered emblematic of the "up for grabs" voters Obama's team always kept a close watch on. The Obama campaign asked the participants to fill out a journal twice a week for three weeks. In contrast to the SEIU project, Benenson decided to do this all online. Twice a week, he sent the participants eight to ten questions, different topics for each session. Rather than asking one broad, open-ended question, the campaign posed an opening question and a series of follow-ups to drill deeply into the topic. The journals provided a revealing body of work about how people were living with the economy day to day, what choices they were making, whether they were putting off purchases or buying a used car rather than a new car, how they viewed their work and their career options, their fears about the future, and their doubts that the American dream still meant something. "If you want to know about being treated unfairly at work," Benenson said, "we would ask, 'When was the last time you felt you were treated unfairly at work? What specifically happened? What made you feel you were being treated unfairly? How was that different or similar to times you were being treated? Was the way you were treated same or different than your coworkers?' It was designed to provoke in-depth responses." The journal entries eventually added up to more than fourteen hundred pages of raw material.

The second phase of the project took place in early June. Benenson and business partner Danny Franklin conducted nine focus groups, three in each of the three locations. Each focus group was limited to just three participants and lasted two and a half hours. These "triads," as they were called, were divided by age and gender: men over fifty or under fifty; women over fifty or under fifty. The sessions allowed for an even deeper conversation about issues the participants had described in their journal entries. "They shared a strong sense that America was changing in a way that was out of their control," Benenson said. "They felt the old rules of the economy and how you got ahead didn't apply anymore. It wasn't so much that they didn't recognize new rules in the economy. They weren't sure there *were* new rules. How to get ahead was more perplexing to them. The ground rules had disappeared and they didn't know what the new ground rules were.

"On the broadest scale, they were really struggling to keep what they had. They were more worried about sliding down the economic ladder than moving ahead. All they wanted was to be able to get out what they put in, and they weren't sure they could." Benenson said a woman in Denver told them, "As a parent you want things to be better for your children. I know my parents did when I was brought up. I don't think most kids are going to be able to buy a house. I think it's going to be really a struggle to be able to do that. So the dream is going to have to be modified. Something is going to have to change dramatically." A Columbus man said, "I'm sick of debt affecting how much disposable income we have. I just want it all paid off." One of the most compelling insights was the degree to which the concept of the American dream did not mean as much for younger workers as it did for older ones. "The language around the American dream wasn't carrying the same resonance," Benenson said. "Some of the symbols of achieving the American dream were becoming burdens—owning that house with the big mortgage was expensive; owning two cars and more debt; having your kid go to college. The cost and burden of taking out those loans was making a lot of Americans ambivalent. They weren't sure a college education was worth it."

In early June, Benenson's team produced a forty-five-page document summing up the findings. There were a variety of implications for the campaign. People prized reciprocity—the idea that hard work would be rewarded—but felt it was no longer part of the basic bargain in society. They wanted to be part of something bigger but saw the sense of community slipping away. They put a higher priority on economic security than on taking risks; just maintaining that security was worth celebrating. As he was finishing, Benenson conducted a benchmark survey that reinforced the conclusion that Obama's message had to be as forward-looking as possible. He had to draw a contrast based on values and visions for the future, not debate what he had done right or wrong. Benenson said, "What we learned in 2011 made us pretty confident that the president's economic values and vision were a lot more aligned with where swing voters were and where most Americans were than anyone in the Republican field," Benenson said. "We didn't have any false sense of confidence. We knew it would be a close race. But we never deviated from that kind of approach and that kind of strategy."

Throughout the spring and summer of 2011, the campaign also conducted other research projects, including a series of more traditional focus groups, to probe political attitudes about the economy, the president, and the Republicans. David Binder ran the focus groups, as he had done in 2008. Binder was the inexhaustible traveler of the Obama research team, originally recruited by Axelrod and, by the assessment of his colleagues, a gifted moderator. Axelrod especially liked that Binder was not a pollster. Pollsters sometimes came to focus groups with an agenda, to confirm what they found in their polls, and their questions sometimes prodded the participants to confirm the numbers. Binder didn't mix quantitative and qualitative research. He was there to tease out what people were really thinking. In the early stages, Axelrod wanted Binder to keep the focus as broad as possible, to allow the participants' true feelings to bubble up naturally. At this stage he did not want a directed conversation about specific issues. The challenge this time was far different from that in Obama's first campaign. "In '08 when we do qualitative research, there's more of the sense of how do we create excitement about this person that's running? Is he risky, and if so, what can we do to bridge that concern that we're trying somebody a little bit too new?" Binder said. "That obviously was not the case this time. This time there's a record to run on that will be attacked, and the methodology's more along the lines of determining to what degree can people reenlist with the president who has potentially disappointed them. It's a very different kind of questioning and probing—kind of emotional investigative."

Over time, Binder's research produced three broad findings about how people felt about the president. The first was, predictably, the enormous dissatisfaction with the state of the economy. This overwhelmed everything else. Debt and deficits would later become a bigger concern for many of the people, but through most of 2011 the economy dominated discussions. Anxiety about the economy pervaded the conversations—concerns that jobs were not coming back fast enough, that salaries weren't going up, that the housing crisis wasn't over, that people felt underemployed. "It was basically a sense that the country wasn't moving forward to the degree that they had hoped, and for some people they felt that the president promised better," said a campaign official.

The second finding was that people had not given up on Obama. Their initial buy-in on his character had not been compromised. They knew his biography. They admired his family. They remembered that each night when he was in Washington he had dinner with his wife and daughters in the White House residence. To some extent the groups were skewed; Obama haters were never included in the groups, so the full fury of anti-Obama sentiment that had fueled the Republican victory was missing from these groups. But those voters were already lost to the president. The question was how many of his 2008 supporters were in danger of defecting. What Binder found was that while there was anxiety about the president and his record, there was almost always the thread in the conversations that voters remained open to him. "They wanted to give him the benefit of the doubt," Binder said. "And part of that was only because they felt he was trying. And when we asked, 'Well, what have you seen to indicate that he's trying?' then they would—even though they'd just [finished] bad-mouthing Obamacare—they said, 'Well, he's trying to do something about health care.' So you find all this conflict, internal conflict among the voters."

But if Obama's 2008 supporters still gave him the benefit of the doubt, they nonetheless had serious reservations about him. His heart may have been in the right place, they said, but was he up to the job? That was the most troublesome finding. Voters questioned whether he really understood how to get the economy moving. They worried that he did not have policies that would work. They feared that the problems were bigger than he was—which was such a profound change from the way they had viewed him in 2008, when they saw him as a transformational figure who was going to be able to radically change Washington. They did not see him as weak—the killing of Osama bin Laden had helped remove that issue from the election—so much as they sensed that he lacked the experience to make Washington work. They recognized, particularly after the debt ceiling fight, that he faced stubborn opposition from the Republicans, that the Republicans were more to blame for the standoff than was the president. But they wanted a president capable of finding a way around that obstacle. "We heard that quite a bit, that he didn't have enough experience to know how to deal with the job," one campaign official said. "And a lot of it I think was you have to knock heads together with Congress, and Obama didn't seem to know how to do that. . . . People brought up Lyndon Johnson, which was interesting. You don't expect a focus group to say he needs to be more like LBJ, especially given the age group here. But it was amazing, some people saying LBJ had it, he knew how to twist an arm in a way to get what he wanted. And Obama doesn't seem to do that." Another campaign official said, "I've never had so many damned references to Lyndon Johnson in my life. All the bloody time. It became like an inside joke, how many times is LBJ going to come up? We were trying to find a way to use Republican obstruction as more of a weapon and people would concede it. 'Yeah, they're horrible, they're terrible, but he's the president, he should be able to figure out a way to get around it. It's your problem. You're the one who wanted the job.'"

"People thought the president was doing a pretty good job under the circumstances," Grisolano added. "They were angry about the economy but fairminded about what he walked into. But they didn't feel they had a sense of the bigger picture. Where was he driving, where was he taking the country, how are we going to get there?" The president's advisers concluded that he would make the campaign less about the state of the economy and all about who would look after the interests of the middle class during a time of economic transition. "The beauty of this framework was that it helped us slip the noose on the economy," Grisolano said. "We knew the Republican message was, 'The economy sucks, Obama's responsible, fire him.' By going to the issue of which candidate could be trusted with the country's long-term economic future, we kind of sidestepped the . . . 'throw the bums out' thinking."

Preparation for the attacks on Mitt Romney also began early. The Democratic National Committee had done some of the initial work before the Obama team decamped for Chicago. Once settled in their new offices, the campaign's opposition research team, led by Elizabeth Jarvis-Shean, dug into the former Massachusetts governor's record. Every Friday, the campaign's different department heads met with Messina to rate the Republican challengers. Romney began as number one and never slipped lower, even when others were ahead of him in the polls. Their reasoning was that Romney had run for president before, could raise the money needed to wage a long campaign, and was running against an improbable group of rivals. As someone with extensive business experience, Romney fit Axelrod's long-held belief that in times of stress or dissatisfaction, voters look for a remedy, not a replica. "He seemed the most distinct from Obama, the solid businessman, no gloss," Axelrod said. Certainly Romney had flaws, and the campaign was looking to exploit them. And they knew that after 2010 the nomination battle would push him to the right. Axelrod said he told the president after the midterms that the seeds had been planted for his reelection, "because the gravitational pull in the Republican Party was now so far to the right that anybody who was going to be the nominee had to go through that tollbooth and they would have to pay a very high toll."

By the fall of 2011, Obama's advisers began to worry that Romney was successfully avoiding attacks from his Republican rivals. Plouffe was concerned that the likely challenger's image was too positive. The team decided they couldn't wait for one of the Republicans to do it. If they wanted their likely opponent framed up for the general election, they would have to take on the job themselves. On October 30, 2011, Plouffe went after Romney on NBC's *Meet the Press*. "He has no core," Plouffe said. "I can tell you one thing working a few steps down from the president, what you need in that office is conviction. You need to have a true compass, and you have got to be willing to make tough calls. You get the sense with Mitt Romney that if he thought it was good to say the sky was green and the grass was blue to win an election, he'd say it." The Democratic National Committee released an online video attack with the same theme. "From the creator of 'I'm running for office, for Pete's sake,' comes the story of two men trapped in one body: Mitt versus Mitt," the narrator said. Using footage of Romney taking positions on both sides of different issues, the narrator added, "Two Mitts, willing to say anything."

Around that time, Bill Clinton met with Messina, Axelrod, and Patrick Gaspard, the former White House political director who was now at the DNC, in Harlem. Be careful here, he told them. You do not want to paint Romney as a flip-flopper. His reasoning was born of his own experience. Republicans had tried the tactic on him and he had learned that people sometimes came to the conclusion that a politician with such a reputation eventually could end up on the right side of an issue. Swing voters, especially, thought that way. If voters thought Romney in the end might do the right thing, they would be more comfortable voting for him, especially if they had real doubts about Obama's ability to deal with the economy. Clinton told the trio from the Obama campaign that they should hold Romney accountable for the conservative positions he was espousing as a candidate, not provide him with an escape hatch by suggesting he didn't believe them.

Clinton's advice helped refocus the Obama team. Going after him as a flip-flopper might be attractive, but Romney's real vulnerabilities were the positions he was taking and his record in private industry. Romney was using his business experience as his principal calling card as a candidate, a way to draw contrast with a president who had no private-sector experience. Obama's team set out to turn it into Romney's biggest liability. Near the end of 2011, I talked with Axelrod about this. He said, "The two things that concern folks the most are an economy that, not just over the last three years, but over the long term, feels like it's been rigged against hardworking, responsible everyday people. And politics in which people too often are willing to subjugate fundamental principles to their own ambition. And when you think about the two things that most distress people, you wouldn't necessarily come up with Mitt Romney as the answer, because he in many ways represents those things in the economy that concern people the most."

Obama's advisers had done their own research on Romney's vulnerabilities. At first blush, voters saw Romney's business experience in a generally positive light. They accepted some of the harsher business practices that Bain and other private equity firms engaged in—the downsizing of companies, layoffs, elimination of benefits—as standard operating procedure in a competitive world. They saw Romney's success as a sign of his toughness, a quality they thought might be useful in a president dealing with such a stubborn economic crisis. Did he break the law? they asked the moderator. The campaign team then decided to ask another series of questions focused not on the legality of what private equity firms did but on the issue of whether it was the right thing to do. It may have been legitimate, but was it right? One Obama adviser told me later, "Once we began introducing that, it allowed us to make the following argument, which was effective: He may get the economy, he may know how to make money, he may have made hundreds of millions for him and his investors. But every time he did, folks like you lost your pensions, lost your jobs, jobs got shipped overseas. And that became the best way for us to define his business experience, his strength, in a way that then served to really hurt him at the same time, to separate technical experience from the values around it." In October 2011, the campaign had conducted focus groups in three battleground states—Ohio, Florida, and New Hampshire—and had shown participants a famous photo taken of Romney and his partners at Bain as they were forming the company. They were holding dollar bills and smiling broadly, and more bills were stuffed in their pockets and in their mouths and in their shirt collars. After seeing that, Messina said, "People were like, 'Game over.'"

CHAPTER 5

Fall Offensive

August 2011 was the lowest month of Obama's presidency, lower even than November 2010, when Democrats lost the House and Senate. At least Obama and his team had seen that coming. August 2011 was worse too than the first month of 2010, when Scott Brown's election in Massachusetts had shocked the Democrats and seemed to signal the death of health care. August 2011 was, in the words of one presidential adviser, "indescribably bad." It was the low point not only because it brought Obama's hopes of a grand bargain on the deficit crashing down, but also because the collapse damaged the president almost as much as it hurt the Republicans—something White House officials had never anticipated. Obama's team worried all summer about a possible default. They were, said another senior official in the White House, "scared shitless" that the government would default, with all the consequences for the economy that would bring. They began the negotiations with minimal expectations; mostly they wanted to avoid a catastrophic default. "It wasn't like this was driven by, 'Hey, let's have something here where we're just dancing with John Boehner and we look like the compromisers and that'll help us politically,'" Plouffe told me at the time. "That's not what drove the strategy. What drove the strategy was, 'Okay, we actually have a chance here to do something meaningful on the debt and the deficit.'" John Boehner's apparent interest in a grand bargain, which the president believed was genuine, raised expectations that something serious might result. When it came crashing down, the debris hit everyone—including the president. "We knew absolutely that when this fell apart we'd be left holding the bag of shit," the president's adviser said. "You just knew you were going to be in terrible shape."

It turned out to be much worse than they imagined. All through the long summer of negotiations, White House officials calculated that Obama's advocacy for a balanced package of spending cuts and tax increases would make him seem to be the reasonable partner, the adult in the room. In contrast to the president's reasonableness, they argued, Republicans were doing something extraordinary by holding an increase in the debt ceiling hostage to their own ideological demands for spending cuts, just as their base expected. As Eric Cantor had told the freshmen at the beginning of the year, they were using their leverage when it could be felt most. No party had ever done that with a debt ceiling increase—posturing, yes,* but never this. White House officials believed that if the talks broke down, the public would blame the Republicans for their intransigence. Instead, the public saw a dysfunctional Washington playing Russian roulette with the good faith and credit of the United States. Obama could not escape the blame.

In the aftermath of the debt ceiling negotiations, Standard & Poor's lowered the country's credit rating for the first time ever. The ratings agency said the decision was based less on economic conditions than on the broken politics of Washington. The country's leaders had failed to instill confidence that they could solve its fiscal problems. Consumer confidence plunged sixteen points, the kind of decline associated with cataclysmic events like 9/11 or the collapse of Lehman Brothers. Almost 80 percent of Americans said they were dissatisfied with the way the political system was working. More than seven in ten said they had little or no confidence in Washington's ability to solve problems. Bill McInturff, one of the nation's leading pollsters, analyzed a month of data and found the numbers appalling for what they said about the country. "The perception of how Washington handled the debt ceiling negotiation led to an immediate collapse in confidence in government and all the major players, including President Obama and Republicans in Congress," he wrote.

The debt ceiling debacle put Obama in a sour mood. He was most frustrated by the failure to strike a deal with Boehner and the Republicans, but he was also deeply unhappy over the portrait that was emerging of him, that of a leader who could not work his will with Congress, no matter that the Republicans were united in their opposition. The public understood the obstacles Obama faced with the opposition party, but many people still thought the president should find a way to make the system work. He was the president, after all. He was the daddy figure. "The president thought he got a good deal, thought he had tried to do the right thing, and was basically being portrayed as feckless and weak by people on his side, driven almost entirely by the editorial board and the op-ed pages of the *New York Times*," one senior White House official said. "The right was saying the same thing about the president the left was saying, and that's a bad place to find yourself in." During the summer negotiations, Obama had met with a group of columnists for an off-the-record

---

*As a new senator, Obama had voted against raising the debt ceiling as a symbolic protest of rising deficits.

conversation. David Brooks made an observation. You've lost control of your narrative, he told the president, according to someone else present. Obama was quick to respond. David, he said, the problem is not my narrative. The problem is the economy. We have a terrible economy. But in fact, Obama *had* lost control of the narrative. "He was very exasperated by how broken Washington was in this case and how Boehner just couldn't make the deal even if it was the right thing to do for the country," a senior campaign adviser said. "And surprised by, with notable few exceptions, how the press never just chased the story full-time. Cable's the biggest driver of this, but there was a controversy, and that just kind of drove a narrative that in our mind wasn't true." Obama was not just exasperated. "He was exhausted," said one person who saw him at the time. "He looked tired, was tired, and I think he had done everything he could to pull that thing together." Another adviser said Obama was "as low as I've seen him."

As long as he had been running for president or in the White House, Obama had experienced trouble during the summer. In 2007, his campaign appeared stalled and his major donors were in rebellion. In 2008, after Sarah Palin's selection as John McCain's running mate gave the Republican ticket a jolt of energy, he had to rally his campaign team to step up its game when polls showed the Republican ticket overtaking him. His first summer as president was marked by the rise of the Tea Party, protests at congressional town hall meetings, and a decline in his poll numbers. The following summer White House officials could see the thunderclouds building for the fall elections. Now there was another summer of discontent. The promise of winter and spring—the eloquent speech in Tucson, the first signs of economic recovery, and the prospect of possible cooperation with the Republicans on deficit negotiations—had given way to an ugly and rancorous summer. He was frustrated at how he was being characterized, frustrated that his party and his allies were so openly attacking him. He thought it was mightily unfair. Could they not see all the things he had accomplished during his first two and a half years in office, from health care—which other presidents over half a century had failed to enact—to saving the automobile industry, to preventing another Great Depression, to passage of financial regulatory reform, all over ferocious Republican opposition?

One article in particular stung the White House, written by Drew Westen of Emory University and published in the *New York Times* on August 6 with the headline, "What Happened to Obama?" It was as searing an indictment as anyone who purported to be an ally of the president had made. "The president is fond of referring to 'the arc of history,' paraphrasing the Rev. Dr. Martin Luther King Jr.'s famous statement that 'the arc of the moral universe is long, but it bends toward justice,'" Westen wrote. "But with his deep-seated aversion to conflict and his profound failure to understand bully dynamics—in which conciliation is always the wrong course of action, because bullies perceive it as weakness and just punch harder the next time—he has broken that arc and has likely bent it backward for at least a generation." He argued that Obama should have dealt harshly with the Wall Street transgressors who brought on the economic collapse. He said Obama had chosen to "avert his gaze" from the economic inequality and corporate influence harming the country. Westen blamed Obama for not listening to those in and out of his administration who had called for a larger stimulus package—without taking into account how difficult it would have been to enact something larger than the $800 billion package. "The result, as predicted in advance, was a half-stimulus that half-stimulated the economy," he wrote. Westen said he and others who supported Obama in 2008 had overlooked "disquieting aspects" of the candidate's biography—"that he had accomplished very little before he ran for president"—and said the country was now led by a president "who either does not know what he believes or is willing to take whatever position he thinks will lead to his re-election." He offered a final thought on why Obama's presidency had come to this point: "He ran for president on two contradictory platforms: as a reformer who would clean up the system, and as a unity candidate who would transcend the lines of red and blue. He has pursued the one with which he is most comfortable given the constraints of his character, consistently choosing the message of bipartisanship over the message of confrontation."

The president's advisers said he was thoroughly irritated with Westen's piece. Once published, it shaped the post–debt ceiling conversation. It was proof, some analysts said, that Obama's base was in revolt. There was little evidence that his real base—African Americans in particular—was defecting. But among liberal elites there *was* great dissatisfaction and disappointment. Westen's piece also burned the president's advisers, who paid far more attention to such writings than many people might assume. "It got to their liberal nerves," a leading Democrat said of the White House staff. The decision was, "We've got to stop the quacking by the professional base."

The White House responded by getting Obama out of Washington. On August 15, the president landed in Minneapolis for the start of a three-day bus tour that would take him to small towns in eastern Iowa and western Illinois. As he traveled across the gently rolling landscape near the Mississippi River, Obama's motorcade numbered almost twenty vehicles. The president rode aboard a new, armored black bus, a behemoth of a vehicle with flashing lights and tinted windows that seemed to match the determined—even dark—mood of the White House team. Iowa was always therapy for Obama, and the bus trip was as much designed as a restorative for the president as it was a time to try to reframe the debate and stand clear of the wreckage back in Washington. But the president received a jarring welcome when he arrived in Iowa—a front-page editorial in the *Dubuque Telegraph Herald* that said he should have stayed in Washington. "While many folks here are flattered that you are spending time with us in the Dubuque area, we respectfully ask what will be accomplished," the editorial said. "Will this be a productive session with positive outcomes and clear direction, or is it a publicity-generating event to bolster your re-election campaign?" The editorial said the money spent on the trip would have been better used for flood victims in the region. It ended with another jab at the president for lack of leadership: "We don't need your attention as much as we need your leadership. We need a president who won't tell the people what they *want* to hear but a leader who tells us what we *need* to hear."

Slate's John Dickerson tweeted, "The president is on a political bus tour which he says isn't . . . political where he will tell Republicans to stop behaving politically." The truth was that the president wasn't quite ready to show his hand for the next battle with the Republicans. He was in Iowa and Illinois in a holding pattern. His White House and political teams were still working out their fall plans. And so for three days, his problems traveled with him. The crowds were generally friendly and polite. It was the Midwest, after all. On his second day, Obama left the Hotel Winneshiek in tiny Decorah, Iowa, and someone shouted out, "Welcome to the 50s." The comment could have been a reference to the time warp of small-town, heartland America. It was actually a reference to the fact that a few weeks earlier the president had just turned fifty, now noticeably grayer than when he first came to eastern Iowa in 2007 to ask people, improbably, to help make him president. He stopped often in between his scheduled town halls. He bought ice cream at DeWitt Dairy Treats. He went into a high school gymnasium to say hello to members of a women's volleyball team. In Decorah, one woman yelled, "We love you. We're behind you."

But if people were friendly, their questions conveyed the seriousness of the times. In Atkinson, Illinois, a Realtor from nearby Geneseo said that after the debt ceiling, the phones in her office had stopped ringing. "We have no consumer confidence after what has just happened," she said. A farmer registered dissatisfaction with government regulations that he said hindered his ability to produce a crop. The *New York Times*' Mark Landler wrote, "Mr. Obama got tough questions from people who said they were fearful about their future, frustrated by the paralyzed job market and fed up with a political culture in Washington that produced the debt-ceiling imbroglio." Obama soaked up the criticism and pushed back against the Republicans. He said some of his opponents were willing to engage in political brinksmanship "even if it costs the country." Many of the people in the audiences expressed support. At his last stop, in Alpha, Illinois, a college student said to Obama, "I just want to let you know one thing. I am not disappointed in you like Michele Bachmann wants everyone to believe." The president responded, with an ironic smile, "Thank you. I appreciate that."

While Obama was on his bus tour, the Gallup organization reported that approval of his handling of the economy had plunged to 26 percent, the lowest of his presidency. The day after he returned to Washington, he left the capital for his summer vacation. The day after he arrived on Martha's Vineyard, the Dow fell more than four hundred points.

As the bus tour was concluding, White House officials put out the word that the president would deliver an economic speech when he returned from vacation. This too was part of the holding pattern as the White House tried to regroup. "There was this huge debate going on about whether the president should have a jobs plan, and so we figured we can suffer through three weeks of jobs planning," said one of the president's advisers. "We also thought it would make it easier for him to be on vacation if everyone knew when he came back something big was going to happen." But first came a misstep that reinforced the impression that Obama's White House was far from ready for the fall battle. On the morning of August 31, White House chief of staff Bill Daley called John Boehner, who was in Ohio, to inform him that a letter would be forthcoming to the leaders of Congress requesting that the president be allowed to deliver a speech to a joint session of Congress on the evening of Wednesday, September 7, the day the House was scheduled to return from its August recess. A little later that morning, White House communications director Dan Pfeiffer sent out a tweet with the news that Obama had asked for the joint session speech.

Almost immediately, a White House official got an angry call from Barry Jackson, Boehner's chief of staff. Why weren't we informed of this? he demanded to know. Apparently Boehner had not relayed to his staff the contents of Daley's call. The real problem, however, was that the White House was asking for a prime-time speech by the president on the night of the first big post–Labor Day debate among the Republican presidential candidates, scheduled for the Ronald Reagan Presidential Library in California. White House officials said the GOP debate was not a factor in the planning, though privately they had begun to explore whether the sponsors of the debate, MSNBC and *Politico,* would consider moving back the start time by an hour. "It is coincidental," White House press secretary Jay Carney told incredulous reporters. Carney said the existence of one debate on one cable channel was "not enough reason not to have the speech at the time that we decided to have it. Again, there's one president; there's twenty-some odd debates."

The White House talking points only made the president look small and petty. Conservative talk radio whipped up opposition, and by the middle of the afternoon Boehner responded by telling the president to move the speech to Thursday, September 8. Daley called Boehner back and pressed him to schedule the speech as requested, but Boehner would not budge. Obama was furious with his staff, feeling they had put him in the position of appearing to try to jam the Speaker. By nightfall, Obama gave up and agreed to move the speech. It was a one-day hiccup, but one that again reinforced perceptions of a weak president. The *New York Times* wrote an editorial castigating Boehner for petty politics, but could not resist a shot at the president. "It was distressing," the editorial said, "to watch President Obama fail, once again, to stand up to an opposition that won't brook the smallest compromise. . . . Mr. Obama's people negotiated with Mr. Boehner's people behind closed doors. When they emerged, the White House caved, to no one's surprise." Daley bore the brunt of the criticism—and accepted the blame. "I'll take responsibility for that," he said. It turned out that his days as chief of staff were numbered, though his departure was not primarily because of this episode.

The flap over the speech may have seemed minor—Washington gamesmanship at its worst—but it had a powerful effect on many of Obama's allies. Some of the president's political advisers were privately critical of the White House, worried that the debt ceiling fight had bled away confidence in Obama's leadership. "I just don't think they looked around the curve on some of the leadership stuff," Robert Gibbs told me a few days later. "What's stunning to me on some of these polls is how much those characteristics have taken a real big hit. I mean, this is the guy who killed Osama bin Laden." Gibbs was frustrated especially about the mishap over the timing of the economic speech. "You want to reset the agenda on jobs," he said. "So you don't pick the single most political time slot possible in the week to do it. That's what I don't get. If you look weak and political all in the same pitch, I mean, what could be worse?" Gibbs knew the president well, having been with him from the 2004 Senate race forward. "My guess is more than anything he's frustrated," he said. "I think for a long time he's been playing this [the battles with Republicans] as if it's a little bit more on the level. I think he is more clear-eyed about the game that's been played."

The day after the standoff over the speech, I sat down with David Axelrod in Chicago. He was furious with the Republicans. "This is the first time they've [Congress] ever turned down a president," he said. "They knew that we ran on this pledge to try and bring more cooperation and less partisanship to Washington, and I think they were never going to let us do that." The lesson from the debt ceiling and the embarrassment over the speech was plain. "It really does take two to tango, and if you're out there on the dance floor tangoing by yourself you look kind of stupid," he said. He was deeply worried about the economy and determined not to let the Republicans turn the coming election into a referendum on Obama. "This is the Romney strategy," he said. "Blame Obama for every ill and offer yourself as the remedy, but mostly blame him for every ill. And if we're passive in the face of that, then we'll certainly lose." He said he did not believe past was prologue and argued that many Americans did not blame Obama for the problems he had been dealing with. That would give the president an opening to climb out of the political hole he was in. "From next week on," he said, "we have to articulate a clear, clarion-clear economic vision that people see themselves in, not a clinical kind of macroeconomic vision but an economic vision for now and the future that they have an investment in. I think we need to recoup the basic themes that drove him all through his political career, about sort of how do you not just recover from the recession but how do you restore the middle class, how do you restore the sense of fairness and opportunity that we've lost? And without clearly articulating that vision—and he hasn't for sure—we can't win."

I said I thought the real question for the president was not whether people blamed him for what had happened as he was coming into office but whether they believed he had the strength of leadership now to do something about it. I said that question seemed more acute now than it had a year earlier. "I agree with that," Axelrod said. Part of the president's problem was that what once was seen as strength—his patience, his calmness, and his willingness to compromise—now seemed evidence of weakness. Was he capable of making a shift? I asked. "Well, I think this is a big thing," he replied. "This is a strategic and tactical question that we have to decide, but it's also a personal question that he has to decide. I find what these guys [Republicans] are doing deeply offensive, I think he finds it deeply offensive, and I think he needs to show some of that. I think he needs to be very passionate about it. And he needs to be passionate about it in a simple and direct way. And if he is, if he does that, I think we will win. If he doesn't I think it's going to be harder. This is not a time for nuance. I think that the battles we're having on the Hill need to be channeled into a larger fight, because they really are. These fights on the Hill reflect what these Republican presidential candidates are all saying, in part because they're all worshipping the same false god of this Tea Party crowd. So it's important that this thing that we're talking about, this sort of sense of passion and edge, extend to how he talks about all the governmental stuff as well. He can't be sort of a narrator of the government four days a week and then a campaigner three days a week. I mean, it's got to be of one piece."

———

Obama addressed Congress and the nation on Thursday, September 8. The speech was ostensibly to present a new package of measures designed to create more than a million jobs. Its other and more important purpose was to make the pivot from negotiation to confrontation, from governing to campaigning. Before the speech, one of his advisers made clear that from that day forward, Obama would not only press for action on his jobs package but also use every tool available to pin the blame on Republicans if his proposals were not passed. He was not going to go behind closed doors with congressional leaders. "We're not going to sit in the Cabinet Room for weeks at a time," the adviser said.

Obama spoke with a new sense of urgency. He offered a package of $447 billion in tax cuts and new spending initiatives. The biggest piece by far was an extension of the payroll tax cut that was initially approved in the 2010 lame-duck session. He proposed including employers as well as individuals in the extension. He told lawmakers that some of his ideas were ones Republicans had supported in the past. "You should pass this jobs plan right away," he said. He talked about the political climate. "The next election is fourteen months away. And the people who sent us here—the people who hired us to work for them—they don't have the luxury of waiting fourteen months. . . . They need help, and they need it now. He drew a contrast between his philosophy and that of the Republicans: "This larger notion that the only thing we can do to restore prosperity is just dismantle government, refund everybody's money, and let everyone write their own rules, and tell everyone they're on their own—that's not who we are. That's not the story of America."

The joint session speech marked the pivot point for Obama. He saw the jobs package as something that might actually kick-start the economy, and he knew that anything that helped the economy made his path to reelection that much easier. But he also needed a new argument for the campaign. And at heart, he needed Americans to look at him anew. "Obama is a reasonable guy, and you've got to be true to who you are," a senior White House official told me later. "You can't light yourself on fire. It's not going to work. But if you focus too much on reasonableness, you can lose strength. Being reasonable in the face of unreasonableness—sometimes you can see how someone can turn that to weakness. That's what the fall strategy was about, that was what the tone of the joint session was. We needed a circuit breaker on our political narrative. We needed something that would allow everyone who commented on it to say Obama learned this. It was one of the toughest things for us, because we're all somewhat stubborn and we all sometimes want to just tell the [Washington chattering class] to go to hell. We were reasonable with Boehner before, we're talking to these guys. Now we're not. Now we're going out to the country and we're going to be tough, so you need the circuit breaker moment to move on. The speech was about the circuit breaker."

Obama had returned from his summer vacation focused on the job ahead. Beyond the joint session speech, his advisers had blocked out the first months of the fall for regular travel outside of Washington to make the case for the jobs package. One trip in late September took Obama to an aging bridge over the Ohio River that linked Ohio to Kentucky and by happenstance the areas represented by John Boehner and Mitch McConnell, the Senate Republican leader. "Mr. Boehner, Mr. McConnell, help us rebuild this bridge," Obama said. "Help us rebuild America. Help us put this country back to work. Pass this jobs bill right away." It wasn't exactly Ronald Reagan at the Brandenburg Gate saying, "Mr. Gorbachev, tear down this wall," but as political theater it got the point across that Obama was now fully in campaign mode. On September 19, Obama defiantly reengaged with Republicans on the deficit. Speaking from the White House Rose Garden, he called for $1.5 trillion in new taxes to help produce overall $3.2 trillion in deficit reduction over a decade. "I will not support—I will not support—any plan that puts all the burden for closing our deficit on ordinary Americans," he said. Republicans accused him of political posturing. White House officials saw it as redefining Obama in the face of criticism that he had been weak—and weakened—in the debt ceiling battle.

Rarely had the president been as blunt in his challenges as he was that day. Rarely had he been so willing to draw such sharp contrasts. In just a few weeks, Obama had transitioned from a president who talked openly about how he was prepared to buck his own party on entitlements to a politician determined to reconnect with his base as the two parties headed toward the election campaign. Attempting to stay above the fray and appealing for at least a temporary cessation in the partisan wars in Washington was no longer an option. Obama's speech also helped reassure some in the Democratic family that he was still one of them, prepared to fight for their values. Daniel Mintz, the campaign director of MoveOn.org, an organization often at odds with the president, issued a statement of praise. "For months, hundreds of thousands of members of the American Dream Movement have been urging Washington to focus on creating jobs and making our tax system work for all Americans, not just the super rich," he said. "Today, we're glad to see this message reach the White House."

That afternoon, I spoke with David Plouffe, who outlined the thinking behind the speech and how it fit together with the jobs package. He said he had never seen the electorate so focused on the issue of fairness and said Obama's positions drew a sharp contrast with the Republicans, whether candidates like

Mitt Romney and Rick Perry or members of Congress like Paul Ryan. Looking ahead, Plouffe talked about the challenges the economy presented to Obama's reelection. "There are two certainties of our life for the next fourteen months," he said. "One, the economy is going to be awfully challenging. Two, we're going to have a really, really close and tough election. That's just a fact." He said that everyone around the president knew people did not give him high grades on the economy, but that the contrast he would draw in the campaign was one the voters would respond to. "I think at the end of the day we can construct a campaign that suggests to people that this is a president who's in alignment with the world you think we live in and where we need to go as a country," he said. "But it's going to be hard. It's going to have to be a much more contrasted message. It just has to be. Right?"

Plouffe caught the moment accurately. The public was focused on fairness, but voters also were not seeing in Obama the leadership skills or strength to do much about it, given the Republican opposition. It was why he and the others around the president knew that they would have to be on the attack in 2012 in ways they never had to be in 2008.

On September 17, 2011, about a thousand demonstrators converged on Zuccotti Park near Wall Street in New York. It was the first Occupy Wall Street protest, and within weeks it became a movement—the Occupy movement— that spread to more than seventy cities around the country. Occupy was both a viral and a virtual movement that exploded almost overnight, drawing attention to the growing gap between rich and poor and the topic of income inequality, which was rarely addressed by politicians. Because it started in New York, the movement drew a huge amount of media attention. The media also covered it because it appeared to be the left's answer to the Tea Party movement. There were similarities, certainly, but as time passed it was obvious that there were major differences as well. The Tea Party movement focused on electoral action. The Occupy movement did not. Occupy protesters set up tented encampments in parks and squares around the country, but there was no organized political strategy behind them.

What the Occupy movement did politically was to introduce new shorthand language to frame the debate about income inequality—the gap between the nation's top 1 percent of income holders and the rest of the population. People rallied under banners and placards that read, "We are the 99 percent." One blog, created by a pair of twenty-somethings, posted photos of people holding up handwritten stories of their struggles, which all ended with the statement, "We are the 99 percent." *Mother Jones* magazine tracked down the founders of the site, who said they had started it in early September and within a month were getting a hundred postings a day, "from the 61-year-old who lost her job and moved in with her kids, to the husband of a college professor on WIC and Medicaid to support an infant daughter, to the 50-something couple living on tossed-out KFC, to a bevy of youths pummeled by student debt and too poor to visit a dentist."

What it all added up to was a matter of interpretation. After the Arab Spring, some Americans wondered if this would be a homegrown version of a grassroots revolt against the power establishment. Some Democrats embraced the movement. Elizabeth Warren, who had been rejected by Republicans in the Senate to head the new consumer protection bureau created by Obama's financial regulatory reform legislation and was now running for the Senate in Massachusetts, said, "I created much of the intellectual foundation for what they do." White House officials maintained some distance from the movement, particularly the most unsavory aspects of it—the vandalism, violence, and breaking of the law. But Obama's advisers recognized that the movement was helping to reshape the political conversation. "I think it had a significant change in the overall climate in that it reframed the discussion nationally and it did two things," said Anita Dunn, who served as White House communications director early in Obama's presidency. "One, it gave people permission to openly discuss something that had not really been openly discussed, which was the growing inequalities and the unfairness. Two, it gave many members of the Democratic Party much more confidence in going to those places in the criticism of the Republican policies."

Though the president was looking to draw sharp contrasts with the Republicans on values and would make raising taxes on the rich a centerpiece of his message, his advisers feared the Occupy movement put too much focus on pure class division. Obama was sounding more like a populist himself at times. He wanted the rich to pay more in taxes. Many Democrats wanted to hear more of that from the president, but he didn't exactly want to alienate the rich either. His advisers worried that if they embraced the Occupy rhetoric directly or indirectly, some of the middle-class swing voters they hoped to attract would turn away. "The one fear about Occupy, would they get violent, would this take a turn that would necessarily rebound against us but generally would taint the whole argument about tax fairness? So there was great concern about that," Plouffe said. When the movement began to fizzle, it was actually to the relief of many in the Obama campaign. But Obama advisers recognized that the movement had some lasting effect. "Occupy had its blazing moment in the sun and then began to peter out, but again, the arguments they were making were in the bloodstream of our politics all through 2012," Plouffe said.

———

Obama completed his pivot to the campaign on December 6, 2011, in Osawat-omie, Kansas, population 4,600, where he delivered a speech that was the culmination of a year of conflict with congressional Republicans, months of research by his campaign, and the president's own frustrations with what he had experienced over the previous three years. Piggybacking on Teddy Roosevelt's New Nationalism theme of a century earlier, Obama drew a line from the economic excesses that had contributed to the collapse in 2008 to the coming election campaign. What had happened then, he said, resulted from "breathtaking greed of a few with irresponsibility across the system." The result was widespread economic pain and, ever since, a raging debate about what to do. "Throughout the country, it has sparked protests and political movements—from the Tea Party to the people who have been occupying the streets of New York and other cities," Obama said. "It's left Washington in a near-constant state of gridlock. And it's been the topic of heated and sometimes colorful discussion among the men and women who are running for president. But this isn't just another political debate. This is the defining issue of our time. This is a make-or-break moment for the middle class and all those who are fighting to get into the middle class. At stake is whether this will be a country where working people can earn enough to raise a family, build a modest savings, own a home, and secure their retirement." He invoked Roosevelt's epic battle against the trusts at the beginning of the twentieth century. He spoke in concrete terms and pointed fingers at his opponents. Whenever there was an economic challenge, he said, Republicans responded with the same prescription: free markets, fewer regulations, tax cuts, especially for the wealthy. "It's a simple theory—one that speaks to our rugged individualism and healthy skepticism of too much govern-ment. It fits well on a bumper sticker. Here's the problem: It doesn't work. It's never worked."

The goal of the Kansas speech was to anchor Obama in a mission to rebuild the economy by rebuilding a stronger middle class. "It was a chance for him to say to the country, 'Here is where we are. Here's where we stand and here's where we need to go,'" Grisolano said. The speech was not overly prescriptive. Obama would wait until his 2012 State of the Union address for that. Instead he hoped to convey a sense of his values and to challenge those of the Repub-lican Party, based on all that the campaign had learned through the year. David Nakamura of the *Washington Post* said the president had "laid out, in his sharp-est language yet, the economic and social arguments" destined to be used against the Republicans in 2012. The headline in the *New York Times* read, "Obama Sounds a Populist Call on G.O.P. Turf." "Obama Says Middle-Class Faces a 'Make or Break' Moment," the *Kansas City Star* headline said.

A transition that began with the shellacking in 2010 and built on the disappointment and frustration over the year's conflict with Republicans in Congress was now done. The Osawatomie speech was the most important of the year for the president, as it laid out the themes for the reelection campaign more robustly than at any time during the fall. The Republicans were just a month away from the first votes in their nomination battle. Obama served notice that he would be ready for Mitt Romney or whoever emerged as their nominee.

A month before Obama's speech in Osawatomie, Nate Silver, the baseball statistician turned political prognosticator, wrote an article in the *New York Times Magazine* that carried the headline, "Is Obama Toast?" The headline was more provocative than Silver's careful analysis. He noted that incumbents are almost always favored for reelection; six of the previous eight presidents who had run a second time had won a second term. But he pointed out that the debt ceiling fight had proved to be a perfect storm of trouble for the president. The outcome had offended Obama's liberal base, frustrated swing voters, and potentially imperiled the already fragile economy, which of course was the worst danger of all. "Obama has gone from a modest favorite to win re-election to, probably, a slight underdog," Silver wrote. He sketched out a series of scenarios, depending on the state of the economy and Obama's potential opponent, Mitt Romney or Rick Perry. Against Romney, with a stagnant economy, the president was a clear underdog. Even with an improving economy, it was no better than a 60 percent probability that he would win.

Obama's advisers well understood the situation. They could see the president's strong points and knew there were certain arguments Republicans might use against him that would not fly with the swing voters they were hoping to woo back to his side. Swing voters in the Obama focus groups rejected the charge being leveled by Romney and the Republicans that the president had made a bad economy worse. They thought that was nonsense. "The great vulnerability for us," a campaign official said, "was what they said at the end of the sentence—'I just don't know if he can turn it around'—which was Romney's great strength, which then became the foundation for our attacks on him to take away that strength."

CHAPTER 6

Building the Army

The campaign never stopped building. From the moment Obama took the oath of office on January 20, 2009, and every day thereafter, his team was always at work preparing for the coming campaign. Everyone said Obama's 2008 operation had rewritten the book on organizing, and in some ways that was accurate. But 2008 was just a beginning, a small first step toward what Obama's team envisioned when they began planning the reelection campaign. In one of their first conversations about the reelection, Messina said he told the president that the reason they could not rerun 2008 was because so much had changed in just two years. Technology had leapfrogged forward, with new devices, new platforms, and vastly more opportunities to exploit social media. And Obama was now an incumbent with a record. The whole campaign would have to be different. The president sent Messina off to Chicago, far away from the hothouse of Washington and Beltway chatter, to use 2011 to build the foundation and reassemble the army from 2008. As the Republican candidates were gearing up and then battling each other through the summer and fall of 2011, Messina and his colleagues were investing enormous amounts of time, money, and creative energy in the development of what resembled a high-tech political start-up whose main purpose was to put more people on the streets in 2012, armed with more information about the voters they were contacting, than any campaign had ever attempted.

In campaigns, the people who design the overall strategy or make the ads or take the polls or appear as talking heads on television become the political celebrities, instantly visible, nationally famous, and highly acclaimed. But for sheer esprit de corps, little tops the people who regard field operations as the soul of a campaign. The word "field" carries special meaning. It is a point of pride, a badge of honor, among those who spend their days thinking about nothing other than how to identify, locate, motivate, register, cajole, persuade, mobilize, and ultimately turn out the voters their candidate will need to win an election. These campaign workers often began their careers working in a remote office in a state with an early primary or caucus—the kids who organized Iowa for Obama in 2007. They moved from one state to the next, gaining expertise and greater responsibility. They became experts on the minutiae of politics—key counties in key states, swing precincts, voting histories, demographics of the electorate, turnout models, ratios of staff to volunteers to voters, door knocks, telephone calls, mail drops, contacts of any kind and which work better than others. Over time, some would take on responsibility for a state. Others would eventually move to headquarters to help oversee a handful of smaller states or several battlegrounds. At the top of the pyramid were leaders who oversaw the extraordinarily complex and ever-shifting matrix of data and people that was all aimed at a single target: maximizing the vote by election day.

At the Obama campaign, Messina was in overall charge of building the ground operation, but a team of experienced professionals backed him up. Jennifer O'Malley Dillon had started out the 2008 campaign running John Edwards's operation in Iowa but was brought into the Obama operation after Edwards quit the race. She became an instant star and, after the election, moved to the Democratic National Committee as executive director. She oversaw the continuation of the Obama field operation, now renamed Organizing for America, and began investing millions of dollars and countless hours on technology and analytics that would eventually migrate to the reelection campaign. When Obama set up shop in Chicago in early 2011, she became deputy campaign manager in charge of all field operations. Three other veterans of 2008 were also part of the core team. Jeremy Bird, a former divinity student at Harvard, had managed the South Carolina operation for Obama during the primaries, and his success there not just in helping win the state but also in creating a model for organizing helped elevate him to national field director for 2012. He shared an office with Mitch Stewart, one of the campaign's most highly regarded organizers in 2008, a strategist who had taken on the task of winning Virginia. In 2012, he would serve as director of the battleground states. Every day Bird and Stewart focused on one number: 270—the electoral votes needed to reelect the president. Buffy Wicks had worked for Howard Dean in 2004 and came to the Obama campaign in 2008 after working on the grassroots project called Wake Up Wal-Mart. In 2012, she became director of Project Vote, a newly created unit in the campaign that was designed to focus on the electorate by demographic groups rather than as individual voters.

The first steps toward building the reelection operation were taken in the months after Obama's 2008 victory. Campaign staffers did a series of after-action reports. "We did very detailed postmortem where we looked at all kinds of numbers, looking at the general stuff like the number of door knocks we made, phone calls we made, number of voters that we registered," Stewart said. "But then we broke it down by field organizer, we broke it down then by volunteer. We looked at the best way or the best examples in states of what their volunteer organization looked like." The project produced a thick three-ring binder that ran to nearly five hundred pages and was filled with recommendations for how to strengthen what was already considered a state-of-the-art field operation. Another early step was the decision to expand massively the investment in technology, digital, and particularly analytics—the top priority of Dillon while at the DNC. "A lot of what we built on the campaign was built on top of or came from the work that we did in '09 and '10," she said.

The 2012 campaign had, as do most now, a digital director in Teddy Goff. But they also had a chief technology officer, Harper Reed, who had never done politics before but was a genius at building the tools Messina and company wanted. Michael Slaby was named chief innovation officer. Rounding out the team was Dan Wagner, who was in charge of the analytics operation, which would become one of the most important additions to presidential campaign operations. Wagner had started in Iowa in 2007 and quickly showed off his expertise in data mining and analytics. The work of his team, which operated out of a windowless area of headquarters known as the Cave, would become an integral part of almost everything else the campaign did. The campaign hired software engineers and data experts and number crunchers and digital designers and video producers by the score—hundreds of them—who filled back sections of the vast open room resembling a brokerage house trading floor or a tech start-up that occupied the sixth floor of One Prudential Plaza overlooking Millennium Park in Chicago.

No campaign had ever invested so heavily in technology and analytics, and no campaign had ever had such stated ambitions. "Technology was another big lesson learned from 2008, and leap of faith and labor of love and angst-ridden entity and all the other things that you can imagine, because we were building things in-house mostly with people that had not done campaign work before," Dillon later told me. "The deadlines and breaking and testing—is it going to work, what do we do?—but we set this course. Some stuff didn't work, but the things that needed to work did. They held up, they load-tested, and there's probably nothing that Jim and myself were more involved in. . . . At the end of the day it was certainly worth it, because you can't customize our stuff, and so we just couldn't buy off the shelf for anything and you know that, and fortunately we had enough time to kind of build the stuff. I don't know who else will ever have the luxury of doing that again."

Messina and Dillon had a vision of what they wanted, based on the changing landscape of technology. Messina was as data driven as any presidential campaign manager in modern times, and Dillon had concentrated her efforts while at the DNC on starting work on the programs that would make Obama's groundbreaking 2008 campaign look old-fashioned in comparison. They wanted to be able to measure everything, and they wanted all the data the campaign accumulated about voters to be integrated. The campaign had a voter list and a donor list and volunteer lists and other lists, but what they wanted was the ability to link all the contacts each person had with the campaign into one vast database. "There's always been two campaigns since the Internet was invented, the campaign online and the campaign on the doors," Messina told me. "What I wanted was, I didn't care where you organized, what time you organized, how you organized, as long as I could track it, I can measure it, and I can encourage you to do more of it. So what I said to them was I want all of our data together, I want for the first time to treat [a voter] like a voter and not like a number, because right now you're just a voter number, your voter ID number in your state, your FEC number for how much you contribute, your census data, whatever we know about you from commercial vendors. But we don't treat [a voter] like a person." It took the technology team nearly a year, but what they produced was software that allowed all of the campaign's lists to talk to one another. The technology team named it Narwhal, after a whale of amazing strength that lives in the Arctic but is rarely seen. Harper Reed described Narwhal as the software platform for everything else the campaign wanted to do and build, "much like the piping of a building or the foundation of a building . . . the stuff that makes it so we're structurally sound."

The next goal was to build a program that would allow everyone—campaign staffers in Chicago, state directors and their staff in the battlegrounds, field organizers, volunteers going door to door or volunteers at home—to communicate simply and seamlessly. The Obama team wanted something that allowed the staff field organizers in the Des Moines or Columbus or Fairfax offices to have access to all the information the campaign had about the voters for whom they were responsible. They wanted volunteer leaders to have access online as well. And if someone didn't want to knock on doors, the campaign wanted them to be able to organize from home, but have the data about the voters with whom they were communicating integrated into the main hub of information. That brought about the creation of Dashboard, which Messina later said was the hardest thing the campaign did but which became the central online organizing vehicle. It was enormously complicated to develop, made all the more difficult because the engineers who were building it had never worked on campaigns and did not instinctively understand the work of field organizers. Some of them were sent out to the states briefly as organizers to better understand the needs of those on the front lines.

"Dashboard is what we needed to communicate," Dillon said. "It was all about the users, so if the users didn't have a good experience there was no point in it. . . . That's why it was the Holy Grail." Reed described it as a way to bring the field office to the Internet. "When you walk into a field office, you have many opportunities," he said. "We'll hand you a call sheet. You can make calls. You can knock on doors, and they'll have these stacks there for you. They'll say, 'Harper, you've knocked on fifty doors. That's great. Here's how you compare to the rest of them.' But it's all very offline. It's all very ad hoc and it's not very modern. And so what we set out to do was create that offline field experience online." Reed said near the end of the campaign they received an e-mail from a wounded Afghanistan war veteran who was in a hospital. He was logging into Dashboard and participating in the organizing effort the way any other volunteer walking precincts was doing. Reed was blown away by the message. He said, "I could have quit that day and I would have been satisfied with my role."

The Obama leadership not only wanted all the lists to be able to talk to one another, they also wanted people to be able to organize their friends and families. This was taking a concept introduced in 2004 by Bush's reelection team—the notion that voters are more likely to listen to people they know than to paid callers or strangers knocking on their door—and updating it to take advantage of new technology, namely the explosion of social media. All current campaigns learn from the best of previous campaigns. Bush's 2004 campaign had taken lessons from the Democrats in 2000, whose ground game was judged superior to the Republicans' despite the loss. Messina was repaying the favor, hoping to make another significant leap into the future of organizing based on some of what Bush had done, at the expense of the 2012 Republican nominee.

Early in 2011, some of the Obama team visited Facebook, where executives were encouraging them to spend some of the campaign's advertising dollars with them. "We started saying, 'Okay, that's nice if we just advertise,'" Messina said. "But what if we could build a piece of software that tracked all this and allowed you to match your friends on Facebook with our lists and we said to you, 'Okay [so-and-so] is a friend of yours, we think he's unregistered, why don't you go get him to register? Or [so-and-so] is a friend of yours, we think he's undecided. Why don't you get him to be decided?' And we only gave you a discrete number of friends. That turned out to be millions of dollars and a year of our lives. It was incredibly complex to do."

But the third piece of this puzzle provided the campaign with another treasure trove of information and an organizing tool unlike anything available in the past. It took months and months to solve this, but it was a huge breakthrough to the campaign team. If a person signed on to Dashboard through his or her Facebook identity, the campaign could, with permission, gain access to that person's Facebook friends. The Obama team called this "Targeted Sharing." They knew from other research that people who pay less attention to politics were more likely to listen to a message from a friend than from someone in the campaign. What the campaign could do was supply people with information about their friends based on data the campaign had independently gathered on those people. They knew who was and wasn't registered to vote. They knew which of these friends had a low propensity to vote. They knew who was solid for Obama and who needed more persuasion—and a gentle or not-so-gentle nudge to go out and vote. Instead of asking someone to send out a message to all of his or her Facebook friends, the Obama campaign could present a handpicked list of the three or four or five people the campaign believed would most benefit from personal encouragement.

Teddy Goff told my colleague Aaron Blake, "For people who allowed us, we were able to say to them, 'All right, you just watched a video about registering to vote. Don't just share it with all your friends on Facebook. We've run a match, and here are your ten friends on Facebook who we think may not be registered to vote and live in Ohio, Colorado, Virginia, Florida.'" This was especially helpful in trying to reach voters under age thirty. On Obama's target lists, the voter file contained no good contact information for half of those young voters—they didn't have landlines, and no other information was available. But Goff said 85 percent of that group were on Facebook and could be reached by a friend of a friend. Reed described another example. Someone interested in health care might click on an ad on Facebook, and up would pop an infographic on health care. At the end of it, there would be a "share" button, and if the person clicked on it, up popped names of friends the person could share the information with. The campaign knew from its own database which of those friends were most likely to respond to information about health care. "We went through and we looked at all those friends and found the ones that were the best matches for that specific piece of content," Reed said.

Google's Eric Schmidt said, "If you don't know anything about campaigns you would assume it's national, but a successful campaign is highly, highly local, down to the zip code. The revolution in technology is to understand where the undecideds are in this district and how you reach them." That was what the integration of technology and old-fashioned organizing was designed to do for Obama in 2012.

At the beginning of the Obama presidency, Organizing for America, the successor to the 2008 campaign organization, was run through the DNC under the supervision of Dillon. Some Democrats hoped it would be the president's secret weapon in helping to win support for his legislative agenda. The results on that front were mixed, and there were few obvious success stories about its political muscle during the disastrous 2010 elections. The losses in the midterms taught another lesson, Stewart said. "Failure is always a better teacher than success, and 2010 was tough," he told me. "We learned tactically some lessons, but ultimately I think what probably helped us more than anything else is a lot of our volunteers and staff had only been involved in the '08 campaign, which was a lot of highs, and unless you were very early on in the process like I was, there weren't a lot of lows. So 2010 was a good learning experience just in that [it showed us] this isn't all rainbows and bubblegum. I think it actually helped harden some of our volunteers and staff to prepare for 2012."

What wasn't seen was all the work that was taking place behind the scenes—work that no Republican presidential candidate would be able to match in 2012, if for no other reason than the amount of time and money and experimentation invested up front by the Obama team. They were able to test and retest everything. Messina said there were other dividends returned by the decision to keep OFA operating between the campaigns. "It kept our super volunteers active in the organization and gave them a reason to talk to their neighbors for two years and continue to grow their ability and talent, and then second, it put a whole bunch of young kids who were kind of the second- and third-level people in the '08 race in analytics and gave them a home at the DNC, a boss in Jen O'Malley [Dillon], and a patron at the White House."

Dan Wagner had come to the DNC after the 2008 election to expand what was initially a tiny analytics operation. David Plouffe had seen the potential for analytics during 2008, and Dillon was a big believer in it as well. In early 2010, others on the Obama team had an epiphany about the value of analytics. It came just before the special election to fill the Senate seat of the late Edward M. Kennedy. Many Democrats were still in denial about the direction of the race, incredulous that a little-known Republican state senator named Scott Brown could have enough momentum to defeat Democratic attorney general Martha Coakley. Wagner, who was operating with the analytics team out of the DNC, analyzed the numbers and concluded that Brown was going to win. He delivered his conclusions and the data to Messina. "He said, 'We're going to lose, and here's why we're going to lose,' and it happened almost exactly like that," Messina said. "That's when we first started saying this model can really *be* something." Later that year, according to Sasha Issenberg, author of *The Victory Lab,* they began modeling seventy-four Senate and House races and pegged the outcomes with extraordinary accuracy.

Dillon and Bird brought Wagner to the reelection campaign, over some internal resistance, when they all moved to Chicago. Eventually the Obama campaign modeled practically everything—voters, states, volunteers, donors, anything that they could think of to improve their efficiency—to give them greater confidence in the decisions they were making. They wanted to know who was most likely to serve as a volunteer, and they created a model to tell them. They established record numbers of offices in the states, and record numbers of staging areas for volunteers, based in part on analysis of how much more likely people were to volunteer if they were close to an office. "We built a model on volunteer likelihood," Stewart said. "We built a model on turnout, we built a model on support, we built a model on persuasion—who's most persuadable." Dillon described the ways in which the modeling aided fund-raising. "We could model the likelihood of someone being at home during the day and more likely to answer the telephone, so those were the people we would call to help our contact rate," she said. The campaign created a system that allowed for tailored fund-raising appeals to individual voters. One voter might get an appeal for, say, $213, and another voter got an appeal for a different amount. "Those weren't random numbers that were being put in there," she said. "Testing had shown us that if you asked for that amount you're more likely to get it based on their previous history." They built a model that told them who was more likely to give online versus who was more likely to respond to direct mail. They saved money by telling their phone vendors not to call certain people; they knew those people wanted to give only online and did not want to be bothered on the phone. In the fall of 2011 the campaign sent out a big direct mail solicitation from Michelle Obama. Half was sent to a list drawn in the traditional way, the other half based on the campaign's analytic model. Messina said, "Wagner said, 'I'm going to overperform them.'" He did, by 14 percent.

Virtually every e-mail sent by the campaign included a test of some sort—the subject line, the appeal, the message—all designed to maximize contributions, volunteer hours, and eventually turnout on election day. There was nothing particularly new about this, but it could mean millions of dollars lost or gained and a more efficient use of volunteers' time. The campaign would break out eighteen smaller groups from their e-mail lists, create eighteen different versions of an e-mail, and then watch the response rate for an hour and go with the winner—or take a combination of subject line and message from different e-mails and turn them into the finished product. Big corporations had used such testing for years, but political campaigns had not. In the Obama tests, the differences among e-mails sometimes were as great as 90 percent. Mitch Stewart said the 2012 campaign was light-years ahead of 2008 in its technical precision and efficiency. "When you're spending hundreds and hundreds and hundreds of millions of dollars, finding 3 percent efficiency, or 8 percent, that's real money," he said.

From modeling and testing, the campaign refined voter outreach. Years earlier, political scientists Don Green and Alan Gerber of Yale had first shown convincingly that there was added value by having volunteers knock on the doors of prospective voters. The Obama campaign discovered that while that was generally the case, it wasn't always so, that some voters were more likely to respond to different kinds of contact. "Up until '12, I would stake my career on the fact that door knocking is the most powerful communication tool that we have, face-to-face communication essentially in terms of grassroots organizing," Dillon said. "[But] I don't think you can say today that door-to-door contact is more effective communication for all voters. You need to understand the way people want to take it in. It doesn't have to be a door knock. It could be a phone call from the person you know or a shared article that you read that they'd be more likely to open because you shared it."

From their post-2008 analysis and other research into management practices, Obama's field team concluded that the best management ratio was six or eight to one. That became the model for building the organization—one field director would have half a dozen deputies. The deputies would have six to eight regional field directors, who in turn would oversee the work of six to eight field organizers. Those field organizers were members of the paid staff and also were the connection between the paid team and the volunteers. They interacted directly with the neighborhood team leaders, who led the campaign in their local areas. As was often the case, these neighborhood team leaders were in their fifties or sixties, being directed by Obama campaign field organizers in their twenties.

With those ratios in mind and with an early estimate of the size of the electorate and the likely vote totals they would need to win specific states, the campaign calculated that it would need to recruit fifteen thousand neighborhood team leaders to oversee hundreds of thousands of volunteers. After continuous tweaking of their models, they ended up at just over ten thousand. By November 2011, they had relatively concrete goals for their field operation. In actual numbers they were far short of what they needed—short too of the size of their army in 2008. Starting early and working methodically, they established goals for organizing, held state organizers accountable to meet them, and eventually filled out the organization. The year before the election, Obama's advisers began setting state-by-state goals. "We didn't care at all [about] national demographics," Bird said. "It needs to be states. How can we get the demographics in a place where we can win?" The campaign looked at three groups: Who was registered and who wasn't? What was the existing and potential electorate? Could they change the composition? Were the people who weren't registered likely to vote Democratic? "That was number one," Bird said. "That was how many people can we register and can we change the pie?" Next they analyzed who had voted for Obama in 2008 but did not vote at all in 2010—the sporadic voters. How many would they need to get to 50 percent? The third group was the pool of potential undecided voters, people who had voted for Obama in 2008 but had voted for Republicans in 2010. Once that analysis was done, the next step was to determine the right blend for each state. "In Nevada the blend was registration and turnout," he said. "We didn't need to persuade a single undecided voter if we did our registration work right. In Florida we had to do all three [registration, persuasion, and turnout], and they were all three huge tasks because just the size of all of them is massive." The campaign established metrics for each state in the early summer of 2011 and then kept refining them. "The worst thing that campaigns do is they set up a plan, they set up a strategy, and they think it's a noun—like, 'I got a strategy'— and it's really a verb," Bird said. "You should be changing it as you move forward." They were trying to create an electorate as partial to Obama as possible so that they could win even if the odds said otherwise.

The campaign's attention to detail rivaled that of the best corporations. Dillon and her team believed in training and preparation and set up a training operation unlike anything campaigns had done previously. "If you think of innovations in campaigns, it could be the biggest we had," Bird told me. The campaign provided volunteers with training on everything from how to use and manipulate all the data available to how to talk to voters on their doorsteps. Over some objections, Messina approved a budget to cover the cost of training directors in the battleground states. Another innovation was the recruitment of corporate trainers or coaches, who volunteered their time to help teach everyone how to manage. "We recruited a whole group of pro bono executive coaches," he said. "These are people that coach Fortune 100 companies." Obama's team recruited them as volunteers, but instead of having them knock on doors, they were asked to provide management training. "We had them partner up with our state leadership," Bird said. "They didn't need to know anything about campaigns, because we didn't want their advice on how to run a campaign. We wanted their advice on how to be a manager."

The better trained the volunteers, the more effective they would be. The campaign prepared another thick binder that described best practices for volunteers. They wrote and rewrote scripts to be used when volunteers went knocking on doors. They embraced the work of social scientists—an increasingly common practice in political campaigns—to help them find the right language for those scripts. They consulted with what the New York Times later called a "dream team" of academics—who called themselves the "consortium of behavioral scientists"—for advice. The group included political scientists, psychologists, and behavioral economists. The campaign was operating well outside of the traditional network of political consultants. Many of the insights came from academic research that was three or four decades old but up to now mostly ignored by political strategists. Obama's team embraced it, as Bush's 2004 campaign had embraced the work done by political scientists on the efficacy of face-to-face communications, and integrated it into its targeting efforts.

Throughout 2011, Obama advisers were baffled by the slow start to the Republican presidential race. They knew from their own experience in 2008 how long it took to build a field operation capable of winning a presidential campaign. They were even more keenly aware of the lead times and money required to build the technological infrastructure to support a sophisticated get-out-the-vote operation for 2012. Republicans could see that the Obama campaign was spending tens of millions of dollars in 2011. They weren't sure on what.

BOOK TWO

THE REPUBLICANS

CHAPTER 7

Mapping the Race

During the Christmas holidays in 2006, Mitt Romney and his family—five sons, five daughters-in-law, and many grandchildren—gathered at their home in Utah. They were there to make a final decision about a campaign for president, which Romney had been pointing toward for more than a year. A video of their activities showed Romney energetically shoveling snow off the deck of their home, Romney sledding with his grandchildren, children sliding down stairs on mattresses, the general chaos of a house filled with people and constant activity. One clip showed Romney saying grace before dinner. Ann Romney narrated most of the video, talking about her relationship with her husband and their experiences traveling the country as they were exploring a candidacy. The video concluded with the family seated in the living room talking about the pros and cons of Romney running for president, with the prospective candidate taking notes on a pad of paper. "If people really get to know who you are, it could be a success," Craig Romney said to the others in the family. Tagg Romney, the oldest son, said in the video, "I don't think you have a choice. I think you have to run." He added, "I look at the way your life has unfolded. You're gifted. You're smart. You're intelligent. But you've also been extraordinarily lucky. So many things have broken your way that you couldn't have predicted or controlled that it would be a shame not to at least try, and if you don't win, we'll still love you." "Maybe," Romney interjected, to chuckles from his family. "Maybe." Tagg picked up again: "The country may think of you as a laughingstock, and we'll know the truth and that's okay. But I think you have a duty to your country and to God to see what comes of it." At that Christmas gathering, the family took a vote on whether Romney should run. The five sons voted yes, their wives voted yes. Mitt and Ann Romney voted yes.

Four years later, when the Romney family gathered for their Christmas holiday, they faced a similar decision. This time they were in Hawaii and they sat together on a balcony one evening to share their thoughts about a second campaign. This time there was no video record of the meeting, and the vote would have shocked a political community closely monitoring the preliminary maneuvering for the 2012 race. Even some of Romney's closest political advisers might have been surprised. When they polled the group in Hawaii, ten of the twelve family members voted no. Mitt Romney was one of those ten voting against another campaign. The only yes votes were from Ann Romney and Tagg Romney. Some of the reservations were personal. All of them knew how disruptive and invasive a presidential campaign would be in their lives. "None of us were looking forward to the process," Tagg Romney said. "We're a pretty private family, to be honest with you. Having that privacy yanked away was not going to be fun. That was an underlying reason—but not the driving reason. You tasted the bitter pill once, you didn't want to go bite into it a second time." The more fundamental reason so many were opposed was that they feared the campaign ahead would be as brutal as it would be uncertain. "The basic reason was I think a lot of them thought, looking at it, saying, 'This is going to be a really tough primary campaign to win,'" Tagg Romney said. And if his father were to win he would face an incumbent with a billion dollars, much of it used to attack and attack and attack.

Mitt Romney had other reasons to think that not running might be the wiser choice. Winning as a moderate from Massachusetts who happened to be Mormon was always going to be difficult. "A lot of the thinking on the part of my brothers and my dad was, 'I'm not sure I can win a primary given those dynamics,'" Tagg Romney said. The prospective candidate also knew the sheer physical and family toll another campaign would take. "He's a private person and, push comes to shove, he wants to spend time with his family and enjoy his time with them," his son said. "Even up until the day before he made the announcement, he was looking for excuses to get out of it. If there had been someone who he thought would have made a better president than he, he would gladly have stepped aside."

Confidence about Romney's commitment to running never wavered in Boston, where his team had been mapping the race for months. On Thursday, December 9, 2010, just weeks before the family vote in Hawaii, Romney gathered his senior campaign team at the family's oceanside home in La Jolla, California, for a full-scale discussion of a 2012 campaign. The team was full speed ahead, and Romney had done nothing to slow the machinery. In fact, he had done everything a likely candidate needed to do. He had spent the previous year helping to elect Scott Brown to fill the seat of the late Massachusetts senator Edward M. Kennedy; meeting with prospective donors; promoting his book, *No Apology;* campaigning around the country for and giving money to Republican candidates. Romney used his national and state political action committees to ingratiate himself with state and local candidates in the early states and elsewhere, giving nearly $400,000 to three hundred candidates, according to Nicholas Confessore and Ashley Parker in the *New York Times*. "State auditors, county commissioners, sheriffs: no Republican candidate, it seems, has been insignificant enough to escape the glow of Mitt Romney's affections," they wrote. To those who followed him on some of those trips to see donors, he was far more focused than during his first campaign. Whatever reservations he may have had about a second campaign, he kept them out of view of the political advisers around him.

In La Jolla, the group was large. The attendees included Matt Rhoades, who ran Romney's political action committee and was slotted to manage the campaign; Beth Myers, who had managed the 2008 campaign and remained one of Romney's longest-serving and most loyal advisers; and Eric Fehrnstrom, a former journalist and longtime Romney spokesman and adviser. Bob White was there. He was Romney's partner when Bain Capital was founded and was the candidate's closest confidant. Stuart Stevens and Russ Schriefer, partners in one of the Republican Party's best-known media firms, were there in their capacity as strategists and message gurus. Stevens would become the campaign's chief strategist. Ron Kaufman, who retained close ties to former president George H. W. Bush and was the Republican national committeeman from Massachusetts, was there as a veteran of many presidential campaigns, an experienced counselor now devoted to making Romney president. Others included Spencer Zwick, the well-regarded finance director whose task would be more difficult the second time around because of a decision that Romney would not, if at all possible, dip into his personal fortune to fund the campaign as he had done in 2008. Zac Moffatt, who would oversee the campaign's digital operation, was part of the group, as was Kelli Harrison, Romney's personal assistant. Family members included the candidate's wife and two of the couple's five sons, Tagg and Matt. The only one missing from this inner circle was Peter Flaherty, who with Myers and Fehrnstrom had served Romney as governor and after the 2008 campaign together had formed their own political consulting firm. A family problem prevented him from being there.

The conversation was broad-based: What's the rationale for the campaign, what would it feel like, when would it have to start? Romney had been expressing his concerns about Obama and the administration's economic policies, but at this first big meeting the focus was less on the president and more on what kind of race Romney would need to run. The group surveyed the field of prospective rivals for the nomination. They discussed whether John Thune, the senator from South Dakota, would jump in. They talked about the possibility that Haley Barbour, the governor of Mississippi, or Mitch Daniels, the governor of Indiana, would join the race. (Stevens always insisted that Barbour, a former client, would not, and had told Barbour he did not think he should run.) But there was no talk about how the entry of one or another of the potential candidates would influence Romney's decision or strategy. Romney had learned that lesson from his first campaign: Above all he had to run his own race.

At that time four years earlier, other candidates, including John McCain, were already running hard, and there was great pressure on Romney, who had no national profile, to move quickly. In December 2010, there was no such imperative. Romney could set his own pace as the nominal front-runner and was content not to force a decision to ramp up early in the new year. "I don't recall leaving California feeling that the throttle had been switched to full steam ahead," Beth Myers said. Mitt and Ann Romney were still weighing the costs and benefits of a second campaign. "It's like a second marriage," one Romney adviser said. "You go into it with your eyes open. It's not as romantic. You realize the toll that the campaign takes on your family, your friends, and you really need to feel that it is an important thing for you to do. I think that's what Mitt and Ann were thinking about: Is this the right thing for us to do for the country? And would we be able to run a race that we'd be able to focus on the things that are important to move the country in the right direction? Or would it be all about issues that were tangential to that? And I think they were wrestling with their ability as a family to make that commitment again."

The experience of the first campaign shaped the second, starting with the most important question of all, which was what the message would be. Romney had struggled as a first-time candidate, veering into social issues in a frustrating effort to demonstrate that he could be trusted on the matters that religious and social conservatives most cared about. At the start of that first campaign, he had been urged by some Republicans with whom he consulted to present himself as what he was, a Mr. Fix-It, an economic turnaround artist, not a conservative ideologue. The issue of authenticity—who was Mitt Romney?—dogged him throughout the first campaign. Romney's advisers concluded that he had not hit his stride as a candidate until he was practically out of the race. That can be common with candidates; only the certainty of losing liberates them to act in ways that are more natural and authentic. Romney's best days as a candidate, his advisers believed, came after losses in Iowa and New Hampshire that had crippled his hopes of winning the nomination. Only when he began campaigning in Michigan and put a focus on economic issues did he seem comfortable. Only then did he find a true voice, they believed. "I think there was a realization then that whatever campaign he was going to run was going to be done playing to his strengths and going back to what makes

Romney uniquely qualified to be president," Schriefer said. That meant Romney 2012 would be focused on the economy. He would keep his eyes fixed on the president and the president's record while stressing his own background in private equity. He would avoid as much as possible getting sidetracked on other issues.

Romney had the luxury to start the campaign on his own timing, not at the frenetic early pace of his first. In his first campaign, he had staged a fund-raising call day in early January 2007 to make a statement that he could compete financially with his rivals, even though he would spend much of his own money. He had begun running television ads that winter in the early states, earlier than any of his rivals, because he wanted to boost his poll numbers and be seen as a top-tier candidate. "That's one thing we learned from last time," Matt Rhoades told me as the campaign was getting under way. "You don't need to be on TV in February, a year out from the primary." Romney planned to house his campaign in the same office building that he had used in 2008, but with far fewer staff for the primaries. Rhoades told anyone who asked that the second Romney campaign would be "leaner and meaner."

Nor did Romney and his team feel any pressure to involve themselves in every controversy, every new development, every trivial matter that caught the attention of the political class and cable television. "I think there was a feeling [in 2008] that you had to be in the news on any given day on whatever the issue of the day was," said one Romney adviser. "The way to be relevant was to comment on whatever happened that day, and by doing that you become [unable] to drive any one particular message." Beth Myers said, "We were constantly trying to not be an asterisk, like anyone who gets into a presidential race for the first time realizes how hard that is, and you have to have a strategy, and our strategy was to be big and play aggressively everywhere. This time we didn't need to do that. We had a very different race." Romney had been following this approach throughout 2010. He avoided injecting himself into the story of the day unless there was a strategic reason to do so. He avoided internal Republican Party fights whenever possible. He wrote an occasional op-ed, mostly on economic issues, but only occasionally made himself available for an interview, even on friendly Fox News. He tried to keep his focus on the president rather than on prospective rivals.

The first quarter of 2011 passed and Romney still had not taken a formal step toward running. By that time, Tim Pawlenty and Herman Cain had formed their exploratory committees; Newt Gingrich had taken a halting step toward doing so; John Thune and Mike Pence had announced that they would not run; Ron Paul had won the straw poll at the annual Conservative Political

Action Conference (CPAC); Rick Santorum was spending more and more time in Iowa, New Hampshire, and South Carolina; Michele Bachmann was suddenly exploring in Iowa; and speculation was building about whether Haley Barbour and Mitch Daniels would run. Romney was the unexciting front-runner and operating contentedly out of the limelight. He was seen as the candidate to beat, but he stirred few passions in the party.

On April 8, 2011, Romney's senior team met again, this time in Boston at Ron Kaufman's apartment near Beacon Hill. The meeting took place three days before Romney would announce the formation of his exploratory committee. Myers had put together a PowerPoint presentation that outlined the campaign's thinking. Two pages were headlined "The Path." One page was mostly a calendar of contests through Super Tuesday, as best as it was known at the time. The other had three subheads: "Assumptions," "Questions," and "Unknowns." Under "Assumptions," the first line read, "No straw polls." This was another lesson learned from 2008—the debilitating cost in time and money of competing in straw polls. Romney had invested heavily to win the Iowa Straw Poll, only to see Huckabee's second-place finish turn out to be the meaningful event of the day. This time he would ignore them.

The presentation outlined the state-by-state strategy Romney's advisers believed he would have to follow to win the nomination. There were five entries under "Must wins": New Hampshire, Nevada, Florida, Michigan, and a "majority of delegates on Super Tuesday." The list was revealing for what it said about Romney's strengths—and weaknesses—as the Republican front-runner. For starters, he was prepared to lose two of the first three contests (Iowa and South Carolina) and still become the nominee. In the modern history of Republican presidential campaigns, no one had ever done that. Four years earlier, he had played hard to win both Iowa and New Hampshire, only to lose them both. This time Iowa would be a wait-and-see state, a target of opportunity rather than a must-win. Iowa's caucus electorate did not favor Romney—too many evangelicals and too many social conservatives for the Mormon from Massachusetts. At that point, Romney's team had decided he would neither write off the state nor commit far in advance to a major effort. But the assumption was that someone else likely would win the caucuses, which made New Hampshire the first firewall of 2012. Given Iowa's treacherous terrain, it was better to throw everything into the Granite State than to shortchange it by spending too much time elsewhere. Romney had made the mistake of getting caught between the two states in the first campaign. New Hampshire would become the first priority for 2012. He would campaign there more frequently than in other states, and the campaign would invest the resources to build a network of support that could withstand a defeat in Iowa.

The other three states on the list highlighted why Romney had doubts about his ability to win over his party. Given the assumption that he might lose both Iowa and South Carolina, he would need a strategy to bounce back immediately. South Carolina had a perfect record in Republican presidential nomination battles, dating back to 1980 when Ronald Reagan won the state. Nobody since had lost South Carolina and gone on to become the nominee. But South Carolina was even more problematic for Romney than Iowa, given its religious and cultural makeup. Romney had ducked the state in 2008 and finished fourth behind McCain, Huckabee, and Fred Thompson. He couldn't exactly duck it as the early front-runner, but his advisers were loath to mark it as a must-win state, despite its history. Could he survive losing South Carolina? They concluded he could, but only if he could rebound with victories elsewhere, which put the focus on both Nevada and Florida. At the time of the meeting in Boston, the nominating calendar was still in flux, caught in the quadrennial jockeying by states jealous of Iowa and New Hampshire's status as first-in-the-nation caucus and primary. Florida was threatening to move into February, in violation of party rules. The timing of Nevada was not set, but it would be one of the first five contests of the year, and fortunately so. Romney had won the caucuses there in 2008, and the state set up well for him because of its sizable Mormon population. Florida also played to other Romney strengths. It was big, diverse, and conservative—but not dominated by the Christian right. It was also hugely expensive. Florida consumed campaign cash, which was needed to run television ads in every market. Romney would have the money to compete there. His team saw it as a place he could not afford to lose—though they were not certain he could end the race there given new party rules about distributing delegates in early states on the basis of proportionality rather than winner-take-all. Among the questions on the agenda that day was, "Do we need to win a southern state? Does FL count?" Romney's advisers were sensitive to the challenge of becoming the nominee of a southern-based party without having any particular affinity with or broad support in the region. The implicit answer to the first question was almost certainly yes, which meant that Florida would have to become that state. There were few others that appeared likely to back Romney at that point.

The calendar posed one kind of threat to Romney. Health care posed another, even larger obstacle as the campaign was taking shape. Health care was to Romney what Hillary Rodham Clinton's vote to authorize the war in Iraq in 2002 was to her candidacy in 2008, a red flag to the party's base that opened a portion of the primary electorate to another candidate with a different position. The Massachusetts health care plan was the crowning achievement of

Romney's single term as governor. He had signed the bill on April 12, 2006, in a ceremony that included Democratic leaders of the Massachusetts legislature and Senator Edward M. Kennedy, who had defeated Romney in the 1994 Senate race and now had come to mark the moment with his onetime rival. Ryan Lizza of the *New Yorker* would later write, "Romney had accomplished a longstanding Democratic goal—universal health insurance—by combining three conservative policies. Massachusetts would help the uninsured buy private insurance; it would create a deregulated online marketplace; and it would require that everyone carry insurance. Uninsured citizens no longer would use the emergency room as a primary-care facility and then fail to pay their bills." Romney said later, "It's a Republican way of reforming the market." Romney was so proud of the achievement that when he posed for his official portrait, which would later hang in the Massachusetts State House, he insisted that a copy of the bill be included in the painting. The portrait shows Romney sitting on the edge of his desk, a picture of Ann Romney off his left forearm and the legislation next to it.

By the spring of 2011, the Massachusetts plan was a problem to be solved rather than an accomplishment to be trumpeted. For advice on his health care plan, Obama had drawn on some of the same people who had shaped Romney's thinking as governor. And he had appropriated many of the main outlines of the Massachusetts plan as the blueprint for the legislation he forced through Congress over united Republican opposition. The parentage was unmistakable. Obama's and Romney's plans were identical in so many ways. Most offensive to conservatives was Obama's individual mandate, the requirement that all Americans purchase health insurance or pay some kind of penalty. As a candidate, Obama had opposed the individual mandate. Clinton had included it in her proposal, but Obama had argued that there were other ways to achieve near-universal coverage. But as president he had pushed hard for it during the torturous deliberations in 2009 and 2010 that finally led to the bill's passage. The individual mandate came straight out of the Massachusetts plan (and out of the conservative Heritage Foundation in the 1990s). But in a Republican Party now infused with the constitutional absolutism of Tea Party activists, the individual mandate was seen as an infringement on individual freedom. Obama's new plan was the target of a series of lawsuits from states led by Republican governors or attorneys general that were working their way toward the Supreme Court. The challenges argued that the individual mandate was unconstitutional and should be struck down. Repealing Obamacare became a rallying cry on the right. Everyone thinking of running for president was committed to dumping the law and going back to the drawing board. Conservatives

competed with one another to declare their opposition to the heinous infringement on individual rights.

Romney was caught in the middle, eager to curry favor with the right but
attached to the Massachusetts plan. He was under enormous pressure to repudiate what he had done. Advisers said the pressure was unrelenting. "Every
single one of the core team probably had fifteen people a day tell them you're
crazy, he needs to repudiate it, it's a mistake, ask for forgiveness," Rhoades
said. Rhoades arrived to run Romney's political action committee a few weeks
after Obama had signed the act into law. "I just had moved into my apartment
here, so it was just about two and a half weeks and Obamacare clears the
Congress. People are like, 'He's done! Come back! It's over!'" he said. Romney
donors saw it as potentially lethal and wanted Romney to give some clear sign
that he regretted what he had done, that he had undergone a change of heart,
that he recognized now that what he had done was in error. Lanhee Chen, the
campaign's policy director, said the team was under "tremendous amounts of
pressure" to back away from the Massachusetts plan.

Romney thought otherwise. Neil Newhouse, who had polled for Romney in
his gubernatorial race, went to Boston in 2009 to make his pitch to become the
pollster for the 2012 campaign. He had conducted a poll on his own to gauge
sentiment about Romney among Republicans in two of the early states, New
Hampshire and South Carolina, and concluded even then that health care could
be a serious problem in the nomination battle. He said Romney had three options: First, embrace it and defend it; second, put distance between the act and
himself by, say, claiming that his successor as governor, Democrat Deval Patrick,
had turned the measure into something unrecognizable; third, say it was a mistake, that he shouldn't have done it, that he had learned an important lesson and
that he was now smarter about how to deal with the problem. "My presentation
is really going well until we get to that point and Mitt says, 'I'm not walking away
from it.'" Romney never wavered on that question, and no one among his core
advisers pressed for a reevaluation of this decision to stand firm. "What would I
say?" one adviser said. "You should pretend you hate it, that you're embarrassed
of it?"

However much Romney believed he had done the right thing, there was
another reason to stand behind it. To admit error, to suggest in any way that
he had had a change of heart on health care, would reopen the criticism of
him as a flip-flopper, as a politician willing to bend his views and his convictions, an ambitious political climber willing to adapt his positions to fit the
circumstances of the next challenge. In 2008, he never quite solved that problem, and it was inevitable that it would arise again in 2012. If he did anything

in the early stages of the race to draw attention to his changes in position on other issues, the consequences could be devastating. Changing his position would expose Romney to the fundamental question for every candidate who seeks the presidency, the question of who you are and what your character is. One adviser said they saw health care as both a character issue and a policy question. If he changed course, it likely would lead to a whole different set of questions that might have been as difficult to deal with as the similarity between the Massachusetts plan and Obama's.

Romney's solution was to defend the Massachusetts law, attack Obamacare, and offer an alternative to it, and he scheduled a speech for May 12, 2011, in Ann Arbor, Michigan, to make his case. The morning of the speech, the *Wall Street Journal* greeted him with a scorching editorial entitled "Obama's Running Mate," which included some of the harshest criticism ever of Romney and his legacy from Massachusetts. "It's no accident that RomneyCare's most vociferous defenders now are in the White House and left-wing media and think tanks," the editorial said. "They know what happened, even if he doesn't. For a potential president whose core argument is that he knows how to revive free market economic growth, this amounts to a fatal flaw. Presidents lead by offering a vision for the country rooted in certain principles, not by promising a technocracy that runs on 'data.' Mr. Romney's highest principle seems to be faith in his own expertise. More immediately for his Republican candidacy, the debate over Obamacare and the larger entitlement state may be the central question of the 2012 election. On that question, Mr. Romney is compromised and not credible. If he does not change his message, he might as well try to knock off Joe Biden and get on the Obama ticket."

Very early on the day of the speech, Tagg Romney, who was heading to the airport for a 6 a.m. flight to New York, got a message from his father. The prospective candidate was scheduled for a conference call with his staff at 7 a.m. to discuss the *Journal* editorial. Romney told his son, "I'm going to tell them I'm out." "He said there's no path to win the nomination," Tagg Romney told me. "At that moment he thought his chances were zero." Tagg Romney was alarmed by his father's statement. He remembers thinking, "This can't happen." He believed that he and his mother were gradually winning the battle to make his father fully comfortable with running again. Now his father was somehow convinced that the party he sought to lead would never accept him as its nominee. Here was the most conservative major newspaper in the country bashing him and calling him a liberal. He didn't see how he could win a primary under those conditions. Why waste everybody's time and money? On the call, his advisers—Rhoades, Fehrnstrom, and Myers among them—were insistent. This will pass, they said. Be patient. This is part of the process. There will be good days and bad. You don't need to worry about it. At the end of the call, Romney accepted their advice. He never shared the private thoughts he had expressed to his son. His campaign advisers never knew that he had awoken that morning ready to quit the race. "There were many other times between December and May where my dad had made up his mind not to run," Tagg Romney said. "He was hoping for an exit. I think he wanted to have an excuse not to run."

Romney's Ann Arbor speech was a PowerPoint presentation with twenty-five slides. He delivered it almost flawlessly in extemporaneous fashion. He had command of the material, even if he was making a questionable political argument. The presentation reflected his true personality, that of the wonkish private equity executive who enjoyed nothing more than breaking down a problem, analyzing numbers, weighing options, and finding a technocratic solution. He drew distinctions between his plan and Obama's. He had solved the problem for Massachusetts without raising taxes. Obama had okayed hundreds of billions in new taxes and in cuts to Medicare. He called for the repeal of Obamacare and then laid out the principles that he said would guide him in trying to provide insurance to the more than forty million Americans without health insurance while doing something to hold down the rising costs of health care.

The next morning, the *Wall Street Journal* carried a story about the speech and a letter from Romney responding to the previous day's editorial. "I was not surprised to read yet another editorial in the *Journal* yesterday criticizing the health-care reforms we enacted in Massachusetts," he wrote. "I was, however, not expecting the distortions of what we accomplished." But the *Journal*'s editorial page editors were still on the offensive, with another editorial critical of Romney's Ann Arbor presentation. "The likely Republican presidential candidate fulfilled the White House's fondest wishes, defending the mandate-subsidize-overregulate program he enacted as Massachusetts Governor in 2006 even as he denounced President Obama's national reprise," the editorial said. "He then proposed his own U.S. reform that is sensible and might do some actual good, but which also runs against the other two plans. These are unbridgeable policy and philosophical differences, though Mr. Romney is nonetheless trying to leap over them like Evel Knievel heading for the Snake River Canyon. . . . Who knows what GOP voters will make of all this, but we won't be surprised if Mr. Romney's campaign suffers as many broken bones (433) as Knievel."

A few weeks after the Ann Arbor speech, I asked one of Romney's top advisers whether the health care issue had been solved. "Listen, every candidate who ever runs for president goes and runs and they have things that they have to overcome," he said. "Either you overcome them or you don't. And as long as—and I do believe this—as long as we keep our head right about that, that attitude, he'll overcome it."

Before Romney's formal announcement, his campaign tested styles of presentation with voters in focus groups and with other research. Which Mitt would voters like best? People did not find Romney particularly appealing speaking directly to the camera. "I think they thought he was overselling," Stevens said. "They discounted what he was saying because he was a salesman, a guy coming to your door. [They were saying], 'I don't care what it is, I don't want to buy it.'" The campaign showed him to people while wearing suits or jeans or other outfits. Voters responded better to him when he was in jeans, and so for the next year and a half Romney mostly wore jeans as he campaigned.

Romney formally launched his candidacy on June 2, 2011, on a farm in Stratham, New Hampshire, owned by Doug and Stella Scamman, both of them former legislators and he a former speaker of the New Hampshire House. The day was sunny and breezy, with big puffy clouds moving across the New England sky. The wind whipped the landscape, blowing down a small tent and putting a snap in a flag planted on the grounds. The guests were served Ann Romney's chili, and she and Mitt dished it up from half a dozen slow cookers that were spread out on a table in a field. A big American flag was hanging from the old barn, with the Romney campaign logo and slogan, "Believe in America," on another barn. Another flag was hanging on the back of the Scammans' 250-year-old house. Romney spoke from the bed of a hay wagon. He wore dark slacks and an open-collared shirt that billowed in the wind, which was so strong that it shook the teleprompters as he delivered the speech.

His focus was on the president, true to the campaign's assessment that Romney would rise or fall as a candidate based on how voters saw him as a potential steward of the economy. He ignored the brewing fight for his party's nomination and the intraparty differences that lay ahead. "A few years ago," he said, "Americans did something that was, actually, very much the sort of thing Americans like to do: We gave someone new a chance to lead; someone we hadn't known for very long, who didn't have much of a record but promised to lead us to a better place. At the time, we didn't know what sort of a president he would make. It was a moment of crisis for our economy, and when Barack Obama came to office, we wished him well and hoped for the best. Now, in the third year of his four-year term, we have more than promises and slogans to go by. Barack Obama has failed America." Obama had inherited a bad economy and made it worse, he said. He and the president had different visions for the country, more government versus less, more spending versus less, more regulation versus less. He offered a litany of economic hardship across the country—

falling home prices, foreclosures, rising unemployment, higher gasoline prices, burdensome federal debt. "These failing hopes make up President Obama's own misery index," he said. "It's never been higher. And what's his answer? He says this: 'I'm just getting started.' No, Mr. President, you've had your chance. We, the people on this farm, and citizens across the country are the ones who are just getting started."

As with all front-runners, no matter how strong or fragile, Romney's struggle would be a familiar one. He was starting off in an enviable position: better funded than his rivals, his message honed and sharper than in his first campaign, the confidence and serenity that come with having run before. He understood the pace of a campaign better than his rivals. But could he truly rally this new and more conservative Republican Party behind him? Or would he find himself in constant conflict over Massachusetts health care, his conservative convictions, and his authenticity? Could he stay on the course he had set? Could he run his race and not the race that his rivals would try to make him run? Romney's family put his chances of winning the nomination at no better than fifty-fifty.

CHAPTER 8

The Apocalypse Party

As the campaign for the Republican nomination first began to take shape in early 2011, the political focus was not on the field of prospective presidential candidates. Instead it was on Congress and the eighty-seven freshman House Republicans who had arrived in Washington as a result of the 2010 elections. The Republican Party was now the Tea Party party, for all intents and purposes, and the newest recruits were cut from a different cloth than those in preceding classes. They were conservative to be sure, but they were also uncompromising, anti-Washington, and antiestablishment in ways previous newcomers had not been—even the class of 1994 under Speaker Newt Gingrich. The Republican congressional leadership was in the grip of this new class, and the presidential candidates were paying close attention.

The mood swings among Republicans—and assessments of the party's future—had come with breathtaking speed over the half-dozen preceding years. When George W. Bush was reelected in 2004, there was talk that Republicans were on the brink of having a durable governing majority in Washington and the states. Then in 2006, with the country souring on Bush's leadership and the Iraq War, with GOP infighting over spending and immigration, and with a series of scandals affecting their elected officials, Republicans were suddenly out of power in Congress. Two years after that, with Obama's historic victory, they were out of power completely in Washington. As Obama took the oath of office in January 2009, the pendulum appeared to be swinging back to the left. Republicans feared they could be facing a lengthy time in the wilderness. In the first year of Obama's presidency, the author Sam Tanenhaus published a work entitled *The Death of Conservatism*. "We stand on the threshold of a new era that has decisively declared the end of an old one," he wrote. "In the shorthand of the moment, this abandoned era is often called the Reagan Revolution. . . . The crisis on the right is the endgame of a long-running debate—not only between conservatism and liberalism but also within conservatism, and sometimes within the minds of individual conservatives—about the nature of government and society, and about the role of politics in binding the two. . . . Today's conservatives resemble the exhumed figures of Pompeii, trapped in postures of frozen flight, clenched in the rigor mortis of a defunct ideology." Tanenhaus wrote with more dramatic flair than some others, but his conclusions were widely shared. Obama's victory in 2008 did seem to mark the endpoint of the conservative ascendance. Republicans seemed divided between their conservative and very conservative wings.

If others were ready to declare the conservative era dead, however, Obama was not—not quite, at least. In a post-election interview in December 2008, I asked him to reflect on the meaning of his victory and whether it marked an end to the Reagan era. He said Reagan had ushered in "skepticism towards government solutions to every problem, a suspicion of command-and-control top-down social engineering." He saw that as a lasting legacy of the Reagan era and the conservative movement, starting with Goldwater. But he saw the 2008 election as an end to knee-jerk reactions toward the New Deal and big government. "What we don't know yet," he added, "is whether my administration and this next generation of leadership is going to be able to hew to a new, more pragmatic approach that is less interested in whether we have big government or small government, they're more interested in whether we have a smart, effective government." Obama got a partial answer to that question twenty-three months after we spoke when resurgent Republicans swept back into power in the House and gained seats in the Senate in November 2010. His failure to persuade the country that he believed in smart government rather than big government had brought the Republicans back to life. But what had the Republican Party become?

The Tea Party movement was born early in 2009, with a rant and a string of rallies. The rant took place on the morning of February 19, 2009, on the floor of the Chicago Board of Trade. CNBC's Rick Santelli started it. "President Obama, are you listening?" His call to arms—"We're thinking of having a Chicago tea party in July"—quickly went viral. Bloggers took up the rallying cry and began to organize protests. Hundreds of thousands of Americans rallied around the country on Tax Day. By summer, Tea Party groups had sprung up across the country, protesting Obama's stimulus package, the auto bailout, what they saw as reckless spending by Washington that was ballooning the deficit and the national debt, and especially Obama's health care reform proposal. The Tea Party became an object of fear and fascination, scorn and admiration—and misunderstanding. Journalists tried to put human faces on the movement and found a mix of emotions and intentions among those newly drawn to political activism. Some scholars saw it as a manifestation of the growing ideological polarization. Others described it as putting a label on a preexisting, ultraconservative wing of the party. Still others noted that it was a reaction against both Obama and the failures of Republican governance during Bush's presidency.

Even without a clear leader, Tea Party activists provided much of the anti-Obama energy fueling the Republican Party's efforts to win back the House and Senate in 2010. They also acted as disciplinarians within the Republican Party. Citing constitutional principles, they demanded political orthodoxy on issues related to government spending, taxation, regulation, and the role of government and invoked litmus tests on elected officials and candidates for office. The demand for purity arose first in the fall of 2009, when Obama nominated John McHugh, a moderate Republican congressman from upstate New York, to be Army secretary. In the ensuing special election in New York's 23rd Congressional District, local GOP leaders put forward as their nominee Dede Scozzafava, whose moderate philosophy matched the district's and McHugh's politics. A skirmish erupted within the party over whether to support her or Doug Hoffman, who was running on the Conservative Party line. Party leaders in Washington, including House Republican leader John Boehner, backed Scozzafava. So did Newt Gingrich. Sarah Palin then endorsed Hoffman, and some other Republicans looking to run for president in 2012 quickly followed her lead, among them Tim Pawlenty, then the governor of Minnesota. Scozzafava dropped out just before the election and endorsed the Democratic nominee, Bill Owens. With the GOP badly splintered, the seat, which had been in Republican hands for a century, fell to Owens and the Democrats in the special election.

The fight in New York proved to be a precursor for other internecine battles that followed in 2010 in Utah, Florida, Kentucky, and elsewhere. Three Senate seats were lost in 2010—in Nevada, Colorado, and Delaware—in large part because Tea Party–favored candidates had won the Republican nomination and proved unacceptable to the overall electorate. But those losses were considered small disappointments in comparison with the overall results in November 2010. The big victory persuaded many Republicans that 2006 and 2008 were aberrations and that the country remained firmly tilted to the center-right. There was only one obstacle, and that was Obama, who they believed was determined to take the country in a radically different direction and had to be stopped.

The Tea Party symbolized the rightward shift in the party, and that movement would shape the nomination battle. The 2010 elections showed that the Republican Party was more conservative than it had been during Reagan's presidency and also more conservative than it had been at the time of Bush's election in 2000. The grassroots movement appeared to be in control, and some elected officials joined them to take on the establishment. South Carolina senator Jim DeMint took an active role in supporting antiestablishment candidates in party primaries, and his support was eagerly sought, to the dismay of the party's established leadership.* Grover Norquist, the head of Americans for Tax Reform, exercised considerable power by asking candidates to sign pledges to voters in their states not to raise taxes. The Club for Growth, whose slogan was "Prosperity and Opportunity through Economic Freedom," took an active role in Republican primary contests, funding television ads against mainstream candidates they regarded as insufficiently conservative on taxes and spending. Americans for Prosperity, funded by the billionaire Koch brothers, worked closely with Tea Party groups from the inception of the movement to prevent ideological backsliding. Talk show hosts, from Rush Limbaugh to Sean Hannity to Glenn Beck, berated Republicans who were straying, as they kept up a steady line of attack against Obama.

But it was more than just a shift to the right. The 2010 midterms produced a party that, at its grass roots, was more militant in its beliefs and less willing to accept compromise in its leaders. In the summer of 2012, the *Washington Post* and the Kaiser Family Foundation did a deep survey examining the political parties. The survey identified five different factions within the Republican Party. Three made up the heart of the GOP coalition and reflected the fissures that the presidential candidates would have to negotiate in the primaries and caucuses. The largest then was labeled "Tea Party Movement" Republicans, accounting for almost 30 percent of the party and clearly the most conservative of the five groups. Ninety-eight percent of them said they wanted smaller government, and just 6 percent said they agreed with the proposition that "the world is always changing and we should adjust our morals and our values to those changes." Another fifth of the party was labeled "Religious Values Voters," though ironically they were not quite as religious as the Tea Party Republicans in our survey. Another fifth was called "Old School Republicans." They were more male than the other groups and somewhat more moderate on social issues. In that sense they were what used to be known as country club Republicans, socially moderate but fiscally conservative. On fiscal and governmental issues, their views were almost as conservative as those of the Tea Party movement group. Moderates barely claimed a toehold in the party and enjoyed no credibility with grassroots activists.

A majority of Republicans in the survey said it was more important for their

---

*DeMint announced his resignation from the Senate in December 2012 to become president of the Heritage Foundation.

elected officials to stick to their principles than to compromise on important issues with the Democrats. The Republican freshman class that was brought to Washington with the 2010 elections reflected these sentiments, and the members were determined not to succumb to the get-along-go-along attitude they believed had affected previous freshman classes. Tom Cole, a Republican House member from Oklahoma, was elected in 2002 and went on to chair the party's congressional campaign committee. During the 2012 campaign, he talked about the difference between his class and those who joined the 112th Congress in January 2011. He arrived in Congress at a time when "our congressional leaders were the leaders that had balanced the budget, had gotten welfare reform passed, and now we were turning to deal with this enormous challenge overseas that hadn't been anticipated. We were doing the right things. That class was very inclined to be supportive of its leadership and its president. Fast-forward to this class. They get here and they're like, 'You guys are part of the problem. On your watch, we lost the majority, we lost control of spending.'"

Some party leaders could see the dangers of a coalition that was overwhelmingly white and had its strongest support among older voters. Tom Davis, a moderate Republican and former Virginia congressman who had run the National Republican Congressional Committee for several cycles, said, "We're going to have to change what we're doing if we want to win. If you want to be a politically competitive majority party, you just take a look at the coalition and the fastest-growing groups and voting. We got the old people; they're dying off. They got the young people; they're going to be voting a long time. They got Hispanics; that's the largest immigrant group. Where are we picking up? You don't pick it up among rural white southerners."

But that was hardly accepted doctrine within the party. Instead, as the campaign was gearing up, the most striking characteristic about the party and its conservative grassroots was the intensity of hostility toward the president. Disgust with Obama had become a dominant strain in the party's personality. Many Republicans, from the leaders of conservative constituencies to newly energized grassroots activists, saw the prospect of another four years of Obama in the White House as disastrous. They feared what he might do if reelected and expressed those fears in apocalyptic terms. Wayne LaPierre, executive vice president of the National Rifle Association, put it this way when he spoke to the annual CPAC gathering in Washington in early 2012: "Our soul is at stake in this election. This campaign is a fight for our country, our values, and the freedom we believe in. All of our Second Amendment liberty, all of the rights we've worked so hard to defend, all of what we know is good and right about America— all of it could be lost if Barack Obama is reelected. It's all or nothing."

Along the campaign trail, ordinary Americans expressed the same fears about a second Obama term, that the country as they knew it would be lost forever. I asked a Michigan Republican what he thought would happen to the country if Obama was reelected. "Additional decay and [loss of] personal freedoms and more growth of dependency on the government, which is sad for America," he said. An Ohio voter, when I asked how he would describe what was at stake in the election, said, "My freedom. I am scared to death of Obama. He has nothing to lose if he gets reelected and I'm just terribly afraid the country will plummet and we won't return. I don't like his health care plan. I don't like the debt that he's put us in. I don't like the control he's trying to take over the American people. I have worked hard all my life and we made it on our own and we didn't come from rich families and he's too much for the entitlements, making people lazy in the United States, which can only lead to others governing us."

For Romney and the others looking to win the Republican nomination, the 2010 elections signaled that the nominating process would be dominated by this grassroots sentiment, as well as by the religious and social conservatives who had risen to power two decades earlier and who had become a force in the presidential primaries. Nomination battles often came down to a contest between an establishment candidate and a conservative insurgent—the business wing or the populist wing. Even for those who came from the business wing of the party, catering to this new party would become the first priority. That meant more than fealty to a conservative philosophy; it meant accommodating to the confrontational desires of those at the grass roots. Romney's advisers believed his conservative views on fiscal issues would find support among Tea Party activists. The worry was how far right he would be dragged in order to defeat more conservative rivals in the field of candidates. Republicans had won the 2010 elections because Obama was seen as having abandoned the center of the political spectrum. Now Republicans were in danger of giving the center back to Obama for 2012.

CHAPTER 9

The First Primary

Politics, like history, is a game of what-ifs, and so one can only speculate about what might have happened if Romney had been pitted against a different field. The reality was that, for all the concerns Romney and his family might have had, he was always the likeliest of the Republicans to become the presidential nominee. For a time in 2011, however, it appeared that Romney could face a more formidable set of rivals. Compared to previous Republicans who had worn the front-runner's label, Romney cast no large shadows.

Potential rivals came from all parts of the party. Former Florida governor Jeb Bush was one. Bush had all the other credentials needed: two terms as governor of a big state, a record as a reformer on education, a politician attentive to the Hispanic community, a realist who understood that nostalgia for the Reagan era did not constitute a winning platform in the twenty-first century. Had his name been Jeb Smith, he might have become the Republican nominee. But his brother's unpopular presidency was only a few years in the rearview mirror. Bush never gave serious thought to running in 2012. He had explored a race for the Senate when Republican Mel Martinez abruptly announced his resignation, but he concluded that the time was not right, for him or for his family. When the 2012 cycle arrived, according to two close advisers, he did not revisit the issue of getting back into politics. Beyond Bush, there were others seen as potential candidates. They included Haley Barbour, then the governor of Mississippi; Mitch Daniels, the governor of Indiana; and Mike Huckabee, the former Arkansas governor whose surprise victory in the 2008 Iowa caucuses helped to cripple Romney's candidacy at the very start of the process. There was Sarah Palin, the former Alaska governor and 2008 vice presidential nominee, a celebrity-politician who was a favorite of the Tea Party movement and knew how to attract the attention of the media. New Jersey governor Chris Christie, the blunt-talking former prosecutor, though not even two years into office, also became the object of a frenzied recruitment effort.

On the night of November 3, 2010, one day after Republicans delivered their shellacking to President Obama and the Democrats, Haley Barbour was sipping whiskey at the Willard Hotel two blocks east of the White House. The Willard is one of Washington's most historic hotels, renovated in the opulent style that recalls the era of President Ulysses S. Grant, who frequented the hotel after hours and coined the term "lobbyists" to describe the influence peddlers who hung out there. Barbour, with a wide girth and deep southern drawl, was at home in such places. Before he was elected governor, he was one of the capital's best-connected lobbyists. His résumé as a party leader was lengthy: Before winning the governorship in Mississippi, he had led the Republicans Governors Association during the 2010 cycle. He had chaired the Republican National Committee when Republicans captured the House in 1994, and before that he had served as political director in the Reagan White House.

Barbour epitomized the business wing of the party, a member in good standing of the Republican establishment, to the extent that there was such a thing. That alone was reason for some Republicans to think he would give Romney a serious challenge. He was a prodigious fund-raiser. He was policy wise and street smart. He knew how to run a tough campaign. Plus, he didn't particularly admire Romney. Barbour was a big-tent Republican. He was conservative in his views but eminently pragmatic when it came to winning elections. When, after the 2008 election, some conservatives were calling for litmus tests for candidates, Barbour took the opposite view. In the summer of 2009, he told me, "Politics is about addition and multiplication; purity is about subtraction and division."

The southerner was a master of the inside game, widely regarded as one of the shrewdest political strategists in either party. He was skilled at the courtship rituals of Washington. The night after the midterm election, he was playing host to more than a dozen reporters. Most had known Barbour for two decades; many called him by his first name. After drinks, the group assembled around a large round table. At each seat, specially printed menus described the evening's four-course meal. The table settings included fine china and silverware. The ostensible purpose was to review the results of the election a day earlier. The real purpose was to continue Barbour's already active exploration of a campaign for the White House in 2012—all on "background," of course. Everyone in the room understood that this was a kind of trial run in the event that he decided to seek the presidency.

Barbour was far from a decision, but had told his advisers that, if he did not run, he didn't want the reason to be that he had not done the necessary preliminary work. He wanted to keep his options open. He had met secretly with Scott Reed, who had managed Bob Dole's 1996 presidential campaign, and with Ed Rogers, his past business partner and a senior White House official in George H. W. Bush's administration, in Birmingham in August 2010 to consider next steps. Those around Barbour saw Romney as "fatally compromised" by the Massachusetts health care plan. Ed Goeas, Barbour's pollster, had conducted polls and focus groups in Iowa. In September, Rogers e-mailed Reed to propose that Reed be hired in November and December to start organizing the calendar. In mid-November, Reed e-mailed Rogers to say, "I personally believe if we build it, they will come." As they prepared, Barbour's team hired the law firm of Williams & Connolly to prepare a vulnerability study. Rogers said, "The vulnerability study confirmed what everybody already knew [about Barbour's potential weaknesses], and they were all problems that were to be managed, not solved, and none of it was fatal in today's world for sure." Most of the problems centered on Barbour's work as a lobbyist. He had earned millions representing tobacco companies. His clients also included alcohol interests, energy companies, and foreign governments.

What wasn't anticipated was that the normally surefooted Barbour would find himself on the defensive over the issue of race three times in a matter of months with a series of missteps. He once explained the South's conversion to the Republican Party as the result of younger whites having grown up with integration rejecting the Democratic Party and joining the GOP. He said it was old Democrats who clung to segregation. His version overlooked the flight of segregationists from the Democratic Party after Lyndon B. Johnson, who knew he was putting his party at risk, signed the 1964 Civil Rights Act. In another case, the *Weekly Standard*'s Andrew Ferguson asked him how his hometown of Yazoo City managed to integrate its schools without violence. "Because the business community wouldn't stand for it," he responded. "You heard of the Citizens Councils? Up North they think it was like the KKK. Where I come from it was an organization of town leaders." In fact, Citizens' Councils in the South had a history of racism that was well documented. Barbour's alarmed advisers put together "an organized walk-back" of the statement. In early 2011, I asked Barbour how such an astute politician had gotten into such a predicament over race. "I have reconciled myself to the fact that some people on the left who don't like me or don't like conservative Christian Republicans from the Deep South are going to criticize anything I do," Barbour said. "Will it have any effect on my deciding whether or not to run? No." Others around him were far more concerned. They worried that Barbour could be badly hurt by running for president, and that if he were ever to become the nominee, the Obama campaign would make the campaign about him rather than the president. Rogers said, "Given his accent and given where he's from, it was always going to be a vulnerable spot for him. . . . It was going to be a problem that was going to be managed, not solved."

Barbour began traveling to test the waters and came back with upbeat reports about the receptions he was receiving but without a commitment to run. After his trips, Rogers would ask, "Well, have you seen a burning bush?" Barbour would reply, "No. I ain't seen no burning bush." Nonetheless, Scott Reed started to plan an announcement tour for early May. A week before the launch, Barbour announced that he would not be a candidate after all. He said he lacked the fire in the belly. "I cannot offer that with certainty, and total certainty is required," he told supporters. There was more to it, according to his advisers. They knew what Obama and the Democrats would do against a portly Mississippian. One close adviser said, "We were never going to be able to make this about Obama and his policies and his bad decisions and the weakness of the economy—everything the campaign should be about."

If Barbour was a serious potential candidate, Donald Trump was the opposite, though his cameo role brought unwelcome attention to the party. The self-promoting businessman waded into the Republican race for seemingly one purpose, which was to flagrantly challenge Obama to prove that he was born in America. That Trump could become the country's most prominent birther *and* the leader in the race for the Republican nomination, according to at least some polls, was the best evidence of just how far out of the mainstream at least some of the Republican base was.

Trump was a clown candidate and his potential candidacy was preposterous, but it clearly irritated the president, who soon vowed to take action. During an overnight visit to his home in Chicago that spring, Obama had found what he thought was the legal document certifying his birth. He brought it back to the White House, where White House counsel Robert Bauer informed him that it wasn't the actual document. Obama said he wanted the real document made public. Many of Obama's advisers opposed the move, believing it would draw more attention to the birther issue and make it seem like the president was being forced to answer to Trump. Obama saw it as an opportunity to demonstrate how much was wrong with politics and the way it was played. He secretly requested the certificate from authorities in Hawaii and quietly ordered a White House lawyer to fly to Honolulu to retrieve it.

On the morning of April 27, 2011, as Trump's helicopter descended on Dover, New Hampshire, for what he hoped would be a grand visit to the Granite State, the White House unexpectedly released a copy of Obama's never-seen long-form birth certificate. Appearing before reporters, the president said, "We do not have time for this kind of silliness." Trump crowed, "I've accomplished something no one else was able to do." But it was Obama who got the last laugh. At the annual White House Correspondents' Association Dinner on April 30, 2011, the president made Trump the butt of his jokes. As Helene Cooper of the *New York Times* put it, "As a hair-gelled, grimly unsmiling Mr. Trump sat at a nearby table—a guest of the *Washington Post*—Mr. Obama ripped one punch after another at the real estate tycoon." Joked Obama, "No one is happier, no one is prouder to put this birth certificate matter to rest than the Donald. And that's because he can finally get back to focusing on the issues that matter— like, did we fake the moon landing? What really happened in Roswell? And where are Biggie and Tupac?" He ribbed Trump for showing decisive leadership in getting rid of actor Gary Busey on *Celebrity Apprentice*. "These are the kind of decisions that would keep me up at night," he said as the audience laughed at Trump's expense. "Well handled, sir. Well handled." He noted that Trump would no doubt bring real change to the White House, and up on the screen popped a photo of the White House that read, "Trump White House Resort and Casino."

Trump's phantom candidacy had peaked. A few weeks later, he announced to no one's surprise that he would not be a candidate. That Trump could become, even for a few weeks, a potentially serious choice in the minds of Republican voters again highlighted a party whose leadership was being overrun by forces they could not control.

Mike Huckabee presented another potential challenge to Romney—a clear contrast in an area that had plagued Romney as a candidate and would continue to do so. Huckabee was an economic populist with a life story the opposite of Romney's. He had an instinctive feel for middle- and lower-middle-class Americans, having grown up without money or connections. Among the field of candidates, he also would have first claim on the party's evangelical base. He resented talk that Romney was "next in line" for the nomination and had tangled frequently with Romney in 2008. "I take a little umbrage about the next in line," he told the *Washington Post*'s Karen Tumulty in February 2011. "I was second, not Romney. I came in second in the number of delegates. It's just pure spin to deny me that. Give me that."

What stood in Huckabee's path was not the confidence that he could compete for votes, but concerns about money—the state of his personal finances and the cash it would take to run again. After his loss in the 2008 race, Huckabee, genial in personality and firm in his conservatism, had gone on to become a Fox News personality. He had his own television program and a contract that finally began to give him the financial security he had lacked his entire life. He and his wife had started to build their dream home in northern Florida. But there were other signs that he wasn't serious about running a second time. Tumulty captured that side of Huckabee in the profile she wrote after interviewing him. "Instead of throwing red meat to the conservative faithful, Huckabee was tucking into a breakfast of eggs and butter-slathered pancakes at a trendy New York hotel overlooking Times Square. His much-discussed diet—he famously lost more than 100 pounds after a diabetes diagnosis in 2003 and wrote a book about eating right—is apparently on hiatus."

Staffers from his 2008 campaign were in regular conversation with him about another campaign, but found little enthusiasm from Huckabee. Ed Rollins, the veteran Republican strategist, said, "Finally I said to him, 'Mike I've been through this. I can't want this more than you want it.'" On May 14, 2011, to no one's surprise, Huckabee announced that he would not run, removing another obstacle from Romney's path.

Sarah Palin rolled into the Pentagon parking lot on the back of a Harley-Davidson on the morning of May 29, 2011, and all hell broke loose. As she prepared to join the annual Rolling Thunder motorcycle event, she was swarmed by a horde of television cameras, still photographers, and reporters. "Get out of here before someone gets hurt," a burly biker in a white T-shirt and black vest shouted angrily, waving his hands at the cameras. A woman shouted above the noise, "We love you, Sarah!" The former Alaska governor was dressed in black—black helmet, black leather jacket, black T-shirt, and black jeans. Large sunglasses shielded her eyes. As she moved through the crowd, she was swallowed up by the gawkers and reporters. She turned to Jason Recher, her traveling adviser. "Okay," she said. "What's the plan?"

That was the question on everyone's mind that morning. Palin was at the start of a campaign-style bus tour that would take her to historic sites and monuments along the East Coast. It had been announced only a few days earlier, and the wild scrum that quickly formed around her spoke not only to her appeal as one of the biggest political celebrities in America but also to the never-ending speculation about whether she too would join the 2012 Republican presidential field. She had ended the 2008 campaign at the center of a raging battle over whether John McCain should have picked her as his vice presidential nominee. Books about the 2008 campaign recounted her missteps, and one of them, by journalists Mark Halperin and John Heilemann, later became the basis of an Emmy Award–winning movie by HBO called *Game Change*.

Palin returned to Alaska to resume her governorship and was hit with a series of ethics complaints. In July 2009, she abruptly resigned her office, drawing more criticism. What kept the interest in her alive was both the media's unrelenting fascination with all things Palin and the passion she stirred among many of the Tea Party activists who had made their influence felt in the 2010 elections. She was the antiestablishment voice at a time when the party establishment was on its heels.

As 2011 opened, Palin suffered another political setback. After the shootings in Tucson in January 2011, some liberals blamed the violence in part on the climate they said had been created by right-wing zealots. Palin was singled out for having issued a list of Democrats she said deserved defeat in 2010, with crosshairs on their congressional districts. Palin was at first perplexed, then frustrated, and finally angry. Advisers warned her to respond carefully. Instead she struck back with a video released the morning Obama was on his way to Arizona to deliver remarks at a memorial service for the victims. In the video, Palin said, "If you don't like a person's vision for the country, you're free to debate that vision. If you don't like their ideas, you're free to propose better ideas. But, especially within hours of a tragedy unfolding, journalists and pundits should not manufacture a blood libel that serves only to incite the very hatred and violence they purport to condemn. That is reprehensible." Palin's reference to "blood libel," which had been used in a *Wall Street Journal* op-ed piece earlier, produced a storm of criticism, and not just from predictable liberal quarters.

For all of the exposure she had gained as McCain's running mate and all of the speculation about her ambitions, she and her husband, Todd, were still just an Alaska couple whose sophistication about presidential politics and campaigns was extremely limited. They knew next to nothing about navigating the early states, the primary-caucus calendar, filing deadlines, delegate selection rules, what it took to build a network of bundlers, or any of the other components of a successful campaign. What she had was an instinctive talent for knowing what she wanted to say and a fearlessness to take on anyone she chose. When she began her Memorial Day bus tour, no one around Palin knew whether she planned to run for president. None of them knew whether she knew, but most doubted that she did either. Even Palin advisers were startled to see the frenzy the bus trip created. They did not expect to see fifty journalists waiting for her when she arrived at the National Archives. They were surprised to see live reports on cable from Gettysburg when they got there. They were shocked at the sight of hovering helicopters as she arrived in Philadelphia.

Political professionals scoffed at the notion of Palin as a serious candidate. They dismissed the bus tour as so unconventional as to be ridiculous as a model for a campaign. Alex Castellanos, a veteran Republican strategist, put it this way in an e-mail to me as the bus tour was under way: "She just repeats what Republicans already believe, in an emotional and energetic way, true. But when she leaves, Republican voters are left right where they were standing when she entered the room. She doesn't take us anywhere. Until she does, her stature will continue to diminish, not because she is not running, but because she is not leading." Palin shrugged off such criticism. "I don't think I owe anything to the mainstream media," she told Greta Van Susteren of Fox News.

She dominated news cycles as she traveled up the eastern seaboard. New Hampshire was her eventual destination. She crossed the New Hampshire state line just after Romney made his formal announcement. There, she invited an eclectic group of people—some political and some not—for a casual clambake in Seabrook. With her daughter Piper at her side, she fielded questions from reporters. "I had a sense the whole thing was ramping up when we started the bus tour, and more so when we ended that bus tour," said one of her advisers.

After the bus tour came a movie called *The Undefeated*, a piece of cinematic hagiography about Palin's tenure in Alaska. Palin's team had approached filmmaker Stephen K. Bannon about making the movie and gave him full access to material. He said he retained editorial control. The premiere was held at the century-old Pella Opera House in Pella, Iowa, on June 28, 2011. By then, Palin had competition from another conservative woman, Michele Bachmann, who had just announced her candidacy in her hometown of Waterloo. The movie premiere drew predictable media attention, but Palin was not satisfied. Acting on an invitation, she decided to return in August for the Iowa State Fair, which has become a favorite stop for presidential candidates the year before every election. She arrived the morning after a candidate debate in Ames and the day before the Iowa Straw Poll. "I don't think I'm stealing any spotlight," she said. She continued to play coy about running for president. She scheduled one more major event in Iowa a month later, a speech on September 3 to a Tea Party gathering in Indianola, south of Des Moines. The night before, she was mobbed by supporters chanting, "Run, Sarah, Run," at a suburban Des Moines restaurant. Some had traveled hundreds of miles to be there, many believing she would use her appearance to announce her candidacy. They were the true believers. One said he was "99.9999 percent sure" she would run. The next day, the Tea Party crowd gathered in the rain in a balloon field to hear her. Palin delivered the best speech she had given in many months, a populist broadside at "a permanent political class" that enriched themselves at the expense of ordinary Americans through "corporate crony capitalism." At that, the audience leaped to their feet, chanting, "Sar-ah! Sar-ah! Sar-ah!"

Two days after Labor Day, Tim Crawford, who was the treasurer of Palin's political action committee, and Mike Glassner, her chief of staff, flew to Phoenix to meet the Palins for the first serious conversation about what running would entail. They presented them with a package of information: deadlines, schedules, what each day might look like. They explained the constant fund-raising demands, the time required to court voters in Iowa and New Hamp-shire, and what those voters had come to expect. They warned that running would mean nonstop travel without weekends off. The meeting went on for several hours. The Palins had many questions, nuts-and-bolts inquiries about what to expect if she ran. That was the last of it. A month later, she issued a statement saying she would not be a candidate in 2012. "I believe that at this time I can be more effective in a decisive role to help elect other true public servants to office—from the nation's governors to Congressional seats and the Presidency." By the time she made the announcement, the political world had passed her by. For once, her sense of timing failed her.

The annual Conservative Political Action Conference in Washington is a win-ter carnival for conservatives, with huge portions of red meat tossed from the podium to a hungry audience of mostly young conservatives. It is a proving ground for would-be Republican stars, a place to compete for outrageous sound bites or the most memorable attacks on the opposition. On the night of Febru-ary 12, 2011, Indiana governor Mitch Daniels broke all the rules—and made himself into a viable candidate for the Republican nomination. Rather than red meat, he talked about a new "red menace," the threat to America from the ocean of red ink produced by a succession of budget deficits that he said under Obama were growing at an alarming rate. "We face an enemy, lethal to liberty, and even more implacable than those America has defeated before," he said. "We cannot deter it; there is no countervailing danger we can pose. We cannot negotiate with it, any more than with an iceberg or a great white."

If Haley Barbour represented a threat to Romney because of his political smarts and fund-raising ability, Daniels offered the potential to challenge Rom-ney because it was so clear what he stood for. He was a politician with a long résumé in and out of government and with deep ties to a generation of Repub-licans who had served in Washington and the states. Before becoming gover-nor, he was George W. Bush's budget director and earned the nickname "the Blade" for his efforts to reduce spending (though spending rose rapidly during Bush's presidency). He was a senior vice president at Eli Lilly, the pharmaceu-tical giant based in Indianapolis, and before that he ran the Hudson Institute, a conservative think tank. On his way up the ladder in Washington, he served as chief of staff to Indiana senator Richard Lugar, as executive director of the National Republican Senatorial Committee, and as political director in Ronald Reagan's White House.

His consideration of a candidacy was anything but conventional. When speculation surfaced in the fall of 2009 that he might become a candidate,

Daniels did everything he could to douse it. His informal kitchen cabinet tried to encourage him that fall, and he was dismissive to them. In January 2010, Daniels had met with a small group of longtime advisers in Scottsdale, Arizona. He told them that if he were to undertake a candidacy, no one around him was going to tell him what to say, and he gave them a taste of it, a chilling warning about the fiscal catastrophe he saw looming. It was a forerunner of the speech he would deliver at CPAC more than a year later. He had another precondition. He would have to have the full support of his family, which was something he knew would be difficult to get, particularly from his wife, Cheri. She and Daniels had married many years earlier, long before elective office was in his future. In the mid-1990s, she had left him and their four young daughters to marry another man. Three years later, after divorcing the second man, she returned to Daniels and their daughters. They reconciled and were married for a second time. It was a happy ending, but it was not a story either wanted to see examined in the glare of a presidential campaign.

Around the same time, Daniels had a conversation with George W. Bush, who also encouraged him to seriously consider running in 2012. I heard about the conversation, and when David Broder* and I sat down with him at the winter meeting of the National Governors Association in February, I asked him about it. He said it wasn't just Bush but others who were encouraging him not to close the door on running. "Just to get them off my back, I agreed to a number of people that I will now stay open to the idea," he told me. Mark Lubbers, a longtime political adviser to Daniels, saw a Google Alert flash on his computer the afternoon an item saying he was open to running was posted on the *Post* Web site. He called Daniels's cell phone. "You just created page-one news in tomorrow morning's *Indianapolis Star*," Lubbers told him. "I didn't make any news," Daniels insisted. "You've got to be kidding me," Lubbers responded. And then, for a year, Daniels did nothing. Good to his word, he concentrated on being governor. One thing he did was to call for a truce on what he called "so-called social issues" to allow politicians in both parties to focus on the fiscal crisis. Social conservatives took it as an expression of unilateral disarmament, and as talk of a Daniels candidacy rose, some of his potential rivals tried to disqualify him. In spite of that, the interest in him continued to build, a function of the weakness of the Republican field and doubts about Romney as a committed conservative who could truly rally the party in a general election.

Daniels wrote the CPAC speech himself, and it was by far the most sophisticated address of the conference, a big-league piece of political and policy rhetoric. Referring to federal entitlement programs, he said an obese Washington

---

*David Broder died on March 9, 2011.

needed "bariatric surgery." He sounded a call to arms but demonstrated flexibility too. "It is up to us to show, specifically, the best way back to greatness, and to argue for it with all the passion of our patriotism," he said. "But, should the best way be blocked, while the enemy draws nearer, then someone will need to find the second best way, or the third, because the nation's survival requires it." He challenged his party to look outward for support. "We must be the vanguard of recovery, but we cannot do it alone. We have learned in Indiana, big change requires big majorities. We will need people who never tune in to Rush [Limbaugh] or Glenn [Beck] or Laura [Ingraham] or Sean [Hannity]. Who surf past C-SPAN to get to *SportsCenter*. Who, if they'd ever heard of CPAC, would assume it was a cruise ship accessory."

Two months after the CPAC speech, I went to Indianapolis to see Daniels. We talked at some length about the issues he had raised in the speech and about the president. I said I had the feeling that he quietly hoped the clock would run out on him, that by the time he finished his legislative business and his deliberations about a candidacy, it would be too late to mount an effective campaign. He didn't disagree. "I don't know about wishing, but I had accepted that that was probable. . . . Look, I have had a sort of 'let this cup pass' feeling. It's a biblical reference." Asked about family considerations, he went quiet. "I don't have much more to say about that," he said. "It's just a very important factor."

Toward the end we returned to the key questions, apart from his family. If none of the other candidates were prepared to address these issues directly, was he obligated in some way to run to ensure that they were aired out under the lights of a presidential campaign? And conversely, did he fear that the cause about which he felt such passion would be set back if he were to run and do poorly? Daniels was forthright in his belief that the debate needed to be at the center of the presidential campaign. "Whether it's me or somebody else, I hope it will become central to the Republican alternative next time. We've got a very fundamental choice to make. It's not just about dollars and cents and safety net. To me the questions that are bound up in that are classic questions—which sector's in charge of life in America, public or private? Is the public sector there to support the flourishing of the private economy, voluntary associations, states, cities, and communities, or is life now so complex that we poor victims out here have to be looked over, tended carefully, and overseen by our benevolent betters? I hope again that it will, one way or another, become a very large part of the alternative that our party, whoever it is, will present to the country. I think it would be a default on our part not to do that."

Six weeks later, Daniels announced that he would not run, citing family considerations. He was never able to persuade Cheri Daniels, who held a veto power over the decision and was reluctant to give up her and her family's privacy. His decision left a void to be filled—a missing candidacy focused on the issue that, other than the state of the economy, defined the differences between Republicans and Democrats. Daniels's candidacy was in many ways a long shot, but the interest in his running reflected the fear among some establishment conservatives—and Tea Party activists too—that their presidential field was defaulting on one of the biggest issues before the country.

For Romney, one less obstacle stood between him and the nomination.

CHAPTER 10

Chris Christie's Story

After Mitch Daniels said no, attention turned to another governor, Chris Christie of New Jersey. He was no ordinary politician, which was why he was in demand even though he had been elected to office only in November 2009. He embodied his state's image with a blunt, in-your-face personality that made him a star in the YouTube era. He relished sparring with political adversaries and ordinary citizens who questioned his decisions, and the confrontations often went viral. Even if they did not, he kept them alive by recounting those moments before other audiences. That he was considerably overweight only added to the intimidation factor that he projected. Republicans loved him.

Christie was born in Newark, son of a father of Scotch-Irish descent and a mother of Sicilian descent. As he once said, that combination "has made me not unfamiliar with conflict." He went to law school at Seton Hall University and started to practice law. In 1992, he took a leave from his firm and volunteered in George H. W. Bush's reelection campaign. Through that campaign he became friends with Bill Palatucci, a politically connected lawyer who ran the Republican presidential campaign efforts in the state during that time and later became a Republican national committeeman. After the 1992 campaign, Christie urged Palatucci to join his law firm, and the two became friends and political allies. "He was a lawyer who was tired of practicing law and wanted to get involved in politics," Palatucci said. "I had been a guy at that point who'd spent over a decade in politics, essentially working for Tom Kean [a former governor of New Jersey], and wanted to know how to practice law. So it was a really good partnership. I kind of showed him the ropes of politics and he showed me the ropes of practicing law. It was very much a mutual relationship." A year after George W. Bush was elected in 2000, Christie was named U.S. attorney for New Jersey. He was a prosecutorial bulldog and relentlessly pursued cases involving corruption by public officials. He won convictions in more than a hundred such cases, including a Hudson County executive, an Essex County executive, a former state senate president, and Sharpe James, the longtime former mayor of Newark.

Republicans approached him to run for governor. "He was indisputably the state's most visible law enforcement officer, a finger-wagging prosecutor with Jersey roots who made a name convicting so many corrupt public officials that state GOP leaders practically begged him to ride his white horse into Trenton," wrote John Martin, a New Jersey political writer.

In January 2009, he filed papers to challenge incumbent Democratic governor Jon Corzine, the former Goldman Sachs executive who had poured tens of millions of his own fortune into winning a U.S. Senate seat and later into his 2005 race for governor. Corzine was vulnerable, but it had been more than a decade since Republicans had won a statewide election in New Jersey. Christie ran as the antithesis of the wealthy Corzine. He was the Springsteen-loving Jersey boy who promised to take on entrenched political interests to bring the state's finances into balance without raising taxes. His upset victory in November 2009, along with that of Robert McDonnell in Virginia, marked the beginning of a Republican comeback that would hit with fuller force the following year in the 2010 elections.

He faced a budget deficit estimated at $11 billion, and to close it he enacted deep spending cuts, layoffs of state workers, and cuts in education. He vetoed a millionaire's tax approved by the Democratic-controlled legislature. He rejected $3 billion in federal assistance when he canceled plans for a rail tunnel between New Jersey and Manhattan, saying his state could not afford its portion of the costs. He belittled critics at town hall meetings around the state, and his staff made sure the videos reached a wide audience. He took on state employee unions with a vigor that caught them and others by surprise. He demanded concessions on benefits and took his fight public. In October 2010, NBC's Jamie Gangel profiled him on *The Today Show*. She asked Christie's wife, Mary Pat, whether she thought her husband would make a good president. "Oh absolutely," came the reply. "But Christie says he's not ready," Gangel reported. To Christie, she said, "Everyone in the Republican Party but you is talking about that you should be on the ticket in 2012 to run for the White House. You say?" Christie responded, "No way."

Chris Christie's position would never change, but it would take a full year finally to bring an end to the speculation that he might run for president in 2012. The story of that courtship by the Republican rank and file, by fellow elected officials, and especially by wealthy contributors and others is best told by the colorful governor, who savored every moment of the experience. I sat down with him in the fall of 2012 to talk about it. When I asked him about his initial reaction to the talk that he should run for president, he said, "Headshaking. I didn't expect it. I've been in the job six, eight, nine months and I just was shocked and I didn't think that's the way it worked. . . . I just remember thinking, 'This is just completely surreal and not what I expected,' and little did I know . . . that it would get a lot crazier." As talk of a candidacy continued, Christie gave a series of responses to say he wasn't going to run. He said he didn't think he was ready. He told reporters in Trenton, "Short of suicide, I don't really know what I'd have to do to convince you people that I'm not running." His wife hated that comment. "It made a lot of people laugh, so I kept using it even if she hated it and making her, as she's done for the last twenty-seven years, just kind of throw up her hands and go, 'I'm doing the best I can.'" He said his comment that he wasn't ready was misinterpreted. "It wasn't me saying I wouldn't be ready to do the job, although I don't know that anybody is ever absolutely ready to do that job," he said. "But what I meant by it was I know what it's going to take to run and you have to absolutely believe in your mind that it's the right time for you to do it and that you're absolutely ready for the challenge and I knew me. If I did it and I didn't feel completely ready, the first time something went wrong, which invariably it would, I would be sitting there in some bad hotel room in Cedar Rapids saying to myself, 'I knew it, I knew it.'"

Meanwhile, the real candidates were courting Christie's favor. He hosted small dinners with some of his New Jersey political allies and brought candidates in individually—Haley Barbour, Tim Pawlenty, Mitt Romney. Christie had some rules of the road for the other candidates. He said he would make a decision about endorsing someone on his own timetable. In the meantime, he didn't want candidates trolling for support or raising money in his state. If and when he endorsed, he would bring everyone with him. "Governor Romney didn't like that too much, and when he came [for dinner], we had a discussion about it," Christie said. "He pressed me really hard that he wanted to start raising money in New Jersey, and I said, 'If you raise money in New Jersey in any kind of aggressive organized way, it's going to make it very unlikely that I'll be able to support you.' So it was a rather tense conversation between the two of us in February of '11 and I heard later from others that he left not very happy with the approach I took. But I took the same approach with everybody."

Christie said Romney was direct in asking for support: "His pitch was, 'I'm the one best prepared for this from having run last time. I know the mistakes I made the last time. I'm not going to make the same mistakes this time.' He told me that he was the one whose experience was best for the problems facing the country economically, that he'd be able to make the best pitch to be the guy who replaces the president, and he told me that he was going to have the best and most successful fund-raising effort that any Republican presidential candidate ever had and that he was not going to be outspent by the president. He said, 'You put those three factors together, Governor, and I think that makes me the likely nominee and a very good chance to be president, and you're going to want to be on board with me before anybody else.'" Christie said he told Romney he was not ready to endorse.

Of all the dinner guests he hosted, Christie said, Barbour was the most entertaining. Compared to the others he was "much more humorous, much more affable, kind of just exactly what you'd expect." He said Barbour broke up the room when someone asked him that night what kind of election campaign he thought it would be if he were the nominee against the president. He said that Barbour replied, "Well, it would remind me of what my high school football coach used to say to us in the locker room before we played a game against our crosstown rival. He would say, 'Boys, turn Mama's picture to the wall, she ain't gonna want to see this.'" Christie added that Barbour was very relaxed and at ease: "He was very conversant in the issues, he answered everybody's questions, but he did it with great humor and kind of what you've come and we've all come to expect from Haley Barbour."

Pawlenty made a different impression. "In the bigger group," Christie said, "he was kind of reserved and actually more reserved than Tim is one-on-one and more reserved than even he was one-on-one with me that night. . . . In fact, the person who really sold Tim that night was Mary [Pawlenty]. She really sold Tim's story much more aggressively than Tim did at that dinner, and everybody walked away impressed with Tim but really impressed with Mary."

Once Daniels and Barbour made their decisions not to run, the pressure on Christie started to ramp up once again. "Craziness," he recalled. "Unsolicited phone calls from people all over the country. One of those, he said, was from Henry Kissinger, who asked Christie to meet him in his New York office. Christie had first met Kissinger in George Steinbrenner's box at Yankee Stadium in 2010: "I walked in and I saw Henry Kissinger in a satin Yankees warm-up jacket, which I just never thought I'd see Henry Kissinger in a satin Yankees warm-up jacket, but there he was in a satin warm-up jacket. . . . When he called me in to his office, he just said, 'The country needs a change and you connect with people in a way that I haven't seen a politician connect with someone in a long time and you need to think about doing this.' I said, 'That's very flattering, but I don't think I'm going to do it. I just think I need to be governor and I love the job I have and I don't see it.' He told me I was wrong and that he had known ten or eleven presidents, I forget the exact number he said, but he said, 'You can do this.' I said, 'I haven't given any deep thought to foreign policy.' He said, 'Don't worry about that, we can work with you on that.' He said, 'Foreign policy is instinct, it's character, that's what foreign policy is.

It's instinct and it's character that determines who are the great foreign policy presidents and who aren't.' I just said, 'It's been great talking to you, thanks.'" He said Kissinger called again and invited him and Mary Pat to dinner. When they arrived, the guests included the CEOs of several major corporations, some of whom urged him to run.

Christie said he continued to get calls of encouragement during the summer, from elected officials in Washington, from politically connected people around the country, from some other governors. He compared notes with Paul Ryan, who was also getting encouragement to run from some of the same people. What was notable about the interest in Christie was that it was taking place as the Republican race was already under way. Romney was an announced candidate, and yet many of the people urging Christie to consider running were donors who could or should have been with Romney but were still on the sidelines. It was a measure of their lack of confidence in the supposed front-runner that they continued to openly push the New Jersey governor, despite his professed lack of interest.* Ken Langone, a wealthy New Yorker who helped found Home Depot, began to apply more serious pressure in private meetings with Christie. In July, he invited Christie to breakfast at the Rocker Club in Manhattan. "The way he sold it to me was that this was going to be a small group of his friends who were going to sit and talk with me about why I needed to do this for our country, and that was Ken's big sales pitch," Christie said.

Christie arrived that morning accompanied by his wife; his son Andrew; Mike DuHaime, his top political strategist; and Maria Comella, his communications director. What they saw and heard stunned them all. "It was jaw-dropping," DuHaime said. Instead of a few people, there were dozens. Christie estimated the group at sixty. Instead of an intimate setting, the room was arranged formally, with the guests' chairs lined up facing a pair of chairs flanking a small table. A telephone sat on the table. "So we sit down and Langone stands up and says, 'Governor, all these people are here today for one reason. If you're willing to announce for president of the United States, we're with you, and everyone in this room has committed that to me and everyone in this room will raise every dollar you need to have raised to have a successful campaign. You won't have to worry about raising the money.'" He said Langone then announced that several people could not attend because they were out of the country. Christie then described what happened. "All of a sudden you hear John Mack [former CEO of Morgan Stanley] on the phone. [Langone] said, 'David Koch is out of the country. David, are you there?' Yes. David starts

*Many of these donors eventually became fund-raisers and bundlers for Romney.

talking." After several others had made the case for him to run, Christie said, Langone asked Kissinger to speak for everyone. "So Kissinger's got the cane and helps himself up, walks to the front of the room," Christie said, "and he says, 'I've known X number of presidents. Being a successful president is about two things, courage and character. You have both and your country needs you.' Then he turned around and sat back down. They all applauded."*

Christie said he was as close to speechless at that moment as he could ever remember being: "I basically said, 'Listen, I don't want to mislead you, I think the overwhelming likelihood is that I won't do this, but I cannot walk out of a room like this after people like you have asked me to consider it and tell you I won't consider it. So I'm going to take some time and Mary Pat and I are for the first time going to deliberate about this and we'll get back to you. I won't hold you for a long time, I'll get back to you as quickly as I can.'"

Christie began to solicit advice about what a campaign would entail. The process lasted many weeks. He said he talked to Karl Rove, the architect of George W. Bush's two successful campaigns, and Ken Mehlman, the former Republican National Committee chairman who had managed Bush's 2004 campaign. He spoke with Rudy Giuliani, the former New York mayor who had run unsuccessfully in 2008 for the Republican nomination. Then one day he got a call from George W. Bush. "He said, 'I'm sitting on the front porch at Kennebunkport, got some time, wanna talk?' 'Yes sir, Mr. President, sure,'" Christie said he replied. "We spoke for probably about forty-five minutes and he just gave me his observations and his advice, didn't say anything like you should or you shouldn't, didn't say he'd be with me or not, just kind of gave me his observations about what he felt the state of the race was, what he thought it would take for somebody like me to get into the race at that point, and then kind of practical things to consider. And he kind of asked me then what was I thinking, what were the impediments in my mind, what were the concerns, so that he could try to play a sounding board for me on that. It was an amazing conversation."

Christie called Palatucci. "I was down on the Jersey shore," Palatucci said. "He called me late that evening and told me he had just gotten off the phone with President Bush. That made him stand up and take notice. Obviously you were talking about someone who had been through the fire of making that decision and then running, and getting the perspective of someone who had been there and done that was very helpful. The president I think helped him to provide a structure for making the decision in his own head. Again, because

---

*Kissinger's office did not make the former secretary of state available for an interview for this book.

the president was taking him so seriously, Chris in his own mind said, 'If people are taking me seriously, I've got to take it seriously.'"

Mary Pat Christie was at work on the trading desk at Cantor Fitzgerald one day when the phone rang. It was Barbara Bush, who had spoken to her son about his conversation with Christie and decided to call Mary Pat. She took no position about whether the governor should run but sought to reassure Christie's wife that living in the White House with children was, on balance, a plus, that she had seen the benefits in her two granddaughters, and that from all she knew about the Christies, they could keep their children well grounded in that environment. "Mary Pat had about a ten-minute conversation with her and called me up and it was probably the most exciting moment of the process for Mary Pat," Christie said. "She called me here [at the governor's office] and I'm sitting at the desk and she said, 'You won't believe who just called me!' I'm like, 'Who now?' I'm thinking it's another incredibly rich person who's trying to convince her that she should get in my ear and get me to run. She's like, 'Barbara Bush called me.'"

The previous April, Christie had received a handwritten note from Nancy Reagan inviting him to give a speech at the Ronald Reagan Presidential Library in Simi Valley, California. The event had been on the governor's schedule for months, set for September 27, 2011. With presidential discussions swirling, everyone around Christie knew the speech would dramatically feed public speculation that he might enter the race after all. Christie also knew that the speech he intended to deliver, in which he would sharply criticize the president, would only add to the frenzy. "I didn't want to come to the Reagan Library and not talk about issues that are bigger than just 'here's what's happened in New Jersey the last year and a half.' We consciously made the decision— this is before the Langone meeting—that we wanted to have a speech that was kind of giving my perspective on foreign policy but from a different perspective, that we're failing at foreign policy because we're failing at home, and that until we get our act together at home we cannot be a dominant force for good in the world because people won't want to emulate us." Christie said he considered whether to scrap that speech and just talk about New Jersey, but decided to proceed with his original speech. "But I knew that the cost of that was you had like a week after the Reagan speech to make a decision and then you were going to start to annoy people," he said.

Christie recalled the trip to California as one of the most exhilarating experiences of his life. The director of the library met him and Mary Pat, and as they came around the first corner they could hear the strains of "Hail to the Chief" and Reagan taking the oath of office. Palatucci noticed that the

Christies were holding hands throughout the entire tour. Nancy Reagan then came to see them. "She came and sat down next to me and she said, 'You know, this is the fastest sellout we've had in the history of these talks at the museum?' I said, 'No, I wasn't aware of that, Mrs. Reagan.' She says, 'Hmmm, that says something, doesn't it, Governor?' 'Yes ma'am, I guess.' Then she turned to me and said, 'Do you know this is the second most press credentials ever asked for for a museum speech, except for when President Bush 43 came here to speak?' I said, 'No, I wasn't aware of that either.' She goes, 'Hmmm, a lot of excitement tonight, do you have a good speech?' I said, 'I think so.' She says, 'It better be.'"

That night he slowly escorted the former First Lady into the room where he was to speak. "Reagan is the first guy I voted for when I was a freshman in college, so there was a lot of emotion running through me," he said. "And then the last thing she said to me was, we sat down and the director of the museum was giving my introduction and she turned to me and she said, 'Do you see that podium?' I said, 'Yes.' She goes, 'That was one of Ronnie's podiums from the White House.' I said, 'Really?' She goes, 'Uh-huh.' I sat there for a second and I just turned to her and I said, 'You're bad, you know that?' She had this big smile on her face. She knew exactly what she was doing."

The speech came little more than a month after the collapse of the debt ceiling negotiations in Washington. Christie slammed Obama and the climate of governing in the nation's capital, which he compared unfavorably to New Jersey. "Still we continue to wait and hope that our president will finally stop being a bystander in the Oval Office," he said. "We hope that he will shake off the paralysis that has made it impossible for him to take on the really big things that are obvious to all Americans and to a watching and anxious world community." In the question-and-answer period, he got a predictable question about running for president. He encouraged everyone to look at a video compilation of his various expressions of disinterest that had been posted on *Politico*'s Web site. But he was stopped short when a woman in the balcony pleaded with him to run. "We can't wait another four years to 2016," she said. "I really implore you as a citizen of this country to please, sir, to reconsider." When she finished, the audience rose spontaneously and applauded. "It's extraordinarily flattering," Christie said in response. "But by the same token, that heartfelt message you gave me is also not a reason for me to do it. That reason has to reside in me."

On the flight home, Christie said he talked with his father: "He said to me, 'Let me just ask you something, do you love your job?' I said, 'Yeah.' He said to me, 'You're forty-eight years old, why are you leaving it if you love it? If you love a job at forty-eight years old why are you leaving it?'" The following Tuesday, October 4, Christie held a press conference to announce, for the last time, that he would not run for the nomination.

Toward the end of our interview, I asked him whether he saw that decision as a gift to Mitt Romney, who was now freed of another potentially strong rival for the nomination. "The enormous gift was the next week," he replied. When I looked puzzled, he reminded me that he had endorsed Romney the following week. "For me to make that decision that quickly and to be willing to put myself out there for him that early, when no one else really had, I think was a real leap of faith and a gift politically because nobody else was willing to do it," he said. "I wouldn't have used the word 'gift,' but since you did it seems to fit, it seems appropriate." The weekend after his decision, after a call from Romney, Christie and his wife hosted Mitt and Ann Romney for lunch at their home. "We talked for two hours before we finally got to the point," Christie said, "and he just said to me, 'You know, I'd love to know what I need to do to get you on the team.' I said, 'Nothing, I'm in.' He got this shocked look on his face and he turned to Ann almost as validation that his ears had worked right, and she had this big smile on her face and she was nodding. And he looked at me and said, 'What can I do for you?' I said, 'You don't have to do anything.' 'You want to be national chairman of the campaign?' I said, 'No. Use that title for somebody who you need to use it for to get them. I'm in.' He turned to Ann and he said, 'Wow, Christmas in October,' and she smiled and she looked at me and she said, 'Governor, you don't know how important and big this is,' and I said, 'I do.'"

CHAPTER II

First Casualty

In the spring of 2010, Mitt Romney came to Minnesota during the promotional tour for his book, *No Apology*. While there he spent some time with Tim Pawlenty, who was in his second term as governor. The two men knew and liked each other, having both been elected in 2002. They were a pair of Republican leaders in northern, traditionally Democratic states. Both were weighing campaigns for the White House in 2012. Pawlenty invited Romney back to the governor's residence, where they talked that day not as potential rivals but as friends. Romney was not dismissive of the younger man's ambitions or prospects and offered advice based on his own unsuccessful campaign in 2008. The most important thing, he told Pawlenty, was to build a campaign structure that could withstand the adversities of a long and grueling battle. "He had done it before and we talked about the magnitude of the effort financially, the magnitude of the effort organizationally, the magnitude of the effort personally, and the importance of having all the tools to go the distance," Pawlenty later recalled. "Clearly that was one thing he was trying to convey to me."

Pawlenty's goal was the same as every other Republican who gave consideration to running in 2012, which was to become the alternative to Mitt Romney. He would need to draw attention to himself as early as possible, as Romney had done in 2008, to establish his political and financial credentials as a potential top-tier candidate. His path to the nomination, like that of other underdogs of the past, depended on the strongest possible finish in the Iowa caucuses. He believed if he moved quickly, he could attract support from Tea Party activists who were skeptical of Romney because of the Massachusetts health care plan, from social and religious conservatives who doubted that Romney's conversions on some of their issues were genuine, and from establishment Republicans who found Romney not to their liking. "We thought that if that non-Mitt space could be aggregated early enough and strong enough, you could put together a viable candidacy," Pawlenty said. Neither he nor his advisers could foresee the potentially catastrophic consequences of acting on those assumptions in a year that would play out against all conventional expectations.

The early months of the Republican race were in many ways the story of what happened to Tim Pawlenty, because his story so clearly helps to explain the unusual nature of the Republican nomination contest. Pawlenty had modeled his campaign on dark horse candidates of the past. Given his limited resources and lack of national recognition, he had no other choice. But he never gave his candidacy what Romney had advised, which was the wherewithal to go the distance. His failure was one more stroke of good fortune for Romney.

Instead of building a campaign capable of surviving, Pawlenty ended up with one that bent with the first signs of trouble and eventually crumpled under the weight of unexpected setbacks, internal tensions, miscalculations, and mistakes. A year and a few months after he and Romney had talked about what it would take to mount a successful candidacy, Pawlenty's campaign for president was in ruins as he became the first of the announced candidates to quit the race. Pawlenty was gone so quickly that he became an asterisk in the campaign. This was a great irony, because in Boston he was regarded as the one likely candidate who might be able to fill the "not Mitt" slot, gain traction, and go the distance. Romney advisers worried about what might happen if Pawlenty began to catch fire. "We always viewed Governor Pawlenty as the strongest, most viable Romney alternative," said Matt Rhoades, Romney's campaign manager, "and we always felt that if he got up around Mitt and ended up winning the Iowa caucuses, he was the type of candidate who could do what we failed to do the last time. That he could come out of Iowa and be a candidate who could then win New Hampshire. He could box us out and he could take over a lot of Mitt Romney space, and that would be a dangerous thing."

Though Pawlenty and Romney were governors of blue states, the similarities mostly stopped there. Pawlenty had none of the privileged aura that Romney exuded. He was blue-collar, not blueblood. He grew up the youngest of five children in South St. Paul, a community of stockyards, Catholic and Orthodox churches, Serbian and Croatian halls. Former Minnesota senator David Durenberger once said of Pawlenty's hometown, "It was the [Minnesota] Iron Range shrunk to the size of one city." Pawlenty's family was classic Reagan Democrat—working class, Roman Catholic, socially conservative—who eventually migrated to the Republican Party. His father was a truck driver, his mother a homemaker. She died when Pawlenty was sixteen, but not before she had made clear her desire to see him become the first in the family to go to college. In high school, he was a good student, active in sports—hockey and soccer—but not stamped with obvious future success. Doug Woog, a South St. Paul native and later hockey coach at the University of Minnesota, once told the *Minneapolis Star Tribune* that rather than seeing Pawlenty as the "most likely to succeed" in his high school class, he would have tagged him as "most unlikely to become governor." "Not because he was negative, but because he wasn't flamboyant," Woog said. "This must be inside [of him], the drive."

An internship in Durenberger's Washington office pushed Pawlenty toward a career in politics. Marriage to Mary Anderson, whom he met in law school, prompted him to leave the Catholic Church to become a member of the evangelical congregation at Wooddale Church in the Twin Cities suburb of Eden Prairie. In 2002, he was elected governor in a three-way race, winning with 46 percent of the vote. He succeeded Jesse Ventura, the independent former wrestler whose publicity-hungry style contrasted sharply with the modest sensibilities of Pawlenty. Minnesota had elected other Republican governors, but none as conservative as Pawlenty. Facing a Democratic legislature, he held the line in his first year against tax increases to deal with a sizable budget deficit that he inherited. He took a hard line during a transportation strike and won. As a Republican in a Democratic state, he could see earlier than many others in his party the wave building in 2006 and felt his party was indifferent to its problems. He gently prodded Republicans to wake up and braced himself for a difficult reelection. He won a second term by just one percentage point after his Democratic opponent imploded in the final week of the campaign. Two years later, he had vetoed thirty-four bills, a gubernatorial record.

After his reelection in 2006, he began to try to raise his national profile. South St. Paul became Pawlenty's calling card as he tried to nudge his party away from its image as the party of the rich. In reality, the party was changing. His roots mirrored the shift within the party to a base that now included more of the white working-class voters who populated the town where he grew up, who made up his own family. Republicans, he said, should become the party of Sam's Club, not the country club. In 2008, he was the runner-up to Sarah Palin in the vice presidential sweepstakes, a competition that in the final stages also included Romney.

Pawlenty left the 2008 campaign empty-handed, but with an appetite to run in 2012. First he had to decide whether to seek a third term as governor in 2010. He sought advice from others, including some who had faced a similar decision. He recalled that one former governor told him, "My third term wasn't my best work. I wouldn't recommend it." Ken Mehlman, the former Republican National Committee chairman, told him, "No good comes from a third term," according to Pawlenty. In Pawlenty's mind, the choice was to run either for president or for a third term as governor. Like Romney four years earlier, he did not believe he could do both. Had he known that Republicans would capture control of the Minnesota legislature in 2010, he later said, he might have made a different decision. Instead, on June 2, 2009, Pawlenty announced he would not seek a third term.

As he mulled whether to run for president, Pawlenty also sought out Mike Huckabee, who had begun his 2008 campaign as a little-known former governor. What Huckabee told him weighed on Pawlenty throughout his campaign for the White House. Huckabee, who like Pawlenty was of modest means as a governor, ended his 2008 campaign with his bank account virtually depleted. He told Pawlenty, Make sure you've got some financial sturdiness under you, because this can get very demanding on your family and on you financially. Otherwise, in the middle of the campaign, you'll be running off to give a speech to the coconut producers somewhere. Pawlenty and his wife persuaded themselves that they had enough at least to start a campaign. But money was always an issue for Pawlenty.

As he sized up the potential field, Pawlenty doubted that any of those most likely to run, other than Romney, could ever become president. (He didn't think either Barbour or Daniels would become candidates.) His advisers came up with the slogan they wished they could use to become the alternative to the front-runner: "Pawlenty. Because there's no one else."

He wrote a book, *Courage to Stand,* and in the first weeks of 2011 did an obligatory tour to attract publicity. On March 21, 2011, he formed a presidential exploratory committee. His embryonic campaign began to produce a series of Web videos, created by then twenty-three-year-old Lucas Baiano, which quickly became the talk of the political community. They included dramatic musical scores that seemed more Hollywood than Washington. As iconic American images flashed across the screen, Pawlenty's amped-up voice provided a message of strength and fortitude: "Valley Forge wasn't easy. Going to the moon wasn't easy. Settling the West wasn't easy. We are the American people. We have seen difficulties before and we have always overcome them. This is about rolling up our sleeves . . . putting our head down, and getting it done." The videos seemed the antithesis of the candidate. He had more fire as a speaker than he was often given credit for, but he could get lost in a party that included media magnets like Sarah Palin and Chris Christie. On one occasion during the 2010 campaign, he nearly faded from view on a stage in his own state when he joined Palin at a reelection rally for Michele Bachmann. "Sarah Palin, Michele Bachmann Rally Thousands in Minneapolis," CBS News reported on its Web site.

Pawlenty formally announced his candidacy on May 23, 2011, at a rally in Des Moines. His advisers called the announcement tour "A Time for Truth." He came out against ethanol subsidies in Iowa. He told senior citizens in Florida that it was time to means-test Social Security. In New York, he told the financial community there should be no more bailouts and that the era of too big to fail was over. In Washington, his last major stop, he took a hard line against federal workers' salaries and benefits. Two weeks later, he delivered a speech about the economy at the University of Chicago, where he called for deep cuts in taxes and spending and a reduction in government regulations. He said the country should not be satisfied with the 2 percent growth rates that existed under Obama. "Let's grow the economy by 5 percent," he said. The wildly ambitious target drew criticism from many economists and editorial writers, but conservative economists and commentators widely praised the speech as a rebirth of supply-side economics. CNBC's Lawrence Kudlow called it a "blockbuster" of a speech. Jack Welch, the former CEO at General Electric, said on CNN, "Everything I see [him] say in the last month appeals to me."

Never before had debates played such a central role in presidential campaigns as in 2012. They had become a staple of nomination and general election battles dating back decades, and virtually every campaign included memorable moments from candidate forums. There was Ronald Reagan's "I am paying for this microphone, Mr. Green" moment in Nashua, New Hampshire, in early 1980. There was Walter Mondale putting down Gary Hart in 1984 with "Where's the Beef?" There was Michael Dukakis's halting answer to a question of what he would do if his wife were brutally raped and murdered. There was Dan Quayle rebuked as "no Jack Kennedy" by Lloyd Bentsen. Barack Obama, never a skilled debater, uttered his most memorable and self-damaging line in a debate in New Hampshire days after his victory in the Iowa caucuses when he turned to Hillary Rodham Clinton and said, "You're likable enough, Hillary." By 2008, debates had proliferated in both parties. They were generally unwieldy and more often than not unsatisfying for the candidates, six or nine or more of whom were arrayed across a stage, mostly looking to avoid a gaffe and if possible put an opponent in an awkward position.

That's what everyone expected again in the 2012 Republican nomination contest: sideshows. Instead, debates became a dominant feature of the campaign, reality TV shows for millions of Americans who followed them week by week, and above all a proving ground for candidates unlike anything seen before. They were often hilarious, sometimes bizarre, always entertaining, and sometimes decisive in winnowing the field of candidates. Cable networks competed to stage the debates, knowing they would produce audience and ratings. Some networks partnered with state Republican parties or Tea Party affiliates and filled the hall with rabid partisans who hooted and cheered or booed the participants, adding to the feel that the debate was an extension of some ancient spectacle of gladiators clashing to the death. CNN debates opened with packaged introductions of the candidates more fitting of the Super Bowl or professional wrestling than the nomination of a major-party candidate for president. Boxing metaphors ran rampant in the pre-debate chatter on television. Performance, not substance, became the measure for judging.

The candidates teamed together to fight back against the debate sponsors, who determined which candidates would and would not be invited, where they would stand on the stage (generally determined by the most recent polls), and the format and ground rules for questioning. When the *Washington Post* and Bloomberg News teamed up to sponsor a debate on economic issues at Dartmouth College in Hanover, New Hampshire, in October 2011, there was a lengthy and sometimes contentious negotiation over a proposal for a segment in which candidates would be allowed to question one another. The candidates' representatives hated the idea. They argued that this would turn the debate into a food fight, as Romney's lead debate negotiator, Ben Ginsberg, argued repeatedly in calls and e-mails with me and Bloomberg's Al Hunt. The segment went ahead as planned. But the conflict between the campaigns and the sponsors reflected everyone's appreciation that the debates could have enormous influence on the outcome of the nomination battle.

The first Republican debate was held on May 5 in Greenville, South Carolina. It was a stripped-down affair. Romney, who had not formally announced his candidacy, declined the invitation. Newt Gingrich wasn't there. Four of the five people onstage—Ron Paul, Rick Santorum, Herman Cain, and Gary Johnson—made up what seemed at the time like a collection of also-rans and fringe candidates. Only Pawlenty was seen at the time as a serious contender for the nomination. His campaign saw the debate as an opportunity for Pawlenty to shine brightest in Romney's absence. He ended up as just one of an unmemorable gang on the Fox News stage.

Pawlenty felt he needed a breakout moment, and to gain one he had to strike directly at Romney. "Our perspective until then was that it probably was not a great idea to pick a fight with Mitt early on because his resources were so overwhelming that until you're strong enough to be able to fight back or sustain the fight, it's not in our best interest to pick a fight," he later told me. "We weren't there yet. But we also started to realize that days and weeks were going on, and if you're figuring to become the main alternative to Mitt, you've got to lay claim to it in some fashion." Pawlenty's team looked to the second debate, scheduled for June 13 in New Hampshire, as the moment. It would be the first in which Romney would participate.

His team arrived in New Hampshire days ahead of the debate and settled into a Manchester law firm for prep sessions. Those in attendance included Nick Ayers, the new campaign manager; Phil Musser, a longtime political counselor to Pawlenty; Sara Fagen, the White House political director in George W.

Bush's administration; Alex Conant, the campaign communications director; and Jon Lerner, the campaign's pollster. All agreed that Pawlenty should confront Romney directly over the Massachusetts health care plan as the template for Obama's new law. Pawlenty came up with the phrase "Obamneycare" to connect Romney to the legislation that conservatives hated. His advisers decided to preview their strategy during Pawlenty's appearance on *Fox News Sunday* the day before the debate. The strategy worked beautifully, setting up a Pawlenty versus Romney narrative for the debate. Pawlenty's advisers, determined to leverage the debate to boost the campaign, had lined up possible endorsements and were ready to drop a new direct mail fund-raising appeal they believed would provide substantial returns.

Behind the scenes, however, another reality was playing out. Nick Ayers had been a late arrival to the campaign, and his presence brought a different tone and tighter circle, to the dismay of some of Pawlenty's longtime friends and advisers. Ayers was considered a wunderkind in the Republican ranks. As a college student he worked in the successful campaign of Georgia governor Sonny Perdue; at twenty-two he was tapped to run Perdue's reelection campaign. He joined the Republican Governors Association in 2007, when Perdue was still the chairman, and remained in that post through the 2010 elections. He was a highly regarded talent. When he was announced as Pawlenty's campaign manager, he sent out an e-mail to his personal network recounting the decision-making process that led him to take the job: "I accepted the position with peace of mind and a deep confidence in the candidate, his family, and the mission ahead, but it was not an easy decision. . . . Opportunities in the private sector were serious and abundant and would have allowed me to achieve a degree of personal financial security that my family has not yet had (at least as much financial security as any of us can have during the Obama presidency). Over the past six months, I have prayed deeply about my purpose in life and how best to utilize the talents God has given me. I wanted my decision to be wholly about how best to serve Him, not what was most politically or financially expedient for my family and me. . . . As He often does in walks of faith, He has called me to a higher purpose. I believe that our Nation is truly on the wrong path. We need a new direction that is positive and hopeful. Simply said, we need new leadership. I believe that Governor Pawlenty is best positioned to provide that leadership." The e-mail ricocheted through the incestuous world of political consultants and reporters, drawing instant scorn and derision for what seemed to be the self-obsession of Pawlenty's new campaign chief. Ayers thought he was doing what Pawlenty wanted by tapping his extensive network of contacts in behalf of the campaign. The e-mail caught Pawlenty's eye, but he chose not to broach it with Ayers. "I know it raised a few eyebrows in some quarters," he said. "But it didn't concern me particularly."

With Ayers's arrival, others who had been part of Pawlenty's wider circle of advisers began to feel frozen out. Among them was Vin Weber, the former congressman from Minnesota, one of the party's most respected strategists and a longtime friend of the candidate. For a time, Mary Pawlenty, the candidate's wife, also was kept on the outside. Dealing with a candidate's spouse is often one of the most delicate jobs campaign advisers face. One member of the team said, "Nick's approach was not, 'How do I turn her into an ally?' but 'How can I sideline her?' He just had no respect for her."

Mary Pawlenty had opposed the decision to denounce ethanol subsidies during the announcement tour that started in Iowa. Her view was that Pawlenty needed all the help and support he could get in that state, given its importance to his strategy. She thought it was foolhardy to start picking fights over something so significant to the Iowa economy and something that presidential candidates dating back many cycles had embraced as the price of wooing Iowa voters. She did not take the rejection of her recommendation on ethanol subsidies well and suggested to others that they not come looking to her for advice. Long after the campaign, Pawlenty tried to explain the situation. "There clearly was miscommunication with respect to Mary and her involvement and all of that," he said. "But it got squared away and got dramatically better." But not before the New Hampshire debate.

The New Hampshire debate was held on the campus of Saint Anselm College just outside Manchester. A huge media contingent filled the gymnasium that served as the press filing center, their appetites whetted by the prospect of a clash between the perceived front-runner and one of his most serious challengers. The script was being written in advance, but what no one could see were two developments backstage. The first, described by two of Pawlenty's advisers, occurred when Romney and Pawlenty met each other before the debate. Romney smothered Pawlenty with kindness. "It was genius. It was genius," Ayers said. "It worried me, because Tim's a nice guy and Tim likes Mitt Romney. I didn't think it would change anything, but I thought in the world of would you rather have them palling around for five minutes or not, you'd choose to not." Pawlenty has no distinct memory of the incident.

The second occurred when Pawlenty's traveling assistant placed a call to Mary Pawlenty so the candidate could have a few words before going onstage. Instead, it became a potentially confidence-shattering moment. "She questioned the strategy," Pawlenty said. "For various reasons she hadn't been as fully in the loop on this as perhaps she should have been." There could hardly have been a more awkward moment for a candidate and his spouse to have this kind of conversation. "It wasn't in the form of, 'You know, don't you dare do this, this is stupid,'" he recalled. "It was more in the form of, 'What's the strategy? Why are you doing this now? How does this help in terms of the overall picture?'" Pawlenty knew there was no way to turn back at that point. "Once you'd teed it up on *Fox News Sunday,* the time to have the concern wasn't in the ten minutes before we started the debate," he said.

CNN played host, with John King as the moderator. The format included questions from citizens in remote locations. A few minutes into the forum, Sylvia Smith, a woman from Littleton, asked the candidates what they would do to defund Obama's health care law. The first response came from Michele Bachmann. "I will not rest until I repeal Obamacare," she said. "It's a promise. Take it to the bank, cash the check." King then asked Romney about Pawlenty's "Obamneycare" comment two days earlier. Romney explained that there were important differences between the Massachusetts law and Obama's. He pledged to repeal the federal law if he became president. King turned to Pawlenty. "Governor, you just heard Governor Romney rebut your characterization, 'Obamneycare.' Why?" Pawlenty faltered. He began to respond to the question. King interrupted. "The question, Governor, was why 'Obamneycare'?" Again, Pawlenty didn't answer directly. Twice more King served up the question that Pawlenty and his advisers had prepped to answer. Twice more Pawlenty flinched. Watching, Ayers turned to another Pawlenty adviser. "Devastating," he said in a whisper. Others on the team could see the damage playing out in real time. "We looked down at our Twitter feeds," one adviser recalled, "and just went, 'Fuck.'"

Only later would Pawlenty recognize the damage he had done to his candidacy. "We set the expectation this was going to happen," he said. "Nobody forced it on us. . . . The frustrating thing is that it was very simple. It was not a complicated deal. We set the expectation. The opportunity arose in a fairly predictable manner early in the debate. Should have just ditched talking to the screen or bashing Obama and said, 'You know, of course it's an appropriate phrase, and here's why.' . . . We teed up the ball and then missed it. I missed it, right? And nothing more complicated than that."

If Pawlenty was the big loser in the New Hampshire debate, the surprise story that night was Michele Bachmann. As Pawlenty stumbled, she turned in a forceful performance. Bachmann was a just third-term member of the House but already a star among conservatives. A devout Christian, she was staunchly opposed to abortion. A former tax attorney, she was a hawk on fiscal issues. An opponent of big government, she was as outspoken as anyone in her party about repealing Obama's health care plan. She was an outsider in the clubby world of Washington politics. After the 2010 elections, she decided to seek a leadership post in the House. Opposition from Eric Cantor, the new majority leader, and Paul Ryan, the new chairman of the Budget Committee, helped defeat her. She formed a Tea Party caucus and on the night Obama delivered his 2010 State of the Union address offered her own "Tea Party" response in competition with the GOP's official response. She was both a fearless advocate for her beliefs and someone with a reputation for playing loose with the facts to fit her ideological leanings.

Bachmann had three goals for the New Hampshire debate: first, to establish herself as a player in the presidential race; second, to dispel perceptions that, as one adviser put it, "she's crazy, says crazy things, is not smart"; and third, to make a splash by actually announcing her candidacy. She drew strong reviews from conservatives and the media. Veteran reporter Walter Shapiro wrote on the Web site of the *New Republic,* "Instead of playing her familiar role as a tea party troubadour, she came across as a right-winger who offered quiet competence and legislative experience."

Bachmann was just beginning to put together a presidential campaign. She had high name identification within the party and an established ability to raise money through direct mail, but lacked virtually everything else. "There was nothing," said Keith Nahigian, who began as a senior strategist and later became her campaign manager. "There was no logo, there was no Web site, there was no infrastructure of any kind." During the spring, Bachmann had reached out to Brett O'Donnell, the former debate coach at Liberty University, to help her prepare for those forums. Like Nahigian's, his role too expanded over time. "His job description is debate coach," wrote Amy Gardner in the *Washington Post.* "But he's more accurately described as the candidate whisperer, because that's what he does all day." Ed Goeas, available after Barbour decided not to run, was hired as the campaign pollster.

She recruited Ed Rollins, who was the campaign manager for Ronald Reagan's 1984 reelection campaign, to run her operation, but only after a wobbly start in their relationship. "It wasn't a great first date," Rollins said of their initial lunch in May in New York. He said they disagreed about how to run the campaign and he told her he would not agree to come aboard unless she agreed to give him full authority, in essence to do as he told her. They parted without a deal. She later called him while he was on a Greek cruise, saying she wanted him and was prepared to work on those terms. "I foolishly said yes quickly," he said. "I should have thought about it." Their relationship never improved. Nonetheless, Rollins recruited others with whom he had been preparing for a Huckabee campaign. Among them were David Polyansky, who became deputy campaign manager, and Alice Stewart, who became Bachmann's chief spokeswoman. There was tension from the start between the candidate and her campaign manager. "Someone had told her, and I don't know who, that she needed to have a big-name strategist to manage her campaign," said one Bachmann adviser. "So she followed that advice, and the only name that she could get to agree to it was Ed."

That mattered little in the days after the New Hampshire debate. Bachmann was now the new and hot candidate of the right. She pulled off a flawless announcement in her hometown of Waterloo, Iowa, and suddenly became a major obstacle in Pawlenty's path. A week before the New Hampshire debate, a *Washington Post*/ABC News poll showed Bachmann with the support of only 4 percent of Republicans, tied with Pawlenty. A month later, she had leaped to second place with 16 percent. Pawlenty, meanwhile, had ticked down to 3 percent.

Pawlenty never thought Bachmann would get into the race. When she did, he judged her as a short-term threat but nothing more than that. He said, "My view was she's going to be formidable at least for a while because she has a lot of skill and ability and appeal at kind of the grassroots organizing level. And so it was a matter of making sure we didn't do things that were disrespectful or unfair or anything like that but just let time take care of itself." Nick Ayers said, "The day she formally announced in Waterloo, we said, 'Look, she's going to be for a while a real problem until she blows herself up.' And we knew that we couldn't blow her up, that we'd have to wait on her to do it, and eventually she would." But instead of letting her burn out naturally, Pawlenty allowed himself to be drawn into a direct confrontation with her. It was perhaps the biggest strategic mistake of his campaign.

On June 9, Romney's campaign manager, Matt Rhoades, announced that his candidate would not participate in the August 13 Iowa Straw Poll. "We respect the straw poll process," Rhoades said. "In the last presidential campaign we were both strengthened as an organization and learned some important lessons by participating in them. This time we will focus our energies and resources on winning primaries and caucuses." One of the lessons Romney and his team had taken away from the 2008 campaign was that the straw polls resulted in an enormous drain in resources and energy for only a modest political return. Romney had won the Iowa Straw Poll in 2007, but not before spending several million dollars and heightening expectations for his performance in the caucuses. Rhoades was determined to avoid that mistake again. Skipping the straw poll was therefore an easy decision.

Another piece of Romney's strategy that was less evident at the time played out in spectacular fashion for his candidacy. Romney's team wanted to consciously increase the pressure on Pawlenty to win in Ames. "We'd been to Iowa before," Rhoades said. "We knew that the straw poll vote, what it took to go into it, the time commitment, the resource commitment to do it the right way. We really kind of hoped to get him out there on the prairie and [let him] essentially use up all his resources and just starve, for a better word." Pawlenty had started the month of June with a strategy of turning the Republican race into a two-person contest between him and Romney. After the debate, he now found himself facing off against Bachmann for a costly and potentially meaningless prize in Ames.

All presidential campaigns hit moments of adversity. The best of them find a way through the problems. Pawlenty's situation now became a downward spiral. Each new development fed on the others. The added pressure to do well at the straw poll meant more resources devoted to Ames. With Bachmann's entry, skipping the straw poll might have been the wisest decision, but because of the disastrous debate performance, that seemed unthinkable. It would be seen as a further sign of weakness by a campaign bleeding openly. "The decision to go all in in Ames was made the day he got in the race and never revisited," said Alex Conant, the campaign's chief spokesman. Only Bob Schroeder, Pawlenty's chief of staff as governor, raised the question of whether they should reconsider the strategy. He was a minority of one. Pawlenty said, "I think in hindsight we would have been better served, once she got in the race, to pull back and live to fight over a longer period of time. But again this is all hindsight. At the time, I was comfortable with the decision, in fact signed off on the decision to keep going full steam ahead in Ames."

On June 25, the *Des Moines Register* published the results of its latest poll of the Republican field. Romney led with 23 percent, but Bachmann had vaulted to second at 22 percent. Pawlenty, at 6 percent, also trailed Cain, Paul, and Gingrich. The *Register*'s Jennifer Jacobs wrote, "Pawlenty has spent 26 days in Iowa during this election cycle, has hired an A-list team of Iowa campaign operatives and was the first major candidate to air television ads in Iowa." It was not quite an obituary. "The *Register* poll was like a two-by-four to the face," Phil Musser said. Pawlenty had staked everything on Iowa and had hired several veterans of Iowa politics, but his campaign was not coming together. After the announcement tour, his advisers had tried to measure the impact in Iowa. "When we started to do some minimal kind of phone calling into Iowa amongst likely caucus attendees, the awareness wasn't high and our support levels were modest," Pawlenty said. Fund-raising was lagging even more after the New Hampshire debate. In early July, little more than a month before the straw poll,

Ayers recruited Sarah Huckabee Sanders, Mike Huckabee's daughter, to over-haul the Iowa operation.

The candidate's fragile position forced another decision that proved fateful. Determined to raise Pawlenty's profile in the weeks remaining, the campaign invested heavily in radio and television commercials. "The idea, rightly or wrongly, behind the TV was we can't get grassroots, on-the-ground support until we create an environment where people feel like they have some familiarity with you," Pawlenty said. "TV was a way to do that." Jeff Zeleny of the *New York Times* starkly explained Pawlenty's position in a July 7 article. "Tim Pawlenty was first in line to enter the Republican presidential race," he wrote. "He is now fighting to avoid becoming the earliest major candidate to be shown the door."

On the morning of August 8, Pawlenty cut into a cinnamon bun the size of a loaf of bread. Around the table at the Machine Shed restaurant in suburban Des Moines was a group of reporters invited to have breakfast with the candidate as he began the final week of campaigning before the straw poll. He struggled to calibrate expectations for the weekend. "I didn't say it's not that meaningful," he said. Then he said, "Well, it's an important event, but it's not the ultimate event. I think we're going to do well, move from the back of the pack to the front of the pack. So we endorse the idea that it's an important measure, but it's not the final measure." His goal, he said, was to finish first, second, or bunched together as part of the top three. Did he regret getting sucked into the straw poll? he was asked. "We didn't get sucked in. We dove in. We want to be in the straw poll," he said.

He was asked about the impending entry of Rick Perry. Would a victory in the straw poll prove fleeting against someone with Perry's presumed resources and big-state experience? "I didn't have a built-in national brand," he said. "I don't have a celebrity status. I don't have personal wealth. I don't have some comedic shtick. This is going to be done the real way. You've got to go meet people and earn their support and earn their trust and earn their vote." Every month, he said, there would be something or someone new, whether Donald Trump in the spring or Perry on the horizon. "We are not ever going to be the cable TV shooting star of the month," he said.

Later that morning Bachmann's campaign bus rolled into tiny Atlantic, Iowa, eighty miles west of Des Moines, the sounds of Elvis's "Promised Land" blaring from the public address system. Her campaign had concluded that its best hope of winning the straw poll was to concentrate on a roughly hundred-mile circle around Ames, figuring that Iowans who lived much farther away were not likely to make the effort to get to the straw poll. That week she was on the cover of *Newsweek* with a controversial photograph that showed her bug-eyed above a headline that read, "The Queen of Rage." Conservatives denounced the magazine. "Is that what's behind your campaign? Rage?" a voter asked. She replied, "I think the power behind our campaign is hope and a future. . . . I haven't read the story. I can only tell you who I am. I am a thoughtful person who is positive. . . . I was mocked. I was jeered. Who cares?"

Inexplicably, the Republican race had become, for the moment, a contest between Pawlenty and Bachmann, with potentially devastating consequences for the loser. Bachmann could not afford a setback, given the momentum she had gained since joining the race. All the other candidates had faded into the background for the week, with the exception of Ron Paul, the libertarian Texas House member with a passionate following but with little ability to expand his appeal. No matter how well he did in Ames, that reality would not change.

On Thursday, August 11, the candidates met for their next debate, hosted again by Fox News. On this night, there were eight candidates onstage: Pawlenty, Bachmann, Romney, Gingrich, Cain, Santorum, Paul, and, for the first time, Jon M. Huntsman Jr., the former governor of Utah, who had recently stepped down as the Obama administration's ambassador to China. Pawlenty was faced with the problem of how aggressively he could attack a female candidate, but after what had happened in New Hampshire, the answer was obvious. "If I get asked to whack somebody, I'm going to whack 'em, because on the heels of that earlier debate we just couldn't afford to have any sense that there was hesitation to be strong and be willing to contrast with your opponents," he said. Pawlenty had talked this through with his advisers. They agreed that they could not allow another round of stories saying he was afraid to take on his opponents.

Within minutes of the introductions, Pawlenty and Bachmann began to spar. "She has done wonderful things in her life, absolutely wonderful things, but it is an undisputable fact that in Congress her record of accomplishment and results is nonexistent," Pawlenty said. Bachmann accused Pawlenty of having embraced views on health care and climate change that were closer to Obama's than to those of true conservatives. "He said the era of small government is over," she said of her opponent. "I have a very consistent record of fighting very hard against Barack Obama and his unconstitutional measures in Congress." Pawlenty then shot back, "She's got a record of misstating and making false statements." He assailed her again for failing to block Obama's initiatives. "She said she's got a titanium spine. It's not her spine we're worried about. It's her record of results. If that's your view of effective leadership with results, please stop, because you're killing us." Pawlenty was a different personality from the candidate who had debated in New Hampshire, but in Bachmann he found a rival who was prepared to hit back as hard as she was hit. "When you attacked her, she was the black widow spider," Nahigian said.

The Ames Straw Poll is an event that long ago outlived its value. By 2011, it was little more than a giant fund-raiser for the Iowa Republican Party and a summer spectacle for political junkies. As a predictor of who might win the Republican nomination, or even the Iowa caucuses, it had a poor record, and it gobbled up precious resources from any candidate who participated. Campaigns bought the tickets for supporters, rented the buses to get them to Ames, and courted them with food and entertainment, all for a few thousand votes. Romney had learned his lesson in 2008, winning the straw poll but losing the caucuses and the nomination. Pawlenty was stuck in a battle that could prove meaningless if he won but deadly if he lost.

When the results were announced late Saturday afternoon, Bachmann led the field with 4,823 votes, or 29 percent of the total, followed closely by Ron Paul with 4,671. Pawlenty was a distant and disappointing third with 2,293 votes, or 14 percent. He and his wife, Mary, were in a hotel room in Ames when the results were announced. They had already agreed that if he fell short of his goal he would quit the race. His lackluster finish made the next step obvious: "We just had it in our mind that I had to have some sort of breakout experience early or the campaign was going to be unsuccessful. We planned for, built up, and spent as if that breakout moment was going to be Ames, and it turned out not to be." He later wished he had announced that he would skip Ames the minute Bachmann got in the race, believing he would have gotten a second look from Republican voters later in the year.

Contributing to the decision to get out was the fact that Pawlenty's campaign was in debt. The candidate said he first heard about it shortly before the straw poll. Some advisers blamed Ayers for letting spending get out of control. Ayers said he had no role in setting up the financial systems for the campaign. "I advised against the way we were managing our resources," he said, "but ultimately the candidate is in charge and I respect that decision and the hierarchy, but I had voiced internal concern." He said that as campaign manager, "Ultimately I'm in charge. The governor and I should have been aware about the numbers. Okay? But we both were given different numbers." Whether Ayers's claim of "different numbers" could withstand scrutiny hardly matters; the Pawlenty campaign was over.

Pawlenty announced his decision to quit on ABC's *This Week* program, hosted that week by Jake Tapper. "We had the wrong strategy," Pawlenty later told me. "Hindsight's twenty-twenty, but we were running on the wrong premise, and the premise was that this thing was going to crystallize early, that somebody—probably Mitt—would be the front-runner and break away from the pack and if you're going to run as a relatively unknown, underresourced candidate from the Midwest, you've got to get some attention early and you've got to put a stake in early. It turned out to be, I think, an outdated model circa 2002, 2004, where you tried to show some progress early, get the buzz going that you're the aggregated challenger to the front-runner, and then try to pivot off of that financially and politically. But things have changed." He had no real regrets about getting out. Had he stayed longer, he still would not have had the financial resources to go up against Romney.

In Boston, Romney advisers were relieved to see Pawlenty on the sidelines. But as Pawlenty exited, another candidate who seemed even more formidable was arriving for his turn at a chance to take down the front-runner.

CHAPTER 12

Candidate "Oops"

C entral casting could not have produced a more ideal candidate for the Republican nomination than Texas governor Rick Perry—on paper, that is. He had led the second largest state in the country for a decade. He succeeded George W. Bush after Bush became president in 2000 and then won election on his own three times. He had rugged good looks and an easy way with people. Born in the tiny town of Paint Creek, he was first elected to the state legislature in 1984 as a Democrat. In his lifetime, he had never lost an election, including a contest for king of the Paint Creek School Carnival when he was in elementary school. The *Dallas Morning News* reported that he had secured that victory "by handing out pennies for votes." To win his third term, he demolished the popular senator Kay Bailey Hutchison in the Republican primary and then defeated Bill White, the well-regarded former Democratic mayor of Houston, in the general election.

Perry was the perfect foil to Mitt Romney. He was a staunch conservative whose convictions were never in question, the leader of a bright red state to Romney's blue Massachusetts, a politician who had nearly perfect pitch with the Tea Party movement and became a national folk hero to those anti-Washington activists after he mentioned secession at a rally in 2009. Perry and Romney had served together as governors, and there was bad blood between them. Romney was chairman of the Republican Governors Association when Perry was running for reelection in 2006. On a trip to Texas, Romney had dropped in to see Perry at the Texas State Capitol. During the meeting, Perry complained to Romney that a consultant on the RGA payroll was also working for one of his opponents, Carole Keeton Strayhorn, who had left the party to run as an independent. Perry asked how was it that a consultant to the RGA could be working to defeat a sitting Republican governor and, by the way, working for a candidate who wasn't even a Republican. Perry and Romney were "two completely different people," a friend of Perry's said.

That was easy to understand given their backgrounds. Perry grew up in hardscrabble circumstances. Paint Creek, which sits north of Abilene, was so small it didn't show up on Texas maps at the time he was born. His father was a dryland cotton farmer, dependent on the Good Lord and the weather to harvest a crop. His home had no indoor plumbing during his earliest years. His mother made his clothes, including underwear. He was an Eagle Scout and an evangelical Christian. But as a boy, asked if he wanted to be a Christian, he said, "Nope, I want to be an Aggie." He fulfilled that dream, attending Texas A&M University, where he was a yell leader (which is what the Aggies called their cheerleaders), an indifferent student, and a member of ROTC. When he graduated, he was commissioned as an officer in the U.S. Air Force and flew C-130 cargo planes around the world. When his time was up, he returned to Paint Creek and went into the farming business with his father. He married his childhood sweetheart, Anita Thigpen, the daughter of a local doctor, after a courtship of sixteen years. In the early 1980s, he took the test to become a pilot for Southwest Airlines and was scheduled for an interview when a huge rainstorm dropped two feet of rain on his hometown in two days. He took that as an omen that he should stay with his father and work the land.

His father and grandfather had been in local and state politics, and when a seat in the legislature came open in 1984, he ran for it and won. He was a Democrat then. Nearly everyone in Texas was. The Lone Star State was undergoing a political transformation that would eventually make it one of the most Republican states in the nation, but in those days the county courthouses and the legislature were still firmly in Democratic hands. The Democratic Party was long split between its liberal and conservative wings. Perry was one of the conservatives. He supported Al Gore's presidential candidacy in 1988, a line on his résumé that later raised questions about his true political leanings. In that 1988 nominating battle, however, Texans remember Gore as the southerner, running against liberals like Michael Dukakis, Richard Gephardt, and Jesse Jackson.

In 1989, Perry joined the exodus of conservative Democrats from their historic home and became a Republican. A year later, he won his first statewide office, defeating Agriculture Commissioner Jim Hightower, the populist Democrat who was seeking a third term. Eight years later, he ran for lieutenant governor in a race that would set him on a fast track to the governor's chair. The office had come open because of the retirement of Bob Bullock, a Democratic legend who had become an ally and a mentor to George W. Bush during his first term as governor. Bush was seeking reelection that year, with an eye on a presidential campaign in 2000, and putting the lieutenant governor's office in Republican hands was crucial to his game plan. Perry's opponent was John Sharp, a classmate at A&M and a shrewd and popular Democrat. On a day that Bush won reelection with 68 percent of the vote, Perry defeated Sharp by

50 to 48 percent. The race resulted in strained relations between Perry and Bush's chief political adviser, Karl Rove, which continued to color Texas politics for a decade and carried into Perry's 2012 campaign.

Six days after his 2010 victory, Perry was in Washington as part of a tour to promote his new book, *Fed Up!*, a screed against Washington and the federal government. The book tour, which included a New York stop on Jon Stewart's *Daily Show,* prompted speculation about a possible presidential campaign. A month earlier, I had interviewed Perry in Texas and asked him about running in 2012. "I don't know how many times you've got to say no," he said. "I have no passion to go to Washington, D.C." At the post-election breakfast, Perry was even more insistent about his lack of interest in seeking the presidency. He suggested that only his untimely passing would prevent him from serving out his term: "Lord willing, I will be governor of Texas."

A longtime Perry adviser said the governor's team had a different role in mind than presidential candidate. "After the 2010 reelect was behind us, I wanted to make sure that if he wasn't going to be the king, I wanted him to be the kingmaker," the adviser said. "I didn't want a repeat of 2008, where he just suddenly endorsed [Rudy] Giuliani. I wanted him to be courted and be a significant national player." A few months later, when Perry's chief strategist, David Carney, and his 2010 campaign manager, Rob Johnson, went off to help run Newt Gingrich's campaign, it seemed to all that Perry was definitely out of the presidential race. Johnson had checked with Perry before taking the job with Gingrich. "Perry said, 'I'm not running.' He gave me his blessing," Johnson said.

Then Perry changed his mind. On May 27, 2011, as the legislative session was nearing its conclusion, he said to reporters that he was "going to think about" running for president. I asked Perry about his sudden change of heart during an interview in the governor's office in Austin months after his campaign had ended. "I truly had no intention of running for the presidency of the United States until May of 2011," he said, "and at that particular point in time it was the phone calls—'we really wish you would consider this,' 'reconsider it,' whatever the words that they used." Perry said his wife, who had never taken such a central role in his political decisions, was among those pushing him. "I wanted to push this off into my corner," he said. "This wasn't something I wanted to do. I think there was a personal pushback that I don't want to go do this because I'm really comfortable where I am and I don't want to go through the trials and tribulations—and even I didn't know the test that would be before me if I decided to make that."

Within weeks, Carney and Johnson were back in Austin and available to lead the exploration, having quit the Gingrich campaign as part of a mass exodus of senior staff. "Rob and I tried to figure out what are the questions," Carney later said. "If you're going to run for president, what are the questions you'd like answered, and ours were: Is there an opening for someone like you to get in a primary; are there the resources there to wage an effective campaign; and is there time?" Johnson went to work contacting potential bundlers who could help raise money quickly. Carney assessed the early states and the potential to build organizations. Deirdre Delisi, a longtime adviser, looked at how quickly Perry could adjust his thinking from state to national policy questions. Perry worked the phones, calling elected officials, activists, evangelical leaders.

Later in July, Perry and his wife met at their residence with Carney, Johnson, and Ray Sullivan, who had been the gubernatorial chief of staff. "Our goal had always been it's a political and policy goal to put him in the strongest possible position to do anything he wanted, and it just so happened that that was a high point in his political life," Sullivan said. "He was as strong and prepared as he'd ever been, I think." By then it was clear that Perry was ready to run. Before he did, however, he decided to have major surgery to repair a bad back, a decision he would come to regret.

Perry's first thought was to announce in Iowa at the Ames Straw Poll. He was told it was too late to be added to the ballot. The conservative blog site RedState had scheduled its annual conference for Charleston the same weekend. Perry decided to make his announcement there. That morning, in declaring his candidacy, he said his goal was "to make Washington, D.C., as inconsequential in your life as I possibly can." The announcement overshadowed the straw poll, and Ames was buzzing with talk about how Perry's entry would affect Romney's candidacy. Mike Huckabee, who was in Ames as an observer, had a different perspective. "The question may be what Romney does to Perry," he said. "One thing Romney's got going for him is that this is not his first rodeo. It's a bruising experience."

Perry joined the race with a burst of energy. His announcement tour took him overnight to New Hampshire and then on to Iowa. His first stop in Iowa was the Black Hawk County Republican Lincoln Day Dinner at the Electric Park Ballroom in Waterloo, which happened to be Michele Bachmann's hometown. Bachmann was also scheduled to speak at the dinner. The press quickly billed it as a confrontation between the surprise winner of the Iowa Straw Poll and the newest conservative threat in the race. Perry arrived early and worked the entire room, trailed by a mob of photographers and reporters. When he spoke, he talked about the economy and Washington as well as his experience as a farmer and an agriculture commissioner and a childhood that included the 4-H Club and the Boy Scouts. Fielding questions, he slipped out of his jacket and noted how wrinkled his shirt was. When he was finished, he sat back down at his table to await the other speakers.

Bachmann was a late addition to the program, and many of her advisers opposed her being there. They knew she was worn out and believed she would be better off doing a victory lap somewhere else rather than muscling in on Perry's night. Ed Rollins had insisted she attend, Bachmann adviser Keith Nahigian said: "Ed's position, I believe, was there's this mythical Perry, we just won the straw poll, let's go crush him." Bachmann waited in her bus until a local Republican told her frantically she was due onstage. Inside, the music announcing her arrival queued up on the public address system, but still there was no sign of her. When she finally got inside, she took the stage without acknowledging Perry and then gave a desultory speech. Ray Sullivan, traveling with Perry, said, "If you could literally see the air come out of the campaign, we were seeing the air come out of the Bachmann campaign." Brett O'Donnell, traveling with Bachmann, said later, "She went up on the stage and she showed that she was fatigued. She didn't really give a very good speech. And it was like the showdown at the O.K. Corral . . . because we had sold it as the showdown at the O.K. Corral. So it was a very bad mistake, very bad mistake, and it was in my opinion one of the biggest mistakes of our campaign." Bachmann never recovered.

The next day, Perry made his first mistake. He was in Cedar Rapids, on a deck around a swimming pool, speaking to a small group of Republican activists, when he was asked about talk that the Federal Reserve might engage in another round of quantitative easing. Referring to Fed chairman Ben Bernanke, Perry responded, "If this guy prints more money between now and the election, I don't know what y'all would do to him in Iowa, but we would treat him pretty ugly down in Texas. Printing more money to play politics at this particular time in American history is almost treacherous, or treasonous, in my opinion." The comment was delivered with a kind of aw-shucks tone, but the words on paper sounded especially harsh, and the comment went viral that night. As Perry's bus moved through other parts of Iowa the next day, he and his advisers watched as the remark was played over and over and over to widespread criticism, including from White House press secretary Jay Carney and Perry's nemesis, Karl Rove. Perry would not back down. "I would use those words again," he later told me. But his advisers were chastened by the experience.

On his first visit to Iowa, Perry also had made the obligatory stop at the Iowa State Fair in Des Moines. A reporter asked whether he was carrying a gun. Perry declined to answer. "That's why it's called 'concealed,'" he quipped, referring to some states' concealed carry laws. Another reporter asked him about Romney. Perry blew an air kiss to the camera. "Give him my love," he said. In Boston, the picture of Perry blowing kisses infuriated Romney's advisers. Campaign manager Matt Rhoades used it as locker room material, something to post on the wall as motivation. He chided the rest of the campaign: "He's blowing kisses at Mitt. Are you guys going to let him get away with that?"

Romney's team took the threat seriously, and for good reason. Within weeks, Perry had eclipsed Romney as the new leader in the polls. The Texan embodied the core region, core constituencies, and core values of the Republican Party of 2011. Perry also could point to success in creating jobs. Texas had accounted for 40 percent of the jobs created in the entire country in the aftermath of the 2008 recession (although some of this was due simply to population growth). Romney's record of creating jobs in Massachusetts, by comparison, was pitifully small. Perry also had the potential to raise the money necessary for a sustained nomination battle. He had some obvious weaknesses. He had never demonstrated a capacity to reach to the middle of the electorate, although that was never a problem in conservative Texas. Nor was it known whether Perry could take his Texas style north to compete effectively in the Midwest, even in the GOP primaries. And of course, there was the Bush factor. Was America ready for another candidate who sounded like George W. Bush? Still, those who had watched him most closely in Texas did not underestimate his skills—or the ruthlessness of his team. Paul Burka of *Texas Monthly,* one of the most astute political writers in the state, understood Perry's strengths and weaknesses as well as anyone. As Perry was preparing to enter the race, Burka wrote that the handsome Texas governor with the big head of hair should not be dismissed as some "soft or feckless" pretty boy, as if he were a Republican version of the Democratic Breck Boy John Edwards. "Perry is a hard man," he wrote. "He is the kind of politician who would rather be feared than loved—or respected."

Romney's team moved quickly to confront this new threat and soon found in Perry's book, *Fed Up!,* the means to take him down. Stuart Stevens was the first to grasp the potential to turn Perry's words against him. Perry's book was an all-out assault on the way Washington had done business for a century, beginning with the enactment of the federal income tax and accelerating with the New Deal. Social Security, the program most associated with Roosevelt's effort to provide economic security to older Americans, became a target of Perry's ire. The program wasn't just on an unsustainable path financially, Perry argued. It was ill-conceived from the start, set up like "an illegal Ponzi scheme" and possibly unconstitutional. To Perry, Social Security was exhibit A in the creation of a new relationship between an oppressive central government and a once free people. "Social Security is something we have been forced to accept for more than 70 years now," he wrote. He argued that the program now stood as "a crumbling monument to the failure of the New Deal, in stark

contrast to the mythical notion of salvation to which it has wrongly been attached for too long, all at the expense of respect for the Constitution and
limited government." Perry was determined to change that equation. The book
had attracted little notice when it was released. Stevens told his colleagues in
Boston that they would make sure it now got the attention it deserved.

Perry had been successful in Texas by not letting opponents get to his right.
Romney's strategy was counterintuitive: to hit Perry from the left. The attack
came at the first of the fall debates, on September 7, at the Ronald Reagan
Presidential Library in California. Perry was the center of attention and the
target of his opponents. At one point he joked, "I kind of feel like a piñata here
at the party." He later told me, "When I took the stage at the Reagan debate I
was the epicenter of every attack from that end to that end and inward. I felt
like the catcher in the javelin contest. I felt more like the pincushion than the
front-runner."

During the first half of the debate, John Harris of *Politico,* moderating along
with NBC's Brian Williams, asked Perry about Social Security. Perry stood by
what was in the book, even repeating that he believed it was a Ponzi scheme
and taking issue with former vice president Dick Cheney and Karl Rove, who
both had disagreed with him on that characterization. Romney looked at Perry
and said, "Our nominee has to be someone who isn't committed to abolishing
Social Security, but who is committed to saving Social Security. We have always had, at the heart of our party, a recognition that we want to care for those
in need, and our seniors have the need of Social Security. . . . And under no
circumstances would I ever say by any measure it's a failure. It is working for
millions of Americans, and I'll keep it working for millions of Americans. And
we've got to do that as a party." Perry plunged ahead. "Maybe it's time to have
some provocative language in this country," he said. In the spin room, Romney's
advisers escalated the attack. Eric Fehrnstrom said, "I think it would be a disaster for the Republican Party to nominate Rick Perry." A few feet away, Stevens offered sarcastic praise for Perry. "I give him credit for standing by his
position," he said. "It's a bold position. It's just a position that places him in a
minority of a minority of a minority."

As the candidates looked to their fall calendars, they saw a succession of debates that would tie them down, limiting the days available for precious fund-
raising or retail campaigning in the early states, while exposing them to
potential humiliation with any misstep. After the Reagan Library forum, the
calendar included two more debates in September, two in October, and three
in November. For Perry, this represented a daunting introduction to the campaign trail. He had debated only a handful of times during his career and in

his 2010 campaign for governor refused to debate his opponents. His advisers saw him as a candidate with retail skills but not an experienced debater who would shine on a stage with the other candidates. His preparation for the debates lacked discipline or any sense of strategy. Recent back surgery had left the candidate unable to exercise—Perry was a fitness freak who released the stresses of his job by long-distance runs—and not sleeping well. For someone who was now at the top of the polls, this proved a lethal combination.

Romney's attack on Perry over Social Security at the Reagan Library debate marked the opening of an extended assault. The campaign would follow with a dozen releases on the topic, magnifying a confrontation that proved irresistible to the media. At the September 12 debate in Tampa, Romney again pressed the Social Security message. Perry's defense was even less effective than it had been in California.* His advisers insisted that Romney's Social Security offensive was having little impact. Days after Tampa, Carney said Perry had jumped nine points in a Florida poll. He said that showed that the public recognized that Social Security needed fixing and was ready to reward someone who said so. It was the elites who were out of touch.

The third post–Labor Day debate was held on September 22 in Orlando, and it coincided with the Florida Republican Party's P5 (Presidency 5) conference, which included a straw poll the day after the debate. Perry's troops arrived confident that he was positioned to win the straw poll and bolster his standing in the race. The day before the debate, Romney's team tried to bait Perry again on Social Security, laying out a list of questions they hoped the moderators from Fox News would pose on Thursday night. They wanted Perry to say whether he believed Social Security was unconstitutional, which his writings suggested. A yes would lead to difficult follow-up questions, which Romney's campaign also posed in its release: If it's unconstitutional, how would you turn the program into something administered by the states? A no would leave Perry open to charges that he was a flip-flopper.

Megyn Kelly, moderating the debate with Fox's Bret Baier and Chris Wallace, put the question to Perry: "Can you explain specifically how fifty separate Social Security systems are supposed to work?" Perry sought to deflect the question, saying those on Social Security would not be affected by any changes. "We have made a solemn oath to the people of this country that that Social Security program in place today will be there for them," he said. "Now, it's not the first time that Mitt has been wrong on some issues before. And the bottom

---

*In Tampa, he also came under attack for having supported mandatory vaccinations for teenage girls to prevent the spread of human papillomavirus, better known as HPV, a common sexually transmitted disease. Had Bachmann, who led the charge, not made a post-debate misstatement of her own, that line of attack might have hurt him more.

line is, is we never said that we were going to move this back to the states."
Romney countered by accusing Perry of changing his position. "There's a Rick
Perry out there that is saying—and almost to quote, it says that the federal
government shouldn't be in the pension business, that it's unconstitutional—
unconstitutional and it should be returned to the states," he said. "So you better
find that Rick Perry and get him to stop saying that."

Social Security, however, would prove to be the least of Perry's problems in
Orlando. At one point, he became tongue-tied as he tried to lay the flip-flop
label on Romney, mangling what was to have been a killer sound bite. "I think
Americans just don't know sometimes which Mitt Romney they're dealing
with," he said. "Is it the Mitt Romney that was on the side of against the Second
Amendment before he was for the Second Amendment? Was it—was before
he was before the social programs, from the standpoint of he was for standing
up for *Roe v. Wade* before he was against *Roe v. Wade*? He was for Race to the
Top, he's for Obamacare, and now he's against it. I mean, we'll wait until tomorrow and—and—and see which Mitt Romney we're really talking to tonight."
"Nice try," Romney said as the audience laughed at Perry's syntactical pileup.

Having first attacked Perry from the left on Social Security, Romney came
to Tampa ready to start another attack from the right, aiming at a long-standing
Texas policy that allowed children of illegal immigrants who had graduated
from Texas high schools to pay in-state tuition at Texas colleges and universities. The law had been on the books for years and had passed the Texas legislature with little opposition. Romney had vetoed similar legislation when he
was governor and accused Perry of offering a $22,000-a-year carrot that would
only increase the flow of illegal immigrants. "That kind of magnet draws people
into this country to get that education, to get the $100,000 break," he said. "It
makes no sense." Fox's Chris Wallace turned to Perry. "How do you feel being
criticized by a number of these other candidates on the stage for being too soft
on immigration, sir?" he asked. Perry began by restating his tough posture on
the border. Then he turned to the tuition issue. "But if you say that we should
not educate children who have come into our state for no other reason than
they've been brought there by no fault of their own, I don't think you have a
heart," he said. From the audience came a round of boos. Democrats might attack Republicans as heartless, but not a fellow Republican.

Perry remembers Orlando as the moment his campaign suffered an irrevers-
ible setback. "We had busted our chops every day. I'm not sure we had any full
day off from the thirteenth of August all the way through this period of time
raising money," he later told me. "We had a really good forty-five-day fund-
raising period and I wasn't prepared to go into the Orlando debate from a rested
standpoint." His back surgery had affected his stamina and overall well-being.

"The biggest impact that the surgery had on me is I had to quit running, and I was a very devout runner," he said. "That's how I managed my stress. From the first of July to about the middle of September, I didn't run, and it had a huge impact on my ability to sleep and my ability to get rid of whatever is eating on me. I had been a twenty-, twenty-five-mile-a-week runner, and poof—it went away." Perry said he could feel the air go out of the hall in Orlando when he made that comment. "There were a lot of people in that room that wanted to be for Rick Perry. We brought to the table the economics, the Tea Party, there was a lot of excitement. And when I said that, there were a lot of people who went, 'Wow!'"

Commentary the next morning from other Republicans was brutal. Pete Wehner, a veteran of George W. Bush's White House, put it this way: "Perry has had three debates. His first was mediocre. His second debate performance was weaker than his first, and last night's debate was worse than either of the first two. . . . He comes across as unprepared, sometimes unsteady, and at times his answers border on being incoherent." Whatever chance he had to come out of Orlando as a winner had been destroyed by the debate. Herman Cain finished first in the straw poll with 37 percent of the vote—more than Perry and Romney combined.

After Orlando, Perry plummeted in the polls. His fading campaign soon became a snake pit of backbiting, second-guessing, and infighting—the worst of any campaign of the 2012 cycle. In mid-October, deeply frustrated with the state of his campaign, Perry called Joe M. Allbaugh, the manager of Bush's 2000 campaign and later Bush's FEMA director and a longtime friend. On Sunday, October 23, Allbaugh met with Perry and his wife at their residence. Allbaugh found Perry unhappy with the operation of the campaign, with his packed schedule, and particularly with the way debate preparations had been managed. Allbaugh said Perry told him, "'If you will come in you have carte blanche to change, do anything to make things happen,' and I said, 'Okay, because that's the only way it's going to.'" Late that afternoon, Perry told his senior staff of the change. The team was caught totally by surprise. "No one on our side knew that was coming and the roles were not well defined," Sullivan said.

Perry's campaign announced the Allbaugh appointment the next day. The release also announced several other additions to the team that had been in the works for weeks and were unrelated to Allbaugh's arrival, which was news to Allbaugh. Among them were veteran GOP consultants Tony Fabrizio, Nelson Warfield, Curt Anderson, and Jim Innocenzi. The latter three were to join

David Weeks as part of the campaign's media team. The whole announcement added up to a major shake-up of a struggling campaign. Perry's spokesmen, Sullivan and Mark Miner, could not explain the changes to inquisitive reporters, insisting that the shake-up was not a shake-up and that Allbaugh's authority did not threaten Carney or any of the others, which as everyone knew was fiction. Perry had bought himself a whole new set of problems, with his campaign now divided into warring camps who were more than happy to air out their differences in the press. The biggest clash was between Allbaugh and Carney, whose personalities were as sizable as their hefty physical bearing. "Dave didn't like it," Allbaugh said of Carney's reaction to his arrival. "I think he was hurt and upset, wounded that he had done all this with Rick. He told me face-to-face in a couple meetings, 'It's just not going to work, it's not going to work.' I said, 'We haven't even tried. How about trying?' He just wasn't interested. I said, 'Dave, we've known one another a long time, I know what you're capable of doing,' and then I started, 'What's the plan, what's the plan?' There wasn't any plan, which is another problem." Carney disputed all aspects of Allbaugh's description of events, saying that no conversation like that ever took place. More than that, he said Allbaugh never showed interest in knowing what the campaign's plans were.

Allbaugh's advocates said he brought order to a campaign that had been mishandled from the start, that he provided more discipline to an operation that lacked it, and that he helped turn the governor's disorderly debate prep sessions into ones that, over time, made Perry a more skilled debater. His detractors said Allbaugh concentrated mostly on administrative matters rather than grand strategy. He required the staff to wear badges with their names on them, changed the key access format for getting into the campaign headquarters, and changed the color of the paper that the block schedules were printed on from red—which made copying more difficult—to white. These critics said he never even met with campaign manager Rob Johnson—that he canceled several meetings—and that he never dug deeply into what the original team's plans and strategy were.

The struggle between Allbaugh and Carney disrupted the whole campaign. Carney decided to disengage once Allbaugh came in, and had told Perry as much. Allbaugh believed Carney had gone AWOL. "They clashed on everything, and it wasn't really any issue or strategy, it was just Dave can be difficult and he decided to be difficult about everything. And Joe overreacted," said one Perry loyalist. "Joe approached it in a somewhat ham-handed way. He has done well at being sort of the battlefield commander, but coming in and giving speeches about taking care of the Perrys and being loyal to the Perrys to people who have been working for them for ten years, when you've been there for ten minutes, doesn't go over very well."

Some of the other newcomers, who had a relationship with neither Perry nor Allbaugh, were equally alarmed at what they found when they arrived. Warfield assumed Perry's team had a comeback to the immigration issue. He assumed Orlando would be a momentary setback. He described what happened: "We're all on board now, we're the team, so okay, and we're all together, we've taken the pledge, we're all part of the brotherhood. Let's see your polling. Well, we don't have any. Aw, come on guys. No, no survey work. None. Zero. Zip. None. Not a national, not a state, nothing. I mean, it is stunning. . . . In Texas obviously it was manageable, this immigration tuition deal, [but] they had no answer because they'd done no polling. They had no awareness of the power of the issue and since they'd done nothing to frame a response they had no chart out of it." One of the veteran advisers said, "If we had had more information, more data, there might have been ways we could have fixed things faster and better. We had to do it from scratch real quick. The [new] team was very critical of that, from day one—to Carney, to anybody that would listen to them. They would say, 'This is nuts.'"

Perry was now a significantly diminished figure, but he survived the two October debates better than those the month before. At the Dartmouth debate on October 11, he no longer was placed in the center—the result of his plunging poll numbers. At the Las Vegas debate on October 18, he decided he would not let Romney put him on the defensive again on immigration. He reprised an old attack against Romney for having hired a lawn service that employed undocumented workers. As Perry kept interrupting, Romney got testy. "I'm speaking. I'm speaking. I'm speaking," Romney sputtered. He explained the rules to Perry, looked plaintively to CNN's Anderson Cooper, noted Perry's poor performances in earlier debates, and generally lost his cool. Perry's charge was mostly spurious, but he had finally gotten under Romney's skin.

The next debate was on November 9 in Michigan. Perry's team vowed that he would be more rested and better prepared than in the first debates and scheduled his arrival in the state well before the forum. But the warfare between Allbaugh and Carney spilled into the debate preparations, at least according to several advisers. "Carney had done something which really ticked me off," Allbaugh said. "I called the governor, who was on his way to the airport, and I said, 'Governor, this is not going to work, I have tried.' He said, 'Well, you do what you need to do, I understand, this is a different game.' I knew better at the time and I knew the governor well enough that he would probably stew about this." The night before the debate, other members of Perry's team got wind of what was happening. "The debate prep room was overflowing with angst," said one person in the room that night. But no two memories of that night are the same. By one account, Deirdre Delisi, the campaign's policy director and a long-standing adviser to the governor, had approached Perry to plead the case for Carney's continued role as the chief strategist in the campaign. By another, Delisi did not think she was trying to get anything reversed. She felt she knew the roles Perry wanted people to play. She felt it was her responsibility to raise it with the candidate.

Perry said he had no recollection of a debate prep room in turmoil. In fact, he said he felt as well prepared for that debate as any other he did. Before going onstage the night of the debate, he took his customary trip to the restroom. He saw Herman Cain standing just behind him. The Michigan debate came shortly after *Politico* reported that two women had accused Cain of inappropriate behavior when he was head of the National Restaurant Association. The Cain campaign accused one of Perry's new advisers of leaking the story, a charge that was denied by Perry's campaign. Perry recounted to me later what happened next. "He looks over at me and he's always got that big smile on his face and I said, 'Herman, how you doing, you big stud?' That's a term of endearment that I would use. Then he kind of had a funny look on his face and I was like, 'God, I bet he thinks I'm making some derogatory remark at him because of what's happened here in the last week.' I walked out of there and I came in and told that story [to his advisers] and everybody was laughing. I walked onto that stage probably as kind of confident and loose as I had been—and then had that little brain fart."

That "little brain fart" was one of the most embarrassing self-inflicted mistakes any candidate has experienced at a presidential debate—a moment that came to indelibly stamp Perry's candidacy as one of the most inept anyone could recall. It happened two-thirds of the way through the debate, as Perry tried to outline the cuts he would make in Washington if he were president. "I will tell you, it's three agencies of government when I get there that are gone. Commerce, Education, and the, um, uh—what's the third one there? Let's see." Ron Paul chimed in. "You need five," he said. "Oh, five, okay," Perry replied, still tongue-tied. Romney suggested maybe EPA was the third. "EPA, there you go," Perry replied. CNBC's John Harwood, co-moderating the debate, sought clarification. "Seriously, is EPA the one you were talking about?" "No sir. No sir," Perry replied, too honest for his own good at that point. Harwood pressed, incredulous that Perry could not remember the third. "The third agency of government I would—I would do away with, the Education." He paused again until someone said, "Commerce." "Commerce," he continued, "and let's see. I can't.

The third one, I can't." He paused again, head down. "Sorry," he said with a sense of finality. "Oops."

In the press area, reporters watched in disbelief as it unfolded. Curt Anderson, a Perry adviser, was at home watching the debate with his wife. He had drifted off just before it happened. He heard his wife shout, "Oh no!" "I'm like, 'What?' She goes, 'Uh, uh, uh, uh.' And she's trying to explain to me. And she says, 'Get the, get the DVR.' So we replayed it, and I was just like everybody else." In the Perry viewing room at the debate, Delisi broke into tears. "It's like people describe earthquakes," said Nelson Warfield, who was in the Perry green room with the others. "The first shake and people go, 'Oh shit, it's an earthquake.' But real bad earthquakes keep going. So it just kept going. He just couldn't get out of it, and the 'oops' put a little cherry on top. Honestly, it's sort of like a collision. I can only remember bits and pieces. I remember my head hitting the computer top." Ray Sullivan and Mari Will, who had been brought on to take charge of debate preparations, spoke to Perry as he came off the stage and urged him to go into the spin room to take some of the sting out of the moment. Sullivan, Will, and Warfield came up with a one-liner to make light of what happened. "I'm glad I've got my boots on, because I really stepped in it out there," Perry told reporters over and over.

Overnight, the campaign team rearranged the governor's schedule. They set up a series of interviews on the morning shows and scheduled Perry to appear that night on *Late Night with David Letterman* to do Letterman's Top Ten list, where after negotiating away a couple of the most noxious suggestions from Letterman's staff, he laughed off his brain freeze with more one-liners. "The governor came down to the live shows on Thursday morning, he was pretty beaten down," Sullivan said. "It would have been really easy for him and to some extent all of us to curl up and ride it out. By the end of the day he felt good. He had a good time. He felt as we all did that it was successful."

But Perry's already reeling campaign could not recover. Jay Root of the *Texas Tribune* later wrote that "oops" turned Perry's misadventures into "a hall-of-fame disaster." Later that month, Carney and Allbaugh had a final parting. The relationship had deteriorated further. Allbaugh said, "I said, 'Dave, you ought to go to New Hampshire and not come back unless you're specifically invited.' That was the last time we had a conversation." Carney said Allbaugh's words were conveyed in a voice mail, not a direct conversation, after he had already decamped back to his home in New Hampshire, having told Perry early on that he did not intend to stay in Austin with Allbaugh in charge. On the eve of the Iowa caucuses, *Politico* ran a brutal story about a campaign that had met none of the expectations set for it. It was, said one beleaguered adviser, "like a nuclear bomb in the middle of the campaign." Long after Perry was out of the race, the divisions remained deep, as Perry advisers played and replayed events, wondering whether it was ever possible for him to have been a serious competitor.

Perry later looked back at the "oops" moment with some humor. His campaign by then, he later concluded, was already fatally wounded. "My low moment happened in Orlando," he told me. "I told somebody the 'oops' moment was kind of just one of those things that happens in life and I knew I was going to see it over and over and over again, but it wasn't anything. I think I went back and actually slept that night."

My interview took place in the governor's office in the Capitol building in Austin in the spring of 2012. Perry was upbeat, as he generally is, showing photos he had taken with his iPhone on a recent trip. I asked him why someone who seemed to fit the party as well as he did could not have been a more serious contender. "I go back and I don't think I'm putting too much emphasis on the "Orlando debate," he answered. I think that was a very, very damaging moment both in words and in visual at the end of the debate when we were trying to tag Mitt [as a flip-flopper]." But he said there were other lessons from his experience. "The big thing that I learned out of this was you got to start early. You've got to start early and you better be prepared for a grinding process, have yourself physically, mentally fit and be ready to go and have a great deal of luck on your side as well." When we talked he was already thinking about another campaign for president. He said, "You would see a substantially different campaign and even a different candidate from the standpoint of preparation and strength of physical and mental capability."

Perry had one brief moment of redemption after he quit the race. He was the Republican speaker at the annual Gridiron Club dinner in Washington on March 24, 2012. He poked fun at others but mostly at himself. One line brought down the house. He said, "It was the weakest Republican field in history, and they kicked my butt!" That was the story of Rick Perry's campaign.

Matt Rhoades kept a memento of Romney's battle with Perry in his office in Boston. It was a fever chart on a single sheet of paper. The headline said, "Rick Perry Decline." It showed Perry's standing in the polls from the day he announced until late November. Perry started at 13 percent in early August, jumped to 38 percent in one poll by the end of the month. Then, as the attacks from the Romney campaign began, he declined steadily until he was at 4 percent in late November. The center of the chart was highlighted in yellow, and in smaller type was a heading that read, "Perry's decline: 6 weeks." The chart noted that Romney's campaign had issued a dozen press releases attacking on Social

Security during September and another seven on immigration in October. The chart underscored what Perry had concluded: He was out of contention long before he ever said "Oops."

"Rick Perry was a formidable opponent," Rhoades said later. "Go back and read all the covers that all of you wrote about him as he got into this. He was the only governor that was creating tons of jobs, conservative from Texas, he was a very formidable candidate. And I think people rewrite his decline and rewrite how potent a candidate he was because of some of the things that happened later in the primary process. But if you look at this graph you can find out what happened to Rick Perry and how it was Governor Romney and the campaign we ran that really diminished Rick Perry's chances of winning, and it was on the issues. . . . So this isn't a trophy, but this is something. It's the truth, and this guy was the eight-hundred-pound gorilla."

CHAPTER 13

Strange Interlude

The demise of Rick Perry left Romney in an enviable position more than two months before the first votes would be cast in Iowa. Five current or former governors, the pool that so often has provided presidential nominees, were now out of the running: Pawlenty, Perry, Christie, Barbour, and Daniels. Left standing in his way was a collection of candidates who were either unelectable, implausible, or simply underfunded long shots to become the Republican nominee. His real opponent then was the sizable portion of the Republican base that remained tepid in its enthusiasm for the former Massachusetts governor. They were still shopping for an alternative, and the final weeks of 2011 would show they were prepared to grasp at almost any shiny object that caught their eye. That produced high drama and low farce, beginning with the rise and fall of Herman Cain.

Without the Tea Party, Herman Cain might not have become a presidential candidate in 2012. Cain was a businessman, a radio talk show host, and a charismatic speaker. He graduated from Morehouse College in Atlanta, did graduate work at Purdue University, and went to work in the food industry. He worked for Coca-Cola and later Pillsbury, where he became a regional vice president for its subsidiary Burger King. With his success there, he was named president and CEO of Godfather's Pizza in 1986 and turned around the failing chain. A decade later he joined the National Restaurant Association as chairman and CEO. Along the way he served as chairman of the Federal Reserve Bank of Kansas City and as an economic adviser to Bob Dole's 1996 presidential campaign. In 2004, he waged an unsuccessful Senate campaign in Georgia.

The rise of the Tea Party fueled Cain's presidential ambitions. His motivational speeches drew enthusiastic audiences. In March 2010, speaking at a forum sponsored by the conservative group Americans for Prosperity, he put on his cowboy hat and said, "I have a message for President Obama. Mr. President, in 2012 there could be a new sheriff in town." Shortly after that appearance, Mark Block, a longtime Wisconsin Republican operative, and fellow strategist Linda Hansen met Cain for dinner in Las Vegas. They asked him how serious he was about running. "I just want to see what kind of buzz I can create," he told them. A turning point came in the fall when several thousand people showed up in Dayton, Ohio, to hear him. On New Year's Day 2011, Cain spoke at a restaurant in Milwaukee, where he got another big reception. He returned to his hotel. "He sat in the atrium, called the producer of his radio show," Block said, "and I'm listening to him and [Cain says], 'Pete, I'm calling to resign.' We all were thinking, 'What the hell are you doing?' And he said, 'I've made my mind up.' And he gave his notice, he quit." A few weeks later, Cain formed a presidential exploratory committee and was off and running.

Few took Cain seriously as a candidate. For all his charisma and his talents as a motivational speaker, he was woefully unprepared for the presidency. But he pursued an energetic travel schedule, while courting conservative bloggers and Tea Party followers, and soon enough was drawing positive notices from Republican activists. He was a hit at the first Republican debate in South Carolina, though the more he was exposed to questioning, the more it became clear he had plenty of rough edges as a candidate, particularly on foreign policy. The day after he formally announced his candidacy, he appeared on *Fox News Sunday*. When the interview turned to Middle East issues, host Chris Wallace asked him, "Where do you stand on right of return?" Cain stared blankly. "The right of return?" He paused. "The right of return?" He paused again until Wallace explained the issue of whether Palestinian refugees who were forced out of their land in the 1948 pact that created the state of Israel should have the right to return to Israeli territory as part of a Middle East settlement. Cain should have known this and would have if he had taken time for a briefing before the program. He was not easily embarrassed by what he didn't know.

By late summer, he had come forward with the signature policy of his campaign, a tax reform plan he called "9-9-9"—a 9 percent individual income tax rate, a 9 percent corporate income tax rate, and a new 9 percent national sales tax. The plan was a huge hit with the party's grassroots economic conservatives and gave Cain something no other presidential candidate had, an easy-to-understand policy that could fit on a bumper sticker. When Perry stumbled at the debate in Orlando, Cain's candidacy took off. In the first post–Labor Day poll by the *Washington Post* and ABC News, Cain had been in sixth place with just 5 percent. Little more than a week after the Orlando debate, he had leaped into a tie for second with Perry at 17. By the first week of November, at 23 percent to Romney's 25 percent, he was in a statistical tie for the lead.

His surprise success brought predictable scrutiny, which he did not handle well. At a debate in Las Vegas in early October, his rivals pummeled him over his tax plan. Rick Santorum said it would mean higher taxes for 84 percent of

Americans. Perry said it wouldn't fly in the states because it created a new tax. Cain said his opponents were mixing apples and oranges—state and federal tax systems. Romney said apples and oranges would be in the same bucket—all taxable. CNN host Anderson Cooper turned to Newt Gingrich. "Speaker Gingrich," he said, "you have said in recent days that Mr. Cain's 9-9-9 plan would be a harder sell than he lets on. How so?" Gingrich replied, "Well, you just watched it."

Weeks later Cain was interviewed on Fox News by Bill O'Reilly and ended up in a verbal joust with the host over his views on Iraq and Iran. O'Reilly challenged Cain over his proposal to put more Aegis warships in the Persian Gulf, which the host suggested would provoke a response by the Iranians. "That would be perfectly all right," Cain said, "because I believe we have a superior capability." Do you really want a shooting war? O'Reilly asked, incredulous. "Well, I don't want that," Cain said. "But if they fire first, we are going to defend ourselves and . . . they are no match for our warships." He had a similar dustup with Charles Krauthammer on Fox News' *Special Report* that same night. He seemed to have contradictory positions on abortion, saying the decision should be left to a woman, her family, and her doctor while also saying he somehow favored outlawing all abortions, too. He hardly looked ready for the presidency.

On the night of October 30, *Politico* posted a story on its Web site that said two women had accused Cain of sexually inappropriate behavior when he was head of the National Restaurant Association and that paid settlements had been negotiated with the women. Cain spokesman J. D. Gordon, who had been alerted by *Politico* ten days earlier, had a response ready. When the story broke, he e-mailed it to about fifty outlets. Exhausted, he fell asleep. As he later recalled the succession of events, he was awakened by a phone call from Geraldo Rivera's brother Craig, who wanted him on Geraldo's program. Gordon, who was friendly with Craig, said he had nothing more to say. Craig said to hold on. "He says, 'Talk to Geraldo at the break.' I'm like, 'I don't want to talk to him.' He says, 'Hold on.'" What he heard next was Geraldo's voice, as he sat up in bed and watched the host holding a BlackBerry up to his lapel microphone on live television. "Geraldo's like, 'You're live, J.D., you're live.'" Geraldo pressed Gordon about whether there had been a settlement. Gordon, who knew none of the details, froze. "It was horrific," he later said.

Cain was in Washington the next day with a full schedule of public appearances and interviews, and the media were in hot pursuit. He found himself confronted by cameras and shouting reporters in a parking garage. Later at a luncheon at the National Press Club, he got more questions. He kept digging the hole deeper with an ever-changing series of explanations. He first said that he was "vaguely familiar" with the incidents. Then he said he knew nothing about a settlement. Later in the afternoon, he told Fox News' Greta Van Sus-teren that he recalled there was "some sort of settlement or termination." Details of the incidents remained hazy, but the candidate was now caught in a familiar scandal routine. Other news organizations joined in pursuit of the story. Within a week two more women were accusing Cain of inappropriate behavior. The fourth accuser, Sharon Bialek, was the first to allow her name to be used. She appeared with celebrity lawyer Gloria Allred at a press conference at the Friars Club in New York. "I want you, Mr. Cain, to come clean," she said. Cain called all the charges "baseless, bogus, and false" and remained defiant. "We are not going to allow Washington or politics to deny me the opportunity to represent this great nation," he said.

In the midst of the uproar over the allegations, Cain committed another major gaffe during a videotaped interview with editors and reporters at the *Milwaukee Journal Sentinel*. He was asked a straightforward question about whether he had supported President Obama on Libya. He paused and stammered, "Okay, Libya." He paused again. "President Obama supported the uprising, correct? President Obama called for the removal of Gaddafi. I just wanted to make sure we're talking about the same thing before I say, 'Yes, I agreed,' or 'No, I didn't agree.' I do not agree with the way he handled it for the following reason— nope, that's a different one." Another pause. "I gotta go back and see. I got all this stuff twirling around in my head. Specifically, what are you asking me that I agree or not disagree with Obama?" His advisers blamed it on lack of sleep.

On November 28, a fifth woman came forward. Ginger White, an Atlanta woman, said she had engaged in a thirteen-year affair with Cain. She had cell phone records showing calls and text messages from a number that belonged to Cain. The candidate again denied the allegations. He said they were friends, that he had tried to help her, but that there was no sexual relationship. Cain's lawyer appeared to contradict the candidate by saying a consensual affair between adults was not a legitimate news story. Four days after White made her statement, Cain told the *Union Leader* newspaper in Manchester, New Hampshire, that he had frequently given her money to help out with expenses. He said he had never told his wife, Gloria, about the payments or about his relationship with White. Cain also said he was reassessing his candidacy.

His campaign was in free fall. Contributions, which had spiked after the first allegations, had dropped off by almost 90 percent within a day or two of White's allegation. On Saturday, December 3, 2011, Cain announced that he was suspending his campaign. He was defiant to the end, saying that he would establish a new organization to promote the ideas he had championed during the campaign. "I am not going to be silenced and I am not going away," he said.

As quickly as he had risen to the top of the Republican field, he was gone and forgotten. His candidacy ended as a bizarre sideshow. Once it was over, it was even more unimaginable that he had virtually led the race for the nomination at least for a few weeks. Such was the state of the Republican Party as the year 2011 neared its conclusion.

What followed Cain's destruction was almost as surprising: the reemergence of Newt Gingrich as Romney's next apparent challenger. No one had started the campaign with more fumbles and missteps than the man who had led Republicans to power in Congress in 1994. His personal balance sheet included as many liabilities as assets. The liabilities included two messy divorces, an admission of adultery, extravagantly harsh and divisive rhetoric toward his opponents, a tumultuous record as Speaker, a capacity to be childish, and, often, turmoil in his wake. The other reality was that by sheer force of intellect, energy, and ambition he had managed to stay in the forefront of the public debate longer than almost any other contemporary member of his party.

For three decades, Gingrich had been a leader of Republicans. He started as a House backbencher roiling the old guard of his party in the 1980s. Once elected to the leadership, he led his party to its first House majority in forty years. After a government shutdown that cost his party politically, he worked with Bill Clinton to produce a major reform of the welfare system and a balanced budget. For a time, he was the face of the GOP, for better and worse. He survived a coup attempt by some of his lieutenants in 1997, then stepped down as Speaker after his party suffered embarrassing losses in the 1998 midterms as he and other Republicans were pushing to impeach Clinton for his dalliance with Monica Lewinsky. Soon after, he left Congress entirely. That could have ended his public career. But he resurrected himself and became the CEO of an idea-generating mini-conglomerate that was uniquely his. He was a brilliant provocateur. The question was whether Gingrich could show the steadiness, the calm, and the maturity that voters seek in a president. Did he have the discipline required of all successful presidential candidates—the discipline to keep his focus, to avoid meaningless fights, to ignore barbs from his critics, to show statesmanship?

In the spring of 2011, the answers all came back negative. He stumbled toward the starting gate, delaying again and again the formation of a presidential campaign committee as he extracted himself from his tangled business empire. In May, more than a month after Paul Ryan put forward his Republican budget plan, Gingrich belittled it on NBC's *Meet the Press*. "I don't think right-wing social engineering is any more desirable than left-wing social engineering," he said. "I don't think imposing radical change from the right or the left is a very good way for a free society to operate." Conservatives trashed him, from Rush Limbaugh to the *Wall Street Journal* to his friend Bill Bennett, who gave him a public tongue-lashing on his radio show the next day. "To salvage your candidacy, say you blew it," Bennett said. Gingrich did. He spent the next few days doing mea culpa after mea culpa with conservative media while apologizing to Ryan. "He called and he was very, very apologetic," Ryan said. "I said, 'Look, that's fine, just take it back, because it doesn't hurt me personally, it hurts our cause, our efforts.'" Gingrich did take it back. He said he was wrong to say what he'd said. He said he liked the Ryan plan and would have voted for it. He said he shouldn't have answered a "hypothetical baloney question," though what David Gregory had asked him was quite straightforward and not in the least a hypothetical. True to form, he found a way to turn his mistake into a warning to the Democrats not to try to exploit it. "Any ad which quotes what I said on Sunday is a falsehood because I have said publicly those words were inaccurate and unfortunate," he told Greta Van Susteren. Meanwhile, spokesman Rick Tyler issued a purple-prose statement attacking Gingrich's critics. "The firefight started when the cowardly sensed weakness," the statement said. "They fired timidly at first. Then the sheep, not wanting to be dropped from the establishment's cocktail party invite list, unloaded their entire clip, firing without taking aim their distortions and falsehoods." He said Gingrich emerged from "the billowing smoke and dust of tweets and trivia" ready to lead "those who won't be intimidated by the political elite." While Gingrich was engaging in damage control over his interview about Ryan's budget, *Politico* reported that he and his wife, Callista, had a revolving line of credit of up to $500,000 at Tiffany's earlier in the decade. Gingrich said his purchasing habits were no one's business and that, anyway, any debts had been paid off.

A week after all this, I sat down with Gingrich to talk about the campaign. He acknowledged again that he had used a poor choice of words when commenting on Ryan's plan. He said what the right had to understand was that imposing dramatic change required them to bring the voters along. "My point is, it's fine to be radical," he said. "Welfare reform was radical, but if you're going to be radical you actually have to spend more time with the American people getting them to understand it." He knew that all his opponents would be waiting to seize on any misstep. "Not just the media but every competitor, White House, the Romney team, the Pawlenty team, et cetera. They're all going to be watching, and any single slip they're going to exploit." He said he learned something else from the firestorm that erupted over his remarks. "There were an amazing number of people waiting to write the 'Newt Is Dead' story," he said. "Whether they wrote it this week, whether they wrote it next week, whether they wrote it a month from now, they wanted to write it. And so I'm now kind of cheerful because in fact it didn't work." As I was leaving, he said to me with a big smile, "All I can promise you is you won't be bored." He said one other thing of note during the hour we spent together: "No normal consultant can work with me, because they have prefixed models of who's allowed to be a Republican."

Those primed to write "Newt Is Dead" stories did not have long to wait. On June 9, his campaign imploded. His entire senior staff quit in a disagreement with the candidate. Those departing included campaign manager Rob Johnson, media adviser Sam Dawson, senior strategists Katon Dawson and David Carney, longtime spokesman Rick Tyler, and leaders of the campaign operations in Iowa and South Carolina. The split was weeks in the making. The campaign was hemorrhaging money. Fund-raising projections were woefully off the mark. "The assumptions about fund-raising were not just off but they were completely wrong," said one of his advisers. The campaign had planned to try to make a splash at the Iowa Straw Poll in August but was so strapped for money it could not afford the entry fee or the list of past caucus attendees. Carney called it "a Cadillac campaign on a Bud Light budget."

The campaign team was in despair when Gingrich insisted on going ahead with a two-week vacation that included a cruise to the Greek isles. They begged him not to go, told him that if he was going to go on vacation at all he should do it in the United States. While he was on the trip, his advisers drafted a long memo that suggested he consider a graceful exit from the race. The only other options were to develop a live-off-the-land strategy or to continue on the current course, which none of the advisers believed was feasible. Gingrich later described the e-mail, which reached him in Istanbul, as, "Money is terrible. Either quit or come back and turn life over to us." When he and Callista returned, they met with Johnson and Sam Dawson at offices that housed the Gingrich business enterprises. The meeting was not acrimonious. There was no animosity. But it resulted in one of the most dramatic walkouts by a campaign team in presidential politics. "I basically told them, 'You would like me to be the candidate for your campaign. I would like you to be the managers of my campaign,'" Gingrich later told me. "I can't be the candidate for your campaign. I have no interest in being the candidate for a traditional Republican campaign." Dawson and Johnson told Gingrich he deserved advisers who shared the same passion and believed in the way he should run the campaign, which they did not. When it was over, everyone shook hands and the departing consultants hugged Callista.

Gingrich had his own, strange ideas about how he wanted to run the campaign. He believed he could find new coalitions of supporters. One was people who owned pets. Another was Chinese Americans in Iowa. He said he would attract new supporters by focusing on the problem of Alzheimer's disease. He believed he could organize and attract support through the Internet, though he had no real strategy for that. He planned to continue to give speeches around the country with his wife to promote the films and books they had produced. He would take advantage of the debates. Everyone thought he was— well, just the same old Newt. Nothing about the opening stages of his campaign reflected well on the candidate. Gingrich had a year or more to get ready for the presidential campaign. Yet when he got to the point of running, he appeared utterly unprepared for the task at hand. He prided himself on being a student of history, but the mass exodus of his campaign team showed that he had not bothered to study what it takes to become a successful presidential candidate. Gingrich had always wanted to do things his way. Now he would have to.

Gingrich called me a week later. He wanted to share how he saw the campaign going forward. "If I fade away, you won't want the chapter," he said, laughing. "If I don't fade away, then you'll want the chapter, right?" He said he had done a comparison of what he called the Goldwater-Reagan-Gingrich model and the standard Republican consulting model. "I was surprised at the virtual impossibility of crossing those two cultures," he said. "The people I brought in were very smart. I have tremendous admiration for them. But it was like bringing in a hockey team and explaining that we're now playing football. But where's the ice?" The past few days had been extremely unhappy ones. "We were being beaten up on every front," he said. "We were getting beaten up by the media, we had consultants who were leaving us in debt while attacking us, which I thought was astonishingly unprofessional." He was determined to follow his own instincts, odd and unproven as they were to veterans of successful presidential campaigns. He said, "We are not trying to hire anyone who is a normal politician, because they're trying to do normal things. We're trying to figure out if we can have a citizen movement that in the age of the Internet can be moved by ideas and concepts." He wanted to focus on big ideas, on a scale of change bigger and bolder than his opponents would ever dare. He ended the call by saying, "At minimum, this will shape the idea environment. If it breaks loose and goes viral, I could be the nominee."

Gingrich soldiered on, participating in debates but otherwise ignored. "We went through the two worst months in my career," he told the *Post*'s Karen Tumulty. "I would say June and July were the hardest months, worse than the two defeats [for Congress] in '74 and '76." He later said to me, "People I had worked with and knew were enthusiastically trashing me. They weren't just trashing me. They were enthusiastically trashing me. And I don't think I'd understood how much hostility the Washington establishment had for me and how much disdain they had for me. . . . It was hard because you'd call friends who'd been told all day by Fox and others that I was dead and how do you raise money for a campaign? So you had to, as an act of will, get up every day knowing that most of the people you were about to call, even if they'd been with you for twenty years, now thought it was sad that you hadn't dropped out and accepted reality."

Debates saved—or resurrected—Gingrich's candidacy. His strategy consisted of the following: Avoid attacking the other candidates. Find ways to attack the media and the moderators. Talk about big ideas. Focus on Obama. From June until early November, he was a bystander on the stage as one after another of the perceived leading candidates drew the attention and the toughest questions. But he was quietly rebuilding his image. No one in the field went after Obama with the intensity of Gingrich, which was exactly what much of the Republican base was looking for. When Cain began his descent into irrelevance, Gingrich was the beneficiary. He became the newest not-Romney in the field, setting up a clash that no one in the party had foreseen.

In mid-November, I wrote about Gingrich's unexpected opportunity and said he still could be his own worst enemy: "He delights in over-the-top rhetoric, stridency, extravagant criticism and condescension toward his enemies. He becomes a scold. Gingrich has various attributes, which have kept him as a prominent voice in the Republican Party for more than two decades in spite of setbacks and self-inflicted wounds. For reasons mostly beyond his doing, he may have been handed a new opportunity for redemption and leadership. Whether he can restrain the impulses that have brought him down in the past will now be his biggest challenge."

The next morning an e-mail arrived from Gingrich. There was no content other than the subject line. It read: "Good analysis newt."

CHAPTER 14

Mitt's Moment

Mitt Romney was the one constant in the Republican race. Through the summer and fall, as his rivals came and went, he remained at or near the top of nearly every poll. He won or tied virtually every one of the fall debates. He did not excite the party's base, but in his steady, unspectacular style he was able to keep his focus on the ultimate prize that had eluded him four years earlier. He had learned well the lessons of 2008. He and his team were digging in for a long battle.

There were now two distinguishing features of the Republican race. One was the absence of a truly strong challenger to Romney. One by one, other candidates had come calling for support. One by one, they had stumbled or been found wanting. Those ebbs and flows contrasted with the other reality of the race, which was Romney's inability to gain additional support when one of his rivals had stumbled. His relative flat line in the polls, with somewhere between 25 and 30 percent support, was considered a sure sign of weakness. The Obama team mocked him as "the 25 percent man." But there was every bit as much weakness, if not more, among those who were seeking to challenge him, which now made his route to the nomination potentially easier. Nothing was guaranteed, but the weakness of the opposition—in particular the failure of anyone to consolidate conservative support in Iowa—gave Romney the opportunity to do something that was not in the original game plan in Boston. It was now possible that Romney could win both Iowa and New Hampshire and set himself on a fast track to victory.

Throughout the year, Romney and his team had played Iowa with considerable deftness. He was neither fully in the race to win the state nor definitely passing on the caucuses, as John McCain had done in both his 2000 and 2008 campaigns. Iowa was not a Romney-friendly environment. Christian conservatives played too big a role in the precinct caucuses, as Romney had learned in 2008. In his second race, he had decided to approach the state cautiously, keeping his options open as long as possible. The strategic conversations had begun in 2010 between Dave Kochel, Romney's lead strategist in Iowa, and the team in Boston. They wanted Romney to campaign in the state just enough to keep himself visible but not enough to suggest that he was going all out there. They wanted to reconnect with Romney's 2008 supporters but needed to stay below the radar so as not to suggest they were making a play to win the caucuses. As other candidates were traveling to Iowa regularly in 2010, Romney stayed away. He made a quick trip in the final month of the midterm elections to campaign for Terry Branstad, who had served four terms as governor in the 1980s and 1990s, retired, and was now trying to win another term. Through the first two-thirds of 2011, as other candidates were swarming the state, Romney was an infrequent visitor. He was there in the spring and came back for the August debate just before the Ames Straw Poll. On that visit he made the obligatory stop at the Iowa State Fair, where he got into a verbal tussle with a heckler and, in trying to defend the free market system, uttered the now-famous words, "Corporations are people, my friend."

Romney maintained a skeletal staff in Iowa, led by Kochel and state director Sara Craig. In the late spring they began to reach out more systematically to their county coordinators from 2008. Over the summer they quietly recruited precinct captains, and in the fall began a more serious effort to canvass potential supporters—all without making any public acknowledgment. Managing expectations became one of the single biggest challenges for the campaign. Campaign manager Matt Rhoades spent considerable time weighing the risks, rewards, costs, and opportunities of Iowa. In November 2011, he vetoed the idea of having Romney attend a sixty-fifth birthday party for Branstad. Ron Kaufman, a Romney senior adviser and former business partner of Branstad, strongly recommended that Romney go to the celebration. To do otherwise would seem to be a snub of the popular governor. Rhoades said no. He knew that if Romney went to the birthday party he also would be obliged to attend a candidate forum sponsored by Family Leader, one of the leading social conservative organizations in the state. Rhoades and others knew it was not a setting that would help Romney. Branstad had already put Romney on notice a few days before the birthday party weekend. "I think he's making a big mistake . . . by not coming here and spending more time," Branstad said at an energy conference in Des Moines. "I mean Romney is dropping in the polls, and I think he wants to keep down expectations—well, his expectations may get really bad if he doesn't get a little more serious." Branstad's public upbraiding, along with Gingrich's emergence, put a noticeable dent in Romney's Iowa support. Rhoades stuck with the plan. "It just seemed like an exercise in jumping through every hoop that people put out in front of you," he said of the Family Leader forum. "That's one of the things that we've not done as a campaign. We didn't do it in Iowa. We didn't go to every forum just because they were in Iowa. We didn't do the straw poll. We learned our lessons [from 2008] and we didn't go."

There was little doubt, however, that Romney would ultimately make a vigorous push in Iowa. On December 1, campaign officials announced the first television buy in the state. In the ad, Romney said, "I spent my life in the private sector. I've competed with companies around the world. I've learned something about how it is that economies grow. We're not going to balance the budget just by pretending that all they have to do is take out the waste. We're going to have to cut spending." The campaign had played the expectations game expertly to that point. The question was whether Romney now risked raising them too high.

On December 10, the candidates met in Des Moines for another debate. Newt Gingrich was now the center of attention and the target of the attacks. A *Washington Post*/ABC News poll of potential Iowa caucus participants showed the former Speaker leading the field, with a ten-point margin over second-place Romney. The Romney campaign's internal polling showed Gingrich ahead by seven points at the time of the Des Moines debate. Interviews with Iowa voters showed how much the debates had helped him. A woman in rural Carroll County who participated in an informal focus group that I convened said, "I think he has shaped these debates. He is making everyone talk about ideas and he is so respectful of the other candidates on the stage and doesn't tear down. . . . He just wants to talk about ideas, and that's so exciting and refreshing." What Iowa Republicans found most appealing about Gingrich was the belief that he would demolish Obama in the general election debates. A woman who lived in the Des Moines suburbs and who participated in another group I met with said, "I think he'd kick [Obama's] butt in a debate, and that's what we need."

With characteristic bravado, Gingrich had called the race all but over. "I'm going to be the nominee," he told ABC's Jake Tapper. "It's very hard not to look at the recent polls and think that the odds are very high I'm going to be the nominee. And by the way, I don't object if people want to attack me. That's their right. All I'm suggesting [is] that it's not going to be very effective and that people are going to get sick of it very fast. . . . They should do what they and their consultants want to do. I will focus on being substantive and I will focus on Barack Obama." Gingrich's hubris angered Romney's Boston team. Rhoades was personally insulted, for his candidate and for the entire campaign.

At the debate in Des Moines, Gingrich was accused of being a career politician who profited by his insider status, a hypocrite, and an intemperate, unreliable leader. Romney led the attacks. "We don't need folks who are lifetime Washington people to get this country out of the mess it's in," he said.

"We need people from outside Washington, outside K Street." Gingrich responded to Romney by saying, "Let's be candid. The only reason you didn't become a career politician is because you lost to Teddy Kennedy in 1994."

The debate also escalated the controversy over immigration that Gingrich had touched off during a forum in Washington two weeks earlier. The former Speaker had said he favored an immigration policy that would allow someone who had been in the country illegally for a quarter century or more and had put down roots in a community to stay to be given a path to legal status—though not citizenship. Romney had been sharply critical of the proposal, as he had been with Perry's in-state tuition program. Asked about his proposal at the Des Moines debate, Gingrich held his ground. "I will just say flatly, I do not believe the people of the United States are going to send the police in to rip that kind of person out and ship them out of this country," he said. Romney continued to take a hard line. "We will then create another magnet that draws people into our country illegally," he said. That was also the night Romney dared Perry to bet him $10,000 to settle a dispute over something in Romney's book.

Five days later, the candidates put on a repeat performance in Sioux City. Gingrich's rivals said he was not a true conservative and would put the entire party at risk if he were the nominee. Michele Bachmann was especially aggressive, attacking him for having been a lobbyist for Freddie Mac, which paid him $1.6 million in consulting fees. Given conservative antipathy toward both Fannie Mae and Freddie Mac for their roles in the foreclosure crisis, this was fertile ground. "The Speaker had his hand out and was taking $1.6 million to influence senior Republicans to keep the scam going in Washington, D.C.," she said. Gingrich replied, "I never lobbied under any circumstance. The truth is, I was a national figure who was doing just fine, doing a whole variety of things, including writing best-selling books, making speeches. And the fact is, I only chose to work with people whose values I shared, and having people have a chance to buy a house is a value I believe still is important in America."

Gingrich's surge in Iowa brought out the newest force in presidential politics, the super PAC, with Romney the first beneficiary. Restore Our Future was explicitly created to help Romney—independent by its incorporation but nonetheless a powerful ally that could spend freely to attack anyone who appeared to be a serious obstacle in the former governor's path to the nomination. ROF began a massive advertising campaign against Gingrich, spending nearly $3 million in December. Romney used his television money to offer positive ads while leaving it to the super PAC to attack Gingrich relentlessly. It was the first clear evidence of the outsized role these groups could play in the nomination battle.

Super PACs grew out of the Supreme Court's controversial 2010 decision in *Citizens United v. Federal Election Commission* and also of a later decision by the U.S. Circuit Court of Appeals in *SpeechNow.org v. Federal Election Commission.* The *Citizens United* decision opened the way for corporations and labor unions to spend as much as they wanted directly on elections. The second decision made it possible for political action committees that engaged only in independent expenditures, and not advocating directly for a candidate, to accept unlimited contributions. Super PACs mushroomed during the 2010 election cycle, with about eighty different ones registered with the Federal Election Commission. Ten of those committees accounted for three-quarters of the roughly $90 million spent on campaigns that cycle. The best known of these committees was American Crossroads, formed by a group that included Karl Rove, the chief strategist for George W. Bush's two campaigns and White House deputy chief of staff in Bush's administration. Like traditional PACs, these super PACs were regulated by the FEC and had similar reporting and disclosure requirements.* The big difference was in the amount of money they could collect from a single individual.

The 2012 presidential election brought another refinement to these super PACs—committees formed for the express purpose of promoting a specific candidacy. Even though they were not allowed to coordinate directly with the campaign of the candidate they were supporting, these PACs were generally created by and staffed with people having close ties to the candidate and his campaign. Romney's super PAC was founded by the general counsel for his 2008 campaign, Charles Spies, and by Carl Forti, who was political director for that campaign. Gingrich's was formed by Becky Burkett, who had run his political action committee at American Solutions, and one of the first to come aboard as its senior adviser and chief spokesman was Rick Tyler, who had long been one of Gingrich's closest advisers and was a member of his campaign team until the mass walkout by senior staff in June 2011. Another twist tied these super PACs even more closely to the campaigns they were aiding: The candidate and his staff were allowed to help raise money for these supposedly independent organizations. Though entirely legal, it seemed a perversion of the system of presidential campaign financing that had been breaking apart since the 2000 campaign.

Iowans were famous for seeing things before voters elsewhere, because they had an early opportunity to examine the candidates repeatedly and up close. But that wasn't the case this time. Until early December 2011, the campaign

---

*Some super PACs also established separate entities that were regulated by the Internal Revenue Service and were not required to disclose the names of their donors.

in Iowa had been far quieter than in previous years. Candidates had spent less time and money in the state. They had held far fewer events, and those events (with a few exceptions) drew smaller audiences and generated less excitement than in the past. Campaign organizing was months behind the pace of the past several cycles. Iowans were moving along with the rest of the country. As Republican voters shifted nationally, Iowa voters changed with them, from Bachmann to Perry to Cain and now to Gingrich. Debates and cable television were supplanting some of the old-fashioned retail campaigning so elemental to Iowa's politics.

The absence of organizational infrastructure was particularly evident. I went to Bachmann's headquarters outside Des Moines in early December and found only a few people making telephone calls. Gingrich's headquarters was even emptier. Scores of cell phones were plugged into outlets in an otherwise barren room. Only two people were making calls to voters, and both were from outside the state. The mismatch between the image of Gingrich as the hot candidate, leading the polls in Iowa, and the support structure he had to turn out voters on caucus night was as great as any I had seen. The Republican race in Iowa was quickly becoming a free-for-all. The attacks on Gingrich drove down his support. Romney's advisers grew increasingly optimistic that he could actually win the caucuses. Meanwhile, two other candidates were beginning to attract attention.

Ron Paul was his own universe as a candidate, but he was becoming a force in Iowa. His brand of libertarianism attracted an intense following, small in numbers but passionate in their support. Paul was the oldest and quirkiest of the candidates. He was out of step with his party on national security issues. His support for legalization of marijuana also put him at odds with most Republicans, though it helped attract young voters. But on the question of government's role, he offered Tea Party activists the purest and most radical platform. He wanted to shrink the government dramatically and balance the budget immediately. He also wanted to abolish the Federal Reserve. In debates, he seemed to enjoy attacking his rivals. He showed no mercy toward Gingrich, who he believed was a hypocrite and a phony conservative. He didn't much like fellow Texan Rick Perry either. The only candidate generally spared from his attacks was Romney. In fact, they acted as allies against the other candidates. In Iowa, Paul was building an organization that was the envy of many of the other low-budget candidates. His supporters had been at work for years. "This isn't a year-and-a-half campaign," Craig Robinson, a former political director of the Iowa Republican Party, told the *New York Times'* Richard A. Oppel Jr. "This is a five-year campaign." The better Ron Paul did in Iowa, the more Romney liked it. Paul had no chance to win the nomination, but in Iowa he had the potential to suppress support for some of the others who were trying to become Romney's principal challenger.

The other candidate on the rise was Rick Santorum, the former Pennsylvania senator. He was as conservative as anyone in the field. He had done his politics in Iowa the old-fashioned way, and for most of the year he had been camped out in the state, drawing little attention. He would go anywhere to meet with one or two or a dozen voters. Reporters rarely followed him around. Romney's campaign advisers thought so little of his chances that they did not even bother to prepare an opposition research book on him. His candidacy seemed improbable from the start. A partisan fighter, he had served Pennsylvania in the House and later the Senate, as one of the most outspoken social conservatives in the chamber. He was the father of seven children, one a special needs child. He and his wife, Karen, lost an eighth child shortly after birth, a wrenching experience that turned him into a more aggressive advocate on some of the social issues he had merely paid lip service to before. When he ran for reelection in 2006, a bad year for Republicans, he lost by eighteen points. He was built like a football player, and his trademark became the sweater-vests that he wore on the campaign trail. Buttons sold at his events said, "Chicks Dig the Vest." By December, he was burrowed deep into Iowa. He had visited all ninety-nine counties in the state, often riding in a Dodge Ram pickup owned by friend and aide Chuck Laudner that became known as the Chuck Truck. He knew Iowa activists by name. When Perry and Bachmann squared off in August in Waterloo the day after the straw poll, Santorum was there too. No one remembered that, but Nick Ryan, a conservative operative in Iowa who was with him that night did. "As he went from table to table, he knew so many people who were in that room. He recognized them, by name," Ryan said. "He shook their hands. He was . . . overlooked by the media but continuing to build relationships."

On December 13, my colleague Phil Rucker and I sat down with Romney for one of a series of interviews he was doing that week with print and Internet publications. He had been criticized for not talking to the press, and this was the week the campaign had chosen for him to check the box. He used the interview to continue his attack on Gingrich, whom he called "an extremely unreliable leader in the conservative world." He also acknowledged that he still needed to persuade some Republicans that he was a true conservative. "There are some elements that create the impression that I may not be a conservative. One is being from Massachusetts. The other is a health care plan that people feel was in some ways a model for what Barack Obama did. And those two things create an image which is not identical to what I'd like to project. . . . People I think question those conservative values, and I have to bring them back to my record and, frankly, my writings. One of the reasons I wrote a book was to make sure people understood what I really believe." Later in the interview he again stressed his conservative position. "I know today there are some of my positions that are not seen as being conservative, and that's the right of people to look at. But if you look at one of the most defining issues of conservatism today, it is whether we're going to reform Medicare and cut back the scale of the federal spending, and the Speaker called that 'right-wing social engineering.' And I applauded the Ryan plan." He also said he was confident he could unite the party as its nominee. "My positions on issues are very much in alignment with the big tent of the Republican Party," he said. "I'm for limiting the scale of government, cutting government spending, dramatically reducing the intrusiveness of government in our lives. My message on the Constitution is entirely consistent with that of the base of my party. And so I don't think there's any difficulty in those in my party coalescing behind me if I'm the nominee."

Matt Rhoades liked to tell people, "Winners close." He was the quiet force inside Romney's headquarters. He had risen through the ranks of Republican strategists, joining the Republican National Committee staff straight out of college. In 2004, he was director of opposition research for George W. Bush's reelection campaign, and four years later he served as Romney's director of communications. He was known for having a pipeline to the *Drudge Report*. He was tough and tough-minded, a man of few words who stayed out of the limelight. When he accepted the job as director of Romney's PAC, he told me he would not put up with the internal chaos that had marked Romney's first campaign. He prized discipline, planning, and execution. As the campaign year neared, he was mindful of 2008, when Romney didn't close, in either Iowa or New Hampshire. He knew Romney was in a stronger position this time, but he was focused on taking full advantage of the governor's position. "We've got to close," he said as he prepared for the last weeks of campaigning before Iowa and New Hampshire. Which is why when Romney set off on a bus tour of New Hampshire on December 21, the name of the tour was "Earn It."

The Republican campaign was running at full speed now in both Iowa and New Hampshire. Romney was making sure his New Hampshire firewall was secure before turning back to Iowa. The night before, he had given what aides had billed as a closing argument speech, though it was mostly a rehash of past themes and rhetoric. Romney still had trouble delivering inspiring speeches on the stump. But the staging, at the picturesque town hall in Bedford, and the advance notice produced a full house of supporters and reporters. Romney's team was in a good mood that night as they kicked off the tour, but one senior adviser remained cautious about Iowa. "I think you could throw a blanket over four or five people, and we could be fifth, we could be first," he said. "I think we're probably going to be in the top two or three but I just don't know. I mean, the stuff that's fallen off Newt is not necessarily going to us." But the more he talked, the more optimistic he sounded. "I mean, it feels weird to me," he said. "I almost think we're on the brink of making this over really fast." He noted that there were eleven days between New Hampshire and South Carolina and that South Carolina governor Nikki Haley, who had endorsed Romney, was bullish about his chances there. "Were we to get these first two, we would have time to get to South Carolina and create something." Romney was not so sure. In our interview with him the prior week, he had offered this view of how long the nomination battle would last: "Traditionally, people who've done well early are able to knock out their opponents because their opponents run out of money. I'm not sure that's the path that will be followed this time, in part because of the availability of Internet, cable, and debate access for campaigns with limited funds. So people may stay in longer than they have in the past, [people] that haven't been able to raise money. So I can't predict what will happen." Romney also thought the race would last longer than many were predicting because of a change in the rules, which now called for delegates to be awarded proportionally in early contests rather than the winner-take-all rules of the past.

The next morning, in Keene, New Hampshire, Romney belittled Gingrich for complaining about the attack ads raining down on him in Iowa. Interviewed by NBC's Chuck Todd, he sent a message to Gingrich that he should be prepared for even tougher attacks. "I know that the Speaker would like to say that we shouldn't have any negativity," Romney said. "But, look, if you can't handle the heat in this little kitchen, the heat that's going to come from Obama's hell's kitchen is going to be a heck of a lot hotter." Later in the afternoon, Gingrich appeared at a press conference in Manchester, New Hampshire, where he was asked about Romney's comments. He smiled. "Look, I'll tell you what. If he wants to test the heat, I'll meet him anywhere in Iowa next week one-on-one, ninety minutes, no moderator, just a timekeeper. If he wants to try out the kitchen, I'll be glad to debate him anywhere. We'll bring his ads and he can defend them." He accused Romney of hiding behind his super PAC. "I don't think he wants to do anything but hide over here and pretend it's not his fault that he is flooding the people of Iowa with falsehoods. That's his money and his staff and it's his responsibility. I can take the heat."

Once Christmas was over, the candidates refocused all their energies on Iowa. The Hawkeye State became a multiscreen political theater as the candidates navigated a turbulent landscape, the most unpredictable anyone could remember. Santorum began the final week of campaigning in a bright orange vest and carrying a shotgun for a short hunting expedition. Rick Perry campaigned with Sheriff Joe Arpaio, the notorious anti-immigration official from Arizona. Arpaio got Perry off to a bad start at a breakfast outside Des Moines when he referred to Iowans as Buckeyes, the nickname of Big Ten rival Ohio State. Santorum and Gingrich attacked Ron Paul, whose growing support threatened both their candidacies. And the sparring between Gingrich and Romney continued. In Dubuque, the former Speaker said of his opponent's attacks, "Frankly, they plain lie." Still stung by Romney's charge that he was an unreliable conservative, Gingrich said, "I don't want to be insidious about Governor Romney, who I think is a very competent manager and a very smart man. But to have someone who is a Massachusetts moderate, who said he did not want to go back to the Reagan-Bush years, who voted as a Democrat for Paul Tsongas in '92, who campaigned to the left of Teddy Kennedy, who as recently as running for governor said [he was] sort of a moderate pragmatic—to have him run a commercial that questions my conservatism? I mean, I've been a conservative all my life." Gingrich said he would not fight fire with fire. He would try to stay positive in his advertising. "We have a lot of time," he said. "I trust in the ability of the people of Iowa to look at something that is baloney and see it as baloney."

By then, Gingrich was already out of time, thanks to weeks of pounding by Romney and Restore Our Future. The landscape changed once again, barely a week before the caucuses. At midweek, a CNN producer called Santorum's campaign urgently trying to book him for an appearance that afternoon. John Brabender, Santorum's chief strategist, remembers the producer saying, "We're coming out with a new poll, we're not going to make it public till four o'clock, all we can tell you is, you really should do Wolf Blitzer." The new poll showed Santorum tripling his support and leaping into third place behind Romney and Paul. "All of a sudden," Brabender said, "what happened is people who wanted to be with us but for the longest time thought we were in last place and so they just really weren't there—all of a sudden they were there."

Perry and Michele Bachmann were fighting desperately to avoid being driven from the race. Bachmann had put herself on a punishing schedule as she tried to match Santorum's feat of campaigning in every county in the state. She was in last place in the CNN numbers, the final indignity for the winner of the Iowa Straw Poll. But there was one more painful moment, an embarrassing defection by her state chairman, Kent Sorenson. Late in the afternoon on December 28, Bachmann arrived at a restaurant south of Des Moines for a quick meet-and-greet before running off to do a live shot for television. Among those waiting was Sorenson. One of Bachmann's advisers asked him if he wanted to say a few words, but he begged off, claiming he had just had some dental work done. A few hours later he showed up at a raucous rally for Ron Paul at the Iowa State Fairgrounds and announced that he was switching sides. "I believe we're at a turning point," he told the audience. Bachmann said Sorenson had been lured away with the promise of a financial payment, which Sorenson denied. Her campaign was expiring amid bitter charges and countercharges.

New Year's Eve brought more shocks when the *Des Moines Register* released its final poll of the Republican race. The *Register* had a notable track record of predicting the outcome of races in Iowa, and when the numbers began to flash on BlackBerries and iPhones at restaurants around Des Moines, where reporters were celebrating the arrival of the election year, it was clear that the caucuses were heading for one of the closest finishes ever. Over the four days of polling, Romney led with 24 percent, followed by Paul with 22 percent and Santorum with 15 percent. Then came this paragraph: "But if the final two days of polling stand alone, the order reshuffles: Santorum elbows out Paul for second." In a year of surprises, why not this latest: a surging Rick Santorum with just days left before the caucuses. Santorum's timing was perfect. It was too late for any of his opponents to launch the kind of air attack that Romney had thrown at Gingrich.

On the evening before the caucuses, Santorum appeared before an overflow audience packed in a steamy side room at the Pizza Ranch. It was a dramatic change from just two weeks earlier when he had trouble holding a lunchtime crowd during a speech at an insurance company in Des Moines. He told the crowd this was his 380th Iowa event. "We haven't speed-dated through Iowa," he said. "We've taken our time. It's been a courtship." With the caucuses twenty-four hours away, he pleaded with Iowans to set aside everything but their own instincts and their own judgments. "You're first," he said. "That is a huge responsibility. I know a lot of people make light of the Iowa caucuses, but as you will see tomorrow night, it will have a huge impact on this race. And so the decision you make, and I know this, cannot and should not be taken lightly. . . . This is the most important election in your lifetime. . . . Do not defer your judgment to people who know less about who these candidates are than you do. Lead. . . . I'm asking you to lead. I'm asking you to be bold."

Caucus night was a blur of precinct results, shifting numbers, and uncertain outcomes. For most of the night, Romney and Santorum were neck and neck, with Paul running third. Santorum hesitated to go out to speak until he knew the final results, but his aides urged him at least to claim a moral victory even if he wasn't in first place. No matter what, he had far exceeded expectations. Brabender reminded him that no matter what he said, the first lines would be the ones television would capture. When he finally addressed supporters, he had a broad smile on his face. "Game on!" he said. It was a remarkable showing for Santorum, but by early the next morning, the near-final count showed Romney with a lead of 8 votes out of more than 120,000 cast.

A few days later, Rhoades told me, "Everything we did in Iowa was to win the nomination, not to win Iowa, to win the nomination. That was our plan from the beginning, keeping our options open was the plan to win the nomination. Popping out there, doing debates, never going the McCain route of writing off the state at some point. We kept our options open from day one because it was all about winning the nomination. And we ended up winning Iowa." As Romney boarded his chartered airplane for the flight to New Hampshire the morning after the caucuses, he was in position to do what no Republican had done in the modern era of presidential politics—win both of the opening contests. The only worrisome thing was that while he had "won" the caucuses, he actually received fewer votes than he had four years earlier. He had momentum, but he did not yet have his party.

Jon Huntsman Jr. awaited the other candidates in New Hampshire. He was the misfit in the Republican race, the lone apparent moderate (other than perhaps Romney) in a party where such species were nearly extinct. Huntsman was a popular former governor of Utah who had been tapped by Obama in 2009 to become U.S. ambassador to China. The appointment was seen as a clever way to fill a critical diplomatic post and sideline a potential 2012 rival at the same time. Then rumors of a possible Huntsman candidacy surfaced in January 2011. Huntsman came to Washington that month for the state visit by Chinese president Hu Jintao. Obama couldn't resist having fun with his envoy to Beijing. "I'm sure that him having worked so well with me will be a great asset in any Republican primary," he said to laughter at a press conference. That night, Axelrod spoke to Huntsman. "I went up to him and said, 'Jon, I want you to know you can have my endorsement too if that helps,'" he said. "And he said, 'Oh, I don't know where all this is coming from, it's way overblown.'"

Meanwhile, a fledgling Huntsman for President operation sprang up under the direction of John Weaver, a veteran Republican consultant who had been a senior strategist for John McCain. The team also included Fred Davis, a Republican ad maker from Hollywood known for his theatrical flair, who had done the "I am not a witch" ad for Delaware's Christine O'Donnell. The Weaver operation technically was not connected directly to Huntsman. In interviews both said there was no direct contact between the two while Huntsman was in Beijing. But Huntsman could easily monitor the press coverage as the team built a Web site, a theme, and the skeletal infrastructure for a candidate who met all of Huntsman's criteria. Huntsman resigned his diplomatic post and returned to Washington at the end of April. The day he landed, he got off the plane, put on a tuxedo, and attended the White House Correspondents' Association Dinner. Late that night he called Weaver and said he wanted to meet the next morning with the team Weaver had put together. Weaver suggested late morning, knowing the likely condition of the others after a night of hard partying. Huntsman insisted on an early start. The group arrived at Huntsman's home in the Kalorama neighborhood in Northwest Washington with various degrees of hangovers. "From 7:30 a.m. onward, it was back-to-back-to-back-to-back meetings, all at his request," Weaver said.

Huntsman was ill-suited to seek the nomination of the Republican Party as it was constituted after the 2010 elections. In Utah he was a fiscal conservative but a moderate in other areas. He had looked favorably on the need to combat global climate change. He supported civil unions for gay couples. Once out of the Obama Foreign Service corps, he took issue with the war in Afghanistan, saying he would bring U.S. forces home as quickly as possible. Stylistically, he lacked the hard edge that some activists on the right expected of their presidential candidates. Long after he had dropped out of the race, he talked with me about the political culture shock he experienced when he returned from China and joined the Republican race. "You come back to the anger and the vitriol," he said. "How you could talk of a president, of any party, as they were President Obama? I just couldn't get my head around that." I asked whether he found the country changed during his time away. "Very much so," he said. "The party structurally was different. It was siloed in different ideological areas. The Tea Party of course had blossomed, and that was a driving sort of vanguard force. The vitriol toward the president, the venom, was something that I had never experienced before, and I had worked for Ronald Reagan as a young guy as an advance man. He was a gentleman, he believed that politics ought to have certain standards for decorum and respect. And what I was hearing just was not out of my world politically. The anger, the town hall meetings with people throwing punches and shouting down politicians."

Huntsman believed this was destructive to the Republican Party. "I came from the Republican Party of ideas," he said. "You think about solutions, you put 'em forward, you fight for them based upon our Republican ideals—that don't include, by the way, hating the other guy, but teeing up something that's bold, courageous, and optimistic. So that's the party I came out of. And when you hit head-on with the reality that you don't just put ideas forward, you rip the guts out of the other guy, you rip him down, you cut him to shreds, you eviscerate him—that wasn't my style. People could say you've got to be that angry, you've got to rip the president. I just worked for him, for heaven's sake. I was his envoy to China. He's a decent man. I can't do that. And even if I did, it would come across as disingenuous. I'm not going to play that game."

Huntsman proved to be an indifferent candidate. Fred Davis later said, "I thought he got more and more uncomfortable as things went on." His announcement day was, in Huntsman's own words, "an utter disaster," a logistical nightmare that included credentials with the candidate's first name misspelled. Huntsman and his father, one of the wealthiest and most powerful men in Utah, were livid over the foul-ups. His operation underwent some staff upheaval, including a change in campaign managers. He had a one-state strategy focused on New Hampshire. His first debate, in Ames the week of the Iowa Straw Poll, was so unmemorable that David Axelrod summed it up with a devastating review: "Smaller than life," he said. At that debate, Huntsman had joined others on the stage in raising his hand to reject a hypothetical deficit reduction deal that would include one dollar in new taxes for every ten dollars in spending cuts. "It was a knee-jerk response to the environment I found myself in," he said. Huntsman said he had two choices: turn his back on a record of not raising taxes as governor by saying yes to such a deal, or respond with what he thought was an absurd answer to an absurd hypothetical question by saying no, along with everyone else onstage. "And it's something I regretted after, because the Republican Party I grew up in was always after solutions. It wasn't after dogmatic approaches where you're ultimately willing to walk the plank if you don't get your way."

Huntsman said he had a revelation onstage that night in Ames as he watched Michele Bachmann tangle with Tim Pawlenty, which was how underwhelming the field of candidates was. "What went through my head—and I hope this doesn't sound egotistical—what went through my head was in this country of 315 million people, Nobel Prize winners, university presidents, CEOs, creative class leaders, innovators, great people, this is what we get to run for president? This is it? How come we've got this? They're all good people, but they're not the best that this country has to offer. I thought, during a time of great need, you know, unlike any other time since maybe 1860, this is what we get?" At that August debate, Huntsman still had hopes of making a mark in the race. By the time the campaign reached New Hampshire, he was running on fumes.

———

When Romney landed in New Hampshire the day after Iowa, he had a celebrity in tow: his old rival John McCain. They were the oddest of odd couples. Romney was buttoned up and buttoned down, a by-the-numbers manager who was driven by data, logic, and hardheadedness. John McCain was a freewheeling and unpredictable warrior, a visceral politician who relied on his gut and his instincts to make his way. At this very moment four years earlier, the two had been sworn enemies, dueling in a nasty New Hampshire primary campaign. On this Wednesday in January 2012, they found political communion on a stage in the Granite State. It is what happens to politicians. After his victory over Romney in Iowa in 2008, Mike Huckabee handed off to McCain the responsibility of blocking Romney's path to the Republican nomination with an exhortation that has been etched into the political history books. "Now it's your turn to kick his butt," Huckabee said to McCain that night. McCain obliged. Now McCain was there to give Romney a pat on the back rather than a kick in the rear.

McCain's embrace of Romney also was a slap at Huntsman, who had been a McCain supporter in 2008. Huntsman complained to his onetime ally: "I took a huge hit by supporting him. Support Romney, that's fine. That's okay. But two or three days before the primary when you knew he was going to win anyway? You've got another guy who bled for you and just cut him a little slack. Give him three days for heaven's sake and then support Romney. And I basically just said, 'You know, I gave a lot to you. We sacrificed a great deal in support of your cause, and I would have expected that maybe you would have been willing to show us a little bit of decency in the final stretch.'" McCain did not respond until some weeks later.

New Hampshire has been the scene of great political battles over the years. In the 1980 Republican primary, Ronald Reagan took over the Nashua debate as he fought back after a loss in Iowa. In 1984, Democrat Gary Hart came from out of nowhere in the final days of the primary to upset the heavily favored Walter Mondale. In 1992, Bill Clinton was almost knocked out of the presidential race because of controversies over his relationship with Gennifer Flowers and the military draft and pronounced himself the "Comeback Kid" after finishing second. In 2000, John McCain demolished the GOP front-runner, George W. Bush, by nineteen points in one of the biggest upsets in New Hampshire history. The Republican campaign in New Hampshire in 2012 had none of the suspense, none of the drama, and ultimately none of the significance of some of those memorable earlier contests. New Hampshire was Mitt Romney's state from start to finish, and his rivals never measured up.

The two non-Romney candidates who had dominated the final weeks in Iowa—Santorum and Gingrich—were virtual nonplayers in New Hampshire. Santorum fell into the same trap that snared Huckabee four years earlier. The victory in Iowa made him want to compete in New Hampshire, but he had no money and little infrastructure. He drew big crowds but had nothing behind them. Gingrich, after his fourth-place finish in Iowa, was considered dead politically—for the second time in the campaign. He had only one asset in New Hampshire, the endorsement of the *Union Leader* newspaper, but little else. That left as Romney's principal competitors Ron Paul and Jon Huntsman. Neither looked formidable. Paul had finished third in Iowa and had a solid base in New Hampshire, where his libertarian philosophy was attractive to the small-government, socially moderate, live-free-or-die segment of the New Hampshire electorate. As in Iowa, Paul's support was a shield for Romney. Huntsman was counting on strong support from independents; Paul was taking some of those from him.

On the weekend before the primary, the candidates faced an overnight debate doubleheader. The first was on the night of Saturday, January 7, at Saint Anselm College, sponsored by ABC News and WMUR-TV. Romney easily survived the test. The second was the next morning in Concord, hosted by NBC's *Meet the Press*. David Gregory opened by saying, "Candidates, good morning. I just want to say, on behalf of all Americans, that I thank you for being willing to debate each other every ten hours, whether you feel you need it or not." Romney was not at his best that morning, forced to defend his record both at Bain and as governor of Massachusetts. Santorum asked why, if his record in Massachusetts had been so good, he did not seek reelection. "I went to Massachusetts to make a difference," Romney said. "I didn't go there to begin a political career, running time and time again. I made a difference. I put in place the things I wanted to do. I listed out the accomplishments we wanted to pursue in our administration. There were a hundred things we wanted to do. Those things I pursued aggressively. Some we won; some we didn't. Run again? That would be about me. I was trying to help get the state into the best shape as I possibly could, left the world of politics, went back into business. Now I have the opportunity, I believe, to use the experience I have . . ." He paused and looked at Santorum.

"You've got a surprised look on your face," he said. Santorum asked pointedly, "Are you going to tell people you're not going to run for reelection for president if you win?" Romney continued to try to play the nonpolitician. "What I'm going to tell you is, this—this for me, politics is not a career." Gingrich had little respect for Romney by now and was incredulous as he listened. "Can we drop a little bit of the pious baloney?" he said to Romney. "The fact is, you ran in '94 and lost. That's why you weren't serving in the Senate with Rick Santorum. The fact is, you had a very bad reelection rating. You dropped out of office. You had been out of state for something like two hundred days preparing to run for president. You didn't have this interlude of citizenship while you thought about what you do. You were running for president while you were governor. You were going all over the country. You were out of state consistently. You then promptly reentered politics. You happened to lose to McCain as you had lost to Kennedy. Now you're back running. You have been running consistently for years and years and years. So this idea that suddenly citizenship showed up in your mind—just level with the American people." Gingrich's withering putdown struck directly at one of Romney's biggest vulnerabilities, his political authenticity.

There were other bad moments for Romney in the hours before the primary, including when he said at a rally, "I like being able to fire people who provide services to me." In full context, the quotation was hardly as damaging as it was in the often-tweeted slam that became the talk of the day. The abbreviated version seemed to play into all of the questionable aspects of Romney's political persona—the wealthy and insensitive business executive who was out of touch with the lives of real people. But with the lead Romney had built up through months and months of political work in the state, nothing like that was going to prevent him from winning.

When the returns came in on the night of January 10, Romney posted an easy victory, winning 39 percent of the vote. Paul finished second with 23 percent, and Huntsman was a weak third with 17 percent, though he called it "a ticket to ride" to South Carolina. Santorum and Gingrich got just 9 percent each. Romney had lapped the two of them and turned south without an obvious rival for the nomination.

CHAPTER 15

The Gingrich Resurrection

South Carolina had produced classic campaigns over the years, most notably the brutally negative face-off between George W. Bush and John McCain in 2000 that left the Arizona senator bitter for years. But South Carolina had never seen anything quite like the events that were beginning to take shape in the days after New Hampshire. The eleven-day clash highlighted all the new forces that were altering the dynamics of the nomination contest, from the power of super PACs to the centrality of the debates to the sharp swings in conventional wisdom to the volatility of the conservative electorate. If people thought Romney was on a glide path to the nomination, South Carolina would remind them that the Republican Party was far from a consensus about its nominee.

Buried in Iowa by Mitt Romney's super PAC and relegated to also-ran status in New Hampshire, Newt Gingrich should have been in no shape to mount another comeback in South Carolina. By any standard assessment, he was now out of the race. But nothing about the Republican nomination battle was either predictable or, apparently, normal. Still, if there was an early state where Romney's profile created a barrier to success even more than in Iowa, it was South Carolina. The electorate was everything that Romney was not: southern, very conservative, and evangelical. But after Iowa and New Hampshire, these vulnerabilities were too easily overlooked, including by some members of the team in Boston. They too were caught up in the moment. Neil Newhouse explained the atmosphere inside the campaign. "Everybody's confidence is up," he said. "Everybody is thinking, 'You know what, we could do this, we could sweep this and we could come through and win South Carolina.' If you win South Carolina, we know we've got an organization in Florida, we know we can do that, that's what we've been ready for. South Carolina is like this added bonus in here, and so we got a little heady."

The first significant boost for Gingrich came as the New Hampshire campaign was nearing its conclusion. Sheldon Adelson, a billionaire casino operator, announced that he would contribute $5 million to Winning Our Future, the super PAC supporting the former Speaker. In Iowa, Romney's super PAC, Restore Our Future, had demonstrated how a well-funded committee could virtually eliminate an opponent by deploying overwhelming resources. In South Carolina, Republicans would learn how one billionaire contributor to a super PAC could help keep an otherwise sinking candidate afloat.

Adelson had given generously to conservative causes over the years but rarely had he taken such a high-profile role. In the 1990s he had sought Gingrich's help in battling labor unions in Nevada. Through that association the two had become friends, and Adelson and his wife subsequently had contributed millions to Gingrich's American Solutions enterprise. Adelson and Gingrich also shared a deep commitment to Israel and its prime minister, Benjamin Netanyahu. When the $5 million contribution became public, Gingrich clearly welcomed it. "If he wants to counterbalance Romney's millionaires, I have no objection to him counterbalancing Romney's millionaires," he said. Adelson's contribution to Gingrich's super PAC began to narrow the advertising gap that had marked the campaign in Iowa, where Romney's super PAC had spent about $3 million on ads, compared to a little over $250,000 by Gingrich's PAC. Thanks to Adelson, spending by the two super PACs in South Carolina was far less lopsided. Romney's spent about $2.5 million, with almost all of it used for negative ads; Gingrich's spent about $1.5 million.

In the final hours before the New Hampshire primary, Gingrich, Perry, and Huntsman all had attacked Romney over the work of Bain Capital. Perry had described Bain's style as "vulture capitalism." Gingrich, on NBC's *Today Show,* said, "I've run four small businesses in the last decade. It gets tough out there. It doesn't always work. I get that. But if somebody comes in, takes all the money out of your company, and then leaves you bankrupt while they go off with millions, that's not traditional capitalism." With Adelson's cash infusion, Winning Our Future took a calculated risk, pouring its money into ads airing portions of a documentary called "King of Bain," an all-out attack on Romney's private equity firm. Gingrich's super PAC also bought the twenty-seven-minute film and put it up on its Web site. "King of Bain" told the darker side of the private equity experience, describing the buying, downsizing, and subsequent selling off of companies or their subsidiaries, often resulting in workers being laid off and pensions and health benefits reduced or eliminated while the partners at Bain walked away with huge profits. The film made Romney look like a rapacious corporate raider, the opposite of the job-creating success story he wanted to tell about his business record. The documentary focused on four case studies and had all the familiar techniques of negative advertising—the ominous voice of the narrator, tales of suffering by real and sometimes tearful people, photos of Romney and his partners looking as greedy as they could be. News organizations gave it negative reviews for truthfulness. Romney called it "probably the biggest hoax since Bigfoot." The *New Yorker*'s Steve Coll wrote that while it was likely not the worst piece of political demagoguery that would air during the election, it was, "like most political speech and argument in the Super PAC era . . . a narrative of noise and emotional manipulation, intercut with jagged shards of truth."

Everyone assumed that Winning Our Future was doing the work that Gingrich wanted done by attacking Romney and Bain Capital. Other Republicans jumped to Romney's defense, accusing Gingrich and his super PAC of doing the Democrats' dirty work. Romney's campaign accused Gingrich and his ally of attacking capitalism and the free enterprise system. But Bain was now seeping into the political bloodstream in a way it had not been—just as the Obama team was hoping.

The Republican candidates were scheduled to debate in Myrtle Beach on Monday, January 16. That morning Huntsman surrendered to the obvious. In some polls he trailed all other candidates, including comedian Stephen Colbert, a South Carolina native who had created a super PAC to draw attention to and parody the influence of super PACs. With his wife and four of his daughters joining him at the lectern and his father and other relatives standing at the side of the room, Huntsman announced that he was withdrawing from the campaign. Disillusioned by his experience, he denounced what he called a "toxic" political process. "This race has degenerated into an onslaught of negative and personal attacks not worthy of the American people and not worthy of this critical time in American history," he said. He called on all the candidates to cease their attacks on one another. He told me later, "I saw the writing on the wall that [Romney] was going to be the nominee and I thought, 'Will I let the pain continue?'" Huntsman announced his endorsement of Romney and then disappeared.

That night, the once unwieldy field of candidates was now reduced to five: Romney, Gingrich, Santorum, Perry, and Paul. Thousands of revved-up Republicans, primed for a confrontation, packed the Myrtle Beach Convention Center. Bain provided the first fireworks. Fox News anchor Bret Baier cited a *Wall Street Journal* editorial that had called Gingrich's attacks crude and embarrassing and invited the former Speaker to defend them. Gingrich said that many of the questions he was raising had come straight out of articles in the *Journal*. "The governor has every opportunity to answer those questions, to give us facts and data," he said. It was better for Republicans to know the answers now, he said, rather than have Bain become a debilitating problem in a general election. Romney tried to put the best light on Bain's work. "Every time we invested, we tried to grow an enterprise, add jobs to make it more successful," he said. "And I know that people are going to come after me. I know President Obama is going to come after me. But the record is pretty darn good."

Everyone assumed Gingrich was following a well-planned strategy on Bain. He told me weeks later that it wasn't, that he got drawn into it because of his super PAC's attacks. "You couldn't back off of it when you had twenty-seven minutes of advertising running," he said. "You either had to be with your team or you had to indicate weakness." Inside his campaign, advisers were trying to persuade him to stop talking about Bain. "It was one of those issues that Newt responded to," said Patrick Millsaps, a Georgia lawyer who later became campaign chief of staff. "But if it had been up to us it was not an issue we would have chosen to lead with." Robert Walker, a former Pennsylvania congressman who was one of Gingrich's chief lieutenants in the House and who had been brought into the campaign just before Iowa as national chairman, said, "There was no doubt that the Romney stuff had gotten in his head. He was really viscerally angry with what Romney was doing to him and he thought this was payback. . . . There were a number of us who kept saying to him, 'But Newt, that isn't the message that any of the voters in these polls are saying is important to them.'" David Winston conducted a poll in South Carolina that showed Bain hurting Gingrich with Republican voters. "It showed we had a problem and it showed that this dynamic was clearly not working and the other things he was saying could work," Winston said.

But it wasn't Bain that made the Myrtle Beach debate memorable. The debate ultimately turned on one exchange, and with it the whole South Carolina campaign suddenly shifted dramatically. On the campaign trail, Gingrich had been routinely calling Obama a "food stamp president" and saying that African Americans should demand jobs, not food stamps, from Washington. He also had sparked controversy by contending that poor children lacked a work ethic. He said schoolchildren should work helping to clean their schools—acting in essence as janitors—to learn work habits and earn some money. Fox's Juan Williams confronted him with those comments. "Can't you see that this is viewed, at a minimum, as insulting to all Americans, but particularly to black Americans?" he asked. "No," Gingrich replied, "I don't see that." He said the schoolchildren would benefit by earning the money and doing the work, "which is a good thing if you're poor. Only the elites despise earning money." The audience began to applaud as Williams persisted. "It sounds as if you are seeking to belittle people," he said. Now the audience was booing Williams. Gingrich, who had mastered the putdown of debate moderators, seized the opportunity. "First of all, Juan," he said, "the fact is that more people have been put on food stamps by Barack Obama than any president in American history." The audience applauded again. "Now, I know among the politically correct, you're not supposed to use facts that are uncomfortable." This brought more laughter and applause. "Second, you're the one who earlier raised a key point. The area that ought to be I-73 [in South Carolina] was called by Barack Obama a corridor of shame because of unemployment. Has it improved in three years? No. They haven't built the road. They haven't helped the people. They haven't done anything." Gingrich was out of time, but Baier let him continue. "I believe every American of every background has been endowed by their creator with the right to pursue happiness," he said. "And if that makes liberals unhappy, I'm going to continue to find ways to help poor people learn how to get a job, learn how to get a better job, and learn someday to own the job." As the television screens dissolved for a commercial break, the audience was giving Gingrich a standing ovation, applauding and cheering wildly. Gingrich said he could feel the applause roll toward him "like the wave of an ocean."

The audience's reaction to the exchange captured the pent-up anger of the party's base. Conservatives wanted a nominee who would go after the president and the liberal elites, and in Gingrich they saw someone doing it. In Boston, Romney's advisers saw an overnight shift in the race. Romney had entered the Myrtle Beach debate with a ten-point lead over Gingrich. A day later, when Newhouse got back the results of his latest survey, the two were in a statistical tie. The race had turned from one with Romney up 32 to 17 percent to a contest that had Gingrich at 23 percent and Romney at 21 percent. "I've never seen numbers like that," Newhouse said. "You just don't see that kind of volatility. You just don't. What it demonstrated is people just weren't anchored and they're paying attention to this stuff."

The morning after the debate, Romney, Gingrich, and Perry all campaigned in Florence. Romney's rally at the convention center drew a sparse crowd that filled only a fraction of the large room—a clear sign of flagging enthusiasm. The front-runner's campaign appeared to be floundering. He had been under fire for weeks for not releasing his tax returns, and his opponents had stepped up criticism. What was this rich man hiding? The issue was a growing topic of debate inside the campaign, but Romney continued to resist. He was hoping to keep the issue at bay until tax time in April, when he assumed he would be safely through the early primaries and on his way to locking down the nomination. Romney's income came mainly from capital gains on the investments in his personal fortune. After the rally he took question from reporters. Time's Mark Halperin asked Romney to estimate his effective tax rate. Romney said it was "probably closer to 15 percent than anything." The figure was far below that of the average taxpayer. Romney told reporters that he also had received speaker's fees but said the amount was "not very much." In truth, he had earned $374,000 from speeches in the previous year—small change to a man who was earning millions on a fortune estimated at more than $200 million, but another example of a candidate totally out of touch with the perceptions of ordinary Americans.

After Gingrich left Florence, Rick Perry arrived. His campaign had lost all its purpose by now, and as a result Perry seemed liberated—more comfortable than at any time since the opening days in August. He ambled into the Drive In restaurant wearing a blue fleece with a Perry campaign logo. He moved from table to table, shaking hands and posing for pictures. He ordered a beef gyro and onion rings for lunch and paid with a $20 bill he pulled from his wallet. Then he plopped down at a corner table with a local couple and two children. He fiddled with his BlackBerry as he chatted. Reporters elbowed one another to catch snippets of the conversation, and photographers pressed up against the windows from outside to shoot photos. When he finished eating, he took questions. Asked about Romney's taxes, Perry said, "Release it all. Not the front page—release all of your income tax, and then the people of America can do the calculations I think rather speedily and figure out what it is and make appropriate conclusions." Told that Gingrich had said that morning that a vote for Perry or Santorum was a vote for Romney, he replied, "That's the reason we have contests. That's the reason we have Super Bowls. That's the reason we have competitions. We'll let the people of South Carolina make that decision."

The next day, Gingrich campaigned at Bobby's Bar-B-Q in Warrenville. When he arrived the parking lot was filled to overflowing. Supporters and spectators packed the banquet room where he spoke, spilling onto the veranda and the parking lot. A new public poll showed Romney still leading Gingrich in the state, but the margin had been cut in half. Gingrich suspected the race was even closer. "I think they have internal polls that show them losing," he said. When a woman in the audience said, "I want to thank you, Mr. Speaker, for putting Mr. Juan Williams in his place," the room erupted with applause.

All of this became the backdrop for the most kaleidoscopic day of the primary—and almost everything that happened that day seemed to further erode Romney's standing. Thursday, January 19, was a day of split-screen viewing and almost hourly recalibration of conventional wisdom. At the beginning of the week, the Republican nomination battle appeared almost as if it were on autopilot, with Romney cruising toward eventual victory. Suddenly the candidates were hurtling toward a Saturday primary now just two days away and Romney was fighting to avoid a potentially costly and unexpected defeat at the hands of the twice-dead Gingrich. South Carolina's reputation for memorable and intensely fought primary campaigns remained intact.

The first news broke while most people were still asleep. Overnight, the *Des Moines Register* posted a report that the Iowa Republican Party had completed a recount of the caucuses and Santorum was now thirty-four votes ahead of Romney. Iowa GOP officials had been struggling since caucus night to determine the actual vote count, and rumors had been circulating for days that Romney's victory was in jeopardy. Just after 9 a.m., the party released its official results, though its statement was ambiguous enough that chairman Matt Strawn had to come forward a few hours later to say definitely that Santorum was the undisputed winner. Santorum had won, but victory seemed to have come too late to make any difference for the former senator, who was gasping for attention at a moment when the nomination contest was seen as a two-person race between Gingrich and Romney.

Meanwhile, another potential blockbuster was unfolding. The *Drudge Report* had posted an item the day before noting that ABC News had secured an interview with Marianne Gingrich, the candidate's second of three wives. Gingrich's personal life was part of the baggage he carried as a candidate. On Thursday morning, Ann Curry of *The Today Show* interviewed Gingrich. "Back in 1995, your ex-wife Marianne told *Vanity Fair* she could derail your campaign with one TV interview," she said. "Tonight she is giving that interview. Is there anything she could say, Newt Gingrich, that could end your campaign?" Gingrich responded, "I'm not going to say anything negative about Marianne. My two daughters, Kathy and Jackie, have sent a letter to the president of ABC News, saying from a family perspective, they think this is totally wrong. . . . People will have to judge me. I'm a sixty-eight-year-old grandfather. See how close I am to my wife, Callista, and how close I am to my daughters and son-in-laws, my two grandchildren. They'll have to make their mind up. But sixteen- and twenty-year-old stories—we have real stories this week on the failure of the Obama administration." Three and a half hours later, ABC's Brian Ross tweeted a link to the most explosive portion of the interview, in which Marianne claimed Gingrich had sought an open marriage. "He said, 'Callista doesn't care what I do,'" Marianne said in the interview. "He wanted an open marriage and I refused."

With fevered speculation about what the ABC interview would do to Gingrich's candidacy, the third big development of the day broke: Perry had decided to end his campaign and endorse Gingrich. Though Perry had little support by then, the symbolic significance of his decision was huge. Reporters quickly descended on the Hyatt Place Hotel in Charleston for Perry's 11 a.m.

announcement. "As I have contemplated the future of this campaign, I have come to the conclusion that there is no viable path to victory for my candidacy in 2012," he said. "Therefore today I am suspending my campaign and endorsing Newt Gingrich for president of the United States. I believe Newt is a conservative visionary who can transform this country. We have had our differences, which campaigns inevitably bring out." Alluding to Gingrich's multiple marriages and the breaking news about Marianne's interview, he added, "And Newt is not perfect, but who among us is? The fact is, there is forgiveness for those who seek God, and I believe in the power of redemption, for it is a central tenet of my own Christian faith."

Perry had come to South Carolina thinking there was still a chance of catching fire. He had seen others rebound after setbacks, notably Gingrich in November. He told spokesman Ray Sullivan the day after the Iowa caucuses that his campaign still had money and he had enough fire left to keep going. "I don't want to wake up five years from now and wonder what if I'd have stayed in," Sullivan said Perry told him. By Wednesday of primary week in South Carolina, Perry saw the futility of continuing. He was out of money and faced another humiliating defeat that could further damage his political reputation. His wife, Anita, agreed. When he told his staff he was pulling out, no one tried to dissuade him. The only thing in question was whether he would endorse Gingrich or remain neutral. An argument was made to stay neutral and see how the race unfolded. Perry came to another conclusion. "I can read polls," he later told me, "and to maintain the race any farther wasn't in my best interest, wasn't in Newt's best interest. And I wanted Newt to be the nominee."

That night in Charleston, the remaining candidates met for the second debate in four days. It took only the opening minutes for a winner to be declared. CNN's John King began with a question for Gingrich about his ex-wife's charges. "Would you like to take time to respond to that?" King asked calmly. "No," Gingrich said. He hesitated for a split second, as if he were going to avoid the whole controversy, but then said, "But I will." With even more righteous anger than he had summoned to put down Juan Williams three nights earlier, Gingrich erupted. "I think the destructive, vicious negative nature of much of the news media makes it harder to govern this country, harder to attract decent people to run for public office," he said. "I'm appalled you would begin a presidential debate on a topic like that." The audience was applauding now as King interjected, "Is that all you want to say, sir?" Gingrich wasn't even close to done. "Every person in here knows personal pain," he said. "Every person in here has had someone close to them go through painful things. To take an ex-wife and make it, two days before the primary, a significant question in a presidential campaign, is as close to despicable as anything I can imagine." As the audience cheered, he added, "My two daughters wrote the head of ABC and made the point that it was wrong, that they should pull it, and I am, frankly, astounded that CNN would take trash like that and use it to open a presidential debate. . . . Now, let me be quite clear: The story is false. Every personal friend I have who knew us in that period says the story was false. We offered several of them to ABC to prove it was false. They weren't interested because they would like to attack any Republican."*

I asked Gingrich later whether he had prepared the response with his advisers before the debate. He said, "Several of my highly shrewd advisers said to me, 'He will lull you to relax and then about two-thirds of the way through the debate he'll ask you.' And I said back, 'No. This involves sex and scandal. He [King] will open with it because he won't be able to help himself.' I hadn't totally thought through how I was going to do it, but I wasn't surprised by it. And I mean, one of the virtues again of being a jazz musician is you eventually get pretty good timing with the audience. And so I came back and said, 'No'—and the audience began to applaud—'but I will.' And if you watch, there's a pause. I didn't expect the intensity of the response, and then, of course, he decided to stick with it, which gave me a second bite at the apple. But the way he came back and said, 'Oh, well, you know they raised it so it's not my fault'—[that] was just too big an opening."

The debate was notable in two other respects. First, Santorum ripped into Gingrich. "I served with him," Santorum said. "I was there. I knew what the problems were going on in the House of Representatives when Newt Gingrich was leading there. It was an idea a minute, no discipline, no ability to be able to pull things together." Santorum then accused Gingrich of not standing up to the Democrats over the check kiting scandal in the early 1990s and said his own work in exposing it had "more or as much to do with the 1994 win as any plan that you put together." Gingrich, who had been the nemesis of the Democrats in the 1980s and helped bring down Jim Wright as Speaker of the House, was outraged by Santorum's putdown. "Each of us writes a selective history that fits our interest," he said as he recounted his many battles with the Democrats. "Those are just historic facts, even if they're inconvenient for Rick's campaign." Santorum was asked to respond to Gingrich's criticism that he lacked the imagination or know-how for something as significant as a presidential campaign. "Grandiosity has never been a problem with Newt Gingrich," he said. Gingrich took that as a compliment. "You're right. I think grandiose thoughts. This is a

---

*A week later, a Gingrich spokesman admitted that the candidate's claim had been false. The campaign had offered only his two daughters to rebut Marianne Gingrich's allegations, not several other people as Gingrich had said.

grandiose country of big people doing big things. And we need leadership prepared to take on big projects."

Romney meanwhile continued to flounder on the issue of releasing his tax returns. "I'll release my returns in April and probably for other years as well. I know that's what's going to come." He said Democrats were trying to demonize success. "I have been successful. But let me tell you, the challenge in America is not people who've been successful. The challenge in America, and President Obama doesn't want to talk about this, is you've got a president who's played ninety rounds of golf while there are twenty-five million Americans out of work, and while the price of gasoline has doubled, he said no to the Keystone pipeline. . . . That's the problem in America, not the attacks they make on people who've been successful." Gingrich, who had posted his returns on his campaign Web site during the debate, put the onus back on Romney: "He's got to decide and the people of South Carolina have to decide. But if there's anything in there that is going to help us lose the election, we should know it before the nomination. And if there's nothing in there, why not release it?"

The next morning, I called an unaligned South Carolina Republican strategist and a Romney adviser for perspective on the week's developments. The strategist said he saw no way Gingrich would lose the primary the following day. He was scathing in his assessment of Romney and the campaign's performance in the state. "I don't know how in the world they can continually flub [the tax issue]," he said. "Both candidate and campaign have done a terrible job." If Gingrich won on Saturday, he said, "Florida is what people thought it would be, an all-out brawl." The glum Romney adviser was critical about the campaign's reluctance to deal with the tax issue. "I would feel a lot better if we'd turned loose some tax returns a couple days ago," he said. "Sometimes I don't understand why the obvious isn't obvious to everybody."

Gingrich campaigned with growing confidence. At a boisterous rally in Orangeburg, he again exhorted conservatives to rally behind him. "The only effective conservative vote to stop the Massachusetts moderate is to vote for me," he said. As he walked away from the microphone, he was asked about Romney's failure to commit to any of the debates scheduled in Florida the next week. "Romney can't claim that he's prepared to debate Obama if he's not prepared to debate Newt Gingrich," he said. Romney, bleeding in South Carolina and nationally, sought to lower expectations. "I said from the very beginning South Carolina is an uphill battle for a guy from Massachusetts," he said after a rain-soaked event in Gilbert. That night in Greenville, in a preview of what was coming, he turned fiery on the stump. It was the first time all week he had shown any life or fight.

On primary day, the candidates held dueling events at Tommy's Country Ham House and then retreated to their hotels to await results. Romney and his wife, Ann, were at the Marriott in downtown Columbia. That afternoon, the *Post*'s Phil Rucker found Romney in the hotel laundry room, feeding quarters into one of the laundry machines. Ann was keeping him company in the tiny room. Romney was fretting about a sock that had slipped between the machines while praising the quality of Brooks Brothers non-iron shirts. Later, as he rode up the elevator with a bag of clean clothes, he foreshadowed the evening's outcome. "We're on to Florida and Nevada," he said. "And where else?"

Saturday night brought a thumping defeat for Romney and a huge victory for Gingrich. The former Speaker captured 40 percent of the vote to just 28 percent for Romney. Santorum ran third with 17 percent. Gingrich, greeted with chants of "Newt can win" from supporters, said his victory was the result of "something very fundamental that I wish the powers that be in the news media will take seriously: The American people feel that they have elites who have been trying for a half-century to force us to quit being American and become some kind of other system." He said, "We don't have the kind of money that at least one of the candidates has, but we do have ideas, and we do have people, and we proved here in South Carolina that people power with the right ideas beats big money." And to the delight of the audience, he went after Obama, the former community organizer on Chicago's South Side. "The centerpiece of this campaign, I believe, is American exceptionalism versus the radicalism of Saul Alinsky," Gingrich said. Romney told his supporters to prepare for a long and difficult fight for the nomination. "I don't shrink from competition, I embrace it," he said.

Gingrich said that night he called Vin Weber, the former Minnesota congressman and a longtime friend and ally during their days in the House. Weber had started the campaign supporting Tim Pawlenty but was now backing Romney. It was the second time he had reached out to Weber. "I called Weber when we were in South Carolina in December," he later told me. "And I said to him, 'These polls mean that I will beat Romney in a positive campaign, and Romney will be told by his guys that he has to destroy me. And I just want you to understand if he does that then there'll be no holds barred.' He said, 'I understand and I will try to communicate.'" Weber remembered that conversation: "He wanted me to convey to the campaign that if they went over the line—and there's no clear definition of what that meant—that he would do significant damage to Romney. I think that's what you saw in Bain. In a calmer environment, Newt Gingrich would have had no problem with Bain Capital. But at that point he was in a mode of creating issues that would hurt Romney. It was a revenge thing on his part." In his call on the night of his

South Carolina victory, Gingrich said he told Weber, "This means they're going to be very tempted to be even worse in Florida. And I just want you to understand I am the best counterpuncher in the modern Republican Party." Weber said he did not remember that call.

Romney had arrived in South Carolina the winner of the first two contests on the primary-caucus calendar, the leader in the polls and positioned to take command of the nomination battle. He was preparing to leave having lost two of the first three contests, now facing a still flawed but rejuvenated opponent in Gingrich and with renewed doubts about his capacity to rally his party behind him.

CHAPTER 16

The Empire Strikes Back

The night after his defeat in South Carolina, Mitt Romney launched an aggressive new attack—the toughest of the campaign—on Newt Gingrich. He landed in Jacksonville and his entourage rolled south to Ormond Beach for an outdoor rally. His rhetoric was harsh and personal. *Politico*'s Reid Epstein said it was as if Romney were reading Gingrich's résumé from a Wikipedia entry and "undercutting each item as he got to it." Romney said the country was electing a leader, not a talk show host. "Speaker Gingrich has also been a leader," he said. "He was a leader for four years as Speaker of the House. And at the end of four years, it was proven that he was a failed leader and he had to resign in disgrace." He said that after leaving Congress, Gingrich had spent fifteen years working as a lobbyist "selling influence" in Washington. In a state whose economy had been hard hit by housing foreclosures, he reprised an attack from earlier in the campaign by noting that Gingrich had worked as a consultant to Freddie Mac, and demanded that Gingrich reveal more of what he had done for the housing agency.

The attacks marked a new phase in the Republican campaign, the result of a week of intense planning by Romney's Boston-based campaign team. Romney's advisers had seen the drubbing in South Carolina coming and began to shift their strategy accordingly. "By the first debate [in Myrtle Beach], it's game over," Matt Rhoades later told me. "I'm not even thinking about South Carolina anymore except for any cleanup duty. We're working on tax returns. I'm working on making sure we have the best kickass events and message strategy and we have all the resources we need to go on TV going into Florida, while we're in South Carolina." When Gingrich blasted John King in the second debate, the Boston team was barely paying attention to South Carolina. Neil Newhouse said, "By the time we got to that point, we knew South Carolina was gone and we had already changed internally. By the time Saturday came, our mourning was over and we were focused on Florida. We didn't even watch the numbers come in on Saturday."

Romney's super PAC had handled the bulk of the advertising attacks on

Gingrich in Iowa and South Carolina. But the Boston team was never fully happy with what the super PAC was doing. Stuart Stevens told the others it was time to shift tactics. His message, according to another member of the team, was: Screw the super PAC. We need to run our own negatives against Newt. We need to start taking the bark off him. Stevens saw Gingrich as an easy target, someone who could not sustain himself in a serious campaign with Romney. "The problem Gingrich has is he's always going to bump up against the idea of what he's saying with who he is," Stevens later told me. "You can't run as an insurgent when you have 'Speaker' in front of your name. You can't run as an anti-Washington guy when you've been there for three and a half decades. You can't run as a closet lobbyist. You can't rage against the machine when you're the machine—against a guy who's never been in Washington."

The team set to work to develop a strategy to take Gingrich down. Advisers began a series of what they called "Kill Newt" meetings. There was a big white-board on the wall of the conference room where the attack strategy began to come together. At the top of the whiteboard was a series of unflattering descriptions: "lobbyist," "undisciplined," "erratic," "opportunist," "arrogant," "unsteady," "what's in it for Newt," "K Street insider," "untrustworthy," "prima donna." Below that were five categories outlining specific lines of attack: "Immig." (for immigration), "Social," "Ethics," "DC Insider," "Conservative." Under "Conservative," the possible attacks included Gingrich's criticisms of on Paul Ryan's Medicare blueprint as right-wing social engineering and his history of supporting more spending. Under "DC Insider" there were three attacks: Freddie Mac, lobbying, and Newt Inc.

Romney's team set out to rattle Gingrich, put him on the defensive, surround him with Romney surrogates as he campaigned in Florida, bombard him on television with attack ads, smother him in the debates and force him, if possible, into mistakes. The Sunday night rally was designed to frame the entire week. "We wanted Mitt to talk about and take it to Obama and focus on jobs and the economy, spending, the issues," Rhoades said. "That just didn't work in South Carolina, not when you've got super PACs dropping on you, not when you've got the press still looking for a fight, not when you have debate moderators serving themselves up on a platter to Newt Gingrich and Newt just cranking it out of the park, to his credit." The Romney team had learned a valuable lesson during South Carolina. "I get lectured all the time during this primary process about Mitt's not being 'big,'" Rhoades said. "We tried it in South Carolina. We got shellacked by Newt Gingrich. So we weren't going to allow that to happen again. And so we went in there, we decided to kick it up a notch on our contrast. The gov, he was just on fire going into Florida."

On the morning after the South Carolina primary, Romney advisers laid out the plan to the candidate in a conference call. It was known as "the path forward" plan, but in reality it was the "Kill Newt" plan. His advisers went through the details department by department. Rhoades offered an overview and turned it over to Gail Gitcho, the campaign's combative communications director. She described what one adviser later called "an entirely negative earned media campaign against Newt." The campaign had lined up a surrogate strike force across the state, with David Kochel flown in from Iowa to manage it on the ground. The plan was to follow Gingrich everywhere he went. "And it was going to be a mind game because we knew that he couldn't handle it," one adviser said. "Our strategy was to go after him with all the earned media* tactics we could employ. We were going to do it nonstop. It was the hardest that we had ever worked, on the entire campaign. We were blowing Newt out over everything. That's what we told Mitt we were going to do."

Romney mostly listened. Okay, he said, let's do it. As the Florida campaign began, Romney was in a tailspin. The campaign's internal polling had shown him leading Gingrich in Florida by 42 to 15 percent before South Carolina. By the night he appeared in Ormond Beach, he was leading by a precarious 37 to 33 percent. Newhouse said he sent an e-mail to others in the campaign that night. It began, "Buckle your chinstraps."

The startling outcome of the South Carolina primary did more than turn the race for the Republican presidential nomination upside down. It also highlighted what by now was the party's yearlong identity crisis in its search for a standard-bearer. If Republican voters seemed confused, it was no wonder. The field of candidates included no one yet who seemed to possess the attributes that could provide a center of gravity to a party still searching for someone to define its post-2010 character. In some respects the contest between Romney and Gingrich had familiar contours: establishment versus insurgents. But neither candidate was the ideal choice to play his assigned role or, more important, to bridge the kinds of internal divisions that had played out in Senate primary contests in 2010. Romney had the breeding and countenance of the establishment, and yet when he first ran for office in 1994 he ran away from Ronald Reagan and the prevailing philosophy and tactics of the Gingrich-led campaign. Gingrich could rightly claim a longer connection to the party's conservative causes, and he embodied the resentment of the grass roots toward the establishments of both parties. He consistently channeled the anger at Obama that had given rise to the Tea Party. But though he had the rhetoric

---

*"Earned media" is a term used by campaign strategists to describe their efforts to produce coverage by the media favorable to their candidates or harmful to their opponents.

of an outsider, he had operated in the corridors of power in Washington for almost three decades, was complicit in some of the actions the Tea Party opposed, and had developed many detractors in his own party.

The two men spoke to contradictory desires within the party. The grass roots yearned for a fighter who could take on Obama in the most strident and confrontational way possible. But other Republicans also knew they needed the steady competence of a leader capable of restraining the worst excesses of the hard-right activists and who could translate conservative rhetoric and ideas into a governing strategy that would appeal beyond the base. At this moment, some of those on the sidelines still seemed better suited to pull the party together. Haley Barbour and Mitch Daniels would have been establishment candidates, yet both had the kind of conservative credentials and credibility that Romney lacked. Chris Christie could be as pugnacious as Gingrich—as rhetorically harsh in attacks on Obama's leadership as anyone. But he would not have been burdened by Gingrich's liabilities. Mike Huckabee could have played the role of populist conservative better than either Romney or Gingrich. No one could at the time say that a Barbour or Daniels or Huckabee or Christie would have done better than any of the existing candidates. But there was no mistaking the feeling that there was still a mismatch between the character and personality of the Republican Party and the people who were seeking to lead it into one of the most important campaigns in years.

Gingrich and Romney had attributes that made them worthy of the coming showdown in Florida. With some exceptions, Romney had been disciplined and patient. He had stumbled in South Carolina over the release of his tax returns, but in other ways he had shown steadiness and intelligence. He was a better candidate than he had been in 2008. Gingrich had shown remarkable resilience throughout the campaign and the spirit that many conservatives were looking for. But it was the other side of the balance sheet that made Republicans nervous about what they might be getting, no matter who they got. Romney lacked real passion in attacking Obama. He was more gentlemanly than many conservatives wanted. He had moved right in the nomination campaign, but many conservatives still didn't trust him. Gingrich had more than enough over-the-top rhetoric to satisfy the base. But he was far from an ideal Tea Party politician. He was not a pure small-government politician. His rivals said his economic and entitlement proposals would blow a big hole in the deficit. And he carried more baggage than the rest of the field combined.

Debates had reshaped the primary in South Carolina. In Florida they did the same—this time to Romney's advantage. On Monday, January 23, the

Republican candidates met in Tampa for their eighteenth debate. There were now four people on the stage—Romney, Gingrich, Santorum, and Paul. But the focus was now only on the two leaders. To prepare for the Florida debates, the Romney campaign had reached out to Brett O'Donnell, previously one of Bachmann's top advisers and the former debate coach at Jerry Falwell's Liberty University. O'Donnell prepared a memo outlining a strategy for attacking Gingrich. Romney was open to the idea but hesitant at first about adopting such an aggressive posture. "He was nervous about executing the strategy, worried that it wasn't the right thing to do," said one person involved in the preparations. "He thought it was very high-risk, that if it backfired people would say, 'Oh, you're the mean guy going after our guy Newt,' or whatever." Russ Schriefer said, "The idea was to prosecute Gingrich on being a Washington insider, having worked for Fannie and Freddie . . . and making sure that when those opportunities presented themselves to take them."

Romney's attacks in Tampa came straight off the whiteboard in Boston. He pursued Gingrich relentlessly. "The Speaker was given an opportunity to be the leader of our party in 1994. And at the end of four years, he had to resign in disgrace," he said. He cited Gingrich's long record in Washington in and out of government and contrasted that with his own record at Bain (which no longer was under attack), the 2002 Winter Olympics, and as governor of Massachusetts. Gingrich accused Romney of spouting falsehoods. Romney seized on the release of Gingrich's contract with Freddie Mac, which showed that he had reported to the agency's chief lobbyist. Gingrich insisted he had not lobbied for the agency, that he was a consultant, but his prior, and laughable, claim that he had been hired because he was a "historian" who could offer strategic guidance on that basis was crumbling. Romney accused Gingrich of being an influence peddler who had lobbied members of Congress in behalf of the Medicare Part D prescription drug benefit that was favored by some of the health care companies that had helped bankroll his American Solutions. "Whoa. Whoa," Gingrich said. "You just jumped a long way over here, friend." Gingrich said he had never lobbied for those companies but acknowledged that he was proud of his support for the new and costly drug benefit.

The atmosphere in the hall that night was totally different from that of the debates in South Carolina. NBC anchor Brian Williams had admonished the audience to be quiet. He said he would not tolerate the kind of cheering and applauding that had occurred in Myrtle Beach and Charleston. Williams's instructions drained from the room the partisan energy that had fueled Gingrich's performances the previous week. The candidates underwent a role reversal. Gingrich was subdued and defensive as Romney went on offense. At one point, faced with a series of attacks, Gingrich said, "I'm not going to spend the evening trying to chase Governor Romney's misinformation." At another point, he said, "Let me be very clear, because I understand your technique, which you used on McCain, you used on Huckabee, you've used consistently, okay? It's unfortunate, and it's not going to work very well, because the American people see through it." Instant analysis gave Romney the victory, though not by a huge margin. But it was clear that there was another momentum shift under way.

There was one other notable moment in the Tampa debate, one that would have lasting consequences for Romney. When the subject of immigration was raised, Adam Smith of the *Tampa Bay Times* asked, "Governor Romney, there is one thing I'm confused about. You say you don't want to go and round up people and deport them, but you also say that they would have to go back to their home countries and then apply for citizenship. So, if you don't deport them, how do you send them home?" Romney replied with a phrase that haunted him to the very end of the general election. "Well, the answer is self-deportation," he said. His response was spontaneous, not something that had been prepared in advance. It came out of Romney's mouth as much to the surprise of his advisers as to everyone else who heard it. Romney went on to say that he would not round up illegal immigrants but that with a stricter system of employer verifications their opportunities for work would dry up. "They're going to find they can't get work here," he said. "And if people don't get work here, they're going to self-deport to a place where they can get work." Romney had given an inelegant description of a process that was already taking place, with many illegal immigrants having returned to their native countries because of the recession that began in 2008. But all anyone would remember was the startling phrase and what people outside his campaign saw as Romney's stubborn resistance to a more humane approach to dealing with the millions of illegal immigrants who were now in the country.

The following day Romney released his 2010 tax returns and an estimate of his 2011 tax liabilities. He said he would release his full 2011 returns when they were completed later in the year, but restated that he would not release returns from prior years, despite the pounding he was taking from the Obama campaign. Still, there was plenty of ammunition for his rivals from the documents he made public. The returns showed that he had income of $21.7 million in 2010 and $20.9 million in 2011, almost all from dividends, interest, and capital gains. He paid an effective rate of 13.9 percent for 2010 and estimated he would pay about 15.4 percent for 2011. The returns highlighted the generosity of the Romneys, who gave away more than $7 million during the two years, most of it to the Mormon Church. The 550 pages of documentation contained more damaging revelations. The Romneys had had a Swiss bank account, which had been closed in 2010. They had had investments in the Cayman Islands, a noted tax haven. The Democratic National Committee produced a Web video asking, "What is Mitt Romney hiding and where is he hiding it?"

The Romney campaign's pummeling of Gingrich carried on nonstop throughout the week. Romney's campaign and his super PAC clogged the airwaves with attacks on Gingrich. The gap between his and Gingrich's spending on advertising ballooned again in Romney's favor. Florida was simply too expensive for Gingrich and his super PAC to keep pace. Romney's campaign had significantly boosted its advertising budget. According to a Republican ad-buying firm, in the final ten days before the primary, the campaign spent almost $4 million on ads in Florida. Gingrich's campaign spent about $1.1 million. Restore Our Future, Romney's super PAC, spent about $6 million in that period to about $5.5 million for Gingrich's PAC. In many markets, Romney was running two, three, or four times as many ads as Gingrich. But the amounts spent in the period after South Carolina hardly measured the totality of Romney's advantage. Romney had been advertising in Florida for weeks. His campaign and super PAC together spent around $15 million in the state over the course of the entire campaign—almost $12 million of it on negative ads. Restore Our Future ran almost twelve thousand ads in the state, and Romney's campaign ran more than nine thousand.

One Romney ad in particular stood out. Neil Newhouse had seen a snippet of a video of the *NBC Nightly News* from the day Gingrich had resigned as Speaker. Tom Brokaw was in the anchor chair at the time. Newhouse asked to see the entire clip. By luck, it ran twenty-seven seconds, perfect for a thirty-second commercial. In his report that night, Brokaw noted that Gingrich, who had once brought down another Speaker on ethics charges, had been "found . . . guilty of ethics violations" by an overwhelming vote of his House colleagues. Newhouse took the segment with him to Florida and showed it to a focus group of voters. Most of the other ads he showed that day did not test well, but the clip of Brokaw drew a strong response. Newhouse came back to Boston and insisted that it be included in the rotation in Florida. NBC and Brokaw protested and asked the campaign to take it down, but Romney's team ignored the request. It worked too well.

On the ground, Gingrich was drawing big crowds, but the Romney surrogates harassed him at every stop. Utah representative Jason Chaffetz, Florida representative Connie Mack, and California representative Mary Bono Mack traveled together much of the week, teaming up for press conferences attacking Gingrich before or after his events. When a frustrated R. C. Hammond, Gingrich's aggressive spokesman, confronted Chaffetz on consecutive days, he managed only to highlight the growing frustrations of his candidate, particularly after an exchange was posted on YouTube. Gingrich's message lost focus. Along Florida's Space Coast, he came up with an exotic idea that seemed to have little to do with the problems voters were confronting. Gingrich pledged that he would establish a permanent moon colony if he were elected president. The grandiose proposal became fodder for a *Saturday Night Live* sketch that portrayed Gingrich as "Moon President." *National Review* featured Gingrich on its cover as Marvin the Martian.

Three nights after the Tampa debate, the candidates squared off in Jacksonville. It turned into a repeat performance of the first debate, though Romney was even more aggressive and Gingrich even more off balance. The former Speaker appeared handcuffed by the harshness of Romney's attacks. After Gingrich defended his proposal for a moon colony, Romney skewered him. "I spent twenty-five years in business," he said. "If I had a business executive come to me and say they wanted to spend a few hundred billion dollars to put a colony on the moon, I'd say, 'You're fired.'" Romney hit Gingrich on Freddie Mac, saying the former Speaker should have protested the policies that he said led to the housing crisis. Gingrich tried to tie Romney to the crisis by noting that Romney had owned stock in both Freddie Mac and Fannie Mae and had profited handsomely by selling some of it. Romney said he had never owned stock in either, that his investments were through mutual funds, and then dropped a surprise on Gingrich that his team had dug out only that afternoon. "And, Mr. Speaker, I know that sounds like an enormous revelation, but have you checked your own investments? You also have investments through mutual funds that also invest in Fannie Mae and Freddie Mac." Gingrich was caught flat-footed. The investment was a minor matter, but one that fed the emerging consensus that Romney had rebounded and Gingrich was reeling.

CNN's Wolf Blitzer tried to get Gingrich to repeat a statement from a campaign rally where he had criticized Romney for his Cayman Islands investments and Swiss bank account. Gingrich said such attacks were fine in interviews but inappropriate at a debate, where, he said, bigger issues should be the topics of discussion. Romney jumped in. "Wouldn't it be nice if people didn't make accusations somewhere else that they weren't willing to defend here?" he said. "Okay. All right," Gingrich said. "Given that standard, Mitt, I did say I thought it was unusual. And I don't know of any American president who has had a Swiss bank account. I'd be glad for you to explain that sort of thing." Romney explained the workings of his blind trust and chided Gingrich to stop attacking his wealth and record of success in business. "It would be nice," Gingrich responded, "if you had the same standard for other people that you would like applied to you and didn't enter into personal attacks about personal activities about which you are factually wrong. So I would be glad to have a truce with you, but it's a two-way truce."

At another point Blitzer asked Gingrich about a Spanish-language radio ad, which the campaign had already pulled down, in which he accused Romney of being "the most anti-immigrant" of the candidates. When Gingrich reaffirmed the characterization, Romney, feigning outrage, responded, "That's inexcusable. And, actually, Senator Marco Rubio [who was neutral at the time] came to my defense and said that ad was inexcusable and inflammatory and inappropriate. Mr. Speaker, I'm not anti-immigrant. My father was born in Mexico. My wife's father was born in Wales. They came to this country. The idea that I'm anti-immigrant is repulsive."

Gingrich knew he was stumbling through the two debates. "I am really good if I'm centered," he told me two weeks later. "I mean, I'm probably as good a debater as there is in the country. If I'm not centered, I'm not any better than anybody else. It was obvious by Monday night [in Tampa] that Romney would attempt to destroy me and would do so—we've now gone from, 'Oh, my super PAC is doing bad things I can't control,' to Romney personally lying, knowing he's lying. I mean making campaign speeches that are lies. In the first debate, I didn't respond to him because I would have gotten so angry that it would have been uncontrollable. And I thought it was better to be passive than to blow up. And it was a conscious decision. In the second one, I was so surprised by his dishonesty, and then suddenly I'm working on the next time we debate, I mean to think through how do you deal with it. Let me give an example. He turns and says, 'I've always voted for a Republican when that opportunity was available.' Well, Larry Sabato tweets within seconds it's not true. Now, in a setting like that where the audience had a fairly large number of Romney supporters, how do you turn to the supposed front-runner for the Republican nomination, former governor and successful businessman, and say, 'You know, you're just a lying sack of shit.' It's just plain not true. And he had two or three other things where he came at me and at the time they all seemed wrong. But I didn't have 'there you go again,' and I couldn't figure out how to cope with it."

Romney wasn't fighting this battle alone. Virtually the entire Republican establishment had joined in the effort to take Gingrich down. Some of the attacks were orchestrated by the Romney campaign. Others occurred spontaneously, spawned by past battles dating back almost two decades between Gingrich and fellow Republicans. From one corner to another, those who had tangled with Gingrich, who felt aggrieved toward Gingrich, or who feared him as their nominee joined to stop him, knowing how much harder it would be to do so if he were to win in Florida. Bob Dole said Gingrich would threaten the election of Republican candidates up and down the ballot. "Hardly anyone who served with Newt in Congress has endorsed him," Dole said in a statement issued through the Romney campaign, "and that speaks for itself. He was a one-man band who rarely took advice. It was his way or the highway."

The establishment message that Gingrich represented a threat to the party was not new, but the intensity with which it was now being delivered certainly was. That he might become the nominee had touched off near panic in the ranks ahead of Tuesday's vote. Party establishments, to the degree they exist, have only limited power to direct the course of events. But to the extent they have power, they were exercising it with a vengeance, ganging upon the Speaker with evident enthusiasm. Former House majority leader Tom DeLay, who had served as House whip under Gingrich, called him erratic. *National Review* attacked him, as did the *American Spectator*. Ann Coulter issued a warning: "Reelect Obama. Vote Newt." In a matter of weeks, what had been talk of whether a stop-Romney movement would materialize on the right became the reality of a stop-Gingrich movement coming from the party establishment.

Some former House colleagues went after Gingrich; others stood by him. The fight for Ronald Reagan's legacy divided old Reaganites. Some derided Gingrich's claim that he was a key lieutenant in the Reagan revolution or his rightful heir, atleast among the GOP candidates. Others still regarded him as the political leader who helped translate Reagan's success into a congressional majority after forty years of Democratic rule in the House. Sarah Palin accused the establishment of trying to crucify Gingrich and said it was far too soon to call a halt to the debate and the vetting of the candidates. "If for no other reason, rage against the machine, vote for Newt," Palin said. She never quite endorsed him, but her husband, Todd, did.

Privately Gingrich was seething at both Romney and his allies. "This may strike you as naïve and this is my bias," he later explained. "I have never dealt at this level with somebody as dishonest as Mitt Romney. And I wasn't prepared. I mean, I don't mind being really tough and I don't mind a brass-knuckles fight, but it is very difficult." He said what people were overlooking was that he had been at odds with the party's establishment for decades. "I've been in this fight now for thirty years," he told me. He added, "Nobody pointed out, for example, when Bob Dole issued his statement, this is a guy who in 1984 I called the 'tax collector of the welfare state.'" He said Dole had never forgiven him for passing the welfare reform bill in the middle of the 1996 campaign, when Dole was the nominee and knew that Clinton's signing would only make his long odds of winning that much longer. "When we made the decision, [Dole's campaign] called in the middle of our conference and said,

'We can't beat Clinton if you pass this,'" Gingrich recalled. "And I said, 'We can't get [the House] reelected unless we pass this.'"

When the votes in Florida were counted on the night of January 31, Romney's strategy produced a decisive victory. Romney captured 46 percent of the vote to Gingrich's 32 percent, a 240,000-vote margin that left Gingrich tottering. Florida was better territory for Romney than South Carolina. And Romney was the superior candidate. But Romney's superior resources also overwhelmed his opponent. Gingrich said he later compared notes with Joe Gaylord, who had been his most important adviser through his career. "We knew of no theoretical model that could have won the Florida campaign," he said, "because . . . [as] Lord Nelson once said, numbers annihilate." Rhoades and Stevens dismissed analysts who credited the bombardment on television for Romney's victory. It was the candidate, they said, who had stepped up when his candidacy was on the line.

As he left Florida, Romney committed another verbal gaffe during an interview with CNN's Soledad O'Brien. "I'm in this race because I care about Americans," he said. "I'm not concerned about the very poor. We have a safety net there. If it needs repair, I'll fix it. I'm not concerned about the very rich, they're doing just fine. I'm concerned about the very heart of America, the 90, 95 percent of Americans who right now are struggling, and I'll continue to take that message across the nation." With what seemed like a dismissive comment about the plight of the poor, Romney continued to provide the Obama campaign evidence to show he was out of touch with people.

Romney rounded off the week with a big victory in the Nevada caucuses. The result was never really in question. He had won the state by a huge margin four years earlier, and none of his rivals had the infrastructure to seriously contest the event. At midweek, in one of the more awkward events of the campaign, Romney received the endorsement of Donald Trump. It was another blow to Gingrich, who had thought he might win Trump's support. Romney looked uncomfortable standing beside the flashy businessman at Trump's casino hotel and appeared eager to get off the stage as quickly as possible. He took no questions from reporters. Trump held forth for the press before and after the formal endorsement. Romney was far more at ease on caucus night, February 4, as he claimed victory before a crowd of cheering supporters. Gingrich passed up the normal election-night rally with supporters in favor of a sometimes bizarre half-hour press conference, where he struck a defiant pose and trashed the winner. He predicted he would once again be at parity with Romney by the time of the Texas primary later in the spring—though Texas officials had not set an exact date for its contest. He vowed to carry his fight all the way to the Republican convention in Tampa. "I'm not going to with-draw," he said. "I'm actually pretty happy with where we are." Gingrich's per-formance was as strange as it was unconvincing, a stark contrast to the Gingrich who just two weeks earlier had stood before supporters in South Carolina as the candidate with new momentum and confidence. No one could explain Gingrich's performance that night—a rambling and confused defense of his candidacy based on a series of implausible scenarios.

By now there was a curious predictability to the Republican race, despite all the unexpected twists and strange moments. The campaign was playing out almost precisely as Romney's advisers had planned it in Boston the previous spring. They may not have known which of Romney's many rivals would become his principal opponent. But they had understood their candidate's strengths and weaknesses as well as the perils and opportunities of the early states. They had built a strategy with the goal of putting Romney in the strongest possible posi-tion by the beginning of February, with the resources to wage a potentially long fight. Which was exactly where he was. The months and months Romney de-voted to raising money, the time he took going from fund-raiser to fund-raiser, the hours he spent on airplanes flying from one coast to another and back again in the space of a week were all designed to put him in shape to run the kind of campaign a winning candidate must run. There was no question about who was positioned to win a battle over delegates. But the first contests also highlighted Romney's vulnerabilities. His favorability rating among independents was taking a beating. He had dug a deep hole with Hispanic voters with his hard-line pos-ture on immigration. He still struggled to connect with voters. He was given to verbal mistakes. He had a biography that his advisers believed could become an asset in a general election, but they were doing little to inoculate him from the coming attacks by Obama.

CHAPTER 17

Santorum's Challenge

Rick Santorum was an also-ran in the New Hampshire primary. Newt Gingrich and Mitt Romney buried him in South Carolina. Santorum bailed out of Florida, leaving Romney and Gingrich to fight it out there. He ignored Nevada and finished in last place. It was a measure of how strange the Republican contest was that after all that, Santorum was poised for a dramatic reentry into the top ranks of the race. He did it three days after Nevada with victories in Missouri, Minnesota, and Colorado, contests in which not a single delegate was actually awarded. Missouri held a beauty contest primary, a mere popularity vote. Gingrich had not even bothered to get on the ballot, and Romney didn't waste time campaigning there. Minnesota and Colorado held caucuses, the first tentative steps in a lengthy process that eventually would award delegates to the national convention. Santorum saw the three states as an opportunity to get back in the competition. His rebound became one more improbable plot twist in a contest that continued to defy every expert's predictions. With those three victories, he became Romney's principal and last significant challenger.

No one had any fixed expectations about the three contests on February 7. They were on the calendar but seen as an interlude in the Republican race, way stations en route to the more significant events in Michigan and Arizona three weeks later. The odds makers gave Santorum a modest chance to pull an upset in Minnesota, if only because the electorate in caucuses was likely to be small and very conservative. Romney, however, was a solid favorite in Colorado, where he had captured 60 percent of the vote in the 2008 caucuses. His team was so confident about the state that on the morning of the caucuses, Rich Beeson, Romney's political director and a Coloradoan, guaranteed victory to the others. The campaign's final numbers put Romney solidly in first, with Santorum and Gingrich splitting most of the rest of the vote. But Gingrich's support was in a state of collapse in Colorado on caucus day, thanks to the fallout from the former Speaker's rambling late-night press conference in Las Vegas.

Cable networks, accustomed to the excitement of primary and caucus nights over the first four weeks of the year, were fully prepared for another night of counting and instant analysis, no matter that these were events that in past years would have drawn little attention. For Santorum, it was a godsend. Missouri's results came in first that evening, and the former Pennsylvania senator was quickly declared the winner. In head-to-head competition, he had defeated the front-runner by 55 to 25 percent. Next came Minnesota and another big Santorum victory. This was instantly interpreted as a sign of further dissatisfaction with Romney among conservatives and, given his performance there four years earlier, an embarrassment. Had Santorum won only those two, the damage to Romney might have been minimal. The big blow was Colorado. Romney's team watched it slip away all day as they checked and rechecked numbers and measured the full extent of the shift from Gingrich toward Santorum. Rhoades was on the phone with Romney during the day, warning him of potential trouble. Romney was greatly irritated when he heard that news. A late surge of votes for Santorum from conservative precincts around Colorado Springs, the center of social and religious conservative activity in the state, completed the day's sweep. At his victory party after the first of the three victories, a heady Santorum declared, "Conservatism is alive and well. I don't stand here and claim to be the conservative alternative to Mitt Romney. I stand here to be the conservative alternative to Barack Obama."

Santorum had followed a strategy of necessity as Gingrich was battling Romney in South Carolina and Florida. He had neither the money nor the infrastructure to compete effectively in either state. Beyond the debates, he was a nonplayer. Santorum left Florida to return home to prepare for a release of his tax returns. At the same time, his daughter Bella, who was born with a genetic disorder, was suddenly hospitalized, seriously ill. Santorum and his wife, Karen, broke off all campaigning to be with her as the Florida primary approached. Meanwhile, his advisers decided to concentrate their limited resources on the three states everyone else was ignoring. Santorum ran ads in all three. "It was very important for us to win a state, and we felt Missouri was our best bet," John Brabender, Santorum's chief strategist, said. "We thought Minnesota was our next best bet and we thought there was a very, very outside chance in Colorado. . . . I got a call as soon as we won Missouri from a number of people, e-mails from the Romney campaign. 'Congratulations on Missouri, you guys did a great job.' . . . Then we won Minnesota and I might have heard from one or two people from the Romney people congratulating us. When we won Colorado it went dark. My belief is they never thought in a million years they were going to lose Colorado."

Even Gingrich was impressed at Santorum's tactical calculation. "You have to give him credit," he later told me. "He did something very bold and it took a lot of guts. He went to three places nobody else was going and they gambled that they'd win a PR victory. It was almost like the Tet Offensive. We're going to win a PR victory and the PR victory will become the war. It was accurate. It was a very shrewd move, but it was made possible in part because I'd been so damaged by that point that the anti-Romney conservatives were desperately looking for somebody. And if Newt can't beat Romney, who can?"

No one thought Rick Santorum was going to win anything in 2012. He began the campaign in obscurity—overlooked, disregarded, and dismissed as a serious candidate, though he had served sixteen years in Congress. He was first elected to the House in 1990 from western Pennsylvania, defeating a seven-term incumbent Democrat in a race in which national party leaders gave him little chance to win and little support to do so. He became a member of the Gang of Seven, a band of freshman Republicans that included future Speaker John Boehner who vigorously protested scandals at the House Bank and House Post Office. He won a Senate seat in 1994, defeating Democratic incumbent Harris Wofford. He brought many of the partisan tactics of Newt Gingrich's Republican-controlled House to the more sedate Senate. He helped lead the effort to pass welfare reform and was elected to the number three job in leadership. He was a committed conservative who nonetheless looked after a state with a strong blue-collar constituency. He backed a hike in the minimum wage and opposed right-to-work legislation (though he later changed his mind on that), and got his share of earmarks at a time when they were commonplace among legislators in both parties.

In 1996, Santorum and his wife had lost a prematurely born son two hours after birth.* Over time, he became a more outspoken advocate on social issues. Though he voted in favor of contraception, he once said of birth control, "I don't think it's a healthy thing for our country." He said states have the right to ban contraception, though he would not vote for such a law. In his 2005 book, *It Takes a Family,* he wrote, "Radical feminists succeeded in undermining the traditional family and convincing women that professional accomplishments are the key to happiness. As for children? Well, to paraphrase *The Wizard of Oz,* pay no attention to those kids behind the curtain." Like many other politicians, he opposed same-sex marriage. But he once accused leaders of the gay community of leading a "jihad" against him over comments he had made in which he appeared to equate gay sex with bigamy, polygamy, and more. Those comments came during an interview with the Associated Press in 2003, after a

---

*At the time of the 2012 campaign, the Santorums had seven living children.

Supreme Court decision that struck down antisodomy laws. "If the Supreme Court says that you have the right to consensual sex within your home, then you have the right to bigamy, you have the right to polygamy, you have the right to incest, you have the right to adultery," he said. "You have the right to anything." In 2005, he intervened in the case of the Florida woman Terri Schiavo, who had been in a vegetative state for years. He and other Washington politicians urged that a federal judicial panel review a state court decision authorizing the removal of her feeding tube. He also met in Florida with her parents, who opposed the removal, to pray with them.

Despite his conservative views, he was able to win reelection in blue-leaning Pennsylvania in 2000. One Pennsylvania Republican described his political deftness as being able to "run through the raindrops without getting wet." Eventually, Santorum's ideology caught up with him and he got soaked. In 2006, a bad year for Republicans, he was crushed in his bid for reelection. He later came to the conclusion that he never should have sought reelection that year. "We should have just said we're not going to run for reelection but we're going to run for president in 2008," Brabender said. "We would have been much further along." That would have put him alongside Romney in both 2008 and 2012. Santorum had been thinking about a presidential run for some time, and in 2009, after consulting with his family, he decided to test the waters. He had been invited to give a speech in October at the University of Dubuque, and his team leaked word of the Iowa trip to *Politico*'s Jonathan Martin, who wrote a small item about it. CNN picked it up and then other reporters began to call for details. After the speech, during an overnight drive in a rainstorm, Santorum and Brabender began to talk more seriously about what kind of campaign he could run. Santorum saw his base for what it was—social and religious conservatives and to a lesser extent Tea Party activists. He decided to start traveling regularly to Iowa and see what would happen. Few took him seriously. I was among those who gave him no chance. In December 2010, we met for coffee one afternoon in Washington. Santorum laid out his agenda and the rationale behind his candidacy. I listened skeptically, and foolishly took no notes.

Two days after Santorum's trio of victories, I sat down with Gingrich to get his assessment of the campaign. He was battered—now in a downward slide—but, typically, optimistic about the overall state of his campaign and his prospects. "As I kept telling all of you guys," he said, "the not-Romney part of this party is huge. And it will be bigger in another few weeks because in the end Romney is in fact not somebody that this party's going to nominate. And so he's been sustained by being the candidate and being the establishment and being inevitable and having huge volumes of money, but in the end he's not going to get there." How did Santorum's success change things? I asked him. "First of all, it really cripples Romney," he said. "I mean, it's really hard for Romney now to turn around and say he's the inevitable nominee. And that's the number one goal. I mean, if we can't get Romney down to a size we can cope with, then there's no second act, okay? So it turns out now there has to be a second and third act. I mean, the second act is the gradual disappearance of Santorum. Santorum is a very good candidate as long as you don't look at him very long. There's a reason he set the all-time Pennsylvania record for losing."

Gingrich said he was through attacking Romney. "I'm done," he said. "Tuesday was the signal that I'm done. Everything we do from here on out will be surrogates. Yes. I don't need to say anything more because that part of the game is set and I'm shifting to a new game." I asked whether he shared the view that the longer both he and Santorum stayed in the race, the better it would be for Romney. "I wouldn't have shared it before Tuesday because he was gradually decaying," he said of Santorum. "It may be true, although I think he may actually be the right way for me to define the difference. See, if it's only right-left, then the two guys on the right have a whole differentiation problem. What we're about to move towards is a timid versus bold argument. . . . I think in that sense what Santorum has done is he has set me up now to draw that sharp distinction and to be able to say, look, it's not just right-left, it's whether you're prepared to fundamentally rethink where we're going."

Nobody in Boston was worrying about Gingrich then or after. Santorum, however, presented a potentially serious problem. He was difficult to attack as insufficiently conservative, one of the lines used against Gingrich. His vulnerabilities as a candidate were sizable, but more as a general election candidate who would be seen as out of the mainstream. In a Republican nomination battle, Romney couldn't go after those weaknesses. That would be attacking the base.

The next contests were three weeks away. Arizona still looked favorable for Romney, but everyone knew the showdown would be in Michigan, and Santorum was on the move there. Blue-collar Michigan seemed ready-made for blue-collar and Catholic Santorum, despite the fact that Romney was born there. Money was pouring into Santorum's campaign again. The day after his trio of victories, the campaign raised about $1.5 million, with an additional $1 million the next day, Brabender said. "So we were raising money at a clip unlike we had ever before," he said. "But we also knew that hell was coming in a sense that we knew that, just like we had said that all these other people were going to go through scrutiny unlike they ever had before, we knew we were going to as well." The media had a new story line and they were pumping it hard. Nerves were on edge in Boston. "They were saying [Michigan] was Waterloo," Matt Rhoades recalled. "Mitt Romney's Waterloo. We thought everything was on the line in Florida. But then it seemed like everything was on the line times two in Michigan."

Days after Santorum's victories, the annual CPAC gathering opened in Washington, D.C. Romney used his speech to reestablish his conservative bona fides. "I know conservatism because I have lived conservatism," he said. He used the words "conservative" or "conservatism" two dozen times. But it was this line that captured the mood of concern inside the Romney campaign. "I fought against long odds in a deep blue state," Romney said, "but I was a severely conservative Republican governor." The word "severely" was not in Romney's prepared text and it grated on conservative activists. Critics accused Romney of trying to impersonate a real conservative with a caricature of what true conservatism represented. Erick Erickson, the founder of the conservative RedState blog, wrote, "Mitt Romney got a warm reception at CPAC, standing ovations . . . the works. He did nothing to calm fears that he is not one of us. In fact, he might have made it worse today. What the heck is a severe conservative?" He said the phrase sounded like a critique from the left. Romney's speech was also notable for the change in tone from his CPAC speech a year earlier. In that speech, he used the word "conservative" once, not to describe himself but to say what Obama's economic policies were not. At that point he was trying to impress conservatives that he was the most electable Republican, not necessarily the most conservative. With Santorum's challenge, he had to demonstrate anew to the base that he could be trusted.

A Romney adviser e-mailed me two days later to take issue with the criticism of the speech. "The subject of this speech is much more about the nature of conservatism and a challenge to conservatives that this next election is a test of an ability to lead, a test that implicitly has been met with mixed results in prior elections. Romney is not tying himself in knots trying to be like many in the crowd. In fact, he is explicitly saying that [they] may come from different backgrounds. And he is offering a criticism of the professional conservative DC class." He added, "It's a simple fact that Romney has received more conservative votes than any candidate in the R[epublican] primary, so it's hard to argue that conservatives have a huge problem with Romney. I believe that a great deal of this comes from the dynamic not so much that Romney isn't a conservative but that Romney is not one of them or does not seem dependent upon their approval. . . . They want to be the vetting authority. Never mind that they never meet voters."

Romney had good reason to be nervous. A public poll of Michigan

Republicans taken at the weekend by Public Policy Polling showed Santorum leading Romney by fifteen points. The campaign's internal poll taken a few days later put Santorum's advantage at eight points—enormously troubling to his team for a state where he had deep family roots and had won in 2008. Katie Packer Gage, who was directing the Michigan effort, was deeply worried and during one morning staff meeting let her emotions get the better of her. "I felt like nobody thought we could win Michigan," she later said. "And I believed that if we lost Michigan that our campaign could be over. Pretty tough to explain to our donors how he would lose a state he won the time before and a state where his dad had been governor and a state we had always sort of said we were going to win. We were very committed to that." Rich Beeson sent her an e-mail at the end of the meeting: Hang in there, he said.

Until now, Santorum had had the luxury of picking his battles as Romney fought state by state. This was another oddity of the 2012 Republican race. Challengers came and went and came back again as the most conservative voters swung back and forth in what seemed an unfocused search for an alternative to the front-runner. Had the old rules applied, Santorum would have been dealt out of the race after South Carolina, having failed miserably to capitalize on his surprise showing in Iowa. But those rules were out the window in 2012. Now, however, Santorum could not avoid certain confrontations with Romney. He could duck Arizona, but not Michigan.

Michigan was the first state in the Republican race where the president's bailout of the auto industry came into play. Romney was a car guy but a small government businessman as well. He had opposed the government bailout of the industry, a position widely shared among conservatives even though the infusion of money had begun under George W. Bush. Romney wrote an op-ed for the *New York Times* in November 2008, before Obama was even sworn in, opposing more government funds and calling for a managed bankruptcy. He submitted the article just after auto executives had testified in Washington asking for more help—having flown in on their private jets in a display of arrogance that turned their appearance into a public relations disaster. "If General Motors, Ford and Chrysler get the bailout that their chief executives asked for yesterday, you can kiss the American automotive industry goodbye," Romney wrote. "It won't go overnight, but its demise will be virtually guaranteed." The headline, which Romney did not write, left a killer impression: "Let Detroit Go Bankrupt." Whenever Romney or his surrogates went to Michigan, all reporters wanted to talk about was his position on the bailout. Santorum too had opposed what Obama did, but on bailouts he at least could argue that he was consistent. He had also opposed the bank bailout. Romney had supported bailing out the banks but not the auto companies. Santorum said Romney was for helping Wall Street while leaving to fend for itself the industry that defined his home state and that had brought power, financial security, and prominence to his father.

Santorum's challenge to Romney, unlike all the others he had faced, seemed to offer the purest example yet in the nomination contest of the long-simmering conflict between the GOP's business and populist wings, the party establishment and its insurgent grass roots, the country clubbers and the religious conservatives. Perry once had the potential to lead that fight against Romney but fizzled as a candidate. Santorum, through dogged determination and little more, now had the opportunity—if he could take advantage of it. One senior Romney adviser said, "It was not inconceivable that the Republican Party could nominate Rick Santorum, whereas I think we all thought that it would be a stretch for the Republican Party to nominate Newt." Romney's team went to work to prevent a potentially devastating defeat. In the words of one adviser, "We built a fortress around Michigan. Mitt was there. Ann was there. We were in every media market. We were in every corner of the state." Another adviser described the strategy this way: "Campaign hard, campaign real hard. I mean, just campaign as much as we could in Michigan. Upped our media buys some. Really worked our local surrogates, our talk radio surrogates. Worked out endorsement networks. But just to try to flood the zone as much as we could."

Romney and his team made one other crucial decision as they looked at the challenge from Santorum, a choice that bought short-term advantages in exchange for long-term problems. The week before the Michigan and Arizona primaries, Romney unveiled a new tax plan that called for cutting marginal income tax rates an additional 20 percent. That would reduce the rate on the highest earners from 35 percent, the level where it had stood since George W. Bush's presidency, down to 28 percent. Romney said he would avoid enlarging the deficit or giving a special break to wealthy taxpayers by eliminating unspecified deductions and exempting those earning less than $200,000 from capital gains taxes while maintaining them on wealthier taxpayers. There were several motivations for a more detailed tax plan, but the timing was dictated by the emergence of Santorum, whom Romney labeled "an economic lightweight," as a credible challenger. Romney was looking for other ways to prove to conservatives that he was truly one of them. "There were certainly some economic conservatives that thought pretty strongly that we need a more forceful articulation of a tax reform proposal," one Romney adviser said. "But there was also a sense beyond what everyone else may have been saying that if we were going to be the candidate of the economy and of improving the economy, it was going to be hard to advance that discussion much further without fleshing out the tax discussion." Romney's team saw it for what it was politically. As the adviser put it, "This was going to be the coup de grâce in some ways. And I think it was very helpful in the primary. There's no question about it."

The only debate ahead of the two primaries was held February 22 in Mesa, Arizona. As in Florida, Romney came well prepared with an intimate knowledge of Santorum's record in Congress. Santorum had spent much of the day campaigning. He was always indifferent to debate preparation and paid a high price for his failure to anticipate Romney's attacks and work up responses. "This day particularly was in my mind idiotic because they flew and did events in multiple cities and [that] should never have been the case," Brabender said. "We would do debate prep right before the debate, literally, and he had not had a chance to read the material that was put together for him."

Santorum had never been in a debate like this in the presidential campaign. Most times he struggled to get the attention of the moderator as he begged to be heard. In Mesa, he was the target of all the attacks. Romney sought to revive his campaign by destroying his opponent's credibility as a fiscal conservative and by painting Santorum as another deal-cutting Washington insider. He attacked Santorum for supporting earmarks, and when Santorum noted that Romney had sought federal money to help the Salt Lake City Olympics, Romney responded, "When I was fighting to save the Olympics, you were fighting to save the Bridge to Nowhere." Romney tripped Santorum up over his true feelings about Title X family planning funding. When Santorum said he had supported it because it was part of a larger appropriation, Romney countered by saying he had recently watched a clip of Santorum stating positively that he had supported Title X itself, not because it was included in a larger bill. Santorum tried to put Romney on the defensive over the Massachusetts health care plan, but he was up against a superior candidate that night. Santorum's worst moment came when the discussion turned to George W. Bush's No Child Left Behind education reform, which most conservatives now saw as a usurpation of the rights of states, localities, and parents to run their schools. "I have to admit, I voted for that," Santorum said. "It was against the principles I believed in, but, you know, when you're part of the team, sometimes you take one for the team, for the leader, and I made a mistake." The audience began to boo him.

Santorum finished the debate believing he had dealt with that question effectively, by suggesting that while he thought the measure could be improved, it was better than nothing at all. "When he came off the stage he thought he did beautifully with that answer," recalled Hogan Gidley, Santorum's spokesman. "He said it was a signature piece of legislation for a Republican president. They understand that. I said, 'No, they don't understand.'" Brabender said of the debate, "Rick was tired, did not prepare particularly well, and was also the centerpiece. You had Romney, who frankly was a little bit on the ropes at that time. They did the right thing. They spent, they prepared well, Romney had a good performance. We didn't. Do I think it affected some votes? Absolutely."

Over the next few days, neither candidate looked like a winner. Romney scheduled a "major speech" on the economy for Friday, February 24, before the Detroit Economic Club. But he had already unveiled the guts of the speech, his new tax plan. The day's story became a logistical foul-up that left the candidate speaking to his audience on the artificial turf of Ford Field, the Detroit Lions' football stadium, with more than sixty thousand empty seats visible all around him. When one of the club officials enthusiastically showed the venue to Katie Packer Gage, she responded, "I don't know. All I can see are sixty thousand empty seats. Can you send some clowns in here so the press will be distracted?" Reporters tweeted photos throughout the speech. Then came questions and answers, and more trouble. "This feels good, being back in Michigan," Romney said, trying to play the hometown candidate. "You know, the trees are the right height. The streets are just fine." He had used those lines before, but not what came next. "I like the fact that most of the cars I see are Detroit-made automobiles," he said. "I drive a Mustang and a Chevy pickup truck. Ann drives a couple of Cadillacs, actually." Once again, inexplicably, he had stumbled into the stereotype his campaign was trying to avoid.

The next morning, Santorum made his own mess. Speaking at a conference sponsored by Americans for Prosperity, a Tea Party group funded in large part by the Koch brothers, he was trying to highlight his blue-collar heritage by talking about his grandfather, a coal miner. He launched into an attack on the country's elites. "Elites come up with phony ideologies and phony ideas to rob you of your freedom and impose government control on your lives." So far not so bad, but then this: "President Obama once said he wants everyone to go to college," he said. And then, oozing contempt, he added, "What a snob!" The conservative, Obama-hating audience loved it, but it was obviously a major mistake on Santorum's part. The next day he made another. On ABC's *This Week* program, host George Stephanopoulos asked him about a comment he had made about John F. Kennedy's famous speech to Baptist ministers in the 1960 campaign, in which Kennedy had talked about his Catholic faith and his belief in the separation of church and state. Santorum had said watching the speech made him want to vomit. Stephanopoulos asked why. "Because the first line, the first substantive line in the speech says, 'I believe in an America where the separation of church and state is absolute,'" Santorum said. "I don't believe in an

America where the separation of church and state is absolute. . . . You bet that makes you throw up." The back-to-back comments underscored the absence of message discipline by the candidate and made clear he had no strategy for or even interest in reaching beyond his narrow base.

As the primary day neared, the polls in Michigan tightened. A week out, Romney's polling showed that his deficit was now just three points. A few days later, Romney's numbers showed him leading Santorum by three points. Santorum's negatives had doubled in that time, though Republicans still had a mostly positive impression of him, as they did of Romney. The more people were hearing from Santorum, the more unfavorably they viewed him. By the weekend before the primary, Romney's advisers were increasingly confident. Then, by Monday, they were nervous again. "I'm not sure any of us understand what's happening," said one Romney adviser I talked to that day. "I don't think anybody puts this away easily." He was puzzled at how candidates who in past campaigns would have been out of the race were able to keep going. "Gingrich is still being treated as a significant figure and he only won one state and he isn't even playing right now," he said. "We were in a stronger position four years ago and [yet] we were out of the race. . . . And yes, some of this is us. We haven't lit up. Mitt Mania has been kept under restraint."

On the Sunday before the primary, Romney's team decided to send him to the Daytona 500. It would be a way to show his affinity for cars and for a constituency important to the Republican Party. But the weather was rainy enough to wash out the race, and Romney managed to commit another of his verbal gaffes. As he was having his picture taken, someone asked him about his connection to NASCAR racing. "I have some great friends that are NAS-CAR team owners," he replied. By the time he returned to Michigan, Romney was in a bad mood, believing he had wasted the day when he could have been campaigning in Michigan, where it counted. On primary day, he spoke with his traveling press corps. One reporter asked what he would say to Republicans who were critical that he so far had not been able to excite the party's base. "You know, it's very easy to excite the base with incendiary comments," he replied. "We've seen throughout the campaign that if you're willing to say really outrageous things that are accusative and attacking of President Obama that you're going to jump up in the polls. You know, I'm not willing to light my hair on fire to try and get support. I am who I am." Another reporter asked whether he realized that comments like those he had made about his wife's two Cadillacs and the NASCAR team owners were hurting him. "Yes. Next question," he replied. Then a reporter tried to follow up about Romney not being willing to light his hair on fire. That produced, finally, a touch of humor. "I'm not going to do it," the gelled candidate said. "I don't care how hard you ask. It would be a big fire, I assure you."

When the votes were counted on February 28, Romney squeezed out a narrow victory—41 percent to Santorum's 38 percent. He won Arizona easily, as expected. The Michigan victory was what Romney needed, but not enough to knock Santorum out or, for that matter, to shut off talk about Romney's weaknesses as a front-runner. Republican gossipers speculated that his vulnerabilities could open the door to a late entry by another Republican. As the campaign turned toward a dozen contests on Super Tuesday the following week, Romney still had work to do. His strategy was the same as always, which was to try to make himself the most broadly attractive candidate. He could divide and conquer as long as Santorum, Gingrich, and Ron Paul remained in the race indefinitely and split the anti-Romney constituency in the party. Or if the race truly was a two-person contest, as Santorum was saying, he could demonstrate his strength by starting to win majorities. It all came down to the same thing. To win the nomination, he had to keep winning primaries.

The weekend after Michigan and before Super Tuesday, I went to Boston to check in with Romney's team. They were hunkered down—not out of concern that the nomination was suddenly in jeopardy; they were still confident of victory. But they were even more keenly aware that the rules governing this battle were conspiring to make Romney's path to victory long and difficult. Russ Schriefer cited four factors that he thought made it impossible to end the battle quickly, despite what people had said after New Hampshire. One was the calendar and the rule change to proportional distribution of delegates. He pointed to the super PACs as the second factor. "If you go back to, like, the Democratic nomination in 2004, when Kerry wrapped it up so fast, if George Soros decided to give Howard Dean another $5 million, Dean could have gone on. Right? If some big donor decided to [give] Gephardt another $5 million, the race would have continued and Kerry wouldn't have been able to wrap it up as quickly as he did." Schriefer cited two other factors to explain why Romney had not been able to wrap up the race quickly. One was the role of the debates. He doubted that Gingrich would have won South Carolina without them. The other was the rise of social media and Internet fund-raising, something that had grown exponentially in just eight years, which he argued also elongated the process. Everyone had had a moment to challenge Romney. Santorum was the latest and, he hoped, the last. Donald Trump. Michele Bachmann. Herman Cain. Rick Perry. Newt Gingrich twice. Rick Santorum now. "The one thing that we saw was that over the course of the campaign these sorts of surges would last anywhere from three to five weeks," Schriefer said. "And then things would start to settle down." By those calculations, Santorum's loss in Michigan marked the beginning of the end of his time in the spotlight.

Matt Rhoades had a similar analysis that day, with one additional insight. "The way the media has changed, the new media and just the constant negative information flow that exists out there, those three things have completely changed the dynamics of the primary process," he said. "That we're still here and we'll be going on past Super Tuesday is not Mitt Romney's fault. Has our campaign made mistakes? Sure. But it's not our fault that [the contest is] going to keep going. That's how the process is designed, that's what they intended it to do, and that's how it'll be." Rhoades wasn't finished. "One thing [that] happened since New Hampshire is everyone started believing that Mitt was going to, like, roll through everything, and I never thought that. But the perception got out there. And it was like, why didn't Mitt win South Carolina? Why does Mitt lose any states? It's an unfair burden people place on him—some of our own supporters, the D.C. crowd who know nothing about presidential politics, they start chattering and it builds and the media then builds. And then you have South Carolina and you have people saying it's over. And then you have a great night [in Florida] and then Rick has a great night, and it's like, 'What's wrong?'"

Ten states held contests on Super Tuesday, March 6. The only one that really counted and was in doubt was Ohio, where once again Santorum was pitted against Romney in a head-to-head contest that neither candidate could afford to lose. It was, presumably, tailor-made for Santorum to spring an upset. Ohio was like Michigan, an industrial state with an older population hard hit by economic decline over a decade and more. Ohio bordered Pennsylvania—and specifically the part of Pennsylvania that was Santorum's home area. Unlike Michigan, Romney had no direct ties to the state, no family connections, no history of doing well there. He had never been on the ballot there. Romney's campaign team did not regard Ohio as an ideal place for a showdown with an opponent who was both more conservative and more blue-collar and who also had a message—at least when he was focused and disciplined—that was aimed directly at culturally conservative, working-class voters. At times during the campaign, Santorum had spoken with passion and eloquence about what had happened to the country's manufacturing base and to the workers who once made good livings in the auto and steel and glass factories. He spoke from the workers' perspective, unlike Romney, whose language reflected that of the entrepreneur and business owner. As important as Michigan had been, Romney's advisers worried more about Ohio—and knew they would have only a week to make their case. He still had one big advantage. He could far outspend Santorum and did. Between his campaign and super PAC, Romney spent almost $4 million on ads in Ohio. Santorum and his Red, White and Blue Fund spent barely $1 million.

The polls in Ohio had shown a pattern similar to those in Michigan. Santorum's victories in Missouri, Minnesota, and Colorado turned the race around in Ohio, with his margin over Romney pegged at anywhere between seven and eighteen points in the two weeks after February 7. Then Romney began to claw his way back. After the victories in Michigan and Arizona, multiple polls showed Romney and Santorum in a virtual tie in Ohio. Romney, with guidance from Ohio senator Rob Portman, made a series of strategic appearances and stepped up appeals to working-class voters. Three days before the primary, he appeared before an enthusiastic audience at a factory outside Dayton. Nick Mangold, an All-America football player from Ohio State University who was now with the New York Jets, joined him. "If I were as big and strong as Nick," he said, "this race would be over." It was a near-perfect rally except when he got a question from the mother of a young woman serving in Afghanistan with the 82nd Airborne Division. What would Romney do to end the war and bring the troops home? she asked. He did not have a coherent policy for the war. "We're going to finish the job of passing it off to them and bring our troops home as soon as humanly possible," he said. On the final day of campaigning, Romney and Santorum continued to bid for blue-collar voters. In Zanesville, Republicans who had turned out to hear Romney openly worried about the negativity of the GOP contest. "We're giving the Democrats all the ammunition they need to fight us," Shirley Labaki, an antiques store owner, told the *Columbus Dispatch*. "We're doing all their research for them." Santorum attacked Romney as a weak general election candidate and highlighted his own conservative credentials. "Liberalism is an ideology," he said. "Socialism is an ideology. Conservatism is simply what works."

Election night produced hours of agony for Romney. Of the ten contests that night, Romney won six, Santorum three, and Gingrich one. But it was not until well after midnight that the networks gave him Ohio. For a time it appeared that Santorum might pull the upset he needed to truly transform the race. Only when Cuyahoga County, which includes Cleveland, reported its final numbers was Romney declared the winner. He won the state by just 10,508 votes, far less than his margin in Michigan the previous week. That night he also won Virginia, Vermont, Idaho, Alaska, and Massachusetts and a majority of the delegates awarded that day (hitting the goal his advisers had set out a year earlier in their analysis of how to win the nomination). But Ohio's result came so late and was so close that Santorum's victories in Oklahoma, Tennessee, and North Dakota, along with Gingrich's in Georgia, left the distinct impression that the Republican race was far from over. Rhoades described the scene inside Romney headquarters. "This is a night where [Romney's] believing in his team," he said. "Because if you're watching TV, Mitt Romney's losing Ohio. But if you've got our apparatus set where we've got all the phones coming in from all the places and all the counties and precincts, Rich [Beeson] is saying, 'We're going to win it.' It's a painful, painful night, and it's painful to go through because Ohio was late and people love a horse race. The slog continues."

As the primaries were playing out, one of Romney's advisers sent an e-mail taking issue with the criticism of Romney as a weak candidate: "When looking back at this campaign, it will seem very odd that the guy who was winning—and most likely will win—was the guy who was constantly criticized the most. Politics is a perfect marketplace. You are worth what you are worth in votes. That's it. Nothing more or nothing less. . . . There is a Green Room culture, which has come to dominate political coverage, which is dedicated to examining what's wrong with Romney every hour. That's fine. But when one reads this stuff in a year or two years or five years, I do think it will seem odd that everyone spent so much time asking themselves why the guy who was 500 yards ahead of everybody else in the mile run was running so slowly. Okay, sure, he could run faster. But the guys behind him are running slower and it would seem not illogical to spend more time asking what was wrong with everyone else that they can't even beat such a slow runner like Romney. Except that Romney isn't slow. The media tend to look at Romney the way that Republicans looked at Clinton. Sort of mystified that he could be winning. But he was and did. Which is not to say that we don't have lousy days as a campaign. Sure, all the time. But Romney is about to win a Republican nomination without a natural base in the party and that's a credit to his pure candidate skills and intellect and personality. Ask yourself—when is the last time we saw that happen?"

In reality, the Republican race was now over. For all the ups and downs, the twists and turns, the seeming strength or weakness of Romney at any given moment, the battle followed a rigidly predictable pattern. Santorum could win some states after Super Tuesday but had no realistic chance to win the nomination unless he could expand his coalition. Romney and Santorum were prisoners of demographics and the divisions within the party. It didn't really matter where they went or what they said or what kind of ads they ran; the rest of the contests were virtually fixed in their outcome, as had been the case since the first votes were cast in Iowa.

The fault line was most easily understood by one single category of voters in the exit polls from all the major states that had voted or would be voting. If evangelical Christians accounted for more than 50 percent of the primary or caucus electorate, Romney lost the state. If they accounted for fewer than 50 percent, he won. The pattern from Iowa through Super Tuesday showed no variation. Romney had won New Hampshire, Florida, Nevada, Arizona, Michigan, Virginia, Vermont, Massachusetts, and Ohio—all with electorates in which evangelicals accounted for between 22 and 49 percent of the voters. He had lost Iowa, South Carolina, Oklahoma, Tennessee, and Georgia. Evangelicals made up anywhere from 57 to 83 percent of the voters in those contests. Romney was criticized through the primaries for his seeming inability to win over the conservative base of the party. In reality, where he found resistance was primarily among those who described themselves as very conservative, not conservatives in general. The only states where he won a plurality of those voters were, generally, states that were more moderate or less socially conservative. Among the roughly one-third of Republican voters who described themselves as "somewhat conservative," he was an almost universal winner, as he was among those who said they were either "moderate" or "liberal."

After Super Tuesday, the race continued for another month. Santorum still believed there was a way for him to win, if he could get beyond the next month of primaries that generally favored Romney. But he needed three things to break his way: He had to win Wisconsin on April 3; he needed Gingrich to drop out; and he needed Texas to make its late primary a winner-take-all contest. None of which happened. Gingrich clung to the fanciful hope that Santorum would crumble and that the non-Romney voters would turn to him again in a last effort to block Romney's path. Advisers to Santorum and Gingrich talked briefly about joining forces, but Gingrich later told me it was never a serious proposition. Santorum won four more states—Kansas, Alabama, Mississippi, and Louisiana. Romney, however, won where it counted most: Illinois and Wisconsin (as well as Maryland and the District of Columbia).

By the weekend before the April 3 Wisconsin primary, Santorum was under mounting pressure to quit. After a lunch in West Bend that included the state delicacy, cheese curds, Santorum was asked again whether he planned to continue. "I'm not talking about this anymore," he said impatiently. Two days later, Romney won an easy victory. Santorum came out of Wisconsin defeated, exhausted, and out of money. Compounding his problems, his daughter Bella was taken to the hospital again three days after the primary. That weekend, he began talking seriously about getting out of the race. His wife, Karen, wanted him to keep fighting on, but his time was over. On April 10, after losing Wisconsin and facing a likely embarrassing loss two weeks later in his home state of Pennsylvania, Santorum announced he was getting out. Gingrich, for reasons only he could explain, stayed on a few weeks longer. He dropped out on May 10, as he had assured Romney the week before in a private telephone call. Only Ron Paul remained. Romney turned his focus to the president and the general election.

The Republicans had provided the country with a political spectacle, a roller-coaster nomination battle with more bizarre plot twists than anyone could have written in advance. But the nomination contest also highlighted the party's weaknesses—the degree to which its conservative base was pushing the party beyond the mainstream. The primaries turned out not to be good for either the party or its nominee.

CHAPTER 18

Etch A Sketch

On the night of April 24, Mitt Romney returned to New Hampshire to mark another turning point in the campaign. Five states held primaries that day, and Romney swept them all with big majorities as he continued to accumulate the delegates needed to secure his nomination. His focus, however, was no longer on his Republican rivals. He had come back to New Hampshire, where he had announced his candidacy the previous June, to signal the unofficial start of his general election campaign. "To the thousands of good and decent Americans I've met who want nothing more than a better chance, a fighting chance, to all of you I have a simple message," he said. "Hold on a little longer. A better America begins tonight." He called President Obama a failure as president. He recalled the goodwill and high expectations at the time Obama was sworn in and compared that with the mood now. "The last few years have been the best that Barack Obama can do," he said, "but it's not the best America can do." He predicted that Obama's record meant that the president's reelection strategy would be nasty and negative. "That kind of campaign may have worked at another place and in a different time, but not here and not now." With a nod to Bill Clinton's 1992 campaign, he added, "It's still about the economy, and we're not stupid."

Romney had weathered a nomination battle lasting far longer than many analysts had assumed four months earlier. From the perspective of his senior team, he was not a surprise winner but an unlikely one nonetheless—moderate Mitt from Massachusetts leading a party whose identity had been stamped by the intransigence of its congressional wing, particularly the militants in the House, whose approval rating was in the low teens. He was not a gaffe-free candidate, but he had demonstrated resilience and the ability to rise to challenges as they appeared. He was clearly the class of the GOP field and had shown skills and perseverance. From another perspective, Romney's victory was less remarkable. He began the race with sizable advantages: the experience of having run before, a seasoned team, and a financial network that dwarfed anything his rivals could put together. He ran against a weak field, the weakest in many years. He was battered by the experience, particularly from the endless debates.

As the primaries were winding down, Eric Fehrnstrom, Romney's longtime spokesman and one of his closest advisers, suggested that voters would be willing to take a fresh look at the Republican nominee once they began to focus on the choice in November—an altogether rational thought, though it didn't quite come out that way. Interviewed by CNN, he said there would be a moment when Romney would be able to "hit a reset button" as he turned from the primaries to the general election. "It's almost like an Etch A Sketch," he said. "You can kind of shake it up and we start all over." What Fehrnstrom said was sensible yet foolish—sensible because all nominees have the opportunity to reintroduce themselves after their nominations are secured, but foolish because of the doubts he raised about Romney's true convictions. Within hours, the comment went viral. Was Romney really not the conservative he portrayed himself to be during the nomination campaign? Was he now about to try to remake himself again?

Nomination battles often strengthen the winner, but many take a toll, and the Republican contest surely was proof of that. Republican pollster Bill McInturff, who conducted the NBC News/*Wall Street Journal* poll with Democrat Peter Hart, was quoted by those two organizations as saying the nomination battle had had a "corrosive" effect on the party. Romney could not escape the fallout. It was like high school, Stuart Stevens said: "You are who you hang out with." The more successful he was at fending off his rivals, and the longer he fought to prove his conservative credentials to a skeptical GOP base, the more he was in conflict with the need to turn his attention to wooing the fall electorate.

Romney wasn't the first recent nominee to start the general election campaign this way. In 1992, Bill Clinton needed a Manhattan Project in the early summer to repair all the damage from the personal scandals that were aired during his nomination campaign. He, of course, went on to win the presidency. But by many measures, Romney appeared to be in worse shape than other previous nominees. Voters still had trouble warming up to him. His wealth was a barrier they could not get past. Voters had trouble relating to him personally, and he had done little to solve that problem. A *Washington Post/ABC News* poll at the time found that he was the only nominee on record to be underwater in his favorability rating at the start of a general election. His image among independent voters was more negative by the spring of 2012 than when the nomination battle began. He had lost ground among women, thanks to his party's mishandling a fight with the Obama administration over contraception coverage in health care and his pledge to defund Planned Parenthood.

He was not as strong as he needed to be among white working-class voters, a group where President Obama has been consistently weak. He was in serious trouble with Latinos.

Given those realities, did Romney do everything he could have done after the primaries to put himself in a stronger position for the fall campaign? Could he have done more to ameliorate the impact of things he had done to win the nomination? If not a wholesale shift to the center, did he miss opportunities to make himself a more attractive candidate for the fall?

One way to answer those questions is to look at Romney's weakness among Hispanic voters—the biggest single demographic challenge that faced the Republican Party. By the time he had the nomination in hand, he and his party were facing a huge deficit with the nation's fastest-growing minority. This was a problem Republicans had been looking at for many years and one that no amount of talk of reaching out had solved. Few Republicans did well attracting Hispanic votes, and survey after survey showed Romney doing far worse than George W. Bush in 2004 and worse than John McCain in 2008. Bush had done well because Texas shared a border with Mexico and he had become used to dealing with immigrant communities—legal and illegal—in his state. Both he and McCain had pushed at one time for comprehensive immigration reform, including a path to citizenship, although McCain had backed away from that position during his 2008 campaign and his share of the Latino vote ended up well below Bush's. Romney had no connection with the Hispanic community, nor did he have a history of supporting any kind of path to citizenship or legal status. His critical mistake was to see the immigration issue as a weapon with which to attack two of his rivals—Rick Perry and Newt Gingrich—rather than something that demanded a different tone and a more deft handling to prevent his ending up in a deep hole for the general election. The policies he attacked seemed humane—Perry's support for in-state tuition for students who were Texas residents and were the children of illegal immigrants; Gingrich's assertion that illegal immigrants who had been in the country a quarter century or more and had established roots in a community should be allowed to stay and gain legal status. Romney's call for self-deportation compounded his problems.

After the election was over, Matt Rhoades was one of the first among Romney's top advisers to publicly express regret at how aggressively the campaign had used immigration (and by implication how far to the right it had pushed Romney) in the primaries. At the quadrennial conference of campaign managers hosted by Harvard's Institute of Politics in November 2012, Rhoades acknowledged the hazard of using immigration the way they did. When I talked to him about it later, he said the decision to attack Perry was a strategic choice made in the heat of battle at a time when the Texas governor appeared to be a serious threat. He later concluded that the campaign's attacks on Perry's stance on Social Security would have been enough to defeat him. "I feel that we could have beat Rick Perry just with the Social Security hit," he said, "because he just could never really answer his own Social Security position. But hindsight is twenty-twenty. The strategic decision was we have to beat Rick Perry." Self-deportation was neither a strategic nor a tactical decision. It was simply a blunder by the candidate, a verbal ad lib in the middle of a debate. Romney advisers still believed the policy he was describing was fair and unobjectionable, if only he had said it differently. A more benign way of saying it, one adviser later said, would have been "attrition through enforcement."

Two other questions flowed out of the decision to attack Perry and Gingrich on immigration. One was whether there was real debate about the potential consequences of the strategy. When I asked one official, he said, "It obviously wasn't enough. I think this was one of those times where we were very good at tactics, and this was a tactical play that was very obvious, right." Given that it came with such an obvious risk, why wasn't there more debate? "The pull was too strong," he said. "It was too alluring [as] a successful tactic . . . in the confines of the primary. It was too irresistible." Lanhee Chen said, "Anytime you discuss immigration, you always run the risk of creating a wedge issue for a general election. But we ultimately felt like it was an important discussion to have, and it was a politically timely discussion to have, given the primary we were in. So we made a decision to go for it."

There was another reason Romney took the positions he did on immigration. They were consistent with where he had stood before. He had attacked Rudy Giuliani on immigration, charging that New York City was one of the nation's leading sanctuary cities when Giuliani was mayor. He had vetoed a bill similar to the one Perry had signed. If he suddenly reversed course in 2012 by giving Perry a pass on the in-state tuition plan or by giving ground on the question of providing a path to citizenship or legal status, he would have opened himself up to new criticism that he was a flip-flopper. The campaign was always sensitive about not allowing that to become a line of attack by any of his rivals—Republican or Democrat.

The other question is why the campaign did not do more to clean up this problem once they were making the pivot to the general election. Romney had an early opportunity to soften his image on immigration when Florida senator Marco Rubio began to float the idea of finding a compromise on the Dream Act, legislation designed to give young people who had been brought to the United States illegally as children and were graduating from high school a chance to stay in the country and eventually to seek legal status. By completing two years of military service or two years of college they could obtain residency

for six years. The measure enjoyed bipartisan support when it was first introduced, but over time Republicans peeled off. Romney had always opposed it.

Rubio said that his idea would not go as far as the one Obama and the
Democrats favored but that he hoped it would go far enough to win bipartisan
support. Rubio's efforts seemed to offer Romney a lifeline on immigration, something that he could get behind to show that. Instead the campaign kept Rubio
at arm's length, at least publicly. "Privately we were very much encouraged by
what Marco was doing," Chen said. "I think part of the challenge is that they
were working through some specifics, and until we saw some of those specifics,
we weren't going to sign on hook, line, and sinker." Fehrnstrom said the campaign saw Rubio's efforts as potentially helpful. "We were curious about it and
wondering if there would be any kind of political cover that he could provide the
governor by bringing forward his own plan," he said. "But it was always very
nebulous to us. We never saw anything concrete." That conservatives were beginning to raise doubts about Rubio's efforts also gave the campaign pause.

Rubio's efforts were cut short when Obama announced in June that he
would act by executive order to stop deportations of young people who had
been brought to the country as children of illegal immigrants. Romney's team
recognized it as shrewd politics that put the governor in a box. He stumbled in
response, denouncing the process that produced the policy—without the con-
sent of Congress—but refusing to say whether he supported the policy itself.
To oppose it outright would have been hugely damaging politically. To support
it would have meant turning his back on his long-standing position that you
should not reward lawbreaking. "What we tried to do was to talk about process,
talk about the importance of a permanent solution, talk about the fact that
what the president had done had chilled the effort of Marco Rubio and others
that would have been potentially more lasting," Chen said. "But that was what
we were going to be confined to. We were going to be confined to talking about
process rather than substance."

Fehrnstrom said the campaign ultimately believed the best way to deal with
Romney's lack of support among Hispanics was to find a better way to talk
about legal immigration and the impact of Obama's economic policies on the
Hispanic community. The team debated whether Romney should come for-
ward with an immigration plan of his own. Romney's inclination was to do so.
He believed he had ideas worthy of airing in the election. But the consensus
was that it would be a mistake to reopen the debate about immigration policy.
Romney would be at a disadvantage no matter what he proposed. Obama's
Dream Act decision also short-circuited that discussion. When Romney ad-
dressed the National Association of Latino Elected Officials shortly after

Obama issued the order, he talked mostly about strengthening legal immigration but offered no new ideas for dealing with illegals. "We thought if we could somehow focus the discussion about illegal immigration on those who were playing by the rules and how unfair the illegal immigration system was to them, that we could form that connection once again with the Hispanic voter," Fehrnstrom said.

Another option was to launch a more aggressive ad campaign targeted at Hispanics. Ed Gillespie, who was brought in after the primaries to help oversee communications and message strategy, pushed hard for spending money on Spanish-language advertising. Gillespie, a former Republican National Committee chairman and counselor to President George W. Bush, was sensitive to the party's overall problems with Latinos and wanted the campaign to take on the issue more directly. By then, the decision not to offer new policies had been made. "We focused less on taking other positions and more on how we get on the air with Hispanic voters," one campaign official said. "And we were never able to force that until when Ed joined the team. He was a consistent and strong voice and strong advocate for making an appeal to Hispanic voters." It wasn't until near the end of the campaign that Romney began running Spanish-language ads. But another adviser was fatalistic. The campaign wasn't going to solve Romney's or the party's problem with a flight of TV ads. On that point, he was correct. The Republican Party's deficiencies with Hispanic voters were years in the making, and extended beyond the issue of immigration. Republicans long assumed that their conservative and family values meshed well with the values of the Hispanic community, but never worked consistently or effectively to appeal to Latino voters. Certainly immigration was a major problem. After then California governor Pete Wilson backed Proposition 187, an anti–illegal immigration ballot initiative, during his 1994 reelection campaign, the Latino share of the state's electorate jumped dramatically—and turned even more against the Republicans. But Republicans were on the wrong side of other issues important to the Hispanic community. In 2012, the Obama campaign focused its Spanish-language ads on the president's Affordable Care Act, not immigration.

So Romney was carrying his own and his party's baggage with Hispanics as he moved from the primaries to the general election. His own research told his team just how bad the situation was. "For a lot of these Hispanic voters, the first thing that came up was 'Romney's wealthy,'" said one senior adviser. "It wasn't the immigration stuff, it was his wealth, the sense that he's out of touch. And then beyond that, it was the health care plan. They loved Obamacare." The campaign could find no solution to these problems.

———

The primary campaign inflicted other damage. Romney's credibility on taxes and deficits was compromised by decisions made as he was fending off his more conservative rivals. In September 2011, he had issued his initial plan for the economy, which drew a tepid response from conservatives. The *Wall Street Journal* editorial page offered this underwhelmed reaction: "The 160 pages and 59 proposals also strike us as surprisingly timid and tactical considering our economic predicament. They're a technocrat's guide more than a reform manifesto." The plan did not flesh out his proposals for cutting taxes or reforming the tax code. The feeling among his advisers was that to start down that path would inevitably lead to a bidding war with the other candidates. Herman Cain had his "9-9-9" plan. Gingrich had his call for a zero capital gains tax rate. Santorum had his proposals to give manufacturers a bigger break than others. "We're just going to get into a shouting match," an adviser said. Romney, for example, was not willing to take the capital gains tax down to zero. He thought it was bad policy and he recognized that it was bad politics for him, given his wealth and earnings, even if conservatives loved it.

As other candidates offered their plans and as Santorum began to rise as a serious challenger, conservative commentators hammered Romney for not being bold enough. He responded by proposing the 20 percent reduction in income tax rates a week before the Michigan and Arizona primaries. "I think there were certainly some economic conservatives that thought pretty strongly that we need a more forceful articulation of a tax reform proposal," one adviser said. "But there was also a sense beyond what everyone else may have been saying that if we were going to be the candidate of the economy and of improving the economy, it was going to be hard to advance that discussion much further without fleshing out the tax discussion. . . . We made the risk-reward assessment at the time."

By some independent analyses, based on their interpretation of the plan, Romney was calling for $5 trillion in new tax cuts, most of it going to the wealthiest Americans. He said he would offset the cuts, particularly for the rich, by eliminating deductions. But he declined to spell out which ones. Once through the primaries, Romney faced continued criticism from Obama and the Democrats that his plan did not add up. Either he didn't have answers to how he would offset the tax cuts or he didn't want to reveal them because they might be politically unpalatable. Lanhee Chen said Romney discussed the conundrum with his economic advisers. Their conclusion was that once he moved off talking about the broad principles of his plan, he was begging for trouble. Even if a single detail came out they would be forced into a cascade of specificity. "We made the decision to articulate the principles and talk about the need for tax reform and our belief that reform was a part of growth, as opposed to getting into a specific discussion," he said. He added that the campaign eventually produced a fully developed tax reform plan, one that he said when dynamically scored met all the requirements Romney had set out—to retain progressivity, to make sure that the top 6 percent of earners continued to pay what they do now under the new system, and to cut tax rates by 20 percent. "We had all of those features in a plan," Chen said. "But we felt like talking about it in details was going to be a challenge for us to sustain. In all truth, it was a pretty darn good plan." He added, "There was no way Mitt was going to let taxes go up on the middle class. It just wasn't going to happen. I can say that in all honesty. It's not just a political statement. He wasn't—he just didn't believe that was the right thing to do."

With scripted silence, Romney remained on the defensive on taxes.

Romney's vanquished rivals eventually offered their praise for the political savvy he and his campaign had shown in winning the nomination. His competitors acknowledged that they had underestimated his dogged determination and his competitiveness. One rival came away impressed that Romney had grasped earlier than any of the other candidates how much the world had changed. "Mitt did something very smart before everybody else," this person said. "He saw the super PAC future. He had the network to fund it, he funded it early, and Santorum and Gingrich kind of got the joke later, but it was too late and too little. Mitt only in his highest-water mark had 30 percent of the market—70 percent of the market share was for somebody else. So if somebody could have successfully kept pace with him for a while, while the 70 percent aggregated and had their resources to endure that, I think he could have toppled them. But that requires an early super PAC, not dollar-for-dollar money but at least proportionate money with Mitt. . . . His lesson from '08 was he let Huckabee out, survived too long, should have pummeled him early, and that super PAC just pummeled anybody who got in the way. For all of the bemoaning about how he won, the so-called power brokers weren't able to coalesce around anybody early."

Newt Gingrich, too, came to a grudging respect for the campaign Romney waged to win the nomination. Even before he quit the race, he was reassessing Romney as an opponent. "Romney's proven a couple of things," he told me shortly before the Wisconsin primary. "He's tougher than I thought he was, which is good, and he'll become president. He is a very good arouser of resources. I mean, I'm beginning to think he may actually be able to match Obama's resources, which would be extraordinary." In that same conversation over breakfast in Milwaukee, he said, "I also had to realize, if ruthlessly relentlessly negative is necessary to beat Obama, he may be the better nominee. I mean, he may just have both the resources and the toughness and the willingness to say and do anything. That may be the only way you beat Obama." Three months later, as we reviewed events after the nomination battle had ended, he offered an additional insight into both Romney and the Republican Party electorate. I recalled that in February he had confidently predicted that the party would never nominate Romney. "I was wrong," he said. "The party was desperately looking for the person who could beat Obama, so the number one criteria wasn't, are you conservative enough? [It was] can you beat Obama?" He said he learned this during his attack on Bain. The ideology fight was being overwhelmed by the Obama fight. Almost overnight the Bain issue was defined as an attack on free enterprise. "Now, part of that was Romney being clever," he said, "but part of it's guys like Limbaugh, who are not particularly moved by Romney but they were responding to, 'My God, how could you sound like Obama?'"

Romney's campaign had other pressing needs coming out of the primaries. It was nearly broke and leagues behind Obama in building a campaign capable of waging the general election. "We had to expand our finance team, digital and political teams," Rhoades said. "Obviously we knew [the Obama campaign was] spending a lot of money on something in 2011 and it wasn't TV commercials at that point. We believed that they were building out an incredible ground floor, so we needed to build out our political teams in new states." Obama's team had a head start of more than twelve months—some would say four years. Rhoades had kept the Romney operation lean through the primaries but now had to expand exponentially overnight. He asked his department heads in the spring to draw up plans for expansion. Zac Moffatt, who ran the digital side of the campaign, told Rhoades he needed his staff to grow from 14 to 110 in fifty days. Moffatt played catch-up through the rest of the campaign. Romney had set up field operations as the primary and caucus calendar dictated, but once those events were over, they often shuttered their offices and moved on to the next contest. Rich Beeson's political department, with help from the Republican National Committee, had to put in place state-by-state units to turn out the vote. Gail Gitcho's communications shop needed more help quickly. Most pressing of all was the need to raise money. Romney had spent $91 million in winning the nomination, but his war chest was now almost empty. Money had been pouring in since April, but most of that could be used only for the general election, and that didn't start, by the rules of the Federal Election Commission, until Romney formally accepted the nomination in Tampa at the end of August. Spencer Zwick put together an ambitious fund-raising plan and it was working, but finding new people who hadn't already given to Romney for the primaries was one of the biggest challenges the campaign faced. He had swamped his Republican rivals with superior financial resources but now was desperately short of money to wage a campaign against the president during the summer months.

One other problem remained unaddressed as the general election campaign began. Voters still didn't particularly like Romney. After running for president almost continuously since 2006, Romney had yet to fully define himself—and to the extent he had, it was as a wealthy patrician who was unapproachable to the average voter. These voters recognized certain attributes—a man of values, a man of faith, a man devoted to his family, a record of success in business—but they still found him buttoned-up, distant, and unimaginably wealthy. Even Romney's research was telling the campaign that. As one focus group participant said, "He's been too rich for too long."

BOOK THREE

THE CHOICE

CHAPTER 19

The New America

P residential elections are often retold from the inside out, as if all power and wisdom flow from the strategists plotting and arguing inside their secured headquarters. But the story is often better told from the outside in, as a way of highlighting how so much that happens in American politics is determined by larger forces that campaign strategists can change only at the margins. This was certainly the case in 2012. For all the drama of any moment, for all the exaggerated attention given to one daily controversy or another, for all the praise heaped on the winners and the second-guessing of the losers, for all the elements that make political campaigns compelling, entertaining, exasperating, and sometimes just plain weird, elections play out against the reality of an ever-changing country that powerfully directs the action.

The economy was one driving force, as it always is in presidential campaigns. But two others came into play as well in 2012. One was the power of demographic change that continued to alter the face of America and the fortunes of the two political parties, irrespective of the candidates. This has long been part of the political landscape, but never quite so clearly as in the first decade of the twenty-first century when a rising Hispanic population and the aging of the baby boom generation brought new issues and a potent new voice to the table. The other factor controlling the election was relatively newer but no less significant. Political polarization, once thought confined to the elites, was a pervasive factor in shaping the political behavior of voters everywhere.

Americans were still in a gloomy mood as the fall election approached, beaten down by the effects of the economic collapse in the fall of 2008 and frustrated with three years of dysfunctional government in Washington. The recession had hit with overpowering force, pushing the unemployment rate above 10 percent for the first time in almost three decades. The collapse forced many families into foreclosure on their homes. Many others discovered that their homes were worth far less than the mortgages they owed on them. They were frozen economically. Retirement accounts shrank by 30 or 40 percent. Most studies had shown that Obama's stimulus package had prevented an even worse collapse, yet the economy was anything but sound. Unemployment had started to tick down from its peak, but in May 2012 it was still 8.2 percent and had been above 8 percent for forty consecutive months. Every poll indicated that voters cared most about one issue: jobs. Nothing else came close to the economy as the greatest concern on the minds of the electorate. No president since Franklin Roosevelt during the Depression had faced reelection with unemployment so high, though there were few examples from which to draw any firm conclusions. Reagan flirted with rates that high when he was reelected, but economic growth was roaring at a pace far beyond that of Obama's economy. There would be no "morning in America" in the president's campaign ads in 2012.

Long-term unemployment had reached epidemic proportions. Forty percent of the unemployed—almost six million total—had been out of work for six months or longer, in danger of becoming part of a permanent class of workers who would become unemployable as their skills failed to keep pace with the changing needs of the economy. Unemployed workers were moving back into the workforce at the slowest pace since the late 1940s. The *Economist* magazine noted that for the first time in decades, unemployed workers were more likely to drop out of the workforce than to find a new job.

Pollster Peter Hart felt the force of this gloom and pessimism when he organized the first in a series of election-year focus groups for the Annenberg Public Policy Center at the University of Pennsylvania. He began the project, which would run throughout the entire election cycle, in the fall of 2011 with a group of twelve people from the Cincinnati area. Eight had supported Obama in 2008, and the other four had voted for John McCain. When Hart first went around the table and asked people to describe the state of the country, he heard a litany of frustration:

"Disappointing," the first woman said.

"Stagnant," said another woman.

A third woman said, "Going poorly."

In rapid-fire order, the others concurred:

"Contentious."

"Outlook is grim."

"Challenging."

"Running in place."

Why were they so downbeat? The general manager at a family-owned garden center responded, "Unemployment, no job creation, the amount of money of the national debt. It's just, everything's compounded." A man who worked in the investment business pointed to a more fundamental problem. "I feel like that the whole system is flawed, and the fact that, when I say that, I mean that

I feel like that the politicians sometimes aren't really the ones. They're just the mouthpiece. But the people behind their campaign, the people who are contributing to their campaign, are actually the people who are running the country. Whether you call that good or bad or right or left, I think that fundamental problem with our government is what's put us in this place that we're in right now." He said America was running in place and seemed destined to stay there until the next election, maybe longer. A woman who worked in retail sales added, "I think the whole contentiousness that we've mentioned several times is building and building and building, and it's almost to a point now where people just really don't know if they can trust anyone in politics."

Hart asked a twenty-five-year-old man what worried him most. "If I'm going to have a job," he said. "In my family, I've seen the economy hounds hit. My father was laid off for many years and then just recently it's come to hit me as well." Hart asked the others how many knew someone in their immediate family who had been laid off or lost a job during the recession. Seven of twelve raised their hands. One woman said, "The America I grew up knowing isn't the America I know today." Hart asked if anyone around the table felt worry-free. "You'd have to define worry-free," a woman said. "I mean, I can put food on my table. I have no problem putting food on my table. But will I able to retire at sixty, seventy, seventy-five? I have no idea." Hart then asked whether they thought the next generation would be better off than they were. This has always been a hallmark of the American experience, the boundless optimism that holds that the future will be better than the present and that each succeeding generation will live more comfortable lives than the previous. Only three hands went up around the table. Nine members of the group were betting against the American dream, saying they believed the next generation would be less prosperous than their generation.

Two months later, Hart convened the second of his groups. This time he invited all Republicans to a facility in Fairfax, Virginia, in one of the most contested areas of the 2012 election. He found the same pessimism around the table that he had discovered in Cincinnati. When he asked for a word or phrase to describe America at that moment, the answers wove another tapestry of fear and disappointment. "How many people say, 'I think this is the start of a downward decline'?" Hart asked. "We're going around. One, two, three, four, five, six, seven, eight—eight out of twelve of you. Why?" A thirty-five-year-old tax preparer was the first to respond. "We're not sure really, as a society, we're not really sure where we should be heading. And we have a leader that's not taking the reins and pointing us in the proper direction." A fifty-nine-year-old realtor, the most conservative member of the group, said, "I think there's too many people on the government dole or on the take. And I'm afraid the balance is already tipped. And when the balance is tipped, then they're always going to be voting for what they're going to get for nothing." One of the youngest people at the table said, "I would say that I'm no longer hopeful that I think things are going to get better before they get substantially worse. I always thought things kind of just got better. I don't think that anymore." Hart then asked the twelve participants the same question he had asked in Cincinnati: Would the next generation be better off than the current? This time, not a single hand was raised.

For the next year, Hart traveled through the battleground states as he plumbed the opinions of voters. He heard a consistent refrain: pessimism bordering on despair about the political system, disappointment in the president, lack of connection with Romney, concerns about the Republican Party. In June 2012, he convened a group in the Denver suburbs. He found that only four of ten people who had supported Obama in 2008 were definitely in his camp again. The members of this group saw the economy as still troubled, but with signs of improvement. "President Obama's challenge is not in the current conditions, but rather, in contending with voters' disappointment in their unmet high expectations," he later wrote. "Even more, these participants have no idea where we go from here. The president has not drawn a roadmap, nor has he provided any real perspective of where we are currently." But Romney had not broken through. "When asked to write down what they know about him, most wrote either nothing at all or broad generalities that could describe any Republican candidate," he said. Obama had not escaped from either the economy or the sense of personal disappointment in his leadership. Romney was, as Hart noted, still just a stick figure rather than a fully formed challenger.

In the spring of 2012, America reached a long-expected tipping point. Minority births outnumbered those of whites for the first time since the founding of the nation. Minorities—blacks, Hispanics, Asians, and others—accounted for 50.4 percent of all births in the country over the previous year. William Frey, one of the nation's leading demographers, described it as a "transformation from a mostly white baby boomer culture to the more globalized multiethnic country that we are becoming." The tipping point had been years in the making. Each census over the past three decades provided more evidence that America was undergoing one of the most important cultural and demographic upheavals in its history.

The 2010 census showed a slowing in the nation's population growth—the lowest rate of increase since the Depression, thanks in part to the impact of the 2008 recession and a reduced rate of immigration. Frey's essay "The 2010 Census: America on the Cusp," which he prepared for the *Milken Institute*

Review, sketched in detail the new America of the twenty-first century. America's population grew by 27.3 million during the decade, but whites accounted for just 2.3 million of the total, or 8 percent. Whites still maintained the majority of the population—64 percent—and would for many years to come. But among those under age eighteen, there was an absolute decline in the number of whites in America during the ten years between 2000 and 2010. And yet that America was aging was also one of the messages of the new census. The fastest-growing segment of the population by age were those forty-five and over, as baby boomers moved toward retirement. The fastest-growing segment of the population by race was Hispanics. The demographic differences between these two groups provided a stark reminder of America's future, with the two poised for conflict over scarce resources as an older, whiter population gradually gives way to rising generations whose members are significantly more diverse and whose attitudes about race and gender are far different. Frey pointed to another tipping point in the country's demographics. "For the first time, households headed by married couples were less than half the total," he said. Only a fifth of all households were what we think of as traditional families: two parents with children. Sixty years earlier, these families made up 80 percent of American households.

All of this added up to trouble for the Republican Party. In the competition for votes, Obama and the Democrats were on the side of the rising America. It was no secret that Obama did better with younger voters, with minorities, with singles rather than marrieds, with women more than men. Meanwhile, Romney and the Republicans represented a coalition that was fast losing numbers and threatened with the loss of political power. When Ronald Reagan won the presidency in 1980, whites accounted for 89 percent of the electorate. When Obama won in 2008, the white share of the vote had fallen to 74 percent. The Republicans couldn't hold back the glacial strength of demographic change that continued to scour and remake the political landscape. Given that, where they had failed was in not doing anything significant to alter the balance of power in the battle for political support among these newer voters.

Frey sketched out Romney's challenge in another research paper. He ran three scenarios for the 2012 election. The first was based on an electorate that looked almost identical to that of 2008 in terms of demographic shares and the candidates' margins among whites, blacks, Hispanics, and Asians. Under those conditions, Obama was headed toward an electoral landslide with more than 350 electoral votes. A second scenario called for an electorate closer to that of 2004, when Republicans equaled the percentage of Democrats. Under that scenario, Romney was the projected winner with 286 electoral votes. A third scenario blended the first two: white turnout and margins similar to 2008, minority turnout and margins what they were in 2008. Obama was the projected winner of that one as well, with 292. The census findings underscored that, at the starting gate, Romney and the Republicans were running uphill.

The other force shaping the election was the deep polarization that affected almost every aspect of American politics—in political terms something nearly as powerful as the demographic changes under way. America was a country of opposing camps. Obama had run with the promise that he would unite red America and blue America. Three years into his presidency, the divisions were more sharply etched than ever. More than any general feelings about the direction of the country or the state of the economy, more than the pervasive frustrations with gridlock and bickering in Washington, these political and cultural divisions profoundly shaped attitudes and set the parameters for the coming clash between Obama and the Republicans. Those on one side believed they were an expression of the values of a new multiethnic, multicultural, and increasingly tolerant America, the rising America of the twenty-first century. Those on the other saw themselves as guardians of the traditional values and traditional families that had built the country into the envy of the world in the previous century and that they believed should remain at its core. These opposing camps were divided almost evenly in terms of size, with a shrinking number of independents in the middle.

The country had seen some of the same during the presidency of George W. Bush. He became the most polarizing president in American history, measured by the gulf in his approval rating between Republicans and Democrats, until Obama came into office. Obama as polarizer was always there in plain sight, particularly in the late stages of the 2008 campaign when there were ugly expressions about him at Republican rallies. But it was either overlooked or ignored. Gary Jacobson of the University of California, San Diego, noted that Obama had won 53 percent of the popular vote in 2008, the highest percentage for any Democrat since Lyndon Johnson's 1964 landslide. But he also pointed out that Obama's coalition included one of the smallest shares ever of voters who did not identify with the party of the winning candidate.

Geographic voting patterns were more fixed than ever. Fewer counties were up for grabs. Bill Bishop, a journalist and geographic demographer and author of the book *The Big Sort,* tracked the change over time in presidential margins by county. In 1976, about a quarter of the population lived in counties where the winner's victory margin was twenty points or more. By 2008, about half the population lived in counties where the winner's margin was twenty or more. A close look at the decade's election returns showed the rigidity of county-by-county leanings. Between Bush's win in 2004 and Obama's in 2008, just 382 of 3,147 counties in the United States went from one party to the other. Most of those—338—had moved toward the Democrats.

Partisan self-identification defined the critical differences in attitudes far more than traditional demographic measures, which once had been the standard. A Pew Research Center study reported, "As Americans head to the polls this November, their values and basic beliefs are more polarized along partisan lines than at any point in the past 25 years. Unlike in 1987, when this series of surveys began, the values gap between Republicans and Democrats is now greater than gender, age, race or class divides." Over a series of forty-eight measures of values, the average difference between Republicans and Democrats had doubled in a quarter century. And nearly all of the increase, the study said, occurred during Bush's and Obama's presidencies. The summer 2012 study by the *Washington Post* and the Kaiser Family Foundation compared attitudes with a similar study done fourteen years earlier. The findings underscored how the partisan divisions had become the new normal in America. In 1998, 41 percent of Republicans and 45 percent of Democrats called themselves "strong" partisans. In the new study, 65 percent of Republicans and 62 percent of Democrats now identified themselves that way. As in the Pew survey, there was a wide and growing gulf in attitudes about the federal government. A solid majority of Republicans offered consistently high scores on limiting government's role, while a solid majority of Democrats were clustered at the other end of the scale—sharp changes from fourteen years earlier. On social issues, the gaps were similarly large.

With so many families worried about the economy, Obama had little hope of matching his performance in his first campaign. He would have to keep his losses to a minimum. With the country divided along partisan and ideological lines, each candidate would have to play to his base. And given the depth and breadth of the polarization, fewer voters were going to be truly up for grabs, no matter how it appeared at first blush. Mobilization would become more important than persuasion. The conditions pointed to an ugly and grinding general election campaign.

CHAPTER 20

Defining Battle

On May 15, 2012, the Obama campaign began airing a television commercial called "Steel." It was unusually long for a political ad—two minutes rather than the customary thirty seconds—and it aired in only a few markets. The ad profiled a steel company, GST Steel in Kansas City, after Bain Capital had purchased it. The story was told from the point of view of workers who lost their jobs and their health and retirement benefits when the company eventually went bankrupt. The ad was understated in tone, devastating in content. It opened with one of the workers, Joe Soptic, who said, "I was a steelworker for thirty years. We had a reputation for quality products. It was something that was American made. And we weren't rich, but I was able to put my daughter through college. . . . That stopped with the sale of the plant to Bain Capital." The ad cut to a still photo of a younger Mitt Romney at Bain and then video of candidate Romney on the stump saying, "I know how business works. I know why jobs come and why they go." As weathered newspaper clips reporting on the plant's closure flashed across the screen, Soptic provided the voice-over: "They made as much money off it as they could and they closed it down and filed for bankruptcy without any concern for the families or the communities." Joe Cobb, identified as a steelworker for thirty-one years, delivered a sound bite that was played over and over in the days following. "It was like a vampire," he said. "They came in and sucked the life out of us." As the screen filled with images of an abandoned factory site, Soptic said with an air of sadness, "It was like watching an old friend bleed to death." Romney reappeared on the screen. "As I look around at the millions of Americans without work," he said, "it breaks my heart." The ad continued on these themes for another minute, ending with more words from Soptic about Romney: "He's running for president, and if he's going to run the country the way he ran our business, I wouldn't want him there. He would be so out of touch with the average person in this country. How could you care? How could you care for the average working person if you feel this way?"

The two-minute ad marked the opening volley in the long-awaited contest to define Mitt Romney and the beginning of one of the most critical phases of the campaign. The general election had been taking shape for several weeks as Romney scrambled to complete a lengthy to-do list—from repairing some of the damage inflicted by the primary campaign to meeting the urgent need to expand a lean operation into one capable of matching the muscle and sophistication of the incumbent, whose team had spent the prior year preparing for this moment. From one angle, and particularly in retrospect, the battle to define Romney appeared to be a one-sided contest. Obama's campaign attacked and attacked and attacked, pouring tens of millions of dollars into the battleground states for advertising that scored Romney's record in business and government—with almost no pushback by the challenger. It was as if the Obama team had caught Romney flat-footed, as if Romney simply forfeited the most crucial definitional period of the election. But the reality was not that simple. Romney's team was short on funds and therefore limited in its ability to respond. But his advisers were hardly caught by surprise. In fact, his advisers had begun preparing for the moment—and even the specific attacks—as far back as the previous fall. How and why they responded as they did was not just because of an imbalance in resources, although that was a critical factor. Their response also grew out of fundamentally different strategic assumptions about what the campaign ultimately was about and how it would or could be won—assumptions that would be the target of criticism and second-guessing once the campaign ended.

"We're going to beat Obama," Stuart Stevens said. It was April 3, the morning of the Wisconsin primary, and we were having breakfast at the Marriott Milwaukee West in Waukesha, a Republican stronghold outside of Milwaukee. Stevens, the chief strategist for the Romney campaign, was a charming and sometimes mercurial political strategist who with business partner Russ Schriefer ran one of the leading Republican advertising firms in the country. At one point in the campaign, he was featured on the cover of the *New Republic* in the likeness of the don in the Dos Equis beer commercials, with the headline "The Most Interesting Man in the World." Stevens, a Mississippi native, indeed was an interesting man. He was a fitness freak. His office in the Romney headquarters was a cross between a workout room and a pharmacy. It included a ski machine and a bicycle, assorted other fitness gear and clothing, and a desk piled with containers of vitamins and other nutrients. In between campaigns, Stevens was an adventure seeker. He roamed the world, competing in marathon cross-country ski races or bicycle races. He wrote a book, *Feeding Frenzy,* about a monthlong dash through Europe in which he ate in twenty-nine different restaurants with Michelin stars. He wrote for the television series *Northern Exposure*. He was part of the advertising team that helped George W. Bush win two elections. In 2008 he started with John Mc-Cain and then jumped to Romney. In the 2012 Romney campaign, he wore many hats, including that of chief strategist, chief communicator, ad maker, and chief speechwriter. Too many, as it would become clear, as others on the campaign chafed at the disorganization he sometimes brought to deliberations. He had the ear of the candidate, though they could hardly have been more different. They were the campaign's examples of left brain versus right brain, seeming opposites in personality and demeanor.

More than anyone else in the operation, Stevens established and articulated the strategic framework that guided Romney. He told others that this would not be a Match.com election, his shorthand for 2008, when so many people felt so positive about Obama. It would be a Monster.com campaign—all about jobs and the economy. "My take on the whole thing has always been it's going to be easy or impossible," he said that April morning in Wisconsin. "It wouldn't seem easy but that it would be. And that it was going to be an economically driven election." During the 2010 election cycle, Stevens had begun traveling to jobs fairs around the country, filming the stories of people in the lines as they sought work. He talked constantly about the suffering of the unemployed and the state of the country under Obama. He urged everyone he knew to read the story by Michael Luo, published in the *New York Times* in August 2010, about one woman's descent from a middle-class existence to life in a cheap motel hundreds of miles from home after losing her job and later her unemployment benefits. He launched a project to find and film people who had gone from hope to despair during Obama's presidency. One member of the creative team at the campaign, Jim Ferguson—"Fergie" to everyone—had read about a young man in Iowa who had lost his job and was now digging graves. Ferguson went to Iowa and somehow found him and filmed him and made a poignant video about how hope and change had not worked out for some Americans. Stevens was virtually certain that the campaign would turn on the economy and voters' dissatisfaction with the president's performance. He ticked through the statistics of Obama's presidency: More Americans were out of work, more Americans had lost their homes, more Americans had fallen into poverty. "They can't blame Romney for that," he said.

Where are you at this point? I asked him that morning. "Doesn't matter where we are, it's just where he is. [If] his job approval's at 43 [percent], the guy's got problems. Forty-eight? That's better for him, if it stays there." He said the president seemed intent on trying to play off dissatisfaction with what George W. Bush had done in office. "He's trying to reformulate an argument here he would use against Bush. The problem is, he's president. It's not an MRI of the soul," he said. "It's an MRI of his record. And they can't change that."

Obama's advisers understood everything Stevens said about the economy. They believed that Obama's biggest opponent would be the economy itself, more than any of the Republicans. But they also saw the challenger as particularly ill-suited to run in a year in which their research showed that people were looking for someone who would champion the middle class, someone whom they could touch and feel, not just a jobs mechanic. It was David Axelrod, Stevens's counterpart on the Obama campaign, who had been saying that presidential elections were an "MRI of the soul" for the candidates, and that summed up precisely how the Chicago team saw the campaign. Though they had long assumed Romney would become the Republican nominee, Obama's advisers also believed he was the wrong candidate for the times. Jim Messina said throughout the spring and summer that Romney was a bad fit in the industrial Midwest, with his profile as a corporate executive who had shuttered factories. Axelrod believed Romney reflected two aspects of contemporary life that were most troubling to people. One was the general unfairness, the feeling that things were tilted toward the wealthy or the bosses. The other was the belief that too many politicians were more interested in self-preservation than problem solving. He believed that voters would come to see Romney that way, particularly if the Obama campaign did its job. They watched him through the nomination battle, as he was pummeled by his opponents or made his own mistakes—dealing with his tax returns, for example—and saw the attacks exposing genuine vulnerabilities that they could exploit in the general election. After the election was over, Axelrod put it this way: "On paper, Romney seemed like a good candidate because of [being a] businessman, job creator, and a lot of that stuff. But at the end of the day he was maybe the worst candidate to speak to this. . . . Nobody knew Mitt Romney really at the beginning. I don't think they knew him at all. [What] they knew in the first instance was businessman, and the businessman patina was valuable. . . . It was very important for us to fill in the blanks. If he had just been allowed to be this cardboard-cutout successful businessman, he conceivably could have won."

The attacks on Romney were months in the making. Obama's advisers assembled a huge database on Romney. They hired financial researchers and experts on SEC filings to pore over the records of Bain's investments. They dissected his record as governor of Massachusetts. When Romney was governor, all his public appearances and statements were videotaped. The Obama campaign got copies of the videos and transcribed them all. They sent people to the Cayman Islands to dig into the investment entities associated with Romney. They began finding and filming people who had been hurt when companies owned by Bain were closed down.

Stephanie Cutter, who shifted from the White House to Chicago in late 2011 to become a deputy campaign manager, pushed hard to drive attention to Bain and Romney's record as early as possible. She was an alumnus of John Kerry's 2004 campaign and knew what an incumbent president's reelection campaign could do to a challenger. She was determined to use whatever resources were available to do the same to Romney, starting long before he was the nominee. She sent what the campaign called "Bain victims" into Iowa and New Hampshire during the GOP caucus and primary campaigns to tell their stories at press conferences. When Newt Gingrich took up the issue as the GOP candidates were moving from New Hampshire into South Carolina, she became alarmed that it could lose its potency because of the way both Gingrich and Romney handled it. Cutter described Gingrich's Bain attack as overshooting the runway. Gingrich's attacks, along with those of his super PAC, allowed Romney to turn the issue in his favor—in a Republican primary at least—by accusing his critics of launching an attack on free enterprise. The Obama campaign intended to fight a different battle. They would marry it with attacks on Romney's unwillingness to release his tax returns and his Swiss bank account and Cayman Islands investments. To them this would be a debate not about the free enterprise system but about the character and values of the Republican nominee.

Romney's team was far from indifferent or lackadaisical about the role Bain would play in the election. They knew it had been a factor in every campaign Romney had run, starting in 1994 against Senator Edward M. Kennedy, and in 2002 when he ran for governor. Like the Obama team, their preparation began in the fall of 2011. Bob White, a cofounder of Bain and one of Romney's closest confidants, oversaw the project. He believed deeply in what Bain had done and in the integrity of the partners and the company. White conducted a seminar for the Romney team: What is Bain Capital? What is a private equity firm? How does one work? The discussions included lines of attack they could expect—such as Bain profiting even when companies went out of business, or the role of outsourcing or offshoring of jobs. They discussed a small group of companies whose stories would provide fodder for Obama's attacks, companies that had been used before by Romney's opponents. White oversaw the creation of an internal team to deal with the coming attacks—a lawyer, researchers, and communications experts who could respond instantly. They put together case studies of companies, timelines of what had happened, all the vulnerabilities they could compile. They reached out to CEOs of companies Bain had owned to check their facts and to find documents. "We had CEOs crawling around up in their attics looking for records," Eric Fehrnstrom said.

The team also searched out the positive stories about Bain. White believed there was a good story to tell—specifically, more than 120 investments in about a hundred companies, the vast majority of which were successful. As the Obama team was filming victims, the Romney team started to film testimonials featuring people from CEOs to middle managers to younger workers. Ashley O'Connor, who coordinated the advertising operation, sent crews out around the country to build an archive of good news. The inventory included nearly two dozen positive statements ready to be used when needed. But they came to realize that tit-for-tat wasn't sufficient. "[The Obama campaign] very cleverly also made it a character issue about Mitt," Fehrnstrom later said, "and I think it contributed to this sentiment that Mitt 'doesn't understand people like me.'"

Bob White argued for another approach as well, which was to do more to fill in Romney's biography. He was a consistent advocate for doing more to introduce people to Romney, to enhance his image, to show him in settings and with stories and language that contrasted with the stereotyped figure in the Democrats' attacks. He believed that the time to do that was in the summer before the conventions—or much earlier. "We need to define him," he would say. Beth Myers and Tagg Romney believed the same thing but were never forceful enough to change things. Tagg had pressed at the earliest stages of the campaign, even before the primaries, for more attention to humanizing his dad. Eventually he stopped getting invitations to campaign strategy meetings.

Obama's two-minute "Steel" ad was intended mostly as a conversation starter and an experiment, rather than a full-fledged paid advertising campaign. The campaign spent less than $100,000 to put it on television. But it was discussed (and played) repeatedly on cable news shows, and the amplification effect gave the topic widespread prominence in the public conversation about the race. The ad produced immediate results—though not exactly as the Obama campaign might have hoped. Newark mayor Cory Booker, on NBC's *Meet the Press,* said he found attacks on the morality of private equity to be "nauseating." Steve Rattner, who had served as Obama's auto czar and was a prominent Democratic donor, appeared on MSNBC's *Morning Joe* the day after Booker made his comments. "I think the ad is unfair," he said. He said Bain had operated within the rules and had earned a good reputation doing so. While decrying the loss of jobs for some workers, he added, "This is part of capitalism. This is part of life, and I don't think there's anything Bain Capital did that they need to be embarrassed about." Ed Rendell, the former governor of Pennsylvania, told BuzzFeed, "I think they're very disappointing. I think Bain is fair game, because Romney has made it fair game. But I think how you examine it, the tone, what you say, is important as well." Those criticisms reflected the long-standing connections many Democrats had with private equity firms. Obama had received a substantial amount of money from Bain employees.

The day after Booker's criticism, Obama was asked about the Bain attacks during a press conference at a NATO summit in Chicago. He said they were not a distraction but the essence of what the campaign was about. "If your main argument for how to grow the economy is, 'I knew how to make a lot of money for investors,' then you are missing what this job is about," Obama said. "It doesn't mean you weren't good at private equity. But that's not what my job is as president. My job is to take into account everybody, not just some." Asked whether he thought Romney was responsible for the job losses cited in the attacks, Obama said, "Mr. Romney is responsible for the proposals he is putting forward for how he says he is going to fix the economy. And if the main basis for him suggesting he can do a better job is his track record as the head of a private equity firm, then both the upsides and the downsides are worth examining."

The next week, Bill Clinton weighed in and appeared to create more heartburn for Chicago. In a CNN interview, he gave Romney high marks for his business record and defended the role of private equity in the economy, noting that not all investments in failing companies turn into success stories. He saw nothing disqualifying in Romney's biography. "The man who has been governor and had a sterling business career crosses the qualification threshold [to be president]," he said. Obama's team stood its ground. His advisers dismissed the criticism by Booker and Rendell and commentators as a conversation among the elites who lived in television green rooms rather than the real world. Three days after the president responded, I was in Chicago and sat down with Axelrod. "All we're saying is, it certainly doesn't qualify him to be president and he's offering it as a qualification," he said. "That really is the linchpin of his whole argument, that he's an economic whiz who can get under the hood and fix the economy, and that's a very dubious proposition. It was dubious ten years ago when he pitched it to the people of Massachusetts, and it didn't turn out well, and it's dubious now." Then he got to the bottom line. "We just got out of the field yesterday in the battleground states and there's nothing in that polling that tells me that this has been a bad week for us."

On May 26, Obama met with his political advisers in the Roosevelt Room in the White House. The campaign had run almost forty hours of positive ads that month aimed at establishing Obama's credentials as a protector of the middle class and reminding voters of the economic conditions when he took office. That same plan, set out much earlier, anticipated a shift to ads attacking Romney beginning in June. But Messina had a significant change in plans to present to the president. What he put on the table was new—a proposal to radically rearrange how and when the campaign would spend its money. Messina, Axelrod, Plouffe, and Grisolano had been talking about the importance of the summer months and the potential for Republican super PACs to bring their collective resources to bear in attacking Obama. "We were concerned that the super PACs would overwhelm us in the summer and we needed to be fortified for that," Axelrod said. "But the bigger thing was, we needed to define him in the race in the summer, because my read of history was that there has never been a race that's been determined by an ad that appeared after Labor Day." Messina told the president he wanted to take $63 million already budgeted for the fall media and spend it during the summer. The proposal called for taking about half of the money slotted for September and about 40 percent allocated for October and shoving it to June and July and August. Messina also made clear that if the president signed off, the campaign risked being dramatically outspent on the air by the Romney campaign in October, unless it exceeded its fund-raising projections, which at that moment appeared problematic. The campaign had missed one of its fund-raising targets that spring, a rarity for an operation that always seemed flush with cash. Messina had quietly ordered a monthlong hiring freeze.

Most of the post-election attention on the May 26 meeting focused on the advertising budget, but another part of the discussion was equally important. Messina also recommended that the president sign off on an immediate and substantial expansion in the field operation. He was worried about the pace of the campaign's grassroots organizing. The number of persuadable voters was minuscule. To win, the Obama campaign needed to change the electorate in the battleground states, and the only way to do that was through a more intensive effort to register voters and then get them to the polls. Without a more robust registration effort, which was labor-intensive, Obama would face substantial difficulties winning several of the battleground states. If the campaign wanted to stay competitive in as many places as possible, Messina believed, he needed Obama to approve this as well. Messina and Plouffe knew how important it was to beef up the ground operation, but they faced strong internal pressure to scale it back. Then and later, others in the campaign pushed hard to take money from the organizing budget—did the campaign really need eight hundred paid staff in Florida?—and put it into advertising. Messina fought hard and prevailed.

Enthusiasm was another problem that a more robust ground operation could address. One official said the campaign also had received a wake-up call on May 5, when Obama formally began his campaign with rallies in Columbus, Ohio, and Richmond, Virginia. Four years earlier, it took almost no effort by the Obama team to build a crowd for campaign events, once Obama was truly launched. But on this Saturday in May, the crowds did not fill either of the arenas. One official said the campaign subsequently made two hundred thousand phone calls to make sure they filled a three-thousand-seat venue in Iowa at one of the president's next events.

Messina succinctly framed the decision he asked Obama to make that day: "Are we going to dump the kitchen sink now?" Obama generally trusted his team and their decisions. He did not get into the weeds of strategy the way Bill Clinton did. In this case, however, he wasn't ready to sign off without raising concerns. "He didn't just say, 'Okay guys, that's great,'" Plouffe said. "He wanted to understand what it would mean. It's one of the few times where after we make a decision he still is asking, 'Are we sure this is going to be okay?'" Obama wanted a better sense of how much he might be buried by Romney ads in the final days if the campaign raised less than projected. He said to Messina, "Jim, what happens if we miss?" Messina said he replied, "Then we're in real trouble, but I don't think we're going to miss." Julianna Smoot, the deputy campaign manager in charge of fund-raising, had come to this meeting specifically to address the president's concerns about the money. We'll be fine, she assured him.*

The same weekend that Obama and his team were making the decision to front-load their spending, the pro-Obama super PAC Priorities USA began its attacks on Romney, using Bain Capital as the foil. Within weeks, it started to air one of the most powerful and effective ads of the campaign. Like "Steel," in shorthand it told the story of what happened when Ampad, which Bain owned, bought a paper company in Indiana. One of the workers, Mike Earnest, was featured in the ad, describing how he and others were asked one day to help build a stage. It was from that stage that a few days later the plant managers announced they were shutting down the factory. Earnest said, "Turns out that when we built that stage it was like building my own coffin—and it just made me sick."

Obama liked to believe—and told people—that he was a better candidate than he had been in 2008. Yet he was anything but mistake-free. On June 8, he held a press conference to warn that economic problems in Europe could spill over into the United States, something both his economic and political advisers were deeply worried about at the time. But he made a mess of it when, in trying to talk about the state of the U.S. economy, he said, "The private sector is doing fine." He was trying to draw a distinction between job growth, however tepid, in the private sector and job cuts in the public sector, but that was quickly lost. Republicans pounced. "Is he really that out of touch?" Romney said in a coordinated attack by GOP leaders. Obama's advisers realized instantly that what the president had said was a big mistake and urged him to

---

*As it turned out, a decision that looked risky in May turned out not to be risky at all. Fund-raising began to surge again in August and never slowed. The campaign had all the money it could spend in the final weeks.

clean it up quickly. Later that day, during a photo opportunity in the Oval Office, Obama tried to walk it back. "Listen," he said, "it is absolutely clear that the economy is not doing well."

The summer months were eventually remembered for the battle over Bain. But a closer look at the Obama ad spending shows a different early focus. The Obama team had prepared various attacks—on Romney's record at Bain, on his tenure as governor, on his tax returns and investments. But before they did that, Obama's advisers ran positive ads whose main purpose was to remind people of the problems Obama had inherited. As bad and as recent as it had been, the campaign's research found that people had forgotten. Once they had laid down that foundation, they would turn to Romney's record in Massachusetts and then his finances and business record. One reason for starting the negative ads with Massachusetts was that at the time, the campaign's research showed that Romney had an advantage over Obama on who was better equipped to create jobs. "We felt that if we exposed people to the Massachusetts record we could erode those attributes, and that taking that away from him would be detrimental to his candidacy," Grisolano said. If they could "pop that balloon," as media adviser Jim Margolis put it, they could undermine the entire rationale for Romney's candidacy. The Massachusetts ads began in early June and continued throughout the month. The campaign invested close to $50 million in attacking Romney's record as governor.

On June 21, the *Washington Post* published an article that caused another shift in the ad strategy. Citing SEC documents, reporter Tom Hamburger wrote, "During the nearly 15 years that Romney was actively involved in running Bain, a private equity firm that he founded, it owned companies that were pioneers in the practice of shipping work from the United States to overseas call centers and factories making computer components." The story went on to say that an investigation of the records "shows the extent of Bain's investment in firms that specialized in helping other companies move or expand operations overseas. While Bain was not the largest player in the outsourcing field, the private equity firm was involved early on, at a time when the departure of jobs from the United States was beginning to accelerate and new companies were emerging as handmaidens to this outflow of employment."

The Obama campaign quickly turned the story into television commercials. Independent fact-checking organizations said the ads distorted the *Post* article, but the Obama camp ignored those critiques. The Romney team attacked both Obama and the *Post*. Gail Gitcho, the campaign's communications director, called then executive editor Marcus Brauchli to say the story was incorrect and needed either a correction or a retraction. Brauchli also said she accused the *Post* of doing the Obama campaign's bidding, and he took umbrage at Gitcho's accusation that the newspaper and the Obama campaign were in cahoots on the story. Gitcho demanded that the editors meet with the campaign the next day. "I said I was sure we could find time, or we could meet later in the week or even next week," Brauchli said. "That set [Gitcho] off. She said, approximately, 'You don't understand. We're taking on water. Every day, every hour we wait, we're taking on water.'" The next day Gitcho and Matt McDonald, whom Bob White had put in charge of handling the details of the Bain issue, came to the *Post*. Before they arrived, someone leaked to *Politico* their intention to demand a retraction. Brauchli, who had been a reporter in Asia when American firms were expanding their overseas production facilities and knew the history of their activities, held firm during the meeting and refused to issue either a retraction or a clarification.

The Romney campaign's relationship with the press was always tense and difficult. Reporters complained that the Romney team in Boston was rarely willing to engage at the front end on investigative stories but was quick to be critical after they appeared. Nor was the campaign particularly effective at pushing positive stories about their candidate, particularly his good work for his church. The traveling press corps was given little access either to the candidate or to senior staffers who could explain what the campaign was doing. From the perspective of Romney's advisers, the press was a hostile group that cut the candidate no breaks no matter what they tried to do.

On June 28, the Supreme Court issued its long-awaited ruling on the constitutionality of Obama's Affordable Care Act. With Chief Justice John Roberts writing the majority opinion, the Court held, by a five-to-four vote, that the law was constitutional. Roberts's reasoning surprised everyone, including many constitutional scholars. The Court held that, contrary to what the Obama administration had long argued, the individual mandate, the provision most disliked by conservatives, was not justified under the commerce clause that gave Congress the power to regulate interstate commerce. But he said it was constitutional under Congress's taxing power. This was novel and unexpected legal reasoning that avoided a huge breach between the executive and judicial branches of government and protected the Court from accusations that it was acting politically as an arm of the Republican Party.

Disappointed Republicans, who had made repeal a central theme of the campaign, nonetheless seized on the chief justice's opinion to attack Obama as a tax raiser. A few days later, Romney spokesman Eric Fehrnstrom told Chuck Todd on MSNBC's *Daily Rundown* that Romney disagreed with the Court, that he believed the mandate was not a tax. He said it should be considered a fee or a fine, as it had been defined in Massachusetts. Republicans responded angrily to Fehrnstrom's comments, which contradicted their attacks on the president and suggested that Fehrnstrom take a vacation. Two days later, Romney reversed course. In an interview with CBS News, he said, "The Supreme Court is the highest court in the nation and it said that it's a tax, so it's a tax."

The Supreme Court decision effectively ended the debate over Obama's health care law. If the decision had gone the other way, if the Court had overturned the law and thus rejected the signature domestic policy accomplishment of the Obama presidency, it might have done considerable damage to the president's prestige and political standing. Instead, what had been seen as a potentially supercharged moment in the campaign quickly faded as a topic of political discussion.

In July a *Boston Globe* story touched off another skirmish—the nastiest yet—between the two campaigns. The story raised questions about when Romney had actually severed ties with Bain. The candidate had said it was 1999, but the *Globe* found documents from 2002 that listed him as the "sole stockholder, chairman of the board, chief executive officer and president." Stephanie Cutter feared that reporters weren't taking the story seriously enough, that they saw it as minor flap. She decided to make certain it got more attention and set up a conference call that included the campaign's counsel, Robert Bauer. "Either Mitt Romney, through his own words and his own signature, was misrepresenting his position at Bain to the SEC, which is a felony," she said. "Or he was misrepresenting his position at Bain to the American people to avoid responsibility for some of the consequences of his investments." That inflammatory charge drew a response from Romney campaign manager Matt Rhoades, who generally stayed out of the press unless he wanted to send a strong message. "President Obama's campaign hit a new low today when one of its senior advisers made a reckless and unsubstantiated charge to reporters about Mitt Romney that was so over the top that it calls into question the integrity of their entire campaign. President Obama ought to apologize for the out-of-control behavior of his staff, which demeans the office he holds." The next morning, Obama was interviewed by Charlie Rose on *CBS This Morning*, and again defended the attacks on Bain. He said the private equity firm's role was to make money, not create jobs. "That's part of the system," he said. "But that doesn't necessarily make you qualified to think about the economy as a whole, because as president, my job is to think about the workers. My job is to think about communities, where jobs have been outsourced." Romney went on Fox News to denounce the Obama campaign. He called Cutter's allegation that he was either a felon or a liar "ridiculous." He said, "And of course it's beneath the dignity of the presidency and of his campaign." He added of the president, "He really needs to rein in his team and to finally take responsibility for what they're saying. This is really absurd."

During the month of July, the Obama attack ad campaign shifted from the governor's Massachusetts record to the Bain record and to his taxes and investments. The campaign poured another roughly $50 million into the July attacks, sledgehammer pounding backed up by a sophisticated ad-buying strategy that ultimately put their ads on more than forty different cable networks—far more than any campaign had ever done. The most memorable ad Obama ran that month was an omnibus attack on Romney's business record and wealth that stood out from the others because the entire audio was of Romney singing (a cappella) "America the Beautiful" at a campaign rally. As Romney's voice played in the background, the mocking ad included text rolling across the screen that said Romney's companies had shipped jobs to Mexico and China and outsourced jobs to India. Citing news accounts, the ad pointed out that the Republican nominee had "millions in a Swiss bank account . . . tax havens in Bermuda . . . and the Cayman Islands." Romney wasn't the solution, the ad concluded. "He's the problem."

The onslaught continued through the end of August, just as the conventions were beginning. In August, the Obama ad campaign shifted again, this time with about another $50 million worth of ads devoted to drawing direct contrasts between Obama and Romney. From May 1 until the end of August, the Obama campaign spent between $125 million and $150 million on its advertising campaign to tear down the Republican nominee. Kantar Media figures show that the campaign ran their ads 247,183 times. In that same period, Romney's campaign spent about $50 million for about 90,500 ads. None of that money went for ads responding to the attacks on Bain. During that period, Republican super PACs stepped in to fill the gap. An analysis prepared by the Obama campaign showed that with the GOP outside groups, Romney and the Republicans remained at parity with the Obama campaign and in some weeks outspent the combined forces of Obama and Democratic outside groups. But in the candidate-to-candidate competition, there was no comparison. Obama overwhelmed Romney during the summer months. He could do that, Rhoades said, because he had the money, not because the Obama team made a brilliant strategic choice to front-load its advertising. "I don't think there were people sitting here like, 'Oh my gosh, TV doesn't matter right now,'" he said. Ed Gillespie said, "To the Obama campaign's credit, they were loaded for bear. They were waiting to unload and we were constantly reacting. For the challenger to be reacting as much as we were was frustrating. We were constantly taking incoming and constantly reacting. . . . I think the summer was pretty decisive."

The Romney campaign's response, or lack of response, to the attacks on him during the summer became one of the biggest questions of the entire election. Why didn't they answer with ads of their own? Why didn't friendly super PACs pick up the slack? Did the Romney team even have a strategy for responding? What was really going on in Boston during three of the most important months of the campaign? If there was one lingering question about the summer battle, this was it.

Through April 2012, the campaign had raised $100 million and spent $91 million. They had just $9.2 million in cash on hand. Stuart Stevens said the campaign had four options for how to spend that money. "There's a Mitt Romney story to be told, and you can break that story into just an overall story, sort of agent of change, turnaround artist," he said. "You can break it down to the business bio stuff, a man for this moment, economic focus, this is what we need, we're at war, this is Patton. You can do it on the personal qualities, this is a good and decent man and here are these ways to tell you about that. You can do the [Massachusetts] record. Here are the things this guy has done, proves he can do it. Overwhelmingly what people wanted to know is what he would do as president, and it became a threshold question that, before they would listen to the other, they needed to know that."

Stevens said it would have been ideal to be able to do everything everyone was proposing (or that critics later said the campaign should have done). "Whenever people tell me things like this, I say, 'You're right about everything,'" he said. "They say, 'It would have been better to talk about the business [record], it would have been better to talk more about his personal life and everything he did in charity.' You're right. It's the same way they say it would have been better to spend more time in Des Moines. Absolutely. It would have been better to spend more time in Richmond. It would have helped. It would have been better to run more ads early. No question. Every day in the campaign, every moment is Sophie's Choice."

The day that Obama's "Steel" ad was unveiled, the Romney campaign responded with an ad of its own. It told the story of Bain's role in helping to build a different steel company, SDI, or Steel Dynamics, Inc., of Indiana. "When others shied away, Mitt Romney's private-sector leadership team stepped in," the ad claimed. It had a positive message, but it was only available online. The response that day set the pattern for the campaign. "We were prepared," Rhoades later said in response to criticism that Romney's campaign had stood by passively in the face of Obama's attacks on Romney's tenure at Bain. "We did everything else but paid Bain [ads]." The communications team, armed with the documents prepared by White's research project, attempted to knock down every charge from the Obama campaign and critical story in the press. The response strategy also included an aggressive digital effort designed to push people toward positive stories about Romney and Bain, using the tools of Internet search. This was based on the theory that once people hear or see something, they look for more information. "When someone was going in to find [information about an attack] we would roadblock in front of it and say, 'If you read one thing this is what you should read,'" Zac Moffatt said. "We would have a very concise response to whatever the allegation was. The links would say something like, 'Learn the facts, learn the truth, learn how Mitt created jobs.'" The campaign hoped that this would leave a psychological impression that the charges lacked merit, or at least that there was a different version of events. One member of the campaign team, however, said, "We could do as many Web videos until we're blue in the face, we could put out as many quotes about Bain as we could. But that wasn't seeping in. It wasn't making a difference. It definitely wasn't breaking through."

Lack of money was a serious problem. Fund-raising picked up immediately after Gingrich and Santorum finally dropped out, but most of the money that was being raised was only for use in the general election. Raising money that could be used between May and the convention was far more difficult. Most of the people who were willing to give Romney the maximum contribution of $2,500 had already done so. At every fund-raising event in the spring and early summer, a portion of what was raised went to immediate use, but at each event much more went to Romney's general election account or to the Republican National Committee's victory fund.

The campaign did have some money for television ads, but decided not to use any of it to respond to the Bain attacks. "There was no umbrella answer that you could give that would put the thing to bed," Russ Schriefer said later. "So the question became, what do you spend your limited resources on? Do you spend them on defending on Bain and let them play this out, or do we try to open up a front on something of our own and try to define Romney as best as we can?" Attacking Obama was problematic as well. The Romney team found in its research that voters were still resistant to direct attacks on the president. Many voters were disappointed in Obama, including supporters from 2008, but they liked him personally and recoiled against some of the kinds of personal attacks common in campaigns. "This guy is a tough guy to hit," Rhoades said of the president. "If it went too far it wasn't going to work."

Romney chose to spend his advertising dollars on commercials explaining what he would do as president, rather than responding to the attacks. The campaign aired a series of commercials called "Day One" that laid out in general terms the actions he would initiate once he became president. Eric

Fehrnstrom said, "We were resource-limited and our research told us that what people wanted to know most about Mitt was not a response to the Bain attacks but what was he going to do as president." Equally important, the Romney team did not want to spend the summer litigating Bain. "That's not where we wanted to fight the campaign, that's not the fight we wanted," Fehrnstrom said. "So we fought back hard in the earned media. We had an aggressive Web video program that we did around Bain. But ultimately the decision was not to go up on TV with the response." Campaign officials also talked about putting together a surrogate operation composed of former business associates of Romney who could tell his story in personal terms. Everyone agreed this was a good idea, but it never got done, another example of a lost opportunity by the Romney team. It was, as one official later said, "the urgent driving out the important." But it came at a cost to the candidate.

The other mystery was why Republican super PACs did not step in more aggressively when Romney was under attack and short of money. The combined forces of super PACs like American Crossroads and its related nonprofit Crossroads GPS, or the pro-Romney Restore Our Future, or Americans for Prosperity, had huge campaign war chests but chose to spend little of it on ads responding to Obama's attacks. Why? American Crossroads and Crossroads GPS concluded that the most effective use of their money was on attacks against Obama, hoping to persuade voters that the president was a failure on the economy. Their own research had found what Romney's campaign had learned—that voters might be disappointed in Obama but they didn't dislike him. Attacking him proved difficult, requiring a more gentle approach that would try to assure voters it was okay to abandon him. Crossroads GPS spent $56 million during the late spring and summer on such ads. But when the Bain attacks began to bite, American Crossroads put together a response ad and placed an $8.7 million buy in July. Campaign finance laws prohibit direct coordination between the super PACs and the campaigns. Crossroads officials and those at Restore Our Future looked to Boston for some kind of public signal. What they inferred was exactly what the Romney campaign believed: If you're explaining, you're losing. So they did not do more.

One big question remains. Was all this advertising effective? Did the summer attacks on Romney fundamentally change the dynamic of the election? Was the campaign decided before the conventions or the debates took place? After the election, everyone had an opinion—and some data to back it up. John Sides of George Washington University and Lynn Vavreck of UCLA, two political scientists who studied the race closely for their book *The Gamble,* argued in a *New York Times* piece in December 2012 that there was no compelling evidence to show that the summer ad wars changed the race. They looked at changes in the overall race and changes in Romney's image, nationally and in the battleground states. "The political science research and this initial evidence from 2012 suggests that the Obama campaign's blitz of early advertising did little apparent damage to Mr. Romney in the minds of voters," Sides wrote.

Leaders of the two campaigns came to a different conclusion. Plouffe said the goal wasn't to increase support for Obama but to make it harder for Romney to overtake him in the end. "We were already bumping up against our ceiling in a lot of these places," he said. "It wasn't that Barack Obama in the summer was going to start pulling 53 [percent]. It was to retard Romney's progress, and that's what we were able to do. Basically putting a lot of weight on him so it's harder for him to elevate. We accomplished that big time. Two, I think we turned the election more into a choice. We know that from our research."

Certainly the overall state of the race remained close. Obama had a three-point lead in the battleground states at the beginning of May and a four-point lead at the end of August, according to the campaign's internal numbers. Romney's campaign research found that the candidate actually gained a tiny bit of ground, though he remained well behind in their numbers. Obama advisers said the summer attacks helped to cement impressions of Romney—wealthy, out of touch, and not the job creator he claimed—that he was never quite able to repair with the voters he needed most at the end of the campaign. Romney advisers agreed that the relatively small changes in the overall numbers masked the real damage that took place. "We knew it had damaged Mitt's image," Neil Newhouse said. "The long steady drumbeat over the summer of negative advertising had a significant impact in the campaign." Romney recovered some ground just before the conventions but was fighting an uphill battle throughout the rest of the campaign. He came out of the primaries with liabilities and did nothing of note to erase them during the heat of the summer.

CHAPTER 21

The Running Mate

The chemistry was unmistakable. Two days before the Wisconsin primary, Mitt Romney and Paul Ryan shared a stage in Middleton, just outside of Madison. Tall and handsome, with dark hair and a lean physique, Ryan looked like he could be another of Mitt and Ann Romney's sons. At forty-two, he was of the same generation as the candidate's children. Chairman of the House Budget Committee and the main architect of the Republican blueprint to shrink government, he was the darling of conservatives. He had endorsed Romney's candidacy a few days earlier and was at Romney's side during the last days of the primary that settled the Republican nomination contest. Before arriving in Madison, he had joined with Romney's staff to play an April Fool's prank on the candidate, giving a full-throated introduction—"and the next president of the United States"—to what Romney thought was a packed pancake brunch rally. Romney learned it was an empty room only when he came out from behind the curtain. Now in the late afternoon they were holding a rally and town hall before a friendly audience in a hotel ballroom. As Ryan introduced him, Romney beamed. The youthful congressman put a positive sheen on Romney's sometimes corny personality. He called it "Midwest earnest." When questions came from the audience, Romney answered but then deferred to Ryan, who picked up where the candidate left off, confident that he was not overshadowing the future nominee.

The next day, as the two continued their tour of the state, the bond seemed to grow. Romney joked about Ryan's youthfulness, noting that the congressman was just ten years old when Ronald Reagan was elected president. "I did have a Reagan bumper sticker on my locker in the third grade," Ryan interjected to laughter. Ryan was part geek, part nerd, and part fitness-obsessed. He drove a truck, enjoyed hunting deer with bow and arrow, and was, like most Wisconsin residents, a devoted Green Bay Packers fan. He connected with his blue-collar constituency in southern Wisconsin in ways Romney couldn't. People in the crowds saw the growing bond as the two men campaigned together. Sherry Magner, a pharmacy clerk, told my *Post* colleague Philip

Rucker, "I was watching each one as the other spoke, and there was not only respect, but a smile they gave each other." Jeff Burns, a boat parts supplier, saw the combo as ideally suited to deal with the economy. "This election's going to turn on the economy, and you've got two guys who know what it takes to fix the economy. You're talking about a very successful businessman and the most knowledgeable congressman available."

Mitt Romney knew something about picking a vice president. Four years earlier when John McCain was deciding on a running mate, Romney saw it from the perspective of someone in the running—the intrusiveness, the uncertainty, the speculation, and of course the media frenzy. He lost that competition to Sarah Palin—though it was his multiple homes that really hurt his chances after McCain was asked and couldn't remember how many properties he and his wife owned. A McCain-Romney ticket would be just too much real estate, McCain's advisers concluded. Romney got enough of a taste of what the process involved to have clear ideas about how he wanted to make his own selection. He wanted it to be as orderly as McCain's was not, as private as he could make it to protect those under consideration, and as contained as possible inside his own operation to guard against leaks that could embarrass those in the running or damage his own political reputation. He started early and hoped to finish early.

In the early stages of the campaign, Beth Myers kept four folders on her desk. One said, "transition." Another said, "convention." The third said, "victory," the fourth, "VP." These were the big projects Romney's advisers knew they would need to manage if, as they expected, he was successful in winning the nomination. Myers was one of Romney's closest and longest-serving political advisers. She had been with him in his campaign for governor, served as chief of staff in the governor's office, and managed the 2008 presidential campaign. She had worked closely with him when he went through the vice presidential process with the McCain campaign and had spent considerable time talking with Romney about what he wanted as 2012 approached. As early as January 2012, she began to compile a lengthy informal list of potential running mates—"a whole host of folks inside and outside the box, expected and unexpected candidates, and that was the Beth Myers view of the world," she said. By early spring, she had compiled general background materials on all of the potential candidates and began to talk more formally to Romney about the process. It was then that he announced she would head the selection team, and by the end of April the initial list had been pared down, though it still numbered in the teens. She then assembled background bios on them, running about twenty-five pages each. Romney looked them over, and around the first of May he created a much shorter list of contenders—none of them out-of-the-box candidates.

Romney personally began making the calls. Tim Pawlenty was at the chiropractor's office, dealing with a bad back from a spill during an old timers' hockey game, when the call came. Pawlenty had been the runner-up to Palin in 2008 and had no burning desire to go through it all again. He had resolved in his own mind that he was an unlikely candidate to be Romney's running mate. He was then a national co-chairman of Romney's campaign, and as he looked at the politics of the choice, he had concluded that, because he was a former governor like Romney and from a state that wasn't likely to be a battleground, he wouldn't ever be the choice. "I had kind of resolved with my wife, Mary, earlier that if I did get asked that we would respectfully decline," he said. When Romney called, Pawlenty tried to put him off. "I said, 'If you're doing this as a friend to throw me a bone, you really don't need to do this. I've been through this before.' It's an honor to be asked, but it comes with a fair amount of distraction because you have to fill out the paperwork and it becomes kind of a press deal. And I said . . . , 'I don't need the headache of the process if it's just a bone.'" Romney was insistent. He assured Pawlenty that he would be under serious consideration. Pawlenty talked to his wife and to Myers, who outlined what kind of documents the campaign wanted him to submit. "I said, 'Tell me a little bit about the process,' and she said, 'Like the McCain form, it's exactly the McCain form,'" he recalled. "'It's the McCain form plus or minus two questions.' I'm like, 'Really?'" Four years earlier, as a sitting governor, Pawlenty and his wife had spent hours compiling everything for McCain's vetting team. "We were buying three-ring binders and going to Kinko's and copying tax returns and writing and word processing answers to questionnaires in our living room. I've got documents kind of spread around the living room trying to compile the years of the taxes and investment forms and other stuff and it was a ton of work." While he was talking to Myers, a lightbulb went off in his head. He remembered that he still had a copy of everything he had submitted to McCain. "I still had the stuff on a disk and I had to go in and update from '08 to '12. Literally we put the whole thing together in a night, so part of the attraction of going forward with it was [that it was] easier than last time."

Chris Christie didn't expect a call either. "I think there's certain personalities that would fit well as vice president, maybe others that would look [like] a little bit more of a tight fit," he said, "and I think I'd be a little more of a tight fit." When I asked him to explain what he meant by "tight fit," he said, "I just think that my personality is kind of big and I don't think that you necessarily always want to pick big personalities for vice president. That can be problematic in the execution of the job if you win, less so in the campaign." So when Romney called him he had the same response as Pawlenty. "I said, 'If this is just like that the guy who endorses you earliest and you want me to be on the list because it would be nice for you to do for me, I get that,' but I said, 'I don't see you picking me.' So I said, 'Why go through it?' He goes, 'No, no, no, that's not it at all, I'm very serious about this and you will be very seriously considered.'"

Romney outlined the documents he would need from Christie, who said he would discuss it with his wife, Mary Pat. The next day Christie told Romney he would be honored to be on the list for consideration. By early June, he had submitted the paperwork—tax returns* and other personal material and a questionnaire that ran to about seventy-five questions. He recalled that the form included a series of questions about the candidates' personal lives, including whether they had had an extramarital affair or whether someone could credibly claim they did. "Asked about stuff with your kids, any issues with your children, obviously criminal record, mental health issues, drinking history, drug history," Christie said. "Their cutoff line on drugs was, 'used any drugs anytime since you graduated from college.' They didn't ask you about college or before, but since you graduated from college have you used any illegal drugs, that kind of thing." Romney's team wanted every tweet or Facebook entry as well. "It was all intrusive stuff," he said.

Rob Portman was at home on a weekend day when Romney called. Romney told Portman he was asking only a few people to go through the process. He said that having been through it himself he knew it wasn't easy. It was as if he were saying he was sorry to have to put Portman through it. Portman too was reluctant to become a candidate, for family reasons. He wasn't going to agree to go through the process unless his wife and children were all in. The family conversations included discussion of one potentially difficult issue. Portman's son Will had told his parents earlier that he was gay. They knew that if Portman was selected, this would become public, but agreed that it should not be a barrier to Portman entering the vice presidential sweepstakes. As the family deliberated, Portman called Beth Myers to tell her about his son. Without checking with Romney, Myers offered an unequivocal response. That was not a problem and would have no bearing on Portman's potential selection. Later Portman called Romney to say he would be happy to undergo the vetting process. Romney also assured him that he considered the fact that his son was gay a nonissue in the selection process.

---

*Christie recalled that Romney's team wanted twelve years of tax returns. This was at a time when Romney had agreed to make public only two years of his own returns.

The vice presidential selection process is one of those irresistible stories for the media, a classic example in which hype, speculation, handicapping, and analysis quickly outrun any facts or real knowledge of the process. The Romney campaign, like others before it, was determined to ignore all this chatter. Its plan was not to respond to leaks or speculation, however accurate or off the mark. That was the plan, at least until June 19, when ABC News reported that Marco Rubio was not being vetted by the campaign. Rubio had seemed an obvious choice to be under consideration. He was a new and fresh face in the Republican Party, wildly popular with Tea Party activists, and a Cuban American who might help Romney solve some of his problems with Hispanic voters. When the news broke early that day, some other news organizations picked it up. It was a textbook case of how the media seize on a single piece of information to make it the only topic of conversation until something else happens along to crowd it out. On this day, there were few "confirmations" of the report but plenty of discussion about its implications. The Romney camp was caught totally unaware. At the time of the report, Rubio had already sent in his questionnaire to the campaign, Myers later said. Romney officials privately warned some reporters off the story but would not respond publicly. When it was clear something more definitive was needed, they sent Romney to snuff it out. "There was a story that originated today, apparently at ABC, based upon reports of supposedly outside unnamed advisers of mine," he said while campaigning in Michigan. "I can't imagine who such people are, but I can tell you this: They know nothing about the vice presidential selection or evaluation process. There are only two people in this country who know who are being vetted and who are not, and that's Beth Myers and myself." He called the story "entirely false" and added, "Marco Rubio is being thoroughly vetted as part of our process." Romney had taken the drastic step of violating the campaign's code of silence on the vice presidential search process, a sign of how sensitive the Latino issue was in the campaign and the regard with which the team held Rubio. "Everyone just felt this is silly," Myers explained to me later. "It's not helpful and it's not true and let's just clear this up."

On July 15, Chris Christie called a close friend. "You won't believe the conversation I just had with Mitt Romney," he said. Christie was in a car on his way back to New Jersey after attending the National Governors Association meeting in Williamsburg, Virginia. Romney wanted to discuss a problem that imperiled Christie's chances of being on the ticket. The problem involved an SEC ruling, known as the "pay to play" rule, an outgrowth of a previous regulation issued by the Municipal Securities Rulemaking Board. In essence, the rule prohibited financial institutions—big banks and bond companies—whose employees contributed money to certain state and local elected officials from doing bond business in those states. The MSRB rule had been in place for years, with only minor effects on some previous candidates, but because all presidential nominees accepted federal funds for the general election until 2008, fundraising for the fall campaign had never been affected, for either a presidential or vice presidential nominee. After the 2008 campaign, the Securities and Exchange Commission put through a more stringent rule that affected more financial institutions and prospective donors. Coincidentally, by 2012, no one was taking federal funds for either the primaries or the general election. The two changes made the rule come into play as never before.

Earlier in the 2012 campaign, it turned into a major headache for Rick Perry. According to William Canfield, Perry's campaign counsel, when Perry began trying to raise money in New York, lawyers for Goldman Sachs told the firm that none of its employees could donate to his campaign. Perry's campaign hired former SEC chairman Harvey Pitt to examine the issue. Pitt said there was no way around it, and Perry's campaign essentially wrote off any efforts to raise money from the financial community in New York, a potentially sizable source of funds for any candidate. Romney was not covered because he was a former governor, but his campaign team wrestled with its limitations whenever it wanted a sitting governor to sponsor a fund-raising event. As Perry learned, the lawyers for the bond houses were extremely conservative in their interpretation of the rule and told their employees not to risk the severe penalties for violations.

Once Romney began his search for a running mate, the rule became a major issue. Before Romney's call to Christie, Myers had raised the issue with Bill Palatucci, Christie's former law partner and one of his closest advisers. Christie had designated Palatucci to handle all vice presidential discussions with the Romney campaign. Are you familiar with the SEC's "pay to play" rule? she asked. Palatucci said he was. She had been made aware of it earlier in the spring. It would have been a problem with any governor under consideration—among those speculated about were Louisiana's Bobby Jindal and Virginia's Bob McDonnell—but it was a particular problem for the governor of New Jersey because of the governor's constitutional powers. Palatucci said Christie had learned to live with it as governor. There was nothing much to do about it. It was just there. He believed Myers was clearly concerned. He remembered her saying, "Are you telling me I have to tell Mitt Romney that he can't select the person he wants as vice president?" Romney's team began to weigh a series of technical questions about the rule and how it might apply. Could they form separate committees—Romney for President and Christie for Vice President— to circumvent the fund-raising prohibitions? Would the rule apply only to contributions after the selection of a vice president, or would it apply retroactively, meaning the campaign might have to give money back to many donors on Wall Street?

Romney's call to Christie was focused on all these issues, according to several people familiar with the contents of the conversation. Romney indicated that his team was still looking for a more precise answer to some of the questions. Romney had come to the conclusion that if the rule applied only to future fund-raising from Wall Street investment banks, he could live with that. He had already tapped that community for a significant amount of money. But if the rule was applied retroactively, that was another matter. He raised the issue of setting up separate committees to wall off Christie from his fund-raising. Christie thought that was too cute by half, that it wouldn't pass the smell test. He thought it would cause a serious political problem for the ticket. He was also worried about the potential impact on his state, that it would put New Jersey at risk in future bond underwriting.

Romney then raised a question that Christie took as a sign that he was at the top of his list of candidates, although accounts of exactly what was said or intended diverge. One version holds that Romney directly raised the issue of resignation. He said that the problem could be solved if Christie resigned as governor. Christie's response was to laugh. After a moment of silence, Romney said directly, "Governor, are you prepared to resign to be my running mate?" Christie asked for more time to consider a response. He was not prepared to give an answer to a question like that on a cell phone connection. Immediately after he hung up, he told his friend that Romney had said to him that he wanted him to be his vice presidential candidate. The friend could not say that Romney had made a flat-out offer, but Christie certainly believed it was the closest thing possible to one. From those familiar with Romney's side of the call, it was not a direct offer. Romney was still mulling his choices. He was in the process of making calls to others on his list to raise other issues that might complicate their selection. He said to Christie that based on what his campaign knew about the SEC rule, there was no way he could put Christie on the ticket unless Christie resigned. But he did not directly ask Christie to do so. Christie's friends and advisers believed the call signified that he was Romney's first choice. Those around Romney disagree. One person familiar with the conversation said "it was conceivable" that Christie came away convinced that he was Romney's top choice and had just been offered the job, but that that was a misreading of events. Romney was not at a point of making any decision. He was only trying to determine whether it was even possible to continue to consider Christie. "I think he was wondering whether Chris was a viable person to stay on the list at all," one Romney adviser said. Romney reported back to Myers that resigning would understandably be a major concern for the New Jersey governor. To Romney's question about resigning, Christie's initial response—a laugh—had made clear he would not do so. After that phone call, Romney and Christie had no further conversations about joining the ticket.

The *New York Post,* citing sources, reported in late August that Christie had declined to resign to become vice president because he doubted that Romney could win the election and didn't want to jeopardize his own political standing or his future options. The story, which included discussion of the pay-to-play rule, infuriated the New Jersey governor, who felt it mischaracterized the position he had been put in by Romney, which was an either/or choice: governor or vice presidential candidate.

A Romney adviser said the campaign never found an adequate solution to the pay-to-play rule as it might affect sitting governors running for president or vice president. They came away convinced that the rule will have a potentially significant effect on sitting governors who decide to seek the presidency in the future.

Romney had thought he might be able to settle on a running mate by early July, but the process ran longer than he and Myers had anticipated. Romney had asked that he be presented with choices, not a consensus candidate. He was personally familiar with all the serious contenders, having actively campaigned with all of them. They had appeared on Sunday shows in behalf of the campaign and done events apart from the candidate, all monitored by Boston. He solicited opinions from his senior staff, listening mostly and never hinting which way he was leaning. He asked friends and family and political associations who they thought would be good and why. Everyone had an opinion, except Myers, who chose to remain neutral throughout the process. The campaign conducted no polls to gauge the strengths of potential running mates, as some nominees had done. Nor did Romney conduct face-to-face interviews with those he was considering, though other nominees usually did them. He had a different view. "The formal interview wasn't going to be as valuable as what he learned from them on the road," Myers said. "So when he was working with these people and campaigning with them, he was taking the measure of [them]. He wanted to reserve the opportunity to do that [interview] with the final person he chose before he made the final ask."

Everyone on the short list had issues, pros and cons. Ryan came with all the controversy surrounding his budget and its radical changes to Medicare. Pawlenty lacked the charisma that would help to energize conservatives and make them feel better about Romney. Christie, in addition to pay-to-play, had a personality guaranteed to overshadow Romney. Portman had the Washington experience that Romney lacked, but was tied to the Bush presidency. Rubio was talented but untested. But he had another issue. As a Florida legislator he had brushed up against a financial scandal involving the Florida Republican Party. In addition, then-representative David Rivera, a close friend and fellow officeholder, was under federal investigation for campaign finance irregularities. There was no evidence of wrongdoing by Rubio, but among at least some Romney advisers there was concern that Rivera could be indicted before the election, and if that were to happen the story could become a major distraction.* Myers said, however, that the issue did not keep Rubio off the short list of contenders. "Mitt received a number of completed vets, all of which were viable candidacies, and Marco was one of them," she said

Myers met with Romney at his summer home on Lake Winnipesaukee in New Hampshire on July 2. She had taken the fruits of all the research—the personal documents, materials from the public search, policy positions—and woven them into narratives for each prospective candidate. Myers said that at that point Romney had all the information he needed if he wanted to make his decision before leaving for a trip to Europe and the Middle East later in the month. For his own reasons, Romney decided he wasn't ready. "He didn't feel he had to do it and he wasn't ready to make it," Myers said.

In the summer of 2008, Obama had taken a trip to Europe, the Middle East, Afghanistan, and Iraq. The tour was a political triumph, capped by an outdoor rally in Berlin with two hundred thousand people in attendance. Obama's overseas journey was so successful politically that John McCain's team decided it had to bring him back down to earth or risk losing the race before the conventions ever took place. The campaign ran an ad calling Obama the biggest celebrity in the world and comparing him to Britney Spears and Paris Hilton. Romney, who was certainly not a world celebrity, was scheduled for a smaller version of the same thing: a trip that would take him to London for the opening of the Summer Olympics, to Israel for meetings with Israeli prime minister Benjamin Netanyahu and a speech about Middle East policy, and a final stop in Poland. He hoped to piggyback off the opening of the summer games to remind voters back home about his success in turning around the 2002 Salt Lake City Winter Olympics and then use the rest of the trip to fill out his foreign policy vision. His schedule included fund-raisers with American expats in London and Jerusalem. The trip also promised to draw attention, wanted or

---

*Rivera lost his bid for reelection in November 2012.

unwanted, to the fact that a horse that Ann Romney partially owned would be competing in the dressage events—otherwise known as "horse ballet"—at the Olympics. The trip had been on the schedule for some time, but as the departure neared there was a debate inside Romney's organization about the advisability of going abroad for nearly a week, given that foreign policy was an afterthought to most voters and that the time could be better spent in the battleground states.

On the eve of the trip, Romney spoke to the VFW convention in Las Vegas and delivered a scathing attack on Obama. "In dealings with other nations, he has given trust where it is not earned, insult where it is not deserved, and apology where it is not due," he said. This was as tough as any speech Romney had delivered in the campaign. He criticized Obama's handling of virtually every region of the world: Israel, Egypt, Iran, Russia, China, Poland. His speech contained some of the muscularity of Reagan's rhetoric, but what many people, at home and abroad, wondered at that moment was whether Romney would model his policies after those of George W. Bush, who often bucked the Republican foreign policy establishment, or of George H. W. Bush, who embodied it. Would he be able to use his trip to offer any clearer sense of whether he would represent a real departure from the policies of the Obama administration, or mostly a rhetorical one? And would anyone care, given the state of the economy?

Romney flew overnight to London, the first bit of bad logistical planning. His policy director, Lanhee Chen, and a few foreign policy advisers accompanied him, but no senior member of the political team was aboard, nor were any of his most senior communications advisers. His schedule called for him to give an interview to NBC anchor Brian Williams the day of his arrival and then on subsequent days meet with a variety of British officials and attend the opening ceremonies at the games. It was a busy but not taxing schedule, with no tricky foreign policy issues to worry about. Romney got off to a disastrous start. During the interview with Williams, he appeared to criticize the host country's security preparations. Citing news reports, he said, "It's hard to tell just how well it will turn out. There are a few things that were disconcerting." The British press erupted. "Mitt the Twit," the tabloid *Sun* trumpeted the next morning. Prime Minister David Cameron offered a snappish comparison of security challenges for the games in a city the size of London versus one the size of Salt Lake City. London mayor Boris Johnson used Romney as a punching bag before a Hyde Park audience the night before the opening ceremonies. "There are some people who are coming from around the world who don't yet know about all the preparations we've done to get London ready in the last seven years," Johnson said. "I hear there's a guy, there's a guy called Mitt Romney who wants to know whether we're ready. He wants to know whether we're ready? Are we ready?" From the sixty thousand people came a thunderous response: "Yeeeeeaaaaahhhh!" they shouted in unison.

In Israel, Romney gave a speech about the Middle East and the Iranian threat. At a fund-raiser for Americans, whose guests included Sheldon Adelson, Romney suggested that the Palestinian culture was inferior to that of the Israelis and that the differences explained why the Israeli economy was far more prosperous. An Associated Press report published as the Romney entourage was heading for Poland quoted Saeb Erekat, a senior Palestinian official, as saying Romney had made a "racist statement." Stuart Stevens, who had joined the trip in London after the first day's troubles, complained bitterly about the coverage, but the campaign could not counter the narrative of ineptitude that had started to take shape in London and had now hardened into conventional wisdom. In Poland, Romney gave an eloquent speech, but by then there was only one story to be written about the week. A *Guardian* writer dubbed Romney's trip the "insult-the-world tour." The pounding he was taking for his perceived missteps and maladroit comments overshadowed any substance he was trying to offer. The trip ended with the traveling press, which had been given no access to Romney the entire week, shouting questions at him as he was leaving Pilsudski Square in Warsaw, where he had laid a wreath at the Polish Tomb of the Unknown Soldier. "What about your gaffes?" Phil Rucker shouted. Romney didn't even look over as he walked to his waiting car. "Governor Romney," Ashley Parker shouted, "do you feel that your gaffes have overshadowed your foreign trip?" Rick Gorka, who was the traveling press person, shouted at the press corps, "Kiss my ass. This is a holy site for the Polish people. Show some respect." Gorka later apologized for his outburst, but the verbal dustup seemed a fitting conclusion to a trip that produced days of ridicule for the candidate.

The next day, August 1, Romney assembled a few members of his senior staff at the campaign headquarters in Boston. The group included Myers, Rhoades, Stevens, Schriefer, Fehrnstrom, Peter Flaherty, Bob White, and Ron Kaufman. Romney went around the table asking for their views about whom he should pick as his running mate and when they should make the announcement. The top four contenders appeared to be Ryan, Pawlenty, Christie, and Portman. Everyone but Myers offered an opinion, presenting pros and cons about the list. Romney asked pointed questions but gave no hint as to his leanings. When the meeting ended, everyone left the room except Romney and Myers. With little fanfare, Romney told Myers he had decided to make Ryan his running mate. Myers urged him to move quickly. She knew that beginning the next week a protective pool of reporters would begin to follow Romney's every movement. Once the pool was in place, she said, it would be harder to keep his vice presidential talks secret.

Romney picked up the phone and called Ryan. He asked the congressman to meet him in Boston the following Sunday. To avoid detection, Ryan, wearing jeans and a baseball cap, flew from Chicago to Hartford, Connecticut, where he was met by Myers's son, Curt, who drove him to the Myers home. Romney drove down from his lake house in New Hampshire and talked with his choice for an hour. When Romney had finished, Bob White, Matt Rhoades, Spencer Zwick, and Ed Gillespie arrived to discuss the rollout and give Ryan an idea of what to expect, from fund-raising responsibilities to campaign appearances to dealing with the media. After the meetings, Myers's son drove Ryan back to Hartford, where he boarded a plane for Chicago and then was picked up there to return to his home in Janesville.

All that week reporters were in pursuit of the choice, and perhaps by coincidence a boomlet arose around Ryan. Conservative commentators and intellectuals knew him and liked him. They saw in him something they didn't see in Romney, which was the ability to articulate his conservative, small-government philosophy with passion, depth, and optimism. Throughout the week, one after another conservative writer urged Romney to go bold and pick Ryan, though it was unusual for a nominee to dip into the House of Representatives for a running mate. (The last candidate to do so had been Walter Mondale, who picked Congresswoman Geraldine Ferraro to be his running mate in 1984.) The *Weekly Standard* had put Ryan on its cover in July to accompany a lengthy article by Stephen Hayes under the headline "Man with a Plan: How Paul Ryan Became the Intellectual Leader of the Republican Party." *National Review*'s Rich Lowry wrote a column in the *New York Post* in which he argued that, contrary to the views of many political consultants, who saw Ryan as a highly risky choice because of his plan to revamp Medicare, Romney should ignore them and tap the congressman. "Romney has to carry the argument to President Obama," he wrote. "The state of the economy alone isn't enough to convince people that Romney has better ideas to create jobs. Neither is his résumé. Romney needs to make the case for his program, and perhaps no one is better suited to contribute to this effort than Ryan." But he said there was another reason to take the gamble: "At times, it has seemed that the Romney team has embarked on an audacious experiment to see if it's possible to run a presidential campaign devoid of real interest. With the choice of Ryan, that would change in an instant."

The campaign team went to elaborate lengths to keep the secret. The plan called for a public announcement on Friday, August 10, in New Hampshire.

But Ryan was obligated to attend a memorial service that day for people killed at a Sikh temple in Wisconsin. That pushed the announcement to the morning of Saturday, August 11, in Virginia, where Romney was already scheduled to attend a rally. By coincidence, the Saturday event was to be held on the deck of the USS *Wisconsin*. On Friday, the Romney campaign began the process of secretly moving Ryan from Janesville to Norfolk. Like the other finalists, Ryan was being followed everywhere by reporters. They had staked out his home in Janesville. No one, however, was watching the back of the house. Ryan slipped out undetected and disappeared into the woods behind his home. From there he was taken to an airport in Waukegan, Illinois, for the flight to the East Coast.

Romney, meanwhile, had begun calling others who had made it to the next-to-final cut to let them know he had selected someone else. He had started with Tim Pawlenty, the former Minnesota governor, soon after meeting with Ryan. Pawlenty was in Colorado at an Aspen Institute conference. He had long assumed Romney would pick Rob Portman on the theory that Portman was both highly qualified and might be able to help deliver Ohio, the most important of the battleground states. Romney told him he had decided to go with Ryan and explained the likely timetable for the public announcement. "I applauded the pick and told him it didn't change my view of him or my willingness to help the campaign, and it really didn't," Pawlenty later said. "People always say, 'Weren't you disappointed?' You can't be disappointed about not getting something you didn't expect."

On Friday, the day before the scheduled unveiling of Ryan, Romney called others who had been in the final cut. Marco Rubio was fishing when Romney called that afternoon. He finally connected around 7 p.m. to learn that he would not be on the ticket. Rob Portman was giving a speech in Columbus to several thousand bicyclists who were preparing for an annual cancer charity ride. He spoke to Romney when he finished and then joined the cyclists for dinner, trying to act as if nothing had just happened. Christie was in the air, flying back to New Jersey from Montana, when Romney tried to reach him that night. The plane had Wi-Fi but no phone service. Russ Schriefer sent an e-mail to Palatucci, who was on the flight, asking that the governor contact Romney as soon as possible. Palatucci e-mailed in reply: Is this about the vice presidency? Just ask him to call Governor Romney, Schriefer said. Christie's plane landed just before 10 p.m. and he immediately called Romney. "He said to me, 'I have some news that I think you'll find both disappointing and a relief at the same time,' and I said, 'What's that?' and he said, 'I've decided to go another direction with the vice presidency,'" Christie recalled. "And I said, 'Okay, I completely understand, I wish you the best of luck.' He said, 'I can't tell you who.' I said, 'I don't want to know who, because then if it leaks I could be on the suspect list, and I don't want to be on the suspect list.'" Romney then asked Christie to deliver the keynote address to the Republican convention.

Ryan reemerged in public the next morning on the deck of the USS *Wisconsin,* coming down a steep set of steps to join Romney as the Republican vice presidential candidate. Romney was so excited, he introduced Ryan as "the next president of the United States," and had to interrupt Ryan to correct himself. "Every now and then I am known to make a mistake," he joked. "I did not make a mistake with this guy. But I can tell you this: He's going to be the next *vice* president of the United States." Ryan told the audience, "The commitment Mitt Romney and I make to you is this: We won't duck the tough issues; we will lead. We won't blame others; we will take responsibility. And we won't replace our founding principles; we will apply them." The choice gave a needed jolt of energy to Romney's campaign. The crowds became larger and more enthusiastic as the two men traveled together. The chemistry, so evident back in April, was just as obvious now. One campaign official used the word "bromance" to describe what they all saw. Democrats were as elated by the choice as were Republicans, seeing Romney's decision as a political gamble that would thrust Ryan's controversial budget plan and its Medicare cuts into the center of the campaign debate.

No one expected Campaign 2012 to be positive or uplifting. But what was most striking at that point in the race was not just the negativity or the sheer volume of attack ads raining down on voters in the swing states. It was the sense that all restraints were gone, the guardrails had disappeared, and there was no incentive for anyone to hold back. Almost immediately after Ryan's announcement, the two campaigns were using some of the harshest language of the year. Vice President Biden started it during a rally in Virginia before a largely African American audience. He said that Romney would "unchain" the big banks if he were elected president and then added, "They're going to put y'all back in chains." Biden later tried to temper his language, but within hours Romney unloaded. Campaigning in Ohio, he said Obama's "angry and desperate" campaign had brought disrespect to the office of the presidency. "Mr. President," he added, "take your campaign of division and anger and hate back to Chicago and let us get about rebuilding and reuniting America." That brought an incendiary response from the Obama campaign. Spokesman Ben LaBolt said Romney's comments "seemed unhinged."

Faux outrage has long been a part of every campaign's toolkit, but now the outrage seemed genuine. Neither side had to look far to find an excuse to launch an attack or cry foul. The most egregious example of a campaign out of bounds was an ad prepared by Priorities USA, the super PAC supporting Obama. The ad tied Romney to the cancer death of the wife of Joe Soptic, the GST Steel employee who had been featured in the Obama campaign's first two-minute ad. Mostly an online and cable talk show phenomenon, it ran only once or twice as a paid commercial, by accident, but it sparked a bitter exchange between the campaigns. Obama campaign advisers at first tried to distance themselves from the ad by claiming they didn't know the details of Soptic's situation. In fact, the campaign had put Soptic on a conference call months earlier. Obama privately told his advisers he thought the ad had crossed a line and he was unhappy that his campaign had been drawn into it. The Obama campaign also refused to denounce a stream of comments coming from Senate majority leader Harry Reid, who charged, with absolutely no evidence, that Romney paid no taxes for a period of ten years.

If anyone mentioned the Priorities USA ad to Obama's advisers, they pointed to the ad Romney was airing that accused Obama of gutting the work requirement in the welfare reform act that was passed by a Republican Congress and signed into law by then president Bill Clinton in 1996. They argued that the ad was patently false, though some conservative policy analysts argued that it wasn't. Fact-checking outlets declared the ad erroneous. Romney's campaign stood firm rather than walking away. Neil Newhouse would later say, "We're not going to let our campaign be dictated by fact checkers." The comment spoke volumes about Campaign 2012.

Partisanship was bred into the electorate and influenced voters' views. When I wrote about the toxic nature of the campaign, I received two e-mails in response. One blamed Obama and his campaign for the tone. "The onus is far and away on the side of the Democrats and you know it," the writer said. "They have called Romney everything under the sun (almost), namely, a murderer, a felon, and a tax cheat. Then, they cruelly made fun of Mrs. Romney's affliction [she suffered from multiple sclerosis] by cruelly castigating the cost of upkeep for her horse, which she uses as therapy. It is the vicious Democratic campaign machine which has denigrated Romney and now his vice president." The writer of the second e-mail took the opposite view. "Have you been completely unaware of all the ridiculous abuse Obama's received over the last 3+ years?" the writer said. "He spent the first 2.5 years trying to get along and asking for Republicans involvement . . . and what he got instead were accusations of death panels in his health care plan, that he's unqualified to be a president, and that he's a secret Muslim trying to steer the U.S. in Al Qaeda's favor. And, Romney has not distanced himself from any of these claims."

Romney's welfare ad was part of a broader August initiative designed to put Obama on the defensive. The campaign also attacked the president over

Medicare, an issue perennially trouble for Republicans, by saying his health care law would slash Medicare spending by $716 billion over ten years. Romney's team also went after the president for seeming to belittle the hard work of entrepreneurs and small business owners when, making a broader point about the role of government and society generally in creating the infrastructure and climate for entrepreneurs to succeed, he said at a rally, "You didn't build that." This was part of the Romney campaign's strategy, to attack rather than defend. His advisers wanted to force Obama to spend money defending himself. Stevens said, "So we hit them on outsourcing, and they spent money on defense. We hit them on welfare, and they spent on defense. We hit them on China, and they spent money on defense. And we hit them on 'You didn't build [that],' and they spent money on defense. You had this Death Star spending vast amounts of money. We had to get them to spend some of that on defense [for us] to try to stay alive." It was the one time during the summer when the Romney campaign's strategy began to move poll numbers, however slightly, in their direction.

But this pointed to another difference between the campaigns. When Romney attacked Obama for his "You didn't build that" comment, the Obama campaign responded immediately by cutting an ad with the president talking on camera. It was an effective response, probably more effective than the attack itself. Romney's campaign, in contrast, had the opposite attitude, that responding was a sign of weakness. There was a mentality that said you should never explain, never play defense, just always try to stay on offense. That mind-set came to frustrate some of those inside the Romney campaign, who argued that Romney needed to answer some of Obama's attacks more directly and more effectively.

The selection of Paul Ryan had presaged a shift to a bigger message and a broader debate between the two campaigns, one in which how to handle debt and deficits and how to restore the economy would be paramount. As August ended, it seemed as if the candidates hadn't gotten that message.

CHAPTER 22

Bill Clinton and the Empty Chair

The next test for the two campaigns took place at the most outdated of all the events on the presidential campaign calendar: the national conventions. Decades ago, these conventions were grand and gaudy spectacles filled with drama, backroom dealmaking, spirited floor debates, occasional fistfights, and at times riots in the streets. They still retained some of the spectacle. The campaigns converted sports arenas into glitzy television studios with high-tech bells and whistles to entertain the delegates and those watching at home. Delegates still wore goofy hats and costumes. There were parties galore stocked with booze and fat-cat contributors. But security concerns had turned the host cities into armed camps and, for the delegates, limited mobility and logistical snarls. Conventions offered no suspense and little drama. The nightly programs were scripted down to the minute. Much of the speechwriting, save for a few big speeches, was pedestrian, repetitive, and uninspired. Conventions were too long and too boring for the major networks to bother devoting hours of their precious airtime to the nightly program. They were nothing more than nightly infomercials for the candidates. And yet they still had an important political purpose with potentially high stakes. A few effective speakers and perhaps a visual moment could resonate long after the convention had ended. After all, it had happened to Barack Obama at the 2004 convention.

Mitt Romney needed a good convention. The summer battles had left the campaign largely where it had been at the start of the general election. For all the money spent on television, the overall race had moved little since the beginning of May. Obama still held a narrow lead, but Romney's team was relieved to have weathered the summer storm as well as it did, though his advisers knew he had sustained damage. The challenger's campaign was still strapped for cash. His advisers had gotten approval for a $20 million loan in August to tide themselves over until they could begin to use the general election funds they had been stockpiling for months. Even so, they would run no ads for two weeks, which astonished the Obama team. Republican super PAC leaders were patting themselves on the back for helping to keep Romney afloat in the face of the

Obama air assault. Obama advisers looked at the tens of millions they had spent over the summer on ads as an investment that had prevented Romney from doing anything to improve his image as the underdog.

For only the second time, the two parties had decided to stage their conventions on consecutive weeks—Republicans the last week of August in Tampa, and Democrats the first week of September in Charlotte. The parties had done the same thing four years earlier, breaking with a long tradition that had seen a gap of several weeks between the two conventions and with both events generally wrapped up by the middle of August. As with so much in politics, money had influenced to the decisions to shift to later conventions. In 2004, George W. Bush decided to stage his convention as close to the anniversary of the 9/11 attacks as possible (and in New York City). John Kerry had held his convention in mid-July. At the time, both candidates were accepting federal funds for the general election, which came with strict spending limits. Kerry realized too late that he would have to spread his funds over a much longer period of time than would Bush: less bang for the buck. Four years later, in part to avoid that problem, the Democrats decided to move their convention to the last week of August, butting up against the Republicans, who again had picked the first week of September. But in 2012, a different reality dawned on the campaigns—particularly Romney's. Neither candidate was taking federal money for the general election—or for that matter for the nomination battle. But campaign finance law still regulated fund-raising and made a critical distinction between money that had been raised for the nomination versus for the general election. Romney was hamstrung over the summer because he couldn't dip into his general election account until he had formally accepted the nomination. Had his convention come in early August or even late July, he would not have been at such a financial disadvantage.

Florida, with its twenty-nine electoral votes, was the biggest of the battleground states and a must-win for Romney. But Republicans made a major miscalculation when they scheduled their 2012 convention in Florida for the end of August rather than earlier in the summer. A convention is one event in which the candidate has control over everything—except the weather. And late August was the height of hurricane season. As party officials and the campaign's advance team began arriving a week before opening night, the threat had become real. Hurricane Isaac was bearing down on the Tampa Bay area. Four years earlier, the GOP had been forced to scrub the first night of its convention program in Minneapolis–St. Paul because of the threat of a hurricane in Florida. With memories of Bush's failure to respond quickly to Hurricane Katrina in 2005, Republicans didn't want any embarrassing reminder of that seeming indifference and incompetence. That was mostly a question of optics and imagery. In Tampa, as the first day of the convention neared, the issue was public safety. Would Republicans go ahead with opening night on a day when Tampa Bay could be underwater? On Saturday evening, August 25, party officials announced that they would delay opening by one day, forcing Romney's convention team, led by Russ Schriefer, to compress four nights into three, tossing aside a summer's worth of careful planning.

The Republican convention opened on Tuesday, August 28. Inside the Tampa Bay Times Forum, there was a distinct lack of energy. The convention floor, normally a bustling obstacle course, was abnormally quiet, with aisles wide open. It was exactly what Romney didn't need as he sought to charge up his party for the final months of the election. The challenger came to his convention with a lengthy to-do list. Most urgently, he still needed to fill in his biography. He needed to make himself a more appealing person, to counter the image projected by the Obama campaign. His campaign advisers had deferred action on this, believing that the convention offered the biggest audience and the best venue to do so. Romney also was under pressure to show that he had a plan to fix the economy. With so much deferred maintenance packed into three nights, he had little margin for error.

Two speakers carried the heaviest load on opening night: Ann Romney and Chris Christie. Originally Ann Romney was slotted for Monday night, subject to network coverage, with Christie the focal point of the second night. In the hastily revised schedule, they were back-to-back, an incongruous pairing that nonetheless promised star power for the GOP. Ann Romney was one of her husband's greatest assets, more natural than he on the campaign trail, blunt and funny, and a behind-the-scenes force. "Tonight," she said, "I want to talk to you about love. I want to talk to you about the deep and abiding love I have for a man I met at a dance many years ago. And the profound love I have and I know we share for this country." She appealed to the women watching, the campaign's effort to do something about the persistent gender gap. "It's the moms who have always had to work a little harder to make everything right. It's the moms of this nation—single, married, widowed—who really hold this country together." Over the applause, she shouted, "I love you women! And I hear your voices." When she talked about her husband, she described him as warm and loving and patient, with values centered on faith and love of family and country. "From the time we were first married, I have seen him spend countless hours helping others," she said. "I've see him drop everything to help a friend in trouble, and been there when late-night calls of panic come from a member of our church whose child has been taken to the hospital." Finally someone was humanizing the Republican nominee. She talked about her husband's success in business and defended him from critics who had tried to undermine that record. As she closed, she said, "I can't tell you what will happen over the next four years. But I can only stand here tonight as a wife and a mother and a grandmother, an American, and make you this solemn commitment: This man will not fail." Ann Romney had done her part, and the applause rained down on her as Mitt came onstage to give her a hug and kiss and wave to the delegates. Backstage, the next mini-drama was beginning to unfold.

Chris Christie had been working on his keynote address for weeks. He had looked at past keynotes to gauge how much they focused on the party's nominee, how stridently they attacked the opponent, how much they were general tone setters for the campaign. He had gone through sixteen drafts by his count, and worked to keep the speech within the time limits imposed by the campaign. He had sent it to Russ Schriefer, who was Christie's media adviser in the 2009 campaign. Schriefer liked what he read, Christie said. His one piece of advice was to slow down the delivery. "He said, 'Not everybody in the convention hall speaks Jersey,'" Christie said.

Christie watched most of Ann Romney's speech from the green room backstage but was moved into a hallway closer to the stage as she was finishing. The program was running long at that point, and the director was worried that the keynote might run past 11 p.m., which was when the networks were scheduled to end their prime-time coverage. As Christie waited, a member of the production team told him that because of time constraints the director was going to cut a three-minute Christie video that had been prepared as an introduction. You're not cutting the video, Christie told her. He was insistent. He thought the video set up the speech. She relayed Christie's concerns to the director, who said there was no way it could run. Christie told her to ask the director if he had ever heard anyone say "fuck" on live television, because that's what he was about to do if the video didn't run. About this time, Romney, on his way to greet his wife, stopped to say hello. Are you going to kill tonight? he asked. Christie assured him that he intended to. As Christie listened to the ovation for Romney, he was told to start walking up the stairs to the side stage for his speech. Christie again said that if the video wasn't shown, he wasn't going to deliver the speech. There were more sharp words between Christie and the director. Someone called Schriefer. "I said, 'Play the video, run it,'" Schriefer said. The director finally relented and allowed the video to be shown. Christie, irritated, assured him that he would finish by 11 p.m. no matter what.

With that he bounded onto the stage and gave fist pumps to the audience. If the delegates expected a withering attack on President Obama, they didn't get it. If the audience expected him to spend most of his time extolling Mitt

Romney's attributes, they were probably surprised that he didn't. Christie's speech was neither a paean to the nominee nor a shredding of the president. He was critical of the president, but not as harsh as he had been in other speeches. Of Romney, he said the Republican nominee would deliver hard truths to the American people to end the torrent of debt and to do what was necessary to fix the economy. He talked much more about New Jersey and the record he had compiled, his battles with teachers' unions, his work with the Democratic legislature. His money line about the president and Romney was this: "We ended an era of absentee leadership without purpose or principle in New Jersey. It's time to end this era of absentee leadership in the Oval Office and send real leaders to the White House." Christie, keeping note of the time and speaking through applause lines, finished at 10:59 p.m. He walked off the stage and offered one last retort to the director. "Ten fifty-nine," he said, as he spit out one last expletive.

The immediate response to the speech inside the Romney campaign was positive. Overnight reviews were far less so. Christie drew criticism for talking more about himself and less about Romney, though Barack Obama had done the same in his celebrated keynote speech at John Kerry's convention in 2004. Christie couldn't understand it. "I was really surprised by it and bothered by it initially because it shakes your confidence," said the man who never seems to lack that attribute.

On Wednesday night, Paul Ryan delivered his acceptance speech. It was notable for two things: some sharply written lines about the president—"College graduates should not have to live out their twenties in their childhood bedrooms, staring up at fading Obama posters and wondering when they can move out and get on with life"—and controversy that erupted afterward about how he had stretched the truth in describing the shutdown of a GM plant in his hometown and Obama's role in it. Inside the hall especially, his speech was enthusiastically received. But the first two nights still left much to be done with Thursday's program.

Schriefer had packed the final night's schedule—testimonials about Romney from people in his church and from Olympic athletes, a candidate video, an introduction by Marco Rubio, the candidate's acceptance speech, and an unannounced surprise speaker that kept the hall buzzing in the early hours of the evening. Long before the networks were scheduled to start their coverage, an elderly couple appeared onstage. Ted and Pat Oparowski seemed nervous at first, not surprising given the magnitude of the moment, but their appearance quickly became the emotional high point of the week. They told the story of their son, David, who was diagnosed with non-Hodgkin's lymphoma in

1979. At the time, they lived in Medford, Massachusetts, and knew Romney through the church. Romney befriended David. He visited him regularly. He learned that David liked fireworks, so he bought some and took the boy to a beach in Maine and set them off. David had a few possessions and he asked Romney to help write his will. Romney returned one day with a yellow legal pad and helped draft it. When David died, Romney delivered the eulogy at the funeral. "You cannot measure a man's character based on words he utters before adoring crowds during happy times," Ted Oparowski said. "The true measure of a man is revealed in his actions during times of trouble. The quiet hospital room of a dying boy, with no cameras and no reporters—this is the time to make an assessment."

Pam Finlayson followed the Oparowskis. Her daughter had been born prematurely and had a brain hemorrhage in the first days of her life. Romney came to the hospital to pray with Finlayson. "I will never forget that when he looked down tenderly at my daughter, his eyes filled with tears, and he reached out gently and stroked her tiny back," she told the delegates. "I could tell immediately that he didn't just see a tangle of plastic and tubes; he saw our beautiful little girl, and he was clearly overcome with compassion for her." Finlayson's daughter went on to live until she was twenty-six. When she died, Romney reached out once again to comfort the family, she said. "When the world looks at Mitt Romney, they see him as the founder of a successful business, the leader of the Olympics, or a governor," she said. "When I see Mitt, I know him to be a loving father, man of faith, and caring and compassionate friend." The two testimonials brought tears to the eyes of many in the arena that night—and raised two questions: Why hadn't the campaign done more with these stories earlier, and why was neither scheduled for prime time that evening?

The biographical video of Romney was beautifully produced and, in its own way, another powerful validator of the candidate that ran counter to the public image. But it too was another lost opportunity because it was not shown in prime time. Romney advisers said later that network officials had told them they would not run the video even if it were shown in prime time. Obama advisers said they were told the same thing before their convention and ignored the warnings. The networks carried Obama's. Romney's was seen only in the hall and among some people watching on cable.

The prime-time hour opened with the unannounced surprise speaker: Clint Eastwood. The appearance of the award-winning actor and director was a major coup for the campaign. During the Super Bowl earlier in the year, Eastwood had appeared in a commercial for Chrysler called "Halftime," which touted the American spirit and said the country was poised for a comeback. Some Republicans saw it as a thinly disguised ad for Obama's reelection.

Eastwood now had the chance to set the record straight in front of millions of people. Just before going onstage, Eastwood asked one of the stagehands to put a chair next to him at the lectern. Schriefer noticed the chair. That's weird, he thought. The actor got a huge ovation when he appeared, and the first minutes went about as expected. He talked about the excitement in the country the night of Obama's election, and the problems of the day—twenty-three million unemployed, underemployed, or not looking for work. Wasn't it time, he asked, for someone else to take over? Then he began to wander off. He earlier had pointed to the chair—"So I've got Mr. Obama here"—and suddenly began talking to the chair as if Obama were sitting there. He looked quizzically at the chair. "What do you mean, shut up?" he asked. Minutes later he paused again. "What? What do you want me to tell Romney?" he said. "I can't tell him to do that. He can't do that to himself. You're absolutely crazy. You're getting as bad as Biden."

The audience was cheering and laughing as the performance continued, but in the Romney box there was considerable discomfort. Eric Fehrnstrom was seated with campaign manager Matt Rhoades and traveling spokesman Kevin Madden. What the hell? Is this on the teleprompter? he wondered. Stuart Stevens, watching in another room in the hall, was literally sickened. He walked out of the room and threw up. Schriefer was just as dismayed as everyone else. He had helped to recruit Eastwood and was confident he knew what the actor was going to say. Eastwood had appeared at two fund-raising events for Romney during the summer and was funny and self-deprecating. Someone suggested that the campaign try to get him to speak at the convention, and when he expressed willingness, Schriefer slotted him for Wednesday night. But when the schedule was redone because of the hurricane, Schriefer moved him to Thursday. That afternoon, Schriefer, Stevens, and Spencer Zwick visited Eastwood in his hotel suite. All seemed well. He tried out some lines: "My friend George Clooney says he likes hanging out with the president. I like hanging out with the next president." When the trio of Romney advisers left they were confident that he would be a big hit. Schriefer visited him again backstage before he was due to go on. He said he just wanted to make sure everyone was clear about what would happen. Eastwood would have five to seven minutes. They were looking for a repeat of what he had done at the fund-raiser. "Yep," Eastwood replied. Eastwood rambled on for almost twelve minutes—an eternity in convention time. His performance was embarrassing enough to draw a comment from Ann Romney the next morning on CBS This Morning. "He's a unique guy and he did a unique thing last night," she said, trying to be as positive as possible. Charlie Rose noted that when the cameras caught her expression while Eastwood was talking, she looked surprised. Ann Romney smiled and chuckled nervously. "I didn't know it was coming," she said. Eastwood's performance was as bizarre a moment at a convention as anyone could remember. No wonder they are so tightly scripted.

Romney's acceptance speech was the product of a chaotic process and one that revealed much about the candidate. Romney was an English major in college and prided himself on his ability to write his own material. For a speechwriter, Stevens had said more than once, Romney was a tough date. Romney rejected one draft written by Pete Wehner, who had been a Bush administration official and was a gifted writer himself, and set aside another draft written by two former Bush White House speechwriters, Matthew Scully and John McConnell. With some input from Stevens, Romney largely wrote the speech himself, which was his way. He spoke of the hopes that had accompanied Obama into office and the disappointment that now surrounded the president. "But today, four years from the excitement of the last election, for the first time, the majority of Americans now doubt that our children will have a better future," he said. "It is not what we were promised." At times he mocked the president. "President Obama promised to slow the rise of the oceans and to heal the planet," he said. "My promise is to help you and your family." He talked about himself and his religion, something he rarely did. He talked about America and community. And then he turned back to the present and the state of the country and the president. "You know there's something wrong with the kind of job he's done as president when the best feeling you had was the day you voted for him. The president hasn't disappointed you because he wanted to. The president has disappointed America because he hasn't led America in the right direction."

To the chagrin of Romney's advisers, the morning-after commentary focused more on Clint Eastwood than on the nominee's speech. But Republicans left Tampa more energized than when they had arrived. Schrieffer assessed the week this way: "I think we got the three things that we had hoped to get out of it. We were able to work on defining Romney. I think we were able to talk about what it is that we wanted to do. And I think that we were able to have some sort of an indictment against Barack Obama. Those were our three goals. And I think we did those."

Charlotte started to welcome the Democrats the day after Republicans finished in Tampa. The choice of North Carolina spoke volumes about the Obama team. Obama had carried North Carolina by just fourteen thousand votes in 2008. Nobody believed he could do it again. But Obama's team had special affection for the state and what it represented. They saw it as prototypical of the coalition that he had attracted in his first campaign and that, if they did their organizing properly, could be reassembled in 2012. Obama's advisers had big plans for Charlotte, including a final-night rally at Bank of America Stadium, where the Carolina Panthers played football. It was to be a repeat of their outdoor extravaganza in Denver four years earlier and a major opportunity for organizing. But they were also looking for ways to revamp the traditional approach to conventions. Much earlier they had decided to convert what was to have been a four-night program into three, turning Labor Day into a day of service and picnicking while shifting opening night to Tuesday. The concept for Charlotte would be different from past conventions. Rather than devote each night to a single theme or topic—foreign policy one night, domestic policy another—the Obama team wanted to pound the same multiple messages over and over at each night's session. Every night would include talk about the economy, about Romney, about women's issues, about Hispanics, about gay rights. Obama still needed more enthusiasm among his base, and Charlotte provided the opportunity to accomplish that, if speaker after speaker hit those themes each night.

The team that led the convention planning consisted of Jim Margolis, Erik Smith, and Joel Benenson. They drew up the program with a strict eye on what television would or would not cover and also on how best to keep the energy level in the arena as high as possible at all times. They studied what the TV networks had covered at the Denver convention. They produced a huge color-coded spreadsheet that went day by day, speaker by speaker, network by network. They calculated how much time the networks devoted to speeches from the podium and how much of their coverage consisted of commentary and analysis. They looked for new ways to inject the stories of ordinary people into the convention and the coverage. They interspersed short videos into the program to help quicken the pace. But they knew, as did everyone else, that their convention would rise or fall on three speeches: Obama's acceptance, which would cap the convention week; Michelle Obama's testimonial, which would open the week; and Bill Clinton's exegesis on Obama and the economy, which would come on the middle night of the convention.

There was no way to replicate Denver. That convention was historic, marking the formal nomination of the first African American for the presidency of the United States. Obama's team knew that Charlotte could not produce that kind of excitement or anticipation. What the Democrats could not afford were signs of disappointment or letdown. Obama's team knew that any slackening of enthusiasm would be magnified many times over by the media horde assembled in the convention city. But if that was a worry, it was quickly eclipsed by opening night. The convention floor in the Time Warner Cable Arena was gridlocked, packed with people and pulsing with energy. The early evening program included a video tribute to the late senator Edward M. Kennedy that suddenly morphed into an anti-Romney ad, featuring footage from the Kennedy-Romney debate in 1994 in which Kennedy demolished his challenger. Former Ohio governor Ted Strickland, swept out of office by the Republican tsunami two years into Obama's presidency, gave a full-throated attack on Romney for hiding his tax returns and putting his money in overseas accounts. "Mitt Romney has so little economic patriotism that even his money needs a passport," he said. Massachusetts governor Deval Patrick went after Romney's record as governor. Rahm Emanuel, Obama's first White House chief of staff and now mayor of Chicago, defended Obama's record.

All that was table setting for the two main speakers of the night: San Antonio mayor Julian Castro and Michelle Obama. Castro and his identical twin brother, Joaquin, were born and raised in San Antonio. Their mother was a political activist in the Hispanic community and helped found La Raza Unida. He and his brother were both achievers: Stanford for undergrad (where they were elected to the student senate, tying with the highest number of votes), Harvard Law School, and then politics. Julian was elected to the city council a year after he finished law school. After losing a race for mayor in 2005, he was elected in 2009. Two years later he won reelection with 83 percent of the vote. Castro was little known nationally when he was chosen to deliver the keynote address; he exceeded all expectations. "Mitt Romney, quite simply, doesn't get it," he said. "A few months ago he visited a university in Ohio and gave the students there a little entrepreneurial advice. 'Start a business,' he said. But how? 'Borrow money if you have to from your parents,' he told them." Castro paused for effect. "Gee," he said with just the right tone of amazement, "why didn't I think of that?" The convention arena erupted in cheers and laughter.

Michelle Obama drew a booming ovation when she came onstage. The First Lady was more popular than her husband, striking in appearance and with obvious stage presence. She also had a powerful message to deliver about her husband, their values, and the contrast with the challenger. She talked about Obama in deeply personal terms, about the man she had fallen in love with, about the fact that neither came from families with many material possessions. She said both had been raised by parents who had made constant sacrifices that had given them the chance to go places they might never have thought of without a familial push. In twenty-three minutes, she was interrupted by applause almost fifty times. But there was no line that drew a greater response than when she said, "Today, after so many struggles and triumphs and moments that have tested my husband in ways I never could have imagined, I have seen firsthand that being president doesn't change who you are. No, it reveals who you are." She closed with a rallying cry for the grassroots Obama network to deliver an election victory on November 6. If they wanted to leave a better world for all their children, she said, "then we must work like never before. And we must once again come together and stand together for the man we can trust to keep moving this great country forward—my husband, our president, Barack Obama."

Geoff Garin, a Democratic pollster, said later that Michelle Obama's speech could be distilled to eleven words: "Barack Obama loves his family and he loves your family too." Harold Ickes, a longtime Democratic strategist, said he had never seen an opening night at a convention as successful as the first night in Charlotte. The Democrats were off to a fast start, with an even bigger night ahead.

Bill Clinton was the one person with the popularity and credibility to defend Obama's economic record and take on Romney's economic program. The irony of Bill Clinton's becoming Obama's validator and protector was not lost on anyone inside the party or out. Four years earlier the two had sparred tensely during Obama's nomination battle with Hillary Rodham Clinton. Clinton was stung by assertions that he had injected the issue of race into the campaign and had a series of charged phone calls with Ted Kennedy as he sought unsuccessfully to head off a Kennedy endorsement of Obama. Though Clinton had delivered a strong speech in Obama's behalf at the convention in Denver, the widely shared belief was that the two men still had a tenuous, awkward relationship. Obama's decision to name Hillary Clinton as his secretary of state certainly helped improve things, but it wasn't clear that the two men fully trusted one another.

The improvement in their relationship had taken time, and there were still difficult moments. When Clinton had described Romney's business record as "sterling" in June, he was shocked by the negative reaction among Democrats. A White House official said Gene Sperling, who was director of the National Economic Council in Clinton's White House and now held the same job in Obama's, spoke to his former boss to explain why people were upset. A friend described Clinton as "shell-shocked" by the commentary that he had undermined Obama. "He was a little baffled and surprised by the reaction," the friend added. Clinton's DNA was not to attack people. He wasn't looking to go after Romney personally. What he was saying was that Romney might be qualified to be president but, given the choice, there was no question that Obama had the better policies. Days after that episode, Obama and Clinton were scheduled to appear together at a New York fund-raiser. Any worries about

Clinton's reliability faded quickly. With Obama at his side, Clinton told the audience that Romney "would in my opinion be calamitous for our country and the world." In Charlotte, the Obama team wanted Clinton to do even more. Clinton took the assignment seriously. Terry McAuliffe and his wife, Dorothy, close friends of the Clintons, visited the former president in the Hamptons before the convention. McAuliffe is an early riser, and when he came into the kitchen one morning he found Clinton working on the speech. "He was at the kitchen table writing it out, by himself," McAuliffe said. "He knew what he wanted to say. He knew what arguments he wanted to make. He was obsessed. He knew how important this was. He took it on his shoulders." McAuliffe was struck by Clinton's focus. "After a couple of days I'd say, 'Mr. President, happy hour, can I get a beer?'"

The day of the speech, the bloggers played a guessing game: When would the Obama team finally get a look at the speech, and what would they do if it wasn't what they wanted? Clinton was notorious for stretching his speech deadlines. He would make last-minute edits on his State of the Union addresses on his way to Capitol Hill to deliver them. A few hours before the evening session of the convention was to begin, there was another report that Clinton hadn't delivered his text. But if there was nervousness, it had nothing to do with content. The Obama team had already filmed Clinton for TV commercials. They knew what he thought and how he wanted to say it. Besides, Sperling and Bruce Reed, Vice President Biden's chief of staff and domestic policy adviser in the Clinton White House, were working on it with him. What the Obama team worried about was length. Clinton was as notoriously lengthy as he was sometimes late. Obama himself kept asking about it. Have we seen the draft? Axelrod said, "I said, 'Mr. President, trust me, we're not going to see the draft until very, very late.'" It was after 7 p.m. when the speech arrived.

Clinton took the stage about 10:40 p.m. The networks were scheduled to end their coverage at eleven, but Obama's advisers were confident they would not cut off the former president. Clinton could barely speak a sentence without being interrupted by applause. "I want to nominate a man whose own life has known its fair share of adversity and uncertainty. A man who ran for president to change the course of an already weak economy and then just six weeks before his election saw it suffer the biggest collapse since the Great Depression; a man who stopped the slide into depression and put us on the long road to recovery, knowing all the while that no matter how many jobs that he saved or created, there'd still be millions more waiting, worried about feeding their own kids, trying to keep their hopes alive. I want to nominate a man who's cool on the outside"—more cheers—"but who burns for America on the inside." The applause continued. "I want a man who believes with no doubt that we can build a new

American dream economy, driven by innovation and creativity, by education, and—yes—by cooperation. And by the way, after last night, I want a man who had the good sense to marry Michelle Obama." The arena erupted again.

Then he turned his fire on the Republicans with an affecting combination of sarcasm and humor. "This Republican narrative—this alternative universe—says that every one of us in this room who amounts to anything, we're all completely self-made." The audience was laughing now. "One of the greatest chairmen the Democratic Party ever had, Bob Strauss, used to say that every politician wants every voter to believe he was born in a log cabin he built himself. But as Strauss then admitted, it ain't so. We Democrats, we think the country works better with a strong middle class. . . . You see, we believe that 'we're all in this together' is a far better philosophy than 'you're on your own.'" He compared the job creation records of Democratic and Republican presidents. He decried the hard-liners in the Republican Party, whom he said seemed to hate the president, and talked about days when Democrats like himself worked with Republicans to get things done. He debunked the Republican argument that Obama had made a bad situation worse. "No president," he said, "not me, not any of my predecessors, no one could have fully repaired all the damage that he found in just four years."

Clinton's speech was a rhetorical tour de force. He covered every possible argument and every possible subject, validating Obama's policies and his commitment to the middle class, challenging the Republicans as a back-to-the-future party that wanted to implement the same policies that had brought about the collapse. He made the argument for more spending on education and technology and training and said Republican spending cuts would hurt the economy and harm the middle class. The Republican plan didn't pass the arithmetic test either, he said. And as he delivered his next line—"We simply cannot afford to give the reins of government to someone who will double down on trickle-down"—the audience cheered loudly—again.

Obama's team, having cut the speech back, estimated that it would run a little over thirty-five minutes. It ran for nearly fifty. Clinton moved back and forth from the prepared text to his famous riffs so often that Obama's team began to have sympathy for the teleprompter operator. Axelrod laughed. "We had given [Clinton] twenty-five minutes and he had written a fifty-minute speech, and so they cut it down to twenty-five minutes. And then of course he got over there, he had memorized everything he had cut out and he gave the fifty-minute speech—every minute of which was worthwhile." No network cut away.

Clinton's speech finally eliminated the enthusiasm gap that existed between Democrats and Republicans. After Charlotte, it was never again a serious worry for Obama. After his speech, Clinton was calm but not ebullient. "It was off his shoulders," said McAuliffe, who saw him that night. "He did what he had to do. He didn't want to talk about it too much." Everyone else did.

Torrential rains on Wednesday washed away the campaign's hopes for another outdoor program on Thursday night like that of 2008. Obama delivered his acceptance speech from inside the arena. It was an anticlimax—serviceable but not soaring, effective but not as much as either Clinton or the First Lady. The speech was short on specifics, though his team had told reporters it included new details of his second-term agenda. That was for another time. He spoke to the disappointment that many voters, even his own, felt. "If you turn away now," he said, "if you buy into the cynicism that the change we fought for isn't possible, well, change will not happen. . . . Only you can make sure that doesn't happen. Only you have the power to move us forward." Earlier in the speech, Obama had spoken also to the feeling that the campaign had not risen to the moment. "I know campaigns can seem small, even silly sometimes. Trivial things become big distractions. Serious issues become sound bites. The truth gets buried under an avalanche of money and advertising. If you're sick of hearing me approve this message, believe me, so am I." At this, the audience began to laugh and applaud. "But when all is said and done—when you pick up that ballot to vote—you will face the clearest choice of any time in a generation. Over the next few years, big decisions will be made in Washington on jobs, the economy, taxes and deficits, energy, education, war and peace—decisions that will have a huge impact on our lives and on our children's lives for decades to come. And on every issue, the choice you face won't just be between two candidates or two parties. It will be a choice between two different paths for America, a choice between two fundamentally different visions for the future."

CHAPTER 23

The 47 Percent Solution

Mitt Romney was in California when the news broke on the afternoon of September 17. David Corn of *Mother Jones* magazine posted the report, along with excerpts of a video recorded during a $50,000-per-person Romney fund-raiser on May 17 in Boca Raton, Florida. The video had been shot surreptitiously, from a low angle at the side of the room. Romney was visible in an at-times grainy image, but most of his words could be heard clearly.

Someone in the audience said to Romney, "For the last three years, all everybody's been told is, 'Don't worry, we'll take care of you.' How are you going to do it, in two months before the elections, to convince everybody you've got to take care of yourself?" Romney replied, "There are 47 percent of the people who will vote for the president no matter what. All right, there are 47 percent who are with him, who are dependent upon government, who believe that they are victims, who believe that government has a responsibility to care for them, who believe that they are entitled to health care, to food, to housing, to you name it. That that's an entitlement. And the government should give it to them. And they will vote for this president no matter what. And I mean, the president starts off with 48, 49, 48—he starts off with a huge number. These are people who pay no income tax. Forty-seven percent of Americans pay no income tax. So our message of low taxes doesn't connect. And he'll be out there talking about tax cuts for the rich. I mean, that's what they sell every four years. And so my job is not to worry about those people. I'll never convince them that they should take personal responsibility and care for their lives. What I have to do is convince the 5 to 10 percent in the center that are independents, that are thoughtful, that look at voting one way or the other depending upon in some cases emotion, whether they like the guy or not, what it looks like. I mean, when you ask those people . . . we do all these polls—I find it amazing—we poll all these people, see where you stand on the polls, but 45 percent of the people will go with a Republican, and 48 or—" At that point the recording broke off for a minute or two.

Corn had been working on the story for some months. After publishing a story about Romney and one of Bain's companies, he had received an e-mail from someone named James Carter, a freelance researcher, who offered information that led to another story. Carter turned out to be the grandson of former president Jimmy Carter. Carter later tipped Corn to the existence of video clips of Romney and in late August put him in touch with someone who had set up a YouTube account under the name "Anne Onymous" and had posted video clips from a Romney fund-raiser. The anonymous source, whom Corn came to call "A.O.," offered Corn the full video of the May fund-raiser. Corn received the video on September 10 after returning from the Democratic convention, according to an account he published in December 2012. When he viewed the entire video, he realized instantly that Romney's 47 percent comments were explosive and damaging. He planned to post something on September 18, but he accelerated the schedule when the *Huffington Post* published an article that referred to some of A.O.'s previous video postings. Within minutes of his posting, it had blown up into a major controversy.

This was more than a gaffe, more than a slip of the tongue, more than Romney's "I like to fire people" comment in New Hampshire or "I'm not concerned about the very poor" after the Florida primary. This seemed to speak to fundamental values of the candidate, a devastating moment when the candidate was speaking before a friendly audience, off the record, with no expectation that his words would become public. The campaign's first response was a statement. "Mitt Romney wants to help all Americans struggling in the Obama economy," it said. Inside the campaign an argument had erupted. Should Romney directly address the video remarks or not? Romney watched a clip of the video on an iPad during a ride between fund-raisers. He tried to explain it to his advisers. "He was very insistent that this was not in the proper context and that what he was saying was being unfairly portrayed as overly negative," said Kevin Madden, who was traveling with Romney that day. "And he was quite animated." Romney said he had been asked how he could win the middle of the electorate (which was not the question, according to the text of the video). He said his words might have been inelegant but hardly as damning as the video made them seem. Campaign officials told Romney that he needed to respond quickly and vigorously. "It was as dispiriting a day as I've ever encountered in working on campaigns for a long time," Madden said. "We were totally under siege."

In Boston, people were caught by surprise by the comments from the fund-raiser, though not by the existence of a video. They had seen something earlier from the event—an innocuous clip that had been posted on YouTube, about a factory in China that Bain had been interested in. That video clip had gotten no pickup. As the new, 47 percent video hurtled around the Internet and took over cable coverage of the race, Romney's advisers set up a conference call with the candidate. "There was broad consensus that Mitt needed to address it," Eric Fehrnstrom said. "The question I remember trying to hash out was should we do it that night or should we wait until the morning, and the news cycle being the way it is we decided that it should be done immediately and if we have to do it again in the morning we'll do it again in the morning."

Stuart Stevens wanted video of Romney responding so that the video posted by *Mother Jones* wasn't the only thing available for television. The campaign hastily arranged for Romney to speak to his traveling press corps as soon as possible. He explained that what he had said was "not elegantly stated" because he had been speaking off the cuff. He had made the mistake, he said, of trying to become a political analyst. He said he was often asked how he could win and this was his effort to explain how he would try to win the small percentage of voters who were not tied strongly to either party. "Of course individuals are going to take responsibility for their lives," Romney said. "My campaign is about helping people take more responsibility and becoming employed again, particularly those who don't have work," he added. "This whole campaign is based on getting people jobs again, putting people back to work. This is ultimately a question about direction for the country. Do you believe in a government-centered society that provides more and more benefits or do you believe instead in a free enterprise society where people are able to pursue their dreams?"

The 47 percent controversy erupted during the rockiest month of the general election for the Republican challenger. After the convention in Tampa, Romney's campaign seemed to slide steadily downhill. His convention bounce, modest as it was, disappeared once the Democrats started their convention in Charlotte. Ed Gillespie said the Republican convention was "a little bit like cotton candy. It didn't end up giving us any sustenance or protein." The Democratic convention produced a much bigger bounce for the president. The Romney team in Boston concluded that Obama had managed to do what they feared, which was to rekindle the flame from 2008, certainly enough to rally supporters who may have been disappointed in his performance. Democrats were now enthusiastically focused on preventing the Republicans from taking back the White House. More worrisome by far, given the underpinnings of Romney's campaign strategy, the polls were beginning to record growing confidence in the direction of the country and more optimism about the state of the economy. Although the mood was still more negative than positive, polls showed a jump of ten points in the number of people who said that things were heading in the right direction. Romney eyed those numbers with considerable concern. If that accelerated, or even held, it would threaten the whole conceptual framework of the campaign strategy. Just as during the summer, the margin between Obama and Romney remained close and competitive, but underneath those numbers there were signs that the contest was slipping away from the challenger.

The 47 percent video hit less than a week after Romney had created controversy over the Obama administration's handling of protests in Egypt over an American-made video attacking the Prophet Muhammad and later that day the killing of four Americans in Libya, including U.S. ambassador Christopher Stevens. On September 11, protests erupted in Cairo as demonstrators angry over the American video stormed the U.S. embassy climbed over the wall, took down the American flag, and replaced it with a black flag bearing an Islamic inscription. Before the demonstrations turned violent, the embassy had issued a statement that appeared to be an effort to mollify the protestors. "We firmly reject the actions by those who abuse the universal right of free speech to hurt the religious beliefs of others," the statement said. Meanwhile, a separate confrontation was unfolding in Benghazi, though it would take hours before either the White House or the State Department realized how deadly it had become.

As reports continued to update developments, the Romney campaign decided to weigh in. This was an opportunity, advisers believed, to attack the president for siding with Islamic militants rather than defending American values of free speech, however repugnant the video that sparked the demonstrations was. Romney had long accused the president of apologizing for America, and this seemed a perfect example. Romney was on an airplane as the campaign worked out the language. When he was able to read it, he gave his approval. The statement was issued at about 10 p.m. that night, though it initially carried a midnight embargo. Within minutes, the embargo had been broken. "It's disgraceful," the statement said, "that the Obama administration's first response was not to condemn attacks on our diplomatic missions, but to sympathize with those who waged the attacks." At that point, the full extent of the tragedy in Benghazi was not yet known. Romney's advisers did not know that the ambassador and the other Americans had been killed. By morning, however, everyone knew. Nonetheless, rather than step back, Romney went before the cameras to repeat his criticism. "Apologizing for America's values is never the right course," he said. His criticism of the embassy's statement was certainly justified—even members of the administration were outraged that it had been issued and told reporters it had not been cleared in Washington—but his timing was poorly chosen. At a moment when the nation was absorbing the shocking deaths of four Americans, Romney appeared more interested in scoring political points. His comments drew a sharp rebuke from the president.

"Governor Romney seems to have a tendency to shoot first and aim later," he said. But criticism of Romney also came from prominent Republicans.

Romney was suffering from other problems in September. On September 17, Peter Hart convened another of his focus groups. He went to Fairfax, Virginia, for a second time, assembling a group of undecided voters. As the two-hour discussion unfolded, two things became clear. Even voters who said they were undecided had more or less made up their minds. Of the twelve members of the group, only four seemed truly undecided. The other revelation was the degree to which Obama's attacks on Romney over abortion, contraception, and family planning had reached the targeted audience of women voters and threatened Romney's hopes of narrowing the gender gap.

The Obama White House had begun the year on the defensive over whether religiously affiliated facilities—mainly hospitals and universities—would be required to provide free contraception even if doing so violated their religious beliefs. But the Republicans in Congress mangled the public relations of their response, turning what had been a problem for the White House into a weapon in the contest to win the women's vote. The Republican-controlled House Oversight and Government Reform Committee scheduled hearings on the contraceptive issue but declined to hear testimony from any women. Sandra Fluke, a thirty-year-old Georgetown University law student, had asked to be included on the list of witnesses. When she later told her story and argued for free contraception, Rush Limbaugh attacked her as a "slut" and a "prostitute" who wanted to be "paid to have sex." (Under pressure, Limbaugh later apologized for the remarks.) Democrats declared that Republicans were waging a "war on women." Romney had stepped carefully through that winter controversy, but he was on record calling for an end to federal funding for Planned Parenthood. The Obama campaign ran a series of ads over the summer attacking Romney and the GOP as extremists. As with other attacks, the Romney campaign decided not to respond, though that was not a unanimous view among the senior staff. Some Romney advisers thought he was taking an unnecessary risk not putting ads on television rebutting the attacks.

Inside the focus group facility in Fairfax, Hart had asked all of the participants to outline the issue of greatest concern to them. Nine people cited the economy, while two said it was health care. But as Hart probed the reasons why the truly undecided still were not certain about their vote, another reality revealed itself. "One thing that hasn't come up is women's rights and women's health," one of the women said. Hart asked which candidate she thought would be better on those issues. "Obama," she said. He asked another woman, a McCain voter from 2008, why she was not yet firmly in Romney's column. "You know, it should be locked down," she replied. "And I think part of it has to do with the Republican platform and the women's health issues, which should not be an issue." An Obama voter from 2008 said there were aspects of Romney's career and ideas that she liked. "One of the things he has going for him is he has a history of working well with the other party, and that's what we need right now. But part of me can't get past some of the other little things." Like what? Hart asked. "Women's health, gay issues, the right for everybody to marry, those types of things kind of hold me back."

Romney's explanation about the 47 percent comment did nothing to quell the controversy. His advisers could see that it seemed to confirm everything his critics had been saying about him, that he was out of touch with ordinary Americans, or that he saw the world through a prism that made it impossible for him to identify with the lives and aspirations of the middle class or the working class. Prominent conservatives in the media joined others to attack him. On MSNBC's *Morning Joe,* host Joe Scarborough, a former GOP congressman, said, "This is dangerous—not because he's going to lose that 47 percent of the vote—but because you're going to start seeing suburban voters, swing voters, storm away from the campaign as quickly as possible unless he fixes it." *New York Times* columnist David Brooks likened Romney to Thurston Howell III, the wealthy, aristocratic New Englander from the old television series *Gilligan's Island.* "Personally, I think he's a kind, decent man who says stupid things because he is pretending to be something he is not—some sort of cartoonish government-hater," he wrote. "But it scarcely matters. He's running a depressingly inept presidential campaign." *Wall Street Journal* columnist and former Reagan speechwriter Peggy Noonan wrote a blistering critique headlined "Time for an Intervention." "What should Mitt Romney do now?" she wrote. "He should peer deep into the abyss. He should look straight into the heart of darkness where lies a Republican defeat in a year the Republican presidential candidate almost couldn't lose. He should imagine what it will mean for the country, for a great political philosophy, conservatism, for his party and, last, for himself. He must look down unblinkingly. And then he needs to snap out of it and *move.*" Leaders of some of the Republican super PACs began to discuss whether they should shift their substantial funds out of the presidential race into competitive House and Senate contests.

As the 47 percent controversy was gathering momentum, Phil Rucker and I met in Boston to take the temperature of the Romney's advisers. In our conversations, they were defiantly upbeat, determined not to show how worried they were. As political professionals, they were trying to win the election, not wallow in their problems. To the outside world, they displayed a united and, without totally straining credibility, positive face. The race was not lost in the least, they asserted. But privately they were deeply worried. They had absorbed the worst body blow of the general election and were not sure at that point how lasting the damage might turn out to be. They had only one night of polling by the time we arrived, so they could be safely constrained in their assessment. Neil Newhouse later said he had actually stopped polling after the video was disclosed. "We know what it's going to look like," he later said. "We've got to dig our way through this, we've got to push our way through it, and there's nothing in the polling right now that's going to [help]. We know what we've got to do and how we've got to do it."

If the Romney campaign stopped polling, nobody else did, and the findings grew progressively worse as the days went along. Every other day a new poll was published showing Romney slipping in one of the battleground states. Within two weeks of the video being revealed, three polls showed Romney trailing Obama in Ohio by eight, nine, and ten points. In Florida and Virginia, two other must-win states for the challenger, Obama was holding a small but consistent lead. More than the poll numbers turned against Romney. It was impossible to find a story or commentary that did not suggest the race was almost over. A Democrat close to Obama called me one day in late September. "Is it over?" he asked. That was typical of the prevailing sentiment, even if the polls didn't quite show it. Romney taped an interview with CBS anchor Scott Pelley for *60 Minutes*. "You are slipping in the polls at this moment," Pelley said. "A lot of Republicans are concerned about this campaign. You bill yourself as a turn-around artist. How are you going to turn this campaign around?" Romney replied, "Well, actually, we're tied in the polls. We're all within the margin of error. We bounce around, week to week, day to day. . . ." "Governor, I appreciate your message very much," Pelley said. "But that wasn't precisely the question. You're the CEO of this campaign. A lot of Republicans would like to know, a lot of your donors would like to know, how do you turn this thing around? You've got a little more than six weeks. What do you do?" Romney wouldn't hear it. "Well, it doesn't need a turnaround. We've got a campaign which is tied with an incumbent president [of] the United States."

Another shift came the week after the video. Gillespie issued a memo that finally jettisoned the idea that the election was largely a referendum on the president's record. "This election is a choice," he wrote, as if starting to take lines from an Obama stump speech. "And the simple fact is we can't afford four more years of Obama's failed policies." Paul Ryan was one of the catalysts for the change. One Romney adviser said Ryan was outspoken during conference calls about the need to draw a sharper contrast. "He didn't see the referendum stuff was working," the adviser said. He thought Romney had specific plans and proposals that were more attractive than the president's but did not think people were hearing the distinctions clearly enough.*

It had become clear to everyone that trying to explain away the 47 percent comment was failing. But it would take Romney almost three weeks to say publicly that what he said at the Florida fund-raiser was wrong, rather than just inelegant. He was asked about the comment during an interview with Fox News. "Well, clearly in a campaign, with hundreds if not thousands of speeches and question-and-answer sessions, now and then you're going to say something that doesn't come out right," he said. "In this case, I said something that's just completely wrong." One adviser likened the decision to finally admit error to trying to land a huge fish. "At some point, you just cut the line and let that fish drop back into the water and not try to get it in the boat," he said.

At Obama headquarters, the president's advisers tried to keep the race in perspective. Their overall battleground state survey showed Romney dropping three points—from 47 to 44 percent—in the days after the video became public, with Obama's number rising from 50 to 51. They dismissed some of the more optimistic public polls from individual battleground states. Their own numbers showed a tighter race. Plouffe warned others that the public numbers were artificial and subject to change. This was still a close race, he told the team. From Boston, I flew to Chicago to see how the Obama team assessed everything. Stephanie Cutter, the deputy campaign manager and a veteran of John Kerry's 2004 campaign, told me, "I'm realistic that Romney's had a couple of bad weeks. But there's lots of time for him to recover. John Kerry was behind George Bush significantly at this point and he completely recovered after the debates. That's what Mitt Romney's banking on." But even for a team that trusted in its data, it was difficult to believe that the massive hit Romney had taken could not be changing the race.

---

*Romney told me later he paid little attention to the ongoing debate in his campaign about whether the election would be a referendum or a choice. He said he also thought it was as much a choice as anything else.

CHAPTER 24

Debacle in Denver

At 6:59 p.m. Denver time on the evening of October 3, Jim Messina tweeted the following message: "We are back stage in our hold room, Obama staff together eating pizza and fired up. 1 minute left. #forwardnot-back." A minute later, a light on a nearby television camera glowed red, and the more than sixty million people watching could hear the familiar voice of a veteran newsman and debate moderator: "Good evening from the Magness Arena at the University of Denver in Denver, Colorado. I'm Jim Lehrer of the *PBS NewsHour* and I welcome you to the first of the 2012 presidential debates between President Barack Obama, the Democratic nominee, and former Massachusetts governor Mitt Romney, the Republican nominee." As Lehrer made the introductions, Newark mayor Cory Booker, as if holding his breath in anticipation of what was about to unfold on the stage, tweeted, "Here we go! #debate."

The incumbent and the challenger were dressed in the team colors of red and blue America. Obama wore a dark suit, white shirt, and blue tie. Romney wore a dark suit, white shirt, and red tie. The political narrative for the encounter had been fixed two weeks earlier with the release of the 47 percent video. Romney had arrived in Denver on the defensive, with his party demoralized. He appeared at risk of letting the contest slip away from him a month before election day. Polls showed the president with his biggest lead of the campaign. But the fired-up message from Messina belied considerable nervousness inside Obama's reelection campaign. Preparations for Denver had gone badly. Everyone around the president was worried about what might happen.

Over the next ninety minutes, 10.3 million tweets would chronicle the Denver debate. At its high point, the debate generated almost 159,000 tweets per minute. This medium, which barely existed four years earlier, became the arbiter and the real-time spin room of one of the most important presidential debates in history, a pithy, running national conversation that was at turns devastatingly incisive in its judgments of the two men or hilariously funny at pointing out their foibles. The 10.3 million tweets eclipsed the tweets-per-minute pace set during the two political conventions a month earlier and marked, if not the coming of age of this medium, then at least an irrefutable confirmation of its power to shape elite opinions and perceptions. As Obama and Romney sparred onstage, they were oblivious to this running stream of commentary that was rendering judgment long before time was called at the end.

"Gentlemen, welcome to you both," Lehrer said. "Let's start the economy, segment one, and let's begin with jobs. What are the major differences between the two of you about how you would go about creating new jobs?" Obama, by coin toss, went first. "There are a lot of points that I want to make tonight," he said, "but the most important one is that twenty years ago I became the luckiest man on earth because Michelle Obama agreed to marry me. And so I just want to wish, sweetie, you happy anniversary and let you know that a year from now, we will not be celebrating it in front of forty million people." He appeared slightly stiff as he delivered his lines. He segued into the economy, reminding viewers of the problems he had inherited. He claimed progress but said it was not enough. He drew a contrast with his opponent. "The question here tonight is not where we've been but where we're going. Governor Romney has a perspective that says if we cut taxes skewed towards the wealthy and roll back regulations that we'll be better off. I've got a different view." When it was Romney's turn, he too began by mentioning the president's wedding day. "Congratulations to you, Mr. President, on your anniversary," he said. "I'm sure this was the most romantic place you could imagine—here with me." The audience laughed. Then he turned to what he called the "very tender topic" of the economy. Romney spoke of people he and his wife had met along the campaign trail who had lost their job or their home. He outlined his plan to restore the economy. He drew a contrast with the president, countering criticism that his approach was a return to "trickle-down economics." "The president has a view very similar to the view he had when he ran four years ago, that a bigger government, spending more, taxing more, regulating more—if you will, trickle-down government—would work. That's not the right answer for America. I'll restore the vitality that gets America working again."

On Twitter, Chuck Todd of NBC said, "An old Clinton trick by Romney, using real people stories to make his point." Jeffrey Goldberg of the *Atlantic* tweeted, "Romney did better on the subject of Obama's anniversary than Obama did on the subject of Obama's anniversary." Conservative commentator Michelle Malkin tweeted, "Obama rambled. Romney gets off to strong start by recounting mtg w/woman in Dayton OH w/hubby out of work." *New York Times* columnist Charles M. Blow noticed Obama's body language. "Obama looks like he's biting his tongue," he tweeted. Conservative talk radio host Laura Ingraham saw Romney in fighting form. "Romney killed first answer," her tweet read.

David Frum, a Bush White House speechwriter, said of the president, "Obama uncombative. He must have good poll news." At 9:14 p.m., Michael Tomasky, editor of the liberal journal *Democracy,* observed, "Obama isn't aggressive enough, not countering Romney enough." A tweeter dubbed @LOLGOP sent out a comparable message: "I think Mitt Romney had his first Frappuccino tonight," suggesting that Romney might have had extra energy because he had violated Mormonism's prohibition on caffeine. In the Obama war room, Stephanie Cutter could see what was happening. The debate was being lost in the opening fifteen minutes because of a medium that had not even played a role in the campaign four years earlier. Cutter exclaimed to her colleagues, "We're getting killed on Twitter!" David Plouffe turned to White House chief of staff Jack Lew. "This is a disaster," he said.

Onstage, the challenger protested Obama's claim that he wanted to cut taxes by $5 trillion, though several independent studies said that was the size of the cuts Romney was proposing. "I don't have a $5 trillion tax cut," he said. "I don't have a tax cut of a scale that you're talking about. My view is that we ought to provide tax relief to people in the middle class. But I'm not going to reduce the share of taxes paid by high-income people. High-income people are doing just fine in this economy. They'll do fine whether you're president or I am." Romney's tax plan had been a potential liability from the day he announced it back in February. He had deliberately avoided filling in the missing details—the deductions he would have to eliminate or cap in order to pay for his tax cuts. Obama's team was dumbfounded by what he was saying. "Mitt Romney just walked away from his $5 trillion tax cut," Cutter tweeted. Those keeping score on Twitter were more captivated by the contrasting performances on the stage than by the substance of what either was saying. At 9:18 p.m., Bill Maher, the caustic comedian and Obama super PAC contributor, began to sound nervous: "Obama's not looking like he came for a job interview, Romney so far does." Two minutes later, Andrew Sullivan, an enthusiastic Obama supporter with one of the largest blog followings in the country, weighed in. "Man, Obama is boring and abstract," he tweeted. "He's putting us to sleep. I get his points but he is entirely wonky tonight. And he is on the defensive."

Obama bore in on Romney's tax package. There was no way for Romney to pay for all those cuts, he said. Romney was sputtering as he tried to break into the conversation. "Virtually everything he just said about my tax plan is inaccurate," he said. Even he would oppose the plan Obama was describing. Obama was incredulous. He said Romney was saying "Never mind" to eighteen months of campaigning. Basic arithmetic, he said, proved Romney was misleading the public. The president's words may have been on point, but he was listless in the face of Romney's aggressiveness. The challenger was on the offensive against the president and even tried to overrule Lehrer. At one point he demanded the last word during one segment. As Lehrer began to protest, Obama said, "You can have it."

"Well, well, well," tweeted Dana Perino, who was White House press secretary for President George W. Bush and was now a Fox News commentator, "who do we have here? Romney is prePARED." Jeff Greenfield, the veteran political reporter and television correspondent, tweeted, "Romney is instructing Obama on how the economy works, and Obama seems unable to wrench the narrative away from him." Actor Albert Brooks observed, "Romney looks like he got more sleep." Hilary Rosen, a Democratic strategist, protested Romney's attempt to rewrite his tax plan. "I'm sorry, are we gonna let Romney get away with a brand new tax plan?" she tweeted. "That all of a sudden he gets to say that he won't cut more?" But a pattern was emerging on the left and right. As the first half hour of the debate was ending, Hugh Hewitt, the conservative talk show host, tweeted, "Romney pounding POTUS. Let the debate go long. What is POTUS thinking right now? 'Help me @davidaxelrod.'" David Corn, the journalist who had broken the story about the 47 percent video, offered this summation: "Romney does seem more passionate about dealing with the economic mess than Obama. He's doing well." And Mike Murphy, the former Romney adviser and GOP strategist and commentator, said what other Republicans were now thinking: "If we had this Mitt Romney for last 60 days, he'd be 5 points ahead."

At this point, some levity crept into the debate—and the Twitter conversation. Romney was ticking through areas he would cut to try to reduce the deficit. "Obamacare is on my list," he said, using the pejorative that conservatives had attached to the president's Affordable Care Act. "I apologize, Mr. President, I use that term with all respect." Inexplicably, the president replied, "I like it." Romney continued, "Good. Okay, good." The audience laughed. "So I'll get rid of that. I'm sorry, Jim. I'm going to stop the subsidy to PBS. I'm going to stop other things. I like PBS. I love Big Bird. I actually like you too. But I'm not going to keep on spending money on things to borrow money from China to pay for it." "Mitt Romney's love of Big Bird just exploded Twitter," said the Web site BuzzFeed. Instantly someone created a Big Bird identity on Twitter (several parody accounts were launched, in fact) and began offering snarky responses to Romney. "Mitt Romney will end Bert and Ernie's right to a civil union," the Twitter Big Bird tweeted.

The debate continued apace. Romney was loaded for whatever Obama offered. He attacked Obama's green energy initiatives. He said a friend had commented that Obama didn't pick winners and losers, just losers. "You put $90 billion into green jobs," he said. "And look, I'm all in favor of green energy.

Ninety billion, that would have hired two million teachers." At times Obama offered detailed rebuttals, filled with facts and figures. It wasn't always his answers that were a problem—reading the transcript, the debate appeared substantive, serious, mostly civil, and more evenly balanced. It was the way he responded, as if didn't want to be there. Obama managed to score some points in the final half hour, once again calling out Romney for lack of specificity. "At some point, I think the American people have to ask themselves, is the reason that Governor Romney is keeping all these plans to replace secret because they're too good? Is it because that somehow middle-class families are going to benefit too much from them? No." But he showed peevishness when Lehrer tried to cut him off. "Two minutes is up, sir," Lehrer said. "No," Obama replied. "I think I had five seconds before you interrupted me." Later the liberal filmmaker Michael Moore lamented in a tweet, "PBO, lemme get this straight. You can send in drones that kill civilians, but you can't stop Romney or Lehrer from interrupting you?" Obama's closing statement drew this from a *Vanity Fair* tweet: "Good LORD Obama wouldn't win a student council election against a chubby nerd with that closing statement."

In the filing center, where hundreds of journalists from the United States and around the world were watching on flat-screen televisions, there was an area at the front of the room for emissaries of the two candidates to spin reporters after the debate. But spin alley was now obsolete, effectively put out of business by the advances in social media. The tweets had rolled out faster than anyone could really absorb them all, as reporters, strategists, celebrities, and ordinary citizens set the narrative in bursts of 140 characters that magnified the consensus: Romney was not just winning the debate. He was crushing the president. The longer the debate went on, the more everyone was expressing the same view. Two-thirds of the way through, David Gregory, the host of NBC's *Meet the Press,* tweeted, "One hour in Romney is far more energetic and aggressive than the president." As the debate entered its final twenty minutes, journalists and others began to point out Obama's missed opportunities. Ashley Parker of the *New York Times* summed it up this way: "Things Obama has not yet mentioned, w 15 min left: Bain, 47 percent, flip-flopping." "I can't believe I'm saying this," Bill Maher said shortly before the debate ended, "but Obama looks like he DOES need a teleprompter." The *Weekly Standard*'s Bill Kristol blogged that Romney was turning in "the best debate performance by a GOP candidate in more than two decades." *Weekly Standard* writer Mark Hemingway joked, "That wasn't a debate so much as Mitt Romney just took Obama for a cross country drive strapped to the roof of his car." That, of course, was a reference to the Romneys' decades-old family car trip in which the family dog, Seamus, had been put on the roof. Roger Simon, *Politico*'s chief political columnist, headlined his sharply written analysis "President Obama Snoozes and Loses." He said the president "looked like someone had slipped him an Ambien."

Seven minutes after the debate ended, as the front of the filing center was being overrun by a platoon of Romney staffers and surrogates, Olivier Knox, chief Washington correspondent for Yahoo! News, tweeted, "Not one Obama surrogate in the 'spin room' right now. Emergency talking points meeting?" Even the hosts on MSNBC were attacking the president's performance. Eleven minutes later, now almost 11 p.m. on the East Coast, Andrew Sullivan offered one more stinging observation: "Look: you know how much I love the guy, and how much of a high info viewer I am, but this was a disaster for Obama."

The president had met with his debate team for the first time in May in the Roosevelt Room, a few steps from the Oval Office. His advisers gave a presentation to set the context of the debates: History showed that incumbent presidents do poorly in the first debate, they told him. The presentation included a slide reviewing the history of first debates: Of six incumbent presidents, five had lost their first debate. The debate team offered reasons. Presidents lose because they're out of practice and the challenger isn't. Incumbent presidents live in a world where people don't stand a few feet from them and berate them or twist their record. Challengers gained stature just by being on the same stage with the president. Finally, incumbent presidents have two jobs— running the country and running for reelection. Challengers have but one job, which is to win the election. They come to the first debate more ready than the president. Presidents think they know the issues; they're dealing with them every day. They often don't prepare or practice diligently enough. Obama absorbed the briefing and then showed his competitive streak. "Let's see if we can break the string," one member of the team recalled him saying that day.

Ron Klain, a former chief of staff to both Vice President Biden and Vice President Gore, led the debate team. He had been co-leader in 2008. Anita Dunn, White House communications director during Obama's first years in the White House and also part of the 2008 debate team, was back again. The two Davids—Plouffe and Axelrod—were key members, as was Joel Benenson, the campaign's lead pollster. Karen Dunn was recruited to assemble the research that the president would be asked to consume and played an invaluable role. Bob Bauer, the former White House counsel and Anita Dunn's husband, was tasked to handle negotiations with the Romney campaign. Jack Lew, a newcomer to presidential debates, became an active participant as well. Chief speechwriter Jon Favreau participated as the time for the debates approached. Plouffe recommended they recruit Massachusetts senator John Kerry to play Romney in their mock debates. As a fellow Bay State politician, Kerry had

studied Romney closely over the years, bore some similar physical characteristics, and was a skilled debater who had overwhelmed George W. Bush in the
first debate in 2004.

Obama's advisers took Romney very seriously as an opponent. "We were all
really worried about it to begin with," said one member of the team. "McCain
was not a good debater in 2008 and he didn't prepare. Romney went into the
debates that mattered with a strategy, he knew exactly what he needed to do,
he worked his tail off preparing." Everyone on the team knew Obama did not
like debates. He disliked having to chop answers into short bites. His speaking
style was that of an orator who built to a crescendo and delivered his best lines
at the end. In debates, the punch line had to come first. Obama saw debates as
performances—all show. "Obama would be the first to say he hadn't performed
well in 2008 in the multicandidate ones during the primary because he didn't
like them," the adviser said. "He didn't like them for the general election but he
performed well. But he didn't have to perform against a really good opponent.
This was just a totally different situation, so we were quite worried."

During the summer, the team began to game out the first debate and lay a
strategy for the president. An early strategy memo called for the president to be
aggressive in the opening debate, to take the fight to Romney and to stay on the
offensive as much as possible. His advisers told the president to challenge Romney in areas where the challenger had expertise, where he didn't, and where he
seemed to have no moorings at all. Obama was given a series of briefing books
to help him become more familiar with what Romney had been saying. Obama
was diligent in doing the homework. "He came back with voluminous questions," Axelrod said. "He'd read these debate books and he'd send back a memo
with forty questions that reflected the fact that he had read every line. So he
worked hard enough. He was taking it seriously, but everything was out of
alignment and you could tell in the debate prep."

In mid-August, the president and Kerry held their first mock debate at the
headquarters of the Democratic National Committee just south of the Capitol.
Obama's performance was underwhelming. Kerry-as-Romney came well prepared. The president tried to overpower him with facts and statistics. His advisers could see his testiness as he listened to Kerry/Romney attack his record.
Obama's irritability was a major concern, a hangover from his 2008 debates
when his most memorable moment was an unintended putdown of Hillary
Rodham Clinton during a debate three days before the New Hampshire primary. Obama's line, "You're likable enough, Hillary," became a lasting image
and one his advisers did not want replicated in any form against Romney.
Obama understood that he couldn't be snarky against Romney, but he asked
his advisers, with evident frustration, how he should deal with someone he

believed was outright lying about his record. It was clear to all that Obama
didn't much like Romney. This too was different from the 2008 debates.
Obama and McCain were far from chummy, but they had worked together on
some things in the Senate and Obama had real respect for McCain's courage
and sacrifice in behalf of his country as a POW during the Vietnam War. He
believed there were lines McCain would not cross in his pursuit of the presidency. He did not believe the same of Romney.

Everyone knew the first mock debate was just the opener in a series, but it
was an unsettling start. "Everyone was looking at each other afterwards like,
'Let's just go kill ourselves,'" said one of the president's advisers. When his advisers critiqued the performance the following week, Obama was receptive to their
suggestions—in contrast to his sometimes prickly reactions of four years earlier.
He said they were right, that he agreed with their criticisms. He said, according
to one advisers, "I get it, I hear you." He promised he would fix it—and then he
kept doing the same bad things over and over and over again. The second mock
debate was a virtual repeat of the first. The third took place on Friday, September 14, after Obama had just returned from an emotionally wrenching ceremony
at Joint Base Andrews, where he and Secretary of State Clinton had received
the bodies of U.S. ambassador Christopher Stevens and the three other Americans killed in Benghazi. He delivered his worst performance yet. His advisers
wrote it off to a president preoccupied with bigger concerns.

"Let's make the debate project the Manhattan Project of our campaign," Beth
Myers remembered Romney saying to her early in the year. "Let's commit the
resources. Let's commit the time. Let's have all the smartest people." Romney
wanted to be sure that when he walked into the debates, he would be as prepared as he could possibly be. Romney enjoyed debates and looked forward to
them. "He'd probably get mad at me for saying that, but when you run for
president there aren't that many things that are intellectually challenging and
exciting as one-on-one debates with your opponent," she said. "He wanted to
be ready, and being ready for Mitt means lots of preparation."

Myers assembled a core team: Chief strategist Stuart Stevens and policy
director Lanhee Chen developed overall strategy. Jim Perry handled preparation of the voluminous briefing materials for the candidate. Austin Barbour,
who was part of the media team, oversaw all the logistics. Ohio senator Rob
Portman was chosen to play Obama in the mock debates. Other senior members of the campaign staff—Matt Rhoades, Bob White, Eric Fehrnstrom, Ed
Gillespie, Peter Flaherty, Ron Kaufman—were brought in once the process
began in earnest to help with the mock debates and strategy sessions. The
core team first met with Romney on June 23 in Utah, more than three months

before the first debate. "We had policy preparation, strategy preparation, and mock debates," Myers said. "And we did enough of all of them." Myers would give Romney briefing books before long flights, and he would spend his time on the plane digesting the material. He didn't memorize so much as he absorbed and recast the material. "He's the kind of guy who really prepared for his exams at Harvard Law School [and] Business School, but also crammed at the end," Portman said in an e-mail message to me. "So he did both. He took notes in our sessions and then he would synthesize comments people had made and consolidate his notes into a few points in his own writing."

Romney did sixteen mock debates overall, ten before Denver. The first ones took place the week after the Republican convention, as the Democrats were meeting in Charlotte. The Romney team decamped to Vermont, to the home of Kerry Healey, who was Romney's lieutenant governor in Massachusetts. Over a three-day period, the Romney campaign staged five mock debates. Each night at dinner they had general discussions. On the first night, they discussed Obama's strengths and weaknesses. The next night they put Romney under the microscope. Throughout the month of September, they were focused on developing a strategy for Denver. Particularly after the 47 percent video, Romney's team saw the Denver debate as a new opportunity to present Romney whole to the voters. He could be the real Mitt, more thoughtful and compassionate, and more moderate than the Obama ads were saying. But they knew the most important goal was to go after the president's record. "We needed to be ready for the first debate to be on attack on all issues and to have a counterattack," Myers said. In the mock debates, Portman played a president on the attack, but as the debate neared, he cautioned Romney to be ready for a different Obama. "I thought it was important to prepare for a more aggressive Obama just in case," Portman said in a message. "But I expressed my opinion that he would be playing rope-a-dope because he was being told by his people that he was ahead in the polls, which he was. He was probably plus eight in Ohio at that point," Portman said. At this point, not many days before the Denver debate, the numbers everywhere were grim, thanks to the 47 percent comment. Matt Rhoades and company developed a turnaround plan. The first point of the plan was: Have a great debate.

The president left Washington on the morning of Sunday, September 30, and arrived a few hours later in Nevada for debate boot camp. Obama's advisers presented him with a new strategy. The changing landscape—Romney's erosion in the polls after the conventions and the 47 percent comment—had prompted a reevaluation of the plan they had settled on during the summer. Though they claimed otherwise, Obama's advisers were, in Axelrod's word, "seduced" by the new polls and by the new narrative of a race that had Obama firmly in command and Romney teetering on the edge of defeat. The debate team had concluded that the goals for Denver should be adjusted to fit the new state of the race. They no longer wanted Obama to be so aggressive. They recommended that he try to stay above the fray, to capitalize on the fact that voters liked him better than Romney. "The goal in this debate," one adviser said, "is to not change that and not leave the people thinking their guy is a nice guy and our guy is an asshole, because if we can just keep this likability thing where it is, we're going to win. So that colors your thinking about how aggressive you want to be in the debate, that colors your thinking about exchanges in the debate, that colors your thinking about how much conflict you want in the debate." This adviser said there was another reason to urge Obama not to be on the attack. "You're watching these practice sessions and when you turn Obama loose or when he goes after Romney, it's horrible," he said. Another adviser said, "Our assessment on the risk-reward, given where the race was, given what we thought we needed to get done in the debates, given how our candidate was performing, our assessment was to really just play it safe and to go into Denver and to try to deliver some message and talk about our plan, do some positive stuff, engage Romney on some issues but not blow it." "What I didn't want was peevishness," Axelrod said. "I didn't want caustic exchanges, and so we kind of warned him off of those, and in a sense he was left in no-man's-land when he got out there."

When his advisers presented Obama with the new plan, he disagreed with their recommendation. "We had a discussion with him about this aggressiveness thing and to his credit his instinct was that the strategy was wrong," one adviser recalled. "His instinct was he needed to be more aggressive. He was right about that. . . . We explained to him that we thought, given where we were in the race, given our lead, given that likability was his strongest asset, that our strategy was not to be too aggressive in the debate, and he was like, 'I don't see how I'm going to win if that's my strategy.'" Sunday's mock debate was passable. Monday's, however, was lousy. Obama seemed to be regressing. On Tuesday, after an outing to see the Hoover Dam, Obama returned for his final mock debate before Denver. This one went better than the previous night, more in line with Sunday's. All three, an adviser later said, were better than his performance in the actual debate.

Romney arrived in Denver on Monday night, after one final mock debate. In Denver he held a rally at which he received the endorsement of John Elway, the celebrated former quarterback of the Denver Broncos. His campaign was having trouble calibrating expectations. En route to Colorado, Kevin Madden had tried to downplay expectations, but a day earlier Chris Christie had set them sky high. "This whole race," he said on CBS's *Face the Nation*, "is going to turn upside down come Thursday morning." The day before the Denver debate, Romney got another confidence booster when he took a call from George W. Bush. Don't worry, Bush told him. You'll do just fine. The former president told Romney that he knew from his own experience how difficult first debates were for incumbents. He doubted that the president would be as prepared as he should be. He predicted Romney would emerge as the winner.

The morning of the debate, Obama and his advisers met for a final critique session before flying off to Denver. His advisers knew they were sending him into the first and most important of the debates unfocused and with an uncertain strategy. "We went into Denver not really with a strategy but with a hope," one adviser said. "A hope that it would all kind of work out."

When the debate ended, Romney's family joined him onstage. Ann Romney effusively praised his performance. Tagg gave his father a hug. "You were awesome," he said. Romney said he wasn't sure it was all that great. "You crushed him," Tagg told his father "Well, I don't know," Romney said. It wasn't until he walked back toward the holding rooms that he got the full sense of what he had done. Romney staffers lined both sides of the corridor, and as the candidate and his wife approached, they broke out into cheers and applause. In the spin room, Stuart Stevens, who had been the target of much criticism over the previous weeks, kept smiling broadly. He had argued for months that Obama's failure to take ownership of his record would prove to be his biggest obstacle to reelection. He said the debate proved that. "I don't think [Obama] had a particularly bad debate," he said. "He has a bad record."

Obama left the arena quickly and returned to his hotel, unaware of the post-debate commentary that was going on nonstop. A senior White House official recalled approaching him as he was walking into a room with family and friends, who were assembled for an anniversary party. "I remember being gentle, but I said, 'The commentary has been pretty rough,' and I just kind of introduced it, and it didn't sink in at that moment." When Plouffe saw him after returning from the spin room, Obama quizzed him about the reaction. "He said, 'I just don't understand,'" Plouffe recalled. "I had to say, 'It's not just the media. This did not go well.'" Obama began to watch and read some of the post-debate commentary. By the time Axelrod saw him, the president was beginning to come to terms with the night. "He said, 'I gather the consensus is we didn't do very well,'" Axelrod said. "I said, 'It appears to be a consensus.'" Plouffe and Axelrod had been through moments like this. They were reminded of the night of the New Hampshire primary, when Hillary Clinton scored a dramatic upset that reshaped the nomination battle and guaranteed a long and brutal fight. "One of the great qualities of Obama is he gathers himself quickly after a setback," Axelrod said, "and so we were up quite late, not him but the group, thinking through the next day."

The next morning, the president asked another adviser whether she had seen the reruns. "I said I did look at it on television and I said it was really bad on TV and he said, 'Why?'" the adviser recalled. Obama was more curious than defensive, still trying to understand better why the judgments were so harsh. "I told him about the split screen, which he did not know that there was going to be a split screen, and he was aware that he was looking down but he wasn't aware of how the looking down would appear in contrast to Romney." The adviser said Obama replied, "I've got to figure out how to deal with this Romney, if that's going to be who he is." He meant the Romney who had shown up in Denver as opposed to the Romney from the campaign trail. Obama had a rally in Denver that morning. The day was cold and raw, matching the mood inside his campaign, but the president delivered a fiery speech, filled with fresh lines written overnight. He was as energized in the chill Rocky Mountain morning as he had been passive the night before. But the harsh reviews and evident discouragement among Democrats dominated the coverage.

Klain flew back to Washington that morning. When he arrived he sent an e-mail to Axelrod and Plouffe, offering to resign from the debate team. Axelrod and Plouffe independently thought the suggestion was ridiculous and dismissed it out of hand. Later that evening, the president called Klain. What happened in Denver, he said, is my fault, no one else's. Obama had asked Plouffe to get him a video of the debate. He called Plouffe on Friday night. "I get it," he said. When the full team met the following week, Obama told them he wasn't just going to do better in the next debates, he was going to win them. The following Friday, Robert Gibbs had lunch with the president. Gibbs could tell that Obama knew what he had done wrong, that he had pulled back too much and that he would be in a much better place for the second debate. "He knew how poorly he had done," Gibbs said. "He had to engage Romney. He had to debate. He knew." Had the first debate not turned out as badly as it did, Plouffe said, "There's no way we would have had a good second and third debate."

In Boston, Romney's team saw an immediate surge of energy around their candidate. "You would not believe the way the numbers changed literally overnight," Newhouse said. "Literally overnight." The campaign's surveys always asked a question that gauged how recent news was affecting their impressions. Based on what they had heard or seen, did they have a more or less favorable impression of the candidate? "We had been minus-twenty on that, thirty-five/fifty-five, whereas Obama was dead even," Newhouse said. And just like that, overnight the numbers flipped." In Chicago, Obama's team was monitoring the numbers just as closely. David Simas, the director of opinion research, kept watch as the Denver debate rippled through the electorate. When the first numbers came back, Obama's margin had narrowed by a point and a half. Simas wondered, Is this the floor? The analytics team said they couldn't tell yet. The next day the margin tightened again. Now Simas wanted to know something else: Who's moving? The answer wasn't yet empirically clear. By the third day, it was: Romney's gains were coming almost entirely from Republicans and Republican-leaning independents. They had peeled off in September and now were enthusiastically coming home. Romney's advisers believed they were seeing something broader and more significant.

Whatever the numbers said, Obama's team knew it had a perception problem and that the second debate could be even more important than the first. Obama had to reverse the impression left in Denver or the race might truly turn against him. A few days after the first debate, Obama again met with his debate team, who presented him with a new strategy. He could be aggressive almost with impunity and go after Romney at every turn. The team decided to concentrate more on the president's style and less on perfecting his answers. His body language in Denver had cost him badly, and his advisers talked about how he could confront the challenger and stay on the offensive in the face of Romney's attacks. Obama, who found so much of the stagecraft of debates distasteful, agreed with the recommendations. His only lament was that the second debate was more than a week away.

As he waited, the two vice presidential candidates met on October 11 at Centre College in Danville, Kentucky. As a House member, Paul Ryan had never been in such a high-stakes debate, and he was nervous. Joe Biden had been debating for years and loved the verbal combat. Ryan had a capacity to memorize huge quantities of information and devoured the briefing books his team had put together. Biden was not a detail person, but his agility on a stage was well known. Even in 2008, when his presidential candidacy had never gained traction, his debate performances were always solid. Knowing the stakes of his debate with Ryan, Biden immersed himself in preparations. The day of the debate, the vice president's plane landed in Kentucky, and as the motorcade was forming, he took a call from the president. He came out smiling and turned to one of his advisers and said, "I know we're in trouble." The adviser asked what he meant and said Biden replied, "I know we're in trouble because the president just told me to be myself, and that's the first time in four years he's ever told me that."

For Biden, "be myself" meant to be aggressive and to speak to the Democratic base, which was exactly what Obama's team needed. Four years earlier, when he debated Sarah Palin, the advice had been the opposite: Be careful, be deliberate, don't be too harsh, don't act like a bully. After Denver, Obama needed Biden to reenergize the Democrats, whatever that took. That night, Biden followed the new game plan, with exaggerated expressions and gestures and interjections meant to show his disbelief or displeasure with much of what Ryan was saying. Ryan's advisers had prepared him for this. Ted Olson, a solicitor general in the Bush administration, had played Biden as a boorish and sometimes obnoxious character. Biden drew some criticism, but overall he was judged the winner. He accomplished two things. One was to make the argument that the Romney people saw in Denver, the more moderate Mitt, was in fact not the real Romney, that the Republican nominee was the "severely conservative" candidate of the primaries and that Ryan only added more conservatism to the ticket. Equally important, he gave reassurance to the Democratic base. "Let me tell you something," said one adviser. "What we did that night and where we were in the race and where we were with our supporters, between being too cold and too hot, there's no question what risk we wanted to take, and we did a really good job of it." Ryan's advisers were happy that the congressman had kept his cool so well and made no mistakes that would cost the Republican ticket. But Biden had done what the Democratic base wanted and what the Obama campaign needed.

Obama's team had learned some things from the first debate and the fallout afterward. One was that playing to the Democratic base was more important than appealing to undecided voters. The country was so polarized, and the undecided voters so few, that nothing was more important than giving every potential Obama supporter a reason to get out and vote. They realized that in this atmosphere, no one would be penalized for being too aggressive in the debates. They also concluded that 2012 was unlike 2008 in another way. The first debate in 2008 took place against the backdrop of the collapse of Lehman Brothers and an erratic performance by McCain in the days after. Looking steady and somewhat ponderous was good for Obama. But this was a different campaign. People wanted someone who they believed would energetically attack the country's economic problems. Debates were clashes between candidates, not college seminars. Obama needed to show more life and fight. When the debate team had looked at the transcript from Denver, they found that Obama had actually talked for about four more minutes than Romney but had delivered, by his campaign's count, roughly a thousand fewer words. Speak faster, Obama's team told him.

All of this crystallized into a fresh strategy for Obama in the second presidential debate on October 16 at Hofstra University on Long Island. Hit

Romney hard; don't try to debunk his policy proposals, just attack them; don't try to answer Romney if he claimed he wasn't proposing a $5 trillion tax cut, attack the philosophy. Explain the choice and be the champion of the middle class. There was one inherent risk, at least according to the conventional wisdom of debates. The second of the three debates was in the town hall format, with questions from citizens on the stage. It was often assumed that attacking the other candidate in such a setting was difficult if not politically dangerous. The weekend before the Hofstra debate, Obama was in California for some fund-raising. While there, Bill Clinton cautioned him about punching too hard in a town hall debate. He reported this when he returned and began final preparations in Williamsburg, Virginia. His advisers persuaded him to dismiss the advice. "We had learned from our mistakes in Denver," one adviser said. "We had learned that Twitter-sphere wasn't really that interested in candidates being nice with one another, and our voters wanted to see him hit Romney hard and hit Romney on the 47 percent and bring all these attacks." The campaign also developed a strategy for Twitter, encouraging supporters to send positive tweets. Plouffe said, "One of our goals for the second debate was within the first ten minutes to have you guys on Twitter saying, 'Okay, Obama is better, he's back.' We need the press corps to say you're off to a good start."

Romney's strategy was condensed into four bullet points in the campaign's debate briefing book: "Meet the attacks from the president head on. Don't just answer the question; speak to the questioner. Give specific contrast points; on each issue make sure you differentiate yourself from the president. Have the same Mitt Romney show up for second debate as first debate." He arrived for the second debate with his team feeling he was as well prepared as he had been before Denver. But Obama was confident as well. In the locker room before the debate, he huddled with Axelrod and Plouffe. "I feel good about it," Axelrod remembers him saying. "We're going to have a good night."

Romney was, if anything, even more aggressive in the second debate, interrupting the moderator, CNN's Candy Crowley, and jabbing hard at the president. His one memorable phrase, however, was when he talked about how he had worked hard to hire more women while he was governor. He said he had "binders full of women" from which to choose. But Romney faced a different Obama, and that made for a far different evening. The president stayed on the attack throughout. Toward the end of the debate, the Benghazi killings came up. "Who was it that denied enhanced security and why?" the president was asked by one of the citizens on the stage. Obama explained the steps he had taken after the killings and poked at Romney's statements on the night of the attacks and the next day. When it was Romney's turn, he accused Obama of being feckless in the face of terrorism. "There were many days that passed before we knew whether this was a spontaneous demonstration, or actually whether it was a terrorist attack," he said. "And there was no demonstration involved. It was a terrorist attack, and it took a long time for that to be told to the American people." Earlier that afternoon, Ben Rhodes, the deputy national security adviser for strategic communication, had pointed out to the debate team the exact words Obama had used in the Rose Garden the day after the four Americans had been killed. Obama had said it was an "act of terror." The president and his team spent time preparing a response. When Romney was finished, Obama pounced. "The day after the attack, Governor, I stood in the Rose Garden and I told the American people and the world that we are going to find out exactly what happened. That this was an act of terror." Romney was incredulous. "You said in the Rose Garden the day after the attack it was an act of terror? It was not a spontaneous demonstration, is that what you're saying?" Obama replied dismissively, "Please proceed, Governor." Romney continued: "I want to make sure we get that for the record, because it took the president fourteen days before he called the attack in Benghazi an act of terror." Obama interjected, "Get the transcript." Crowley stepped in. "He did in fact, sir. So let me call it an act of terror." Obama said, "Can you say that a little louder, Candy?" "He did call it an act of terror," she repeated.

In pure debating terms, Obama had the advantage that night. In political terms, it was a clear victory for the president. He had avoided another calamity and reassured his supporters.

The third debate took place six days later at Lynn University in Boca Raton, Florida. Romney's team was more nervous about this debate because it would focus on foreign policy, a natural advantage for an incumbent commander in chief. Obama's team believed Romney could approach the debate in one of two ways. He could continue his aggressive attacks on Obama's conduct of foreign policy, or he could try to hug the president on everything except Benghazi in an effort to reassure voters that he would not pursue a reckless foreign policy. The debate team asked Kerry to practice both ways. Their conclusion was that even if the gentler Romney showed up, Obama would still attack him at every turn, which was exactly how the debate played out. Benghazi came and went quickly. CBS's Bob Schieffer raised Libya in the opening segment and it largely disappeared. Romney tried to assure people watching that he would be a prudent and restrained commander in chief. Obama kept on savaging him as reckless, uninformed, and unready. When Romney charged that Obama was dangerously allowing the Navy to shrink in size and that there were now fewer ships than in 1916, Obama replied caustically, "Well,

Governor, we also have fewer horses and bayonets, because the nature of our military's changed. We have these things called aircraft carriers, where planes land on them. We have these ships that go underwater, nuclear submarines."

As the debate ended, Tagg Romney went onstage and approached the president. The week before, during a radio interview, he had been asked what it was like to hear his father called a liar repeatedly during the Hofstra debate. Tagg said it made him want to take a swing at the president. He immediately regretted the comment and wanted to make amends directly: "He was shaking hands and I just leaned in and said, 'Mr. President, I hope you know how sorry I am for what I said. I didn't mean what I said. I would never want to punch you or anybody else and hope you understand it was an expression that was used badly on my part.' He looked at me and said, 'Oh, don't worry about it. If someone said that about someone in my family I'd feel the same way. You're just protecting your dad. You're a good son. I hope my daughters are as protective of me as you are of your dad.' Michelle Obama looked at me and said, 'Thank you for saying that. That means a great deal to us.'"

If Romney had won Denver decisively, Obama carried the night in Boca Raton just as decisively. With the debates now over, both campaigns were looking to their ground forces in the battleground states to carry them to victory.

CHAPTER 25

Ohio and the Path to 270

On an unseasonably warm evening in late October, two dozen people gathered in the backyard of Wanda Carter's home in Columbus, Ohio. They were part of the frontline forces Barack Obama was counting on to deliver the state on November 6. They were all volunteers, with the exception of a twentysomething young man who was a paid staffer with Obama for America. Over hot dogs and other picnic fare, they shared stories and swapped ideas. Then Carter stood up on the deck to give them a pep talk. "If you are reading the newspapers and watching TV, what are you always hearing?" she said. "Get out the vote. Ground game. It's the ground game. It's the ground game. It's the ground game. And that is us. At this point, we and all the other people who are doing what we are doing are the most important people in the campaign." Jim Messina had always said that while he loved the campaign's paid staff, when the operation met the voters on their doorsteps, it was much more effective if the people knocking on the doors were the volunteers— friends, neighbors, relatives of those they were encouraging to vote for the president on election day.

The group in Carter's backyard represented that strategy. Carter, a lawyer, was a neighborhood team leader in Upper Arlington—an NTL in the vernacular of the campaign. NTLs were at the top of the Obama volunteer organizational chart. They had considerable autonomy over how to implement the campaign's voter contact program, but were held accountable in meeting the campaign's goals almost as if they were paid staff. After Carter spoke, Carol Mohr, another neighborhood team leader, outlined to the other volunteers where they had to concentrate their efforts during the final days. "We really care about you if you vote every time, but we're not going to come knock on your door during the get-out-the-vote period," she said. "We care about you until we find out that you're for Romney, and then we'll never knock on your door again. We care about you if you're undecided and we'll come back to you and talk to you several times until after this weekend. Then we don't care about you if you're undecided. If you haven't made up your mind by Sunday night at seven o'clock, we don't care about you. After that we only care about those people who are for Obama but are sporadic voters."

The election was now less than two weeks away. The debates had come and gone. Early voting was well under way. What was left was the last big push. The election had come down to just a handful of states. Florida, Virginia, and Ohio were the big three. Others in play were Colorado, Nevada, Wisconsin, Iowa, and New Hampshire. Obama's inner circle refused to give up on North Carolina, but everyone else believed it would tip to Romney. Four years earlier, Obama's campaign had shaken up the electoral map—winning Indiana and Virginia, two longtime Republican strongholds (although Virginia was turning purple), and conservative North Carolina. His advisers even made forays into states like North Dakota and Montana. Early in the 2012 cycle, they talked about expanding the map again. Those dreams quickly gave way to reality. The economy and the dissatisfaction with the president made holding territory more important than seeking out new states.

The electoral calculus would turn on two questions. First, which of the nine states that Obama had turned from red to blue in 2008 could Romney and the Republicans put back in their column? Indiana was a certainty, North Carolina a probability. New Mexico was lost for the Republicans because of the Latino vote. That left six of the nine to fight over. Second, could Republicans put any Democratic states in play? Wisconsin seemed a possibility. It had backed Democratic presidential candidates since 1988, but the margins were razor thin in both 2000 and 2004. Wisconsin's controversial Republican governor, Scott Walker, had just survived a recall election by a surprisingly large margin, the culmination of a sixteen-month battle over collective bargaining rights of public employees. The state was deeply polarized around Walker, but Republicans had fresh momentum from the recall and a tested organization. With Ryan on the ticket, Romney hoped to add it to his column. Another possibility was New Hampshire. The Granite State had voted Democratic in the 2004 and 2008 presidential elections, but Republicans had swept the state clean in 2010. Romney, from neighboring Massachusetts, hoped to take advantage of the conservative uprising and his own familiarity with the state.

That made eight true battlegrounds, the smallest number in years. But Ohio stood out above all the others. A cartoon by Rob Rogers of the *Pittsburgh Post-Gazette* in early October captured the state's symbolic significance. Three schoolchildren stood before a map of America, outlined in black but with no state boundaries delineated. The map said, "Ohio." "I like the new map," one of the youngsters said. "It's a lot easier than memorizing fifty states." This was a familiar role for the Buckeye State. It was ground zero in the 2004 campaign, the state that ultimately broke John Kerry's heart. Early exit polls on election day 2004 had given Kerry the advantage. In Boston, his advisers were calling him "Mr. President." But when the votes were finally counted, George W. Bush's campaign had outmaneuvered the Democrats with a superior get-out-the-vote operation.

Ohio had been a battleground in 2000 and in 2008 as well, but it took on greater significance in 2012 because of its potentially pivotal strategic importance. Obama had multiple paths to the 270 votes needed to win in the Electoral College. In the spring of 2011, Messina showed me five maps representing five different paths to an electoral majority: the West path, the Florida path, the South path, the Midwest path, and the Expansion path. Each was narrowly drawn to make a point: Obama could lose any number of battleground states and still get to the minimum of 270. Romney had to win most of the likely battlegrounds. Beyond that, no Republican had ever been elected president without winning Ohio. It may have been mathematically possible for Romney to win the election without Ohio, but politically it was almost unthinkable; the combinations of states he would have to win without it made it foolhardy to think about a strategy that did not make the Buckeye State a strategic priority. If the Obama campaign could roadblock Romney in the heart of the industrial Midwest, the challenger's hopes likely would die there.

The campaigns weren't ignoring other battlegrounds, but there was hardly a day in the final month of the election that one of the four candidates—Obama, Romney, Biden, Ryan—was not in Ohio. Political ads ran nonstop; local news programs were so clogged with ads that the time devoted to the news shrank noticeably. From April until late October, ads by the two campaigns had run 187,000 times, according to Kantar Media's Campaign Media Analysis Group. In October alone, at least seventy different ads had been shown there. Radio ads were as prevalent. Anyone driving the jammed roads in the fast-growing suburban and exurban areas around Columbus quickly got a taste of that—one ad piled up on another and another. Direct mail filled mailboxes. One Romney supporter estimated that he had received fifty different pieces in the fall. Phone calls to voters were incessant. One day in late October, a woman who lived near Cincinnati was telling my *Post* colleague Felicia Sonmez that she and her husband were receiving ten to twelve calls a day. At that point, her cordless phone rang. She looked at the screen and saw a 202 area code—Washington, D.C. "And here's what I do with these calls," she said as she clicked the "on" button and then quickly hit the "off" button. "I've been doing that a lot in the last month," she said.

Ohio became the focal point of the campaign for another reason: No battleground state better encapsulated the debate over the economy and the contrasting arguments by the president and his challenger—with Obama's bailout of the automobile industry at the very heart of their disagreement. Ohio had a diverse economy of manufacturing, agriculture, health care, and coal, but the auto industry still played a significant role in the state's well-being. One of every eight jobs was tied directly or indirectly to the auto industry (though that was down from one in five in the previous decade). The industry had at least some presence in eighty of the state's eighty-eight counties. Half of those jobs were in just ten counties, most of them running across the state's northern tier. The entire presidential race might come down to one issue, the auto bailout, and a handful of counties in Ohio. That too made the state the focus of so much attention. "It's so rare that in presidential politics you have such a state-specific message," Aaron Pickrell, Obama's chief Ohio strategist, told me over coffee one morning a few weeks before the election. "The auto bailout gave us that contrast."

The writer Susan Orlean once said of her native state that it "conveys a certain regularness, a lack of wild distinction, a muting of idiosyncratic extreme. The state is a sample of nearly every American quality and landscape but it levels out to be something quietly and pleasantly featureless rather than creating a crazy quilt of miscellany. It is an excellent place to live and a less excellent place to describe, since nothing stands out in that theatrical way that allows for easy description."

But for all its regularness, Ohio was a complex megastate. Pickrell liked to say that running a campaign in Ohio was like running a national campaign. An analysis by the Bliss Institute at the University of Akron noted, "Each region has a distinct political ethos and votes in a different fashion." Northeast Ohio encompassed Cleveland, Akron, Youngstown—cities closely identified with the steel and heavy manufacturing muscle that were once the core of the state economy. Northwest Ohio, which was close to Detroit, was long reliant on autos and manufacturing as well, but it was more rural, less populated, and more Republican than northeast Ohio. Southwest Ohio, including Cincinnati, was more classically midwestern. Southeast Ohio was coal country and part of Appalachia. Central Ohio, anchored by Columbus, had a younger population with a larger percentage of white-collar workers and was home to the state's premier institution of higher education, the Ohio State University. It was no accident that Obama held the first official rally of his campaign at Ohio State on May 5, 2012. Winning the Columbus market was now key to winning the state. The Bliss Institute broke the state into five regions, but political analysts added a sixth in west central Ohio, nestled between Toledo in the north and Cincinnati in the south, with Dayton at its heart.

Ohio was not well suited to Obama. In other states, the president looked to a coalition of minorities, young people, and affluent, well-educated white

voters. Ohio had a sizable African American community, but the white population did not fit the model for Obama's winning coalition. The 2010 census
showed that whites without college degrees—a particularly challenging group
of voters for Obama—accounted for 54 percent of the population, one point
higher than it had been a decade earlier. Ohio was also emblematic of the
economic hardship of the entire industrial Midwest and of decades of decline
as manufacturing jobs disappeared and young people moved away in search of
better opportunities. During the first two years of Obama's administration,
Ohio's unemployment was well above the national average. It peaked at 10.6
percent and held there for seven consecutive months. Polls showed sustained
pessimism in Ohio—years and years in which more people thought the state
and nation were going in the wrong direction. "After 2010, we were very, very
worried about Ohio," said Mitch Stewart, the battleground state director. "We
thought we were in a very difficult spot there."

The Obama campaign's route back in Ohio began with two state-specific
fights. The first was a ballot initiative in November 2011 to repeal Senate Bill
5, which restricted collective bargaining rights by public employee unions.
Obama's campaign helped labor unions collect enough signatures to put the
initiative on the ballot. The measure was convincingly repealed and gave Republican governor John Kasich a black eye. One Romney adviser said later that
the fight cost Romney and the Republicans among some of the working-class
voters they hoped to attract—police and firefighters who were angry over the
collective bargaining restrictions. The second was a fight over House Bill 194,
legislation passed in the spring of 2011 to change Ohio's voting laws, including
restrictions that would have limited early voting. The Obama campaign wanted
as much time and opportunity for early voting as possible, and helped organize
an effort to collect signatures for a citizen veto. Faced with the opposition, the
Republican-controlled legislature repealed the law in May 2012, though bitter
court fights over early voting regulations that pitted the Obama campaign
against Jon Husted, the Republican secretary of state, continued almost to
election day.

During the summer, the Obama campaign bombarded Ohio voters with ads
attacking Romney. The attacks on Bain's role in investing in companies that
had outsourced jobs had particular resonance. Ted Strickland, the former governor, believed that Romney's Swiss bank account and Cayman Islands investments alone could beat him, if enough people knew about them. From May
through August, the campaign spent about $30 million on ads in Ohio. Rom-
ney's pre-convention cash-strapped campaign could spend barely $10 million,
according to Kantar Media's CMAG counts. Republican super PACs could not

make up all the difference. A top Romney adviser said later, "By the time we sort of engaged in the campaign our problem was that Mitt Romney's favorables were impossibly low," he said. "In other words, you couldn't win a campaign even if you won on all the issues with his favorables as low as they got. I think it was high thirties at the time we engaged. That's pretty tough to overcome."

Ohio's economy was improving, and the president was quick to claim credit for saving the auto companies. The state's unemployment rate dipped below the national average in November 2010, and just before the election it ticked below 7 percent. Obama hit Romney for his opposition to the bailout. "When the American auto industry was on the brink of collapse, and more than one million jobs were on the line, Governor Romney said we should just let Detroit go bankrupt," he said at a rally in Maumee during a July trip to the state. Someone in the audience shouted, "That's what he said!" Obama said, "Governor Romney's experience has been in owning companies that were called 'pioneers' of outsourcing. That's not my phrase—'pioneers' of outsourcing. My experience has been in saving the American auto industry." Romney tried to explain that Obama had eventually embraced what Romney had long advocated, a structured bankruptcy. But he never effectively rebutted Obama's argument that the auto companies would not have made it into bankruptcy proceedings without an infusion of government money.

Ohio was critical to Romney, and yet into the early fall his campaign advertising was hit or miss in the state. In September, Rob Portman began to analyze where the campaign was spending its money. He was shocked to see that Romney was not running ads in secondary markets that were critical to Bush's success in 2004. He learned that for months Romney had not been on the radio in rural areas that were vital to his turnout operation. Portman, supported by state director Scott Jennings, became a fierce advocate for a new approach in Ohio. The candidate had to spend more time in the state, and his campaign had to spend more money in more places on TV ads, they told Boston.

But lack of money wasn't the only problem with Romney's advertising. His ad buying was a source of consternation inside the campaign. Late in the race, when Romney's senior advisers learned to their dismay that radio ads they thought were running in rural areas in western Ohio were not actually on the air, there was a major blowup. Romney also was paying significantly more for his ads than Obama, which meant that even if the money spent had been equal, Obama would have run many more ads. *Politico* reported that Romney was paying two, three, even five times more than the Obama campaign to place a thirty-second ad in the same time slot. Obama paid $1,200 for an ad during the Emmy awards. For the same program, Romney paid $3,600. Obama had thirty people working on placing the ads, and they got lower rates in part because they negotiated station by station rather than buying what are called lock-in rates. Obama's team had tapped into a huge dump of data to help guide their ad-buying strategy: the click-by-click habits of individual viewers, with a firewall to protect privacy, gleaned from the information contained in set-top boxes on people's TVs. With those data, Obama's ad buyers dramatically expanded the number of cable networks where they placed ads, beyond the traditional handful of networks campaigns had been using. Romney's team never caught up, and by the end of the campaign, frustrations with the ad-buying strategy were legion.

After Portman's complaints, Boston responded. Advertising increased, as did Romney's time in the state. After the Denver debate, enthusiasm surged and the size of Romney's crowds increased dramatically. But if the first debate changed the psychology of the campaign, it had not changed the underlying arithmetic in Ohio or other battlegrounds. Romney was still trailing and saddled with an image problem. Geoff Garin, who was working with Priorities USA, the pro-Obama super PAC, said he did a focus group in suburban Cleveland shortly after the second debate. The participants were Obama voters from 2008 who were not yet back in his column. Garin asked them about ads. Of all the scores they had seen, were there any they remembered? They responded by talking about Priorities USA's infamous "Stage" ad, in which a worker who had been asked to build a stage used to announce the closing of his plant said he felt like he had built his own coffin. Priorities USA had not run the ad in Ohio for seven weeks and yet the participants could cite specific details. The ad was sixty seconds long and costly to put on television. Garin earlier had recommended against running it anymore because of the cost. After the focus group, he e-mailed: "I think we cannot afford not to run it again."

Romney's advisers were putting on a brave face in Ohio, hoping that the enthusiasm they were seeing at their rallies meant a surge in turnout. But they were still trailing narrowly and were still perplexed about the bailout. The question was whether to take it on directly or avoid turning over the hornet's nest. Portman had been urging the campaign for some time to deal with the bailout. The campaign produced a series of scripts for commercials, but the policy shop, which had signed off on the questionable ad accusing Obama of gutting the work requirement in the welfare law, would not approve any of them.

In late October, the campaign seized on a Bloomberg News story that said Chrysler was planning to shift production of Jeeps from the United States to China. Romney mentioned it at a rally in tiny Defiance, Ohio. The initial Bloomberg story, however, was incorrect, and Chrysler officials immediately denied it. They were planning to produce Jeeps in China for the overseas market, not take jobs out of the United States. Romney's campaign cut an ad—the most controversial of his campaign and one that was the subject of great debate inside the campaign. The ad was carefully and narrowly written. The key sentences were "Obama took GM and Chrysler into bankruptcy and sold Chrysler to Italians who are going to build Jeeps in China. Mitt Romney will fight for every American job." Though the words were literally accurate (and approved by the policy department), the impression left was totally misleading. The ad exploded in the campaign's face. Sergio Marchionne, Chrysler's chairman, issued this statement: "I feel obliged to unambiguously restate our position: Jeep production will not be moved from the United States to China. . . . Jeep assembly lines will remain in operation in the United States and will constitute the backbone of the brand. It is inaccurate to suggest anything different." A General Motors spokesman offered a more caustic response: "We've clearly entered some parallel universe during these last few days. No amount of campaign politics at its cynical worst will diminish our record of creating jobs in the U.S. and repatriating profits back to this country." Newspapers around the state hammered Romney for the ad. Commentators condemned him for playing fast and loose with the facts. When that happened, the Romney campaign, whose style was never to show weakness or admit error, refused to back away. His advisers were sick and tired of being preached at by a media establishment they believed had treated their candidate unfairly.

When it came time to turn out the vote, the challenger was at a major disadvantage. Obama's campaign team had been on the ground in Ohio for almost five years. Jeremy Bird had been the Ohio state director in 2008. Pickrell had run Ted Strickland's campaigns. Greg Schultz, the state director, had been deputy state director in 2008 and had remained in place as state director for Organizing for America until the reelection campaign began. Obama had at least 130 offices around the state, plus five hundred or so staging areas for volunteers working the final days. He had almost seven hundred staffers on the Ohio payroll alone. The only other state that roughly matched that level was Florida, which had eleven more electoral votes. Thousands of volunteers— the Wanda Carters and Carol Mohrs—carried out the duties of contacting the voters. Romney had to build an organization in a matter of months. He had about forty offices and 157 paid staff, though most of those were on the payroll of the Republican National Committee. Scott Jennings said after the election that there was no way the Republicans could overcome Obama's head start. "Our ground game was as good as it could have possibly been, given the time and resources we had to work with," he said. "There's just no substitute for time. Six months . . . wasn't enough to overcome six years of a constant campaign run by the other side. Truly it is remarkable to see what they did, in the rearview mirror."

Beyond the disparity in sheer numbers, the Obama campaign had another advantage. What Messina and Dillon and the field people and the tech people and the analytics people had built over the previous eighteen months provided greater precision in targeting voters. Pickrell told a story about himself that illustrated the disparity between the two campaigns. He was someone who always voted—primary elections and general elections. He was also someone who always voted Democratic. Once during the summer, an Obama volunteer knocked on his door, just to check in and see if he had any questions. The volunteer, of course, did not know that Pickrell was senior strategist for the campaign in Ohio, only that the computers had spit out his name and address as someone who needed one contact but probably nothing after that. Pickrell and his wife later requested absentee ballots. When the ballots arrived, they put them aside on a kitchen table, where they sat for two weeks. The Obama team had a program to monitor absentee ballot returns and to prod people who were slow in turning them back in. "I got thrown back into the database of people who needed to be contacted," he said. "So one afternoon when my wife was home one of the Obama canvassers knocked on our door." The canvasser wanted to remind them to turn in those ballots. Once they did, there were no more contacts. That was the level of efficiency of the Obama organization—targeted and precise. Meanwhile, Pickrell said he received a dozen direct mail pieces from the Romney campaign, a waste of money and effort on the Republicans' part. "Half of those pieces were about Medicare," he said. "I did turn forty last year, but I'm not sure I'm a Medicare voter." He got no direct mail solicitations from the Obama campaign because the database said he didn't need persuading. The Romney team was proud of what it was doing. In the final weeks, Rich Beeson, Romney's political director, said Romney's campaign was getting more data about voters than any previous Republican campaign. Later they learned the scope and sophistication of the Obama campaign. "We didn't have the number of analytics people they did and couldn't collect the amount of data they did," he said. "They took that to another level."

The Obama campaign also had tools no previous campaign had to work with. Through modeling, voters were rated on a scale of 1 to 100 on the likelihood they would support Obama. A similar scale was used to predict turnout. So if someone had a high support score and a low turnout score, meaning that person was very likely to support Obama but not so likely to vote, the campaign tried to make sure that that person got registered and then got out and voted, preferably during the period for early voting. Banking those sporadic voters became a top priority. "They were voting because a neighborhood team organizer on the south side of Columbus was chasing them every single day," Messina said.

The Obama team had done something similar in 2008 but more experimentally. This time the campaign added a third measure, a persuasion score. This helped weed out people who said they were independent but who really were not. Early in the year the campaign ran a test to see who was most likely to be persuaded by certain messages, based on contacts with half a million people in the battlegrounds. "We were able to refine our model from that to see who were actually the best targets for persuasion work," Bird said. "And then we really worked those lists from top to bottom rather than what our gut said [about who was undecided and persuadable]." In the final weeks of the campaign, the Obama team focused on voters with persuasion scores of between 40 and 60. Those with higher scores were likely to vote for Obama without needing much persuasion. Those below probably weren't going to back the president no matter how open they said they were. "In the old days you would say here's a list of people we think are independents, go to those houses," Messina said. "But you waste your volunteers' time all over the place because despite what someone says, there are a very small amount of undecided voters." By knowing the voters and modeling the electorate, the campaign reduced wasted time on the streets. "You're a volunteer knocking on doors in Columbus and you are asked to knock on two doors on one street," he said. "One was to chase an absentee ballot request, the other one was an undecided voter, and you were told what to say."

No get-out-the-vote operation works precisely as planned—or as described in after-action reports by the winning campaign. It always sounds better than it is. Back at headquarters, the Obama field leaders talked about the precision and sophistication of their ground game. On the streets and in the neighborhoods, it never looks as smooth. Much is left to the volunteers, who may or may not carry out the directives with the rigor that the designers expect. But the payoffs for Obama were real on election day.

CHAPTER 26

The Vote

Just after sunset on October 23, Mitt Romney's motorcade, red lights flashing in the dark, began the steep and winding climb up the hills west of Denver. It was the day after the last debate and he was coming back to the city where he had jump-started his campaign three weeks earlier. Earlier that day, Romney had flown from Florida to Nevada for a rally in Las Vegas, but the big event of the day was scheduled for early evening in the Denver suburbs. On the way up the hills, he could see lines of cars parked along the road far from the entrance. His destination was the Red Rocks Amphitheatre, a spectacular natural setting used for concerts and other big events. That night, blue lights bathed the vertical rock walls flanking the sides of the seating area at the rear of the amphitheater. The Romney campaign's stylized signature "R" logo was projected in white against the softly glowing backdrop. Five American flags were hanging high up at the back of the big stage, which was decorated in a western, faux-autumn theme with fenceposts, artificial grass, rocks, and shrubs. More than ten thousand people were jammed into the outdoor concert venue, with thousands more turned away. People began arriving long before dark, their cars quickly overflowing the parking lot. After leaving their vehicles along the road, some people hiked straight up the sharp incline rather than follow the twisting pavement. In the center section of the seating area, supporters were given colored T-shirts to create a huge living image of the Colorado flag—big circles of yellow and red against a white rectangular background. Thunderous applause greeted Romney as he came onstage after being introduced by Paul Ryan. "What a place this is!" Romney shouted above the deafening roar. He patted his heart as the applause swept down across him. Spectators enthusiastically smacked red and white thunder sticks. Taylor Havens told a *Denver Post* videographer, "Red Rocks is on fire because Mitt Romney is here."

There had been other moments almost like this since the first debate, rallies where the size and enthusiasm of the crowd told Romney he had lit a spark with his Denver performance. The day after that first debate, he held a huge outdoor rally in Fishersville, Virginia. On his way to the event, Romney's bus got snarled in traffic. His advisers feared there had been an accident up ahead and wondered if they could find an alternative route. It turned out that thousands of people were trying to get there. They wanted to see Romney, the man who had demolished the president in debate! That was a first for the candidate who had such a tenuous relationship with the Republican base.

The rally at Red Rocks was a notch above everything that preceded it. Yes, the campaign had put a huge effort into the event and a film crew was there to shoot it for commercials. But even accounting for the extra effort by the advance team, the whole scene at Red Rocks—the crowd, the cheers, the energy, the noise, the sense of possibility—looked and felt different. Even the jaded press corps traveling with Romney, by now weary from long days, short nights, endless rallies, and repetitious speeches, took notice. Romney pointed to the debates as the turnaround moment. "They have supercharged our campaign," he exclaimed. Republicans were now embracing Romney in ways they never had before, and his campaign believed that the burst of energy from the first debate had turned into lasting momentum. After Red Rocks, they began to believe not just that the challenger could win, but that he would win.

Reporters had seized on the new narrative in the days after Denver. The story was all about a changed race. Down and almost out in September, Romney was now on the comeback, and that story line colored interpretations of everything. Small changes in the polls were interpreted as big signs of the momentum shift. Not that anyone was calling Romney the likely winner, but the media's hunger for a compelling story down to the last day of the campaign affected the broad sweep of the reporting and analysis. Polls added to the confusion. A Gallup poll in mid-October found the president leading among female voters by a single point in swing states. That was an astonishing result, one that ran counter to everything political strategists knew about the voting patterns of the electorate. But it was something new to talk about, and for a few days cable TV ran with it. Commentators struggled to find an explanation, because there was none—nor was there any other evidence to back it up. Public polls in Ohio tightened, though they still showed the president with a lead of several points. In Florida, a public poll taken immediately after the first debate showed Romney leading by seven points. It was an outlier but it captured the theme of the moment. In Virginia, the public polls in October, with a few exceptions, showed Romney now leading narrowly, after he had trailed throughout the month of September.

Many Americans are skeptical of polls. How could a sample of a thousand or fifteen hundred people speak for a nation? But as the 2012 campaign unfolded, polls became yet another point of contention in the battle between red and blue America. Never had partisanship so colored interpretations. Party loyalists picked polls that reinforced their biases. That was particularly true of conservatives, who weren't buying the evidence of an Obama lead in the preponderance of polls and who deeply distrusted the mainstream media. A new Web site, Unskewedpolls.com, sprang up to challenge data by the mainstream media, particularly any survey in which Democrats significantly outnumbered Republicans. Conservatives claimed the polls showing a sizable Democratic edge in turnout were more evidence of the media's liberal bias and favoritism toward Obama, however methodologically sound they appeared. Gallup's tracking poll consistently showed Romney doing better than did almost all other polls, which gave the poll doubters all the justification and evidence they needed that the media was anti-Romney.

In the final weeks of the campaign, the disparity in polls became a point of contention between the Obama and Romney campaigns because of competing assumptions about the shape and composition of the likely electorate on election day. Only in 2004 had the percentage of self-identified Republicans equaled the percentage of self-identified Democrats on election day. In all other years, Democrats had outnumbered Republicans. But Republicans were certain that the electorate in 2012 would not be anything like 2008. Romney's advisers believed that, at worst, Democrats would outnumber Republicans by two to three points. Obama officials were baffled by the reports coming from the Romney campaign of surging momentum and polls continuing to shift and sought to assure reporters they were not spinning their own numbers. Axelrod thought Romney's team was foolish to put its credibility on the line based on faulty data. If he had any doubts about the outcome, he told me in the last days of the campaign, he would find a way to hedge his language about Obama's prospects of winning. Instead he was more than bullish and ready to stand behind his campaign's numbers. "Everybody's entitled to their own interpretation of whatever they're looking at," he said, "but I wouldn't trade places with them for anything."

For good reason: Romney's polls were more optimistic than Obama's but hardly made the election look in the bag. Neil Newhouse said the campaign's last Ohio poll showed Romney down two points. In Virginia, the last track showed Romney up one, while a separate survey based on internal calls by the campaign showed Romney a point down. In Florida, Romney was up two in the final track and ahead in the second measure. Colorado looked better, with Romney up three in one measure and plus one in the second. The campaign had conflicting data on New Hampshire and had Romney trailing in other states. Beeson and Newhouse estimated that the polling alone put Romney's chances at one in four or a little better, but they were counting on the enthusiasm they were seeing in their polls and in Romney's crowds to give them an added boost. "We thought that voter intensity would put us over the top," Newhouse said.

The "October surprise" is part of the lexicon of presidential politics, the notion that in the final weeks of the campaign something could happen—a terrorist attack or a dramatic revelation about a candidate—to change the trajectory of the race. No one expected what happened in October 2012. On October 29, eight days before the election, Hurricane Sandy slammed into the East Coast, causing widespread damage and devastation. New Jersey, New York, and parts of Connecticut bore the brunt of the storm's fury. More than a hundred people lost their lives during the storm, millions were left without power, lower Manhattan was flooded, and sections of the Jersey shore were wiped out. The hurricane brought the campaigns to a halt. Obama cut short a political trip and returned to Washington to monitor the storm. On October 31, he flew to New Jersey, where he surveyed the damage accompanied by Chris Christie. The New Jersey governor offered unbridled praise for the president that week, piling one superlative on another in television interviews or standing at Obama's side. Obama had been "outstanding," he said. Coordination had been "wonderful." He talked about how often he and the president had been on the phone during the storm and immediately after. "I cannot thank the president enough for his personal concern and compassion," he said at a press conference with Obama. Republicans winced as Christie continued to heap praise on the man he had so often accused of lack of leadership. He told Fox News at one point, "If you think right now I give a damn about presidential politics, then you don't know me."

The storm effectively grounded Romney. As Obama went about his business—being presidential and drawing accolades from all sides—Romney was forced to the sidelines. His advisers could only watch helplessly as Obama soaked up positive coverage carrying out his official duties. Romney and Christie had spoken on the Sunday night before the storm hit. Christie was scheduled to campaign that week but told Romney he wasn't sure whether he would be able to do so. Romney told him to do what his state needed. Later there were reports that the Romney campaign wanted Christie to do one big rally with the Republican nominee on the final weekend. There had been no formal invitation, but when the rumors started, one of Christie's advisers was told to call a senior member of the Romney team with a message: Don't invite Christie to campaign with Romney because he will have to say no.

Some Romney advisers later pointed to Sandy as the moment the campaign was lost. They argued that the storm stalled their momentum and kept them from driving home their message in the crucial last week of the campaign while putting the president in the best possible light. They pointed to exit polls as evidence that the storm badly hurt Romney. Fifteen percent of voters cited the hurricane as the most important factor in their vote—and they backed the president by 73 to 26 percent. But those exit polls also showed that 78 percent of all voters said they had made up their minds before October— before the hurricane and before the debates. Obama won those early deciders by 52 to 47 percent. Of those who said they made up their minds in October or in the last few days of the campaign, Romney would have had to win almost 65 percent of them to claim an overall majority. There was no question that Obama's ratings rose in the wake of the storm, but available evidence suggests that by the time it hit, the election was largely decided. Sandy did not defeat Mitt Romney.

The election turned out almost precisely the way the team in Chicago had predicted—and the way many of the public polls of the overall national vote and in the battleground states were predicting as well. The president won the popular vote by 51 to 47 percent, a smaller margin than in 2008 but bigger than many had been predicting until the final week. He got 65.9 million votes to Romney's 60.9 million. The total vote of 129.1 million, which included other candidates on the ballots, was down slightly from the 131.3 million people who turned out in 2008. The raw vote totals declined in the non–swing states but rose slightly in the battlegrounds, according to calculations by David Wasserman of the *Cook Political Report* and *National Journal,* which may have reflected the money, advertising, candidate time, and mobilization efforts in those states compared with elsewhere. In the Electoral College, Obama won by a landslide. He carried twenty-six states plus the District of Columbia for 332 electoral votes. Romney won twenty-four states and 206 electoral votes. Obama's total was down from 365 electoral votes in 2008 but again was higher than many had been predicting. All the hot air and spilled ink about a razor-thin outcome and a late night of counting was for nothing.

Obama nearly swept the battleground states, to the great surprise of the Romney campaign. Of the nine states that had switched from Republican to Democrat in 2008, only two reverted to the Republican column: Indiana and North Carolina. The Obama campaign had conceded Indiana from the start, but fought to hold North Carolina. In the end, Romney carried it by two points, 50 to 48 percent. Of the most contested of the battleground states—Ohio, Florida, Virginia, and Colorado—Romney's share fell well below what his team had expected.

Obama won Ohio by 51 to 48 percent, almost matching his national numbers. Exit polls showed that African Americans composed 15 percent of the Ohio electorate in 2012, compared to 11 percent in 2008. An analysis of Ohio voting statistics by Mike Dawson, an Ohio voting expert, found no surge at all in the actual number of African American votes cast. Certainly strong support from African Americans and young voters was crucial to Obama's victory in Ohio, but he also was aided by the fact that Romney did worse among white working-class voters than he should have. Nationally, Obama won 36 percent of whites without college degrees. In Ohio he captured 42 percent of those voters. Romney was hurt by a decline in turnout among white voters, whose participation rate lagged blacks', according to a Census Bureau report. That too hurt Romney. It lends credence to the idea that the auto bailout and Romney's image helped the president with that constituency and suggests that the attacks during the summer did more damage than some of the polling at the time indicated. Romney won independents in Ohio, which was always the campaign's top priority, and yet lost the state. "Romney actually had some success in the battle for voters who were open to being persuaded," Scott Jennings, the campaign's Ohio director, said. "Where Obama really hurts us was by turning out base voters where persuasion wasn't the issue. . . . Now we know which strategy gets more votes."

Obama won Florida by a point, 50 to 49 percent, with a margin of about seventy-four thousand out of a total of 8.4 million votes cast. He captured this biggest of the battleground states by winning the Hispanic vote, including the Cuban American vote, which long had been part of the Republican base in the state but was trending blue. Exit polls showed that the Hispanic share of the vote in Florida jumped from 14 to 17 percent. Obama's margin among those voters was twenty-one points, compared with just fifteen points four years earlier. Obama lost the white vote in Florida by twenty-four points, compared with fourteen points in 2008. The swelling Hispanic population and Obama's ability to attract a larger share of it were enough to offset his decline among whites. Virginia was another must-win for Romney, but Obama took it by 51 to 47 percent. Colorado turned out not to be very close at all. The president won it by 52 to 46 percent. The share of the Latino vote rose only a percentage point between 2008 and 2012, but Obama's margin among those voters leaped from twenty-three to fifty-two points, a reminder of the crippling Republican deficit among the nation's fastest-growing minority group.

Obama won New Hampshire and Iowa by six points. He carried Wisconsin and Nevada by seven points. Nevada was never likely to go for Romney. By one estimate, the minority share of eligible voters jumped by nine percentage points between 2008 and 2012 and accounted for 40 percent of all eligible voters in the state. Those demographic changes sealed off the state from

Romney's appeals. Obama's margins were down everywhere, but that was little consolation to Romney. Beyond the principal battlegrounds, Republican efforts to put Pennsylvania into play came up short. Obama won there by five points, although his margin was just half as large as it had been four years earlier. Michigan turned its back on native son Romney and showed its continuing allegiance to the Democrats. Obama won there by almost ten points. Minnesota, another state where Republicans had run some ads, went for Obama by eight points. Nothing changed the overall pattern of the vote from 2008.

Party loyalty was stronger than in any election since exit polls began, with more than 90 percent of Republicans and Democrats supporting their nominee. More than 90 percent of Obama's and Romney's voters also backed the candidate from the same party in Senate elections. The election highlighted the deep geographical divisions as well—the preponderance of deeply red and deeply blue states and counties. Even fewer counties shifted in 2012 than in 2008—a total of 207 compared with 382, according to data compiled by the *Post*'s Ted Mellnik. Of those 207 that changed, 198 moved from Democratic to Republican. That represented about 7 percent of all counties that shifted, the lowest in a hundred years, according to Bill Bishop. The historical average had been almost 25 percent of counties switching parties from one election to the next. Despite the relative closeness of the national popular vote, only four states were decided by a margin of less than five points. Alan Abramowitz, a political scientist at Emory University, pointed out that close elections of the past had a very different pattern. In 1960, the margin between John F. Kennedy and Richard M. Nixon was five points or fewer in twenty states, which included the three most populous: New York, California, and Texas. In 2012, the winner of each of the three states won by a landslide—California and New York to Obama and Texas to Romney.

Obama won reelection despite winning just 39 percent of the white vote and recording the worst margin among whites of any successful Democrat. He offset that by winning 80 percent of the votes of nonwhites. Mitt Romney got almost nine of every ten of his votes from white voters, an untenable position for a party that seeks to lead the nation whose minority population is steadily growing. Among Hispanics, Romney got just 27 percent. That was less than John McCain's 31 percent in 2008. Even as most demographic groups voted slightly more Republican in 2012, Latinos went the other way. The shift toward a more nonwhite electorate continued, as Obama's political team had predicted. On election day 2012, whites made up just 72 percent of the electorate, and this evolution will continue into the future.

When Romney and his strategists looked at the exit polls, they found evidence to claim that he had won the economic argument. After all, they said, he won a majority of those who said the economy was the biggest issue in the election, and that bloc of voters accounted for almost 60 percent of the electorate. And just over half the country said they agreed that government was trying to do too much, as he had preached throughout the campaign. But running counter was other, stronger evidence of why he fell short. A majority of voters still blamed George W. Bush for the economic mess, and only 38 percent blamed Obama. Beyond that, Romney won by just a single percentage point on the question of who would better handle the economy. The challenger needed a much bigger margin on that question to oust an incumbent president, even in difficult economic times. Most telling was the question about which candidate was more in touch with "people like you." Fifty-three percent cited Obama and only 43 percent Romney. A majority said Romney's policies would favor the rich. Voters may have seen Romney as a successful businessman, but Obama's middle-class message had gotten through to people in ways Romney's had not. As Kevin Madden put it after the campaign, "We were teaching an economics class, they were writing love songs."

Mitt Romney spent election night with his family in a suite at the Westin Hotel in Boston. Confidence was so high heading into election day that Romney had not taken the precaution of writing a concession speech in advance. He had made a few stabs at it, but it would not come together. "I can't write it," he told someone close to him. "It doesn't seem right." Paul Ryan was, if anything, more confident. As he was preparing to fly to Boston in the late afternoon of election day, he was openly talking about resigning his chairmanship of the House Budget Committee immediately after the election and was already thinking of possible replacements to head the committee during the budget fight coming in the lame-duck session. By evening, however, Romney and those around him knew that the odds of winning looked much longer than they had at the start of the day. The early exit polls and the campaign's soundings from some of the battleground states painted a picture far different from their internal models and polls in the final days.

During election day, a technological breakdown hit the Romney campaign. The technology team had built software that was supposed to provide near-instantaneous reports on who had voted and who hadn't, invaluable information to assist in getting out every Romney voter possible. But the system, called ORCA, had never been fully tested—"We were building the aircraft as we were taking off from the carrier," Rich Beeson said later—and when thousands of volunteers began trying to file their reports, the system crashed. Some angry volunteers began tweeting out their dissatisfaction, and for a few days there was a story line developing that it was ORCA's crash that helped lose the election for Romney. It may have been one more embarrassment for a campaign that was judged to be leagues behind the Obama campaign in its technological prowess, but it was hardly the catastrophe described. A smoothly running ORCA would not have made Romney president.*

The Romney team monitored the vote count from a boiler room at the TD Garden in Boston, with other senior staffers in a suite at the Westin. Beeson had seen voting patterns during the day that worried him. Turnout in Philadelphia was huge, a sign of enthusiasm in the African American community. In Miami-Dade, an Obama stronghold in Florida, Democratic turnout also looked strong. The campaign had prepared for the possibility of recounts. Staffers had been given assignments and had packed and deposited their luggage, ready to depart in the middle of the night if necessary. As the evening went on, it became clear those contingencies weren't likely to be activated. Romney began to write his concession.

In Chicago, the Obama team operated from its boiler room in the Prudential Building while Obama was with his family and some close friends at the nearby Fairmont Hotel. In the early evening, Obama talked with Plouffe, who told him things looked good. "Can I talk to the First Lady?" Obama asked. Plouffe said not yet, but soon. He wanted to see more definitive results before telling the president that he could pass the good news along. Shortly thereafter, the president spoke to Messina. "I said, 'Mr. President, I have bad news for you,' and he goes, 'You do?' I said, 'Yeah, I think you're going to have to put up with those assholes in Congress for four more years.' He laughed and I said, 'But look, exits are exits, they've always been wrong, they told Al Gore he was going to be president.' I said, 'The model says our people turned out, and I said that's all we cared about, and I said to you, if our people turn out you're going to win, so if I tell you something different now you should think I'm crazy.'"

New Hampshire and Iowa were called for Obama relatively quickly in the evening, but for several hours, the big four—Ohio, Florida, Virginia, and Colorado—were all considered too close to call by the networks. Then at 11:12 p.m., NBC called Ohio for Obama and projected him as the winner of the election. Other networks quickly followed, including Fox News. At Romney headquarters and on the Fox News set, there were dissenting voices. Karl Rove, the architect of Bush's two victories, was working as a Fox News analyst. "I think it's premature," he said. His comments prompted Fox anchor Megyn Kelly to double-check with the network's decision desk, which stood behind its call. Obama was in his hotel suite watching the television screen as the race was being called. He was standing with Valerie Jarrett and her daughter and

---

*The Obama campaign had a similar breakdown with similar technology on election day 2008. An Obama official told me after the 2012 election, "That's not why they lost. It was never going to be a reason they were going to win either."

son-in-law. Jarrett was gesturing enthusiastically at the screen. "You've won!" she exclaimed. Obama stood impassively, arms folded across his chest. Jarrett said, "He said, 'Let's wait and see what everybody else says.' Then when Fox called it he was like, 'Okay, I guess I probably won.'" Messina, Plouffe, and Axelrod quickly hiked over to the hotel. Plouffe, ever mindful that this was the proudest moment for a campaign manager, signaled that Messina should talk to Obama alone first. Then Axelrod, Plouffe, and Robert Gibbs—the original trio from 2008—joined them for a round of photographs.

And then they waited—and waited—for the customary call from the loser to the winner. Jarrett was getting impatient, as was Axelrod. In Boston, they were discussing how quickly Romney should concede and appear in public. But they were also deflated. Ryan was distressed at the projections showing Obama as the winner. One person remembers him saying, "This is wrong. This is bad for the country. This is really, really bad." As the discussions in Boston continued, Messina sent a text message to Matt Rhoades. He tried not to push too hard but reminded Rhoades that both candidates had rallies to address and the hour was late. He asked, "What's your timeline for making a decision about what you're going to do?" Rhoades sent a reply a few minutes later. Romney would be calling the president shortly. "Garrett," Romney said to Garrett Jackson, his body man. "Get me on the phone with the president." Jackson called Marvin Nicholson, Obama's trip director. After pleasantries, Jackson said, "Is your boss available?" He came to regret the brusque-sounding words. He said he was not trying to be disrespectful or abrupt. Obama took the call in the bedroom of his suite. Messina snapped a photo showing the president with the phone on his left ear and his hand covering his right as he strained to hear Romney above the din of the adjacent room. Romney offered congratulations, said he knew the president had hard decisions ahead, offered to be helpful in any way he could, and told Obama he and Ann would be praying for him. Later Obama called Bill Clinton to thank him for all he had done. That's one more chapter for your legacy, he told the former president, according to someone Clinton later told about the call.

Romney delivered a short and gracious concession speech at the Boston Convention and Exhibition Center. He paid tribute to Obama and his campaign team and thanked his staff and supporters and family. He called for an end to partisan bickering and called on leaders and citizens to work together. "I ran for office because I'm concerned about America," he said. "This election is over, but our principles endure. I believe that the principles upon which this nation was founded are the only sure guide to a resurgent economy and to renewed greatness. Like so many of you, Paul and I have left everything on the field. We have given our all to this campaign." The room erupted in applause. He continued, "I so wish—I so wish that I had been able to fulfill your hopes to lead the country in a different direction, but the nation chose another leader. And so Ann and I join with you to earnestly pray for him and for this great nation."

After Romney had finished his speech, Ron Kaufman, Bob White, and Kaufman's daughter Katie went looking for a quiet place to have a drink. They ended up in a staff room on the eleventh floor of the hotel. There were no beers to be had and so they sat and talked. Later, Romney joined them. "Well, now what's the country going to do?" Kaufman remembered Romney saying. "This is scary. This is a bad thing for the country." Romney thought the nation's problems were huge and wasn't convinced that Obama and the Democrats were going to solve them. Kaufman said, "He was talking in this kind of worried grandfather way about this is really not good and this is a real problem for a lot of folks who don't realize." He said the people who would be hurt weren't like himself or White or Kaufman, all financially comfortable. It was younger people and future generations. They talked for a half hour or so. Ann Romney joined them, and then Beth Myers and Spencer Zwick also came by. "It was a really interesting conversation," Kaufman said. "Just the opposite of the 47 [percent], if you will. It wasn't the takers and the givers. The point was no bitter[ness], no anger, disappointment, frustration. His first instinct is, what's going to happen to our country?"

Obama delivered his victory speech at 12:38 a.m. Chicago time at a noisy rally in the sprawling McCormick Place along Lake Shore Drive. There was something different about the president that night, especially in comparison to the same night four years earlier when he addressed more than a hundred thousand people on that balmy night in Grant Park. The crowd that night was ecstatic and there were tears flowing among many who stood in the park. Obama, however, looked sobered, as if the weight of all the problems before the country were settling on his slender frame. This time, in McCormick Place, he was more animated and seemingly more ebullient. Axelrod noticed. The president, he thought, was happier on this night than he had been four years earlier. "I felt the weight of the burden on him more than I felt the elation four years ago," he said. "I know he believes this was a more satisfying win even than that one because of all the obstacles. A year ago the sainted Nate Silver was writing a magazine piece the headline of which was, 'Is Obama Toast?' To be written off and degraded and all that and come back and win . . ." He didn't need to finish the sentence.

CHAPTER 27

Romney's Take

Mitt Romney greeted me at the door with a big smile and firm handshake. It was late January 2013, almost three months after the election. He was at his home in Belmont, Massachusetts, after a weekend in Washington where he had been feted at a luncheon hosted by his friend Bill Marriott and attended the annual dinner of the Alfalfa Club. He was dressed in blue jeans and a checked shirt. He motioned me to one of the big easy chairs in the living room, pulled an ottoman between us to hold my digital recorders, and sat back. For the next hour and a half we talked about his campaign.

I asked him what made him want to be president and why he thought he didn't become president. "I wanted to be president because I believe that my background and experience and my perspective and point of view would be helpful to get America back on track, to keep America the economic power-house it's been and the champion of freedom here and around the world," he said. "I happen to believe that America is on a course of decline if it continues with the policies we've seen over the last couple of decades, and we need to take a very different course, returning to more fundamental principles, if you will." I asked whether part of his decision to run was an effort to fulfill an ambition that his father never did. "I love my dad. It's fair to say that I probably would not have thought of politics had I not seen my mom and dad involved in politics," he said. "But my decision to run for office was really in no way a response to my father's campaign. It was instead a recognition that, by virtue of a series of fortunate events, I was in a position to run for president and potentially become president. And I felt if I didn't do so, given that opportunity, I would have been letting down my country, my family, and the future."

He attributed his loss to a series of factors. "There are almost any number of things which, had they been different, might have yielded a different result," he said. "One, the president ran an effective campaign and did a number of things very well. He was able to appeal directly one on one to key members of the voter base and turn voters out. And so you give credit where credit is due. Number two, there were events outside either one of our control that helped his effort.

One was the perception that the economy had suddenly gotten a lot better. If you looked at the wrong track/right track numbers, they shifted quite dramatically in the final month. Unemployment at 8 percent dropped to 7.9 or 7.8, and that somehow was heralded as a major change in the economy and changed people's perception. That's clearly something you can't control. And the hurricane [Hurricane Sandy] also put us on a bit of a stall in terms of our prosecution of our case and provided an opportunity for incumbency to have a normal advantage. . . . And then of course, there were the things that our own campaign should have done differently or could have done differently. We weren't as effective at turning people out as was the president's campaign. We didn't do as well with Hispanic voters as we probably could have. And then of course the inevitable mistakes that I made. I know the president also made mistakes, but you can say, well, if I wouldn't have made any mistakes, that might have led to a different result as well."

We then went back to the beginning of the race, during the formative months as he was preparing to run again. I reminded him of the family gathering at Christmas in 2010 when everyone had taken a vote on whether or not he should run. There were only two yes votes: Ann Romney and Tagg Romney. He had been one of the ten to vote no. Why? "I knew how grueling the process was, and I felt that there may be others who could be more effective in actually winning and then getting America on course. And I thought, for instance, if someone like Jeb Bush were to have run, that he might well be able to do what was necessary to get the country on track. I got into this out of a sense of obligation to the things I believed in and love for the country, but not because it was something I desperately wanted so that I could feel better about myself." Eventually, after looking over the field of candidates, he decided he was the right candidate for the time. "I didn't think that any one of them had a good chance of defeating the president . . . and in some cases I thought that they lacked the experience and perspective necessary to do what was essential to get the country on track."

He confirmed that at one point in the spring of 2011, he was so pessimistic about his chances that he called Tagg early one morning to say he thought he was not going to run after all. "I recognized that by virtue of the realities of my circumstances, there were some drawbacks to my candidacy for a lot of Republican voters," he said. "One, because I had a health care plan in Massachusetts that had been copied in some respects by the president, that I would be tainted by that feature. I also realized that being a person of wealth, I would be pilloried by the president as someone who, if you use the term of the day, was in the 1 percent. Being Mormon would obviously be a challenge for some evangelical voters. I didn't know whether that would persist or whether that would go away during the primaries. I think it was Stuart Stevens who said, 'You know, our party is more southern, and you're from the North. It's more evangelical, and you're a Mormon. And it's more populist and you're a rich guy. This is going to be an uphill fight.'" Romney laughed. "And so I didn't want to get into the race and make it more difficult for the leader of our party to beat the president. And so for me the gating issue was, am I the person best able to defeat President Obama and therefore get the country on track?"

We talked at some length about the issue of immigration and whether he had compromised his chances of winning more Hispanic votes in the general election by what he had done to win the nomination. His answers offered his perspective on how events had unfolded and how he perceived it at the time and later. Long before he announced his candidacy, he said, he had learned there was to be a meeting in Florida of Hispanic leaders. "I went to see Jeb, I flew down to see him and said I'd like to take immigration off the issue list for the primaries. And wouldn't it be great if Republicans could come up with an immigration plan that all of the contenders could say, 'Yeah, I agree.' And then we could sweep that aside. And we were unable to get there. I mean, there just wasn't enough consensus among Republicans generally."

Once the debates began, Romney aggressively prosecuted the immigration issue against two of his rivals, Rick Perry and Newt Gingrich. Why had he taken the positions he did? I asked. He said in essence that he was only being consistent with things he had said during his first campaign or done as governor of Massachusetts. He said he believed that those previous positions would be used against him in a general election regardless of what he did in the primaries. "I was convinced by one of the colleagues in the campaign who said, 'Mitt, the things you said before about immigration, you will be, quote, hung with in the general. It's not like people will forget what you said in 2008.'" One example was his veto of legislation providing in-state tuition for children of illegal immigrants, which was the initial focus of his attacks on Perry. "If you have those views, which I do, and you've said them before, the idea of not saying them now is kind of silly. . . . You've got video of me having this debate with Mike Huckabee on that topic [in 2008]. Why would I not have the same debate with Rick Perry on that topic?" Did he agree with Matt Rhoades, his campaign manager, that the immigration attacks against Perry were both damaging and unnecessary, that he probably could have beaten back Perry's challenge just on the issue of Social Security? "Looking back, I think that's right," he said. "I think that I was ineffective in being able to bring Hispanic voters into our circle and that had I been less pointed on that in the debates, I would have been more likely to get more Hispanic voters."

Romney drew a distinction between using immigration in the debates and using the issue generally in his effort to win the nomination. "There was a time when our ad people said, 'Look, in South Carolina, we're falling behind Newt. We need to run ads on immigration.' And I said, 'No, I will not run an immigration ad. I'm not going to make this a campaign about immigration. Will I stand for the positions I stand for? Absolutely. I will defend. But I'm not going to go out with a series of immigration ads. Will not do it.' And I had to make the decisions as to whether we're going to go that course or not. And so I decided not to—I mean, I did not run an immigration campaign."

Romney is best remembered on immigration for his comment on "self-deportation" in one of the Florida primary debates. I asked him if he thought that was what had damaged him the most on the issue. He said he was still puzzled by the reaction to the comment. "I thought of it as being a term that is used in the community of those discussing immigration," he said. "I hadn't seen it as being a negative term. You have two options of dealing with those that have come here illegally: deportation or self-deportation. The president has deported more I think in four years than President Bush did in eight years. So the president was using a deportation method. The view of others is, no, let people make their own choice, let them self-deport if they will go to the country that has better economic opportunities than the U.S. might at the current time [or] family connections. And so let people make their own choice, as opposed to deporting them. So I was looking for a more, if you will, compassionate approach, which is let people make their own choice, as opposed to deporting people. And that was seen as being, I think by some, as being punitive. I still don't know whether it's seen as being punitive in the Hispanic community. I mean, I know it is in the Anglo community. . . . I didn't recognize how negative and punitive that term would be seen by the voting community."

There was another moment when he might have repaired some of the damage, which was when Marco Rubio began to talk about trying to find a new version of the Dream Act that could win bipartisan support. I said it seemed as if his campaign kept Rubio and his efforts at arm's length. "Au contraire," he said with a laugh. "We were very much encouraging [Rubio chief of staff] Cesar Conda, who was an old adviser to my campaign in 2008, and the Rubio camp to come out with what I think you call the Dream and Achieve Act. We wanted to see him come out with his own version. Very anxious for that to happen." He said his campaign tried to work with Rubio's staff to come up with something close to where he was on the issue. "But if they came out with something which was a little different than what I had already laid [out], I would at least be able to say directionally, 'What Marco's doing makes a lot of sense and I encourage that process and it seems like there's common ground here.' I could warm myself to what Marco Rubio was saying, even if it wasn't precisely the place I'd like to end up." Obama's executive order, which stopped deportations of students, "knocked Marco's legs out from under him," Romney said. "He decided not to proceed. Now we encouraged Marco's team, 'Please come out!' Yeah. But they already felt that was not a wise move once the president [had acted]."

Romney said there were several times during the early stages of the nomination contest when he thought he might lose. "Almost everybody was ahead of me at one time or the other," he said. "And so I'd look at those and say, 'Well, right now they're more likely to get there, but I'm going to keep on battling.'" He said a betting person might not have put much money on him at those moments, though he always had confidence he eventually would prevail. "But I think for certainly two or three weeks there—maybe longer—I thought it was more likely that Rick Perry would be the nominee, or even Herman Cain or Newt Gingrich." He paused. "I have to tell you that, in the discussions I had with my senior staff, people like Stuart Stevens and Russ Schriefer said, 'Look, Newt is not going to be the nominee. I don't care what the polls say, he's not going to be the nominee.' I was far less sanguine about that."

He said he was most worried about losing the nomination after Gingrich won the January 21 primary in South Carolina. He said that led to what he still believes was the campaign's biggest mistake during the nomination contest, which was to ignore the February 7 contests in Missouri, Minnesota, and Colorado. Romney easily defeated Gingrich in the January 31 primary in Florida, but he was still worried about avoiding a setback in Nevada (though he was heavily favored). "I've got to stop Newt, so we made a real effort in Nevada and said these other contests in Colorado and Minnesota, Missouri, these are nowhere near as significant," he said. "These won't make any difference. Well, in fact, they did make a big difference." When Santorum won all three, Romney got nervous again and insisted he be sent to Maine to make sure he did not lose there the following weekend. He flew across the country and marshaled his forces there against Ron Paul, enough to prevail. Meanwhile, Santorum had taken the lead in Michigan, the next important contest, which caused another moment of deep concern. "I looked and said, 'Look, if he wins Michigan, it may be over.' I mean, this is a state where I'm supposed to win, because I was born there, my dad was governor there. If he wins, what'll happen to Ohio? He'll win Ohio. If he wins Michigan and Ohio, I've probably lost. Any one of these could send the nomination to Rick. So in terms of strategic mistake in our primary campaign, I think probably the most significant one was not devoting the attention and energy we should have to Minnesota, Missouri, and Colorado events and instead focusing all of our effort in Nevada."

———

We talked about the Obama campaign's attacks during the summer of 2012 and why he responded the way he did. He said, "The question is, all right, what do we want to do? Do we want to respond to the attack, where they're saying that Bain is an outsourcer? The fact checkers are saying that's inaccurate. We've responded in the earned media that it's inaccurate. And the earned media stood with us on that—Obama ads are wrong.* But he kept running them. And then, so Romney's this bad guy, outsourcer. Do you respond to the attacks? My own view was that rather than our precious dollars being used to respond to attacks, that we should attack on our own and, number two, lay out what I would do to get the country on track." Those were the so-called Day One ads. Wasn't there a third option, I asked, which was to run positive biographical ads to fill in his profile for voters who were just starting to look at him more closely? "We looked at, quote, bio ads," he said. "And it's, you know, 'Here I am with my family,' and 'Bain is a nice place that started Staples.' And they're hitting me as the outsourcer in chief." Romney said he concluded that any biographical ads he might run would not be as compelling as fresh attacks on the president. "If I'm out there explaining, I'm losing," he said.

If he was short of money, why not dip into his personal fortune to provide the campaign with funds until the convention, something he had done in 2008 to the tune of nearly $45 million? He and his advisers talked about this a number of times, he said, but always believed he would be pounded by the media and the Obama campaign. "Look, if I put $25,000 in, the Democrats would say Romney's trying to buy the election," he said. "It would connect with their narrative that I was out of touch, that I was this wealthy guy, different than anyone else, [that] I was in the 1 percent. And so we were very concerned about doing something that would create that narrative." Eventually he personally guaranteed the $20 million loan that provided the campaign fresh funding in August. In any case, Romney said he did not see the summer as decisive, just part of the ebbs and flows of every campaign. "There are so many things you could point to as being decisive. For instance, I had a lousy September; I had a great October."

His great October began in Denver, and, not surprisingly, he remembered the first debate as the high point of the year. "People would get a chance to see that I was not the person that President Obama had been portraying me as being, and the things he was saying about me and my positions were wrong. I mean, his ads were not accurate. His ads were just pillorying me, saying things

---

*The *Washington Post*'s Fact Checker said the Obama ads were a distortion of an article the *Post* had run describing companies in which Bain had invested as "pioneers" in outsourcing and offshoring.

that were simply not true, and so I recognized this as a chance for people to see who I really am, and understand what I really believe." When I said he seemed to reappear in that debate as "moderate Mitt," he offered this interpretation of what happened. "People saw the entire me as opposed to an eight-second clip of me. . . . The clips are just a little piece, and I don't want to say distorting, but they're not the full picture. And if people watched me on the campaign trail and heard my stump speech, what I said in my stump speech was the same thing I said in that debate. I'm the same guy. But in the debate, they saw the whole thing."

He believed the debates produced a fundamental change in his relationship with the party's rank and file. "What had begun as people watching me with an interested eye had become instead more of a movement with energy and passion," he said. "The rallies we'd had with larger and larger numbers and people not just agreeing with me on issues, but passionate about the election and about our campaign—that was something that had become palpable. We had a rally in New Hampshire [the night before the election]. I mean, this was not just, 'Hey, we're happy with our nominee.' These were people saying, 'We love this. This is great.'" As a result he woke up on election day thinking he would win. "I can't say 90 percent confident or something like that, but I felt we were going to win. . . . The campaign had changed from being clinical to being emotional. And that was very promising."

His last hours on the trail, especially the arrival at the Pittsburgh airport on the afternoon of the election, where he was greeted by a spontaneous crowd of supporters, gave him added confidence. "We were looking at our own poll numbers, and there were two things that we believed," he said. "We believe that some of the polls that showed me not winning were just simply wrong, because they showed there was going to be more turnout from African American voters, for instance, than had existed in 2008. We said no way, absolutely no way. That can't be, because this was the first time an African American president had run. Two thousand eight—that had to be the high point. . . . We saw independent voters in Ohio breaking for me by double digits. And as a number said, you can't lose Ohio if you win independent voters. You're winning Republicans solidly, you're winning independents, and enthusiasm is overwhelmingly on your side. . . . So those things said, okay, we have a real good chance of winning. Nothing's certain. Don't measure the drapes. But I had written an acceptance speech and spent some time on the acceptance speech. I had not written a concession speech." Once he landed back in Boston, a different reality set in. "I called Matt [Rhoades] and Rich Beeson, and we all got on the phone together and talked about what we were seeing. . . . We're seeing much more turnout from groups that we thought would not be voting in as large numbers. The enthusiasm gap is not playing out in who's voting as we might have expected. And it's going to be a lot closer. . . . This is not the picture we had expected."

I asked Romney whether he saw the defeat as a loss for the Republican Party or a loss for Mitt Romney. "I don't think I'm qualified to make that assessment," he said. "I think political scientists will draw those conclusions. I'm sure there are lessons for the Republican Party or for any future nominee in my loss. But I mean, I take responsibility for my own loss. I don't look to the party as being responsible. Clearly some things that happened in the Republican Party were not helpful to my campaign." But did he think the party was on the wrong side of history, fighting demographic trends or trying to push against changing opinion on some of the social issues that would make it more difficult to win the White House in the future? "Well, I feel very deeply that our principles are the right principles for the country and the right principles for the people of America," he said. But he noted again that the party had not effectively appealed to the Hispanic community.

I asked also about the comments attributed to him on election night, that he was now deeply worried for the country. "I'm fearful that unless we change course, if we keep borrowing a trillion dollars a year, this is—we're walking along a precipice. I can't tell you we'll fall over it. Maybe we just walk along it for a year and the private sector will be able to pick up the gap and things will work out. That's possible. But as a guy who's occasionally walked the mountains, I don't like to walk along the precipice. I like to walk back from the precipice." Had the election resolved any of the big choices that he and the president had said the campaign was about? He paused. "There's so many ways of defining what was concluded," he said. "I think a lot of voters voted on things other than the biggest issues. I don't think that if you were to go out and say, 'Look, we're going to have a vote in this country. Do you think we should continue to spend a trillion dollars more than we take in and pass those burdens on to the next generation?' I think my position would win handily. And I think that was one of the measures that was in this election. But I think other issues diverted from that fundamental issue. I believe the American people would line up with the Republican Party on the major issues of the day. But I think oftentimes the opposition running a very effective campaign is able to confuse some of those issues and take us away from that very fundamental issue, which is, do you want to continue to spend and borrow more than we can afford?"

When Romney had mentioned his "lousy September," it was an evident reference to what may have been the low point of his campaign: the infamous 47 percent video. He was in California and said at first he couldn't get a look at the actual video. His advisers were pushing him to respond as quickly as he could. "As I understood it, and as they described it to me, not having heard it, it was saying, look, the Democrats have 47 percent, we've got 45 percent, my job is to get the people in the middle, and I've got to get the people in the middle," he said. "And I thought, well, that's a reasonable thing. . . . It's not a topic I talk about in public, but there's nothing wrong with it. They've got a bloc of voters, we've got a bloc of voters, I've got to get the ones in the middle. And I thought that that would be how it would be perceived—as a candidate talking about the process of focusing on the people in the middle who can either vote Republican or Democrat. As it turned out, down the road, it became perceived as being something very different."

You mean that you were insensitive to a whole group of people? I asked. "Right," he responded. "And I think the president said he's writing off 47 percent of Americans and so forth. And that wasn't at all what was intended. That wasn't what was meant by it. That is the way it was perceived." I interjected by saying, "But when you said there are 47 percent who won't take personal responsibility—" Before I finished, he jumped in. "Actually I didn't say that. That's the perception. I actually, thinking you might raise that, looked up the quote. Let me get it." With that he got out of the chair and went over to the kitchen counter where his iPad was charging. "That's how it began to be perceived, and so I had to ultimately respond to the perception, because perception is reality."

He sat back down and began to look for the quotation, speaking to himself as he scrolled. "There it is, c'mon Notes, there it is, 47 quote—it's this." He began to read the long quotation, offering commentary as he read. At one point he focused on the question posed at the Florida fund-raiser. "Audience member: 'For the last three years, all of us have been told this: Don't worry, we'll take care of you. How are you going to do it in two months before the elections to convince everyone you've got to take care of yourself?' And I'm saying that isn't my job. In two months, my job is to get the people in the middle. But this was perceived as, oh, he's saying 47 percent of the people he doesn't care about or he's insensitive to or they don't care—they don't take responsibility for their life. No, no. I'm saying 47 percent of the people don't pay taxes and therefore they don't warm to our tax message. But the people who are voting for the president, my job isn't to try and get them. My job is to get the people in the middle. And I go on and say that. Take a look. Look at the full quote. But I realized, look, perception is reality. The perception is I'm saying I don't care about 47 percent of the people or something of that nature, and that's simply wrong."

I asked whether he thought that video helped to crystallize another issue he faced: Was it possible for someone with his biography and background and wealth to win the election at a time when there were widespread feelings that struggling families were being left behind while the rich were doing just fine? "Well, clearly that was a very damaging quote and hurt my campaign effort," he said. "I came back in October. I led in a number of polls. I think I could have won the presidency. We came remarkably close. Would I like to have been closer? Absolutely. But the number of votes that could have swung to our side could have made a difference. You have to congratulate the president on a very good turnout effort. We were not competitive on our turnout effort with his. So could I have won? Absolutely. And did I recognize that coming as a person who has a great deal of wealth that in that environment that would be an obstacle? Yeah, I recognized that. But I thought I could get over it."

Epilogue

Into the Future

Campaign 2012 settled little. Billions were spent to produce a status quo outcome in the balance of power in Washington. Obama remained in the White House; Democrats held the Senate; Republicans maintained control of the House. The divisions that had gripped the country through Obama's first term appeared as deeply entrenched after the election as before. Dysfunctional government seemed to be a permanent part of the political landscape, as the weeks immediately after the election demonstrated anew, when Obama clashed with congressional Republicans over the so-called fiscal cliff—expiring Bush-era tax cuts coinciding with a deadline to begin implementing automatic across-the-board spending cuts. The resolution of that round of budget negotiations produced another unsatisfactory outcome, with Obama winning his fight to raise tax rates on the wealthiest Americans and another kick-the-can-down-the-road decision on spending that ensured more fights in the future. Obama was in a more favorable position politically, having won reelection after a campaign in which the choices were unmistakably drawn and facing an opposition held in low regard by the public. But he faced the same intractable opposition from the Republicans, who pointed out that they too had been put back in power in the House. Whether he would use his power differently in a second term and whether he would be more successful remained open questions.

The election changed few minds. If it was status quo in terms of the balance of power, it was also status quo in the philosophical gulf that separated the two parties over issues of economic policy, the federal budget, and the size and scope of government. America was still divided—culturally, ideologically, and racially, as Alan Abramowitz pointed out in his post-election analysis—and that condition was reflected both in the election returns and the way the two parties approached the country's problems. Ideologically red and blue America were no closer to resolving their differences. On the continuum from conservative to liberal, the gap was as wide as ever. Conservatives dominated the Republican

Party—three-quarters of Republicans identified themselves as conservatives, according to a post-election study cited by William Galston of the Brookings Institution. Meanwhile, liberals now constituted the biggest bloc—though only a plurality—in the Democratic Party, the first time that was the case in decades. Political scientists who charted the ideology of House members had noted earlier that the prospects for cross-party coalition building were greatly diminished. The most conservative Democrats were generally more liberal than the most liberal of Republicans. It was no wonder that every budget fight seemed to be a repeat of the previous one.

Culturally, the divisions were almost as significant, although rapidly changing attitudes on gay and lesbian issues, particularly same-sex marriages, had shifted the political balance in the direction of the Democrats. That marked a sea change from only a few decades earlier, when the sixties counterculture, antiwar protests, and battles over busing and affirmative action split the old Democratic coalition, gave rise to the Reagan Democrats, and helped accelerate the conservative ascendance that dominated the political life of the country into the first decade of the twenty-first century. Republicans began to talk openly about the need to adapt to the country's shifting cultural attitudes, though they risked rupturing their conservative coalition by doing so. Many conservatives still believed their party should continue to be a movement of restoration, as *National Journal*'s Ronald Brownstein put it, with the goal of preserving and protecting traditional values.

The changing country and the evident racial divisions within the electorate put the Republicans most at risk. The Grand Old Party remains the party of white voters at a time when the face of America continues to change rapidly. Democrats have tapped into this new America, which in a matter of decades will no longer be a majority-white nation. Republicans awoke to this demographic deficit after the election as if it had caught them unawares. In fact it has been a persistent and visible problem for years, which, with some notable exceptions, has been either ignored by the party or dealt with in such superficial and ineffective ways that it has done them no lasting good. Nothing threatens the party's future hopes more than the party's shortfall among minority voters, and no amount of public relations alone can solve this problem for the Republicans.

Republicans faced a robust internal debate about their future as they looked toward the next presidential election. Political parties are organic, not static, and election losses act as catalysts for change. For that reason, no one could predict the future with any certainty. But the burdens on Republicans to adapt to the new order pressed hard on party leaders in the wake of Obama's victory. Democrats, meanwhile, were mindful that the coalition Barack Obama assembled for two elections may be uniquely his and not wholly transferrable to future presidential aspirants, particularly his support among minority voters.

Was Campaign 2012 a look into the future of politics? It was the first presidential race to be waged under new rules for outside political committees, the result of the Supreme Court's decision in *Citizens United v. Federal Election Commission*, which gave rise to super PACs and to even more shadowy committees that did not report the names of their contributors. Their influence was either enormous or insignificant. Romney's advisers maintained that the nomination battle could have ended much earlier had super PACs not helped prop up rivals who otherwise were woefully short on money. But in the general election, pinning down exactly what difference all the outside spending made is far more difficult. Yet they are part of the new world. Obama's decision after the election to reconstitute his campaign's grassroots organization as a committee able to take unlimited contributions was another decisive step in institutionalizing the financing of politics through big and sometimes disguised money,* with all the corrosive effects that such practices can have on public confidence.

The campaign was significant in one other area involving money. It brought the final steps in the decade-long shredding of the public finance system for presidential campaigns that had been established after Watergate. That system was based on an explicit bargain: The federal government would help to underwrite the cost of campaigns in exchange for candidates' agreeing to limits on spending. It lasted a quarter century and then collapsed in the last three presidential cycles. George W. Bush started by opting out of public financing during the 2000 nomination battle. In 2004, John F. Kerry and Howard Dean followed suit. Then in 2008, Obama decided to forgo public financing for the general election, choosing political advantage over principle. In 2012, Romney adopted the same approach, giving rise to a $2 billion campaign by the major-party candidates. All future candidates—and the country—will live with the consequences.

Presidential debates played a bigger role in 2012 than ever before. They were reality TV for political junkies. Debates certainly affected the course of the Republican nomination battle—Newt Gingrich would not have risen from the dead without them—and they shaped the media's narrative of the race, if not the actual state of the race, during the last month of the general election. Cable networks hyped their debates during the Republican primaries as if they were confrontations between gladiators, complete with video introductions that

---

*Organizing for Action pledged transparency by making its donors public.

included plenty of battlefield metaphors. The Denver debate between Barack Obama and Mitt Romney may have been the single most interesting ninety minutes of the campaign. But how much do debating skills tell us about what it takes to be president? And what is the cost in other opportunities lost—more time spent in conversation with voters or in offering fresh ideas—of all the time spent on them?

New technologies and social media blossomed even more fully into a central feature of politics in 2012, and one can only imagine how coming iterations of technology will affect future campaigns. Internet fund-raising began to take root in 2004. The 2008 campaign was the first in which Facebook and YouTube played a big role. The 2012 election was the first in the age of Twitter, which became the virtual town square for the political community, a transmission belt of news, gossip, opinion, and distortion. This new medium showed its power throughout the year, but especially during the debates. Twitter became the new wire service ticker, the medium that first alerted the world to breaking news. But it also created endless sideshows and diversions and in so doing enlarged the gulf between political insiders and the public at large.

The preponderance and influence of polls increased dramatically in Campaign 2012, and so did controversy about them. There were more polls and more bad polls, and often there was little effort to distinguish between the two. Consumers of polls brought their own political biases to their judgments of which polls to trust. That was particularly the case among conservatives, who discounted any poll that suggested there could be a significant difference in the number of Democrats and Republicans who would turn out on election day. It turned out they were incorrect about who would vote. The emergence of poll analysts marked another change. Two weeks after the election, Richard Thaler, a professor of economics and behavioral science at the University of Chicago, wrote a *New York Times* piece titled "Applause for the Numbers Machine," in which he praised the work of statistical analysts like Nate Silver and other poll analysts working in universities who not only evaluated state and national polls but also set the probabilities for who would win. "They are like the meteorologists who forecast hurricanes," Thaler wrote. For many Obama supporters, Silver's probability charts showing Obama the likely winner were a lifeline during the final weeks of the campaign as the Republicans talked up Romney's chances of winning. More significant may have been what the Obama team did with its heavy investment in data collection and analytics. What they did will become a standard that alters the way future campaigns do business.

The candidates and their allies aired more television commercials than ever before, and focused them on a smaller number of states and a smaller percentage of the population than ever. "Never before will so much money be spent by so many to persuade so few," Peter Hart had said as the general election began. He was so right. The percentage of truly undecided voters shrank to single digits, as low as anyone could remember, with weeks still left in the campaign. Political strategists have long talked about reaching the persuadable voters as their top priority, and still do. But mobilizing the base has become even more important in an age of polarization, and the techniques used to motivate left and right are not ones designed ultimately to bring the country or the parties together once the election is over. Slash-and-burn attacks and the demonization of the opposition have made it all the more difficult to overcome genuine philosophical differences. But there is nothing on the horizon to suggest that any of this will change quickly. All of this may explain why Campaign 2012 did so little to actually improve the prospects for good governance.

The one area in which there was little noticeable competition or innovation was in the battle for ideas. Neither candidate fully rose to the moment. Each pursued a strategy designed for one thing: winning. The president was reluctant to offer a clear outline of a second term, either with fresh economic policies to stimulate faster growth or a blueprint to deal with the deficit and entitlements. The challenger offered Republican orthodoxy at a time when its salience and effectiveness were in question. Both operated within comfortable boundaries at a time of intractable problems.

Inauguration day is often a time of renewal and national unity. That was hardly the case when President Obama was sworn in 2013. Too much had happened during his first term—too many battles and too much strife. Then too were the events between election day and inauguration day that colored the ceremonies—the horrific shooting in December at an elementary school in Newtown, Connecticut, that left twenty children and six adults dead, and the maddeningly inconclusive fiscal cliff negotiations. The pomp and pageantry of inauguration day marked only a temporary cessation of the political strife that had gripped and at times paralyzed the federal government throughout Obama's presidency.

Obama's second inaugural address was far different from the one he delivered four years earlier, when the country was in the depths of an economic crisis and he still talked of fulfilling the post-partisan promise of his first campaign. Scarred by the battles of his first term but newly resolved after winning reelection, the president put forth a message that was not so much one of "Let us reason together" as it was of "Follow me." He offered to work with those willing to work with him, but he rebuked the hard-liners in the Republican Party. He said, "We cannot mistake absolutism for principle, or substitute spectacle for politics, or treat name-calling as reasoned debate." He said there should be no trade-off between providing assistance to the oldest generation and making investments in the youngest—although of course there was—and he threw back in the faces of the Republicans words they had used during the campaign. Safety net programs or entitlements like Medicare, he said, "do not make us a nation of takers." Most arresting was his call for full equality for gays and lesbians. This was a topic never before mentioned during an inaugural address, and the president linked that cause to the earlier struggles for civil rights and women's rights that helped define the American story—from "Seneca Falls to Selma to Stonewall," as he put it. Obama's speech and the attendant ceremonies seemed designed to highlight the emerging America that was at the heart of his winning coalition. The scene at the Capitol was notable for its multicultural cast of performers, a celebration of this new America. When the ceremony ended and Obama was entering the Capitol, he turned and stopped for a long, slow look at the panoramic scene spread out before him on the National Mall. "I want to take a look, one more time," he said. "I'm not going to see this again."

The headline in the next day's *Los Angeles Times* read, "For His Second Term, a Sweeping Liberal Vision." Republicans, whose House majority was now more conservative than ever, said the speech confirmed their long-stated contention that at heart the president was a big-government liberal. Obama's advisers, pointing to the election returns, argued that the president was merely reflecting values that were now in the political mainstream. At the end of it all, the great divide still existed. Whether Obama and the Republicans could change that awaited the next chapter in democracy's ongoing story.

Afterword

Political polarization has become the new normal in American politics—polarization in political attitudes, in voting behavior, and in political geography. This problem once seemed confined mostly to elected officials and the elites. But as political scientist Alan Abramowitz of Emory University wrote a few years ago, "The argument that polarization in America is almost entirely an elite phenomenon appears to be contradicted by a large body of research by political scientists on recent trends in American public opinion. . . . These divisions are not confined to a small minority of elected officials and activists. They involve a large segment of the public and the deepest divisions are found among the most interested, informed, and active members of the public."

The two parties have moved further and further apart. Almost six in ten people described the Republican Party as conservative, according to the post-2012 American National Election Studies survey, while 57 percent—the highest ever—called the Democrats a liberal party. The gap between how voters see Republicans and Democrats along an ideological scale is wider than ever. The gap between Republicans and Democrats in the House has grown steadily wider. Surveys show that more and more people identify themselves as independents, but those findings are misleading. The middle of the electorate has shrunk, despite what those surveys show. Behaviorally, most voters fall into either the Republican or Democratic camp.

In many ways, the polarization is the result of a shift to the right among Republicans. Conservatives now comprise 70 percent of the people who identify themselves as Republicans, according to Gallup. That percentage has increased substantially in a little over a decade. After more than two decades of antigovernment rhetoric, it's little wonder that the attitudes of Republicans toward government's role have become more hostile.

Meanwhile, the public sees Democrats as having moved further to the left, according to the 2012 American National Election Studies survey. For the first time, a majority described the Democrats as a liberal party. In early 2014, Gallup reported that the percentage of Democrats who call themselves liberals had reached an all-time high, at 43 percent. Moderates once comprised the biggest group of Democrats, but over the course of a dozen years the percentage of Democrats who described their ideology as moderate fell from 44 to 36. Conservatives within the party declined from 25 percent to 19 percent.

In March 2014, Andrew Kohut of the Pew Research Center wrote in the *Washington Post*, "While Republicans have become more conservative, Democrats have grown more liberal. The Pew Research Center's values survey, spanning 1987 to 2012, show that Democrats as a whole have moved to the left in recent years. They are much more socially liberal than they were even a decade ago, more supportive of an activist government, more in favor of increased regulation of business."

Two other factors have helped to deepen the red-blue divide. One is the decline in split ticket voting. Over a period of two decades, self-identified Republicans and Democrats have voted for their presidential candidates in ever greater percentages, rising from the mid-70s to more than 90 percent in each of the past three elections. Election 2012 stands out because voting patterns for House and Senate candidates reached almost identical levels. Only about 11 percent of the electorate split their tickets. Gary Jacobson, a political scientist at the University of California, San Diego, described 2012 as "the most partisan, nationalized . . . election in at least six decades."

Because there is less ticket splitting, there are fewer House districts that go one way in the presidential vote and a different way in the vote for who represents the district in the House. In the current House, there are only seventeen districts that Obama won that are held by the Republicans. Democrats hold just nine of the districts won by Romney. The *Cook Report*'s David Wasserman has noted that, during Bill Clinton's first term, when partisan fighting led to a government shutdown, 79 of 136 Republicans came from districts Clinton had won in 1992—a third of the entire GOP conference. "If you look at the people who elected Obama and the people who elected the Republicans in the House, there's very little overlap," Jacobson said. "They owe their victories to very different constituencies, to folks who are pretty divided on every political issue." No wonder finding compromise has become so difficult.

Redistricting and gerrymandering often get the blame for this polarization, and they are definitely factors, but less so than some people suggest. Congress would be a polarized, warring institution even with a more rational system of drawing district boundaries. Even though the presidential election in 2012 was closer than in 2008, three quarters of Democratic districts became more Democratic and three-fifths of Republican districts became more Republican. The truth is that we often now live in clusters of people who think (and vote) the same.

Another factor affecting the political dialogue is that partisans see the opposition in ever more negative ways. Republicans and Democrats are no more or less enamored with their own parties than they were in the past, but they are significantly harsher in their assessment of the opposition. Forty years ago, partisans put the opposition party midway along the thermometer scale of one to one hundred, or at about fifty degrees. By 2012 it had fallen to about thirty degrees. "The American electorate is now more partisan in its behavior than at any time post-World War Two," Abramowitz told an audience at the University of Akron's Bliss Institute in late 2013.

The geography of politics has created the potential for a lengthy period of divided government and polarized politics. Democrats now have an advantage in the electoral college that determines the outcome in presidential elections. Eighteen states and the District of Columbia have voted Democratic in six consecutive elections. They add up to 242 electoral votes. Add only Florida, with its 29 electoral votes, and you've just elected a president. This is no guarantee that Democrats will continue to win the presidency, but it shows that the party's path to 270 has become easier than the Republicans'.

At the same time, Republicans have a built in advantage in the House. Democrats actually won the popular vote in the House elections in 2012 but failed to win the majority of districts. Wave elections can sweep aside these advantages, and the country experienced them in 2006, 2008, and 2010. But the current conditions heighten the likelihood of a continuation of divided government.

Others have made this point but it is worth stressing again: This country now has the equivalent of parliamentary parties—voting in virtual lockstep on every major issue and pushing very different agendas—without a parliamentary system. Both sides are more resistant to compromising, hoping that with the next election they will amass enough power to have their way legislatively. Neither party has the votes to enact its agenda without being required to compromise. The tea party faction of House Republicans in particular is the most resistant to compromise. Gridlock in Washington is more the rule than the exception.

In individual states, however, a different phenomenon is taking place. Three quarters of the states operate under unified party control—one party holding the governor's office and both houses of the legislature. Three decades ago, not quite half the states were under the control of one party. Elected officials are moving to enact conservative or liberal agendas. On economic and social issues, there are now competing models. One is based on principles of limited government, friendliness to business, and cultural conservatism. The other sees an essential role for government in economic and other areas and prizes the growing cultural diversity of a changing America. Red states are enacting tax cuts, sharper spending reductions, and restrictions on abortion or voting rights. Some blue states have raised taxes; others have resisted deep cuts in education. Blue states are moving in the direction of legalizing same sex marriage and in some cases recreational use of marijuana.

Congressional scholars have attacked this topic from various angles, trying to understand why polarization has led to gridlock. Thomas Mann of the Brookings Institution and Norman Ornstein of the American Enterprise Institute describe the problem as asymmetric polarization, which is to say the Republican Party is the principal offender in the breakdown of governance. In their book *It's Even Worse Than It Looks,* they argue that both parties engage in political posturing and game playing. But Republicans, they say, have gone far off track, substantively and procedurally. Mann and Ornstein put the blame for Washington's gridlock squarely on the GOP. Sean Theriault of the University of Texas argues that polarization is less the problem than is partisan warring by politicians who not interested in trying to find common ground with the opposition.

Despite his 2012 victory, Obama had a lousy year in 2013. His legislative priorities were either stalled or rejected. He successfully stared down Republicans over a government shutdown in the fall of 2013, but the fruits of that victory were short-lived. The initial rollout of his health care law was a disaster. Whatever momentum he believed he had when he delivered his second inaugural address the previous January seemed gone. His approval ratings had dropped to the low forties. When he met reporters for his year-end press conference in December 2013, Julie Pace of the Associated Press asked him pointedly, "Has this been the worst year of your presidency?"

That was the big story as the second year of his second term began: Obama in decline. Or so it seemed. But it begged another question. Could the political system be made to work more effectively or was America in a period of near-permanent gridlock, paralysis, and polarization? Americans once believed that campaigns had consequences and that elections mattered. Elections were one way of helping to resolve political differences. After a hard-fought campaign, voters provided politicians with a sense of the direction. It was assumed that politicians—losers as well as winners—would respond, even if grudgingly, to what appeared to be the will of the people and get on with enacting it.

Election 2012 suggested otherwise. By the time Obama had finished his inaugural address, the window for cooperation and possible progress had already closed. The Republicans simply refused to acknowledge that they had lost. The president, with considerable justification, blamed implacable opposition from a Republican Party still heavily influenced by its Tea Party wing. Through the course of the year, Republicans repeatedly showed they would resist compromise at almost any cost. Others saw weakness in the president as a contributing factor. At home, the president was criticized for failing to find a way around the impasse of divided government. Abroad, there was talk of America in decline, with hesitant leadership. His cool, no-drama style of leadership was now seen more as a liability than an asset.

Obama was dealt his first setback early in 2013—and not by the House Republicans, as had so often been the case. This time the Senate—the Democratic-controlled Senate—rebuffed him. The issue was gun control, newly added to Obama's second-term agenda as a result of the horrible killings of schoolchildren at the Sandy Hook Elementary School in Newtown, Connecticut. Obama had seen too many of these mass shootings play out during his presidency—in a shopping center in Tucson and a movie theater in Aurora, Colorado—and he was moved to act despite long odds. His advisers knew he had limited time to win support in Congress for additional restrictions on guns, given the strength of the National Rifle Association. Public opinion overwhelmingly favored what Obama proposed, but when Democratic leaders in the Senate tried to move, they could not muster the required sixty votes to begin debate on any of three measures—expanded background checks, a ban on high-capacity magazines, and a ban on assault weapons. The threat of repercussions by the NRA lobbyists was too strong. "Shame on you!" came a cry from two women in the Senate gallery. Both women had been touched by gun violence. At that point, two months after taking the oath of office for a second time, Obama had to acknowledge there was no way he could win this battle. Public opinion alone could not overcome the entrenched power of the pro-gun forces who would take no prisoners in bringing down candidates who opposed them.

Second-term blues are common among presidents and for good reasons. A president's most significant priorities usually have been dealt with during the first term. Turnover in the cabinet and the White House staff often leaves a president with fewer strong hands to rely on in a second term. Lame duck status is sometimes imposed long before it is reasonable to do so. More than ever, there is a hunger to look ahead to the next presidential election. Obama needed only to look back at his predecessor to see a trajectory of decline. By the beginning of George W. Bush's second year of his second term, Iraq had become a terrible burden, his call for Social Security reform had stalled, and Hurricane Katrina delivered a devastating blow not just to the Gulf Coast but also to perceptions of the Bush administration's competence.

Scandals and controversies marked the first year of Obama's second term. His administration was thrown on the defensive when it was revealed that the Internal Revenue Service appeared to have singled out Tea Party groups for special examination among the many organizations seeking tax-exempt status. No evidence showed any direct White House involvement but the revelations became a rallying cry among conservatives about the intrusiveness of Big Government and the politicization of one of the most feared agencies in Washington.

Republicans pressed the administration over the September 11, 2012, raid on the U.S. consulate in Benghazi that left four Americans, including U.S. Ambassador J. Christopher Stevens, dead. Republicans charged that Obama and his administration had deliberately misled the country about the nature of the attack and the role that al Qaeda terrorists had played in it. Among the charges they sought to prove was one that said CIA officials had wanted to respond to the attacks at the time they were taking place but were ordered to stand down by senior officials. Later reports concluded that the attack could have been prevented but did not pin the blame on Obama or then Secretary of State Hillary Rodham Clinton. A Senate report flatly disputed the claim that CIA personnel had been ordered to stand down. But the Republicans weren't satisfied, and there was no sign that Republicans would stop their calls for further investigations, particularly not when they could keep both Obama and Clinton on the hot seat.

Obama's team found itself embroiled in an even bigger controversy over leaks of classified documents by Edward Snowden, a former contract employee at the National Security Agency. This controversy alarmed both the right and the left. Stories based on the documents that were published in the *Washington Post* and the *Guardian* revealed massive surveillance by U.S. intelligence that included far more extensive electronic data mining of telephone calls of Americans than had previously been revealed. U.S. officials condemned Snowden, who fled the country and eventually ended up in Russia, for damaging national security. The surveillance programs were begun before Obama became president. But because he had campaigned in 2008 suggesting he would strike a different balance between pursuit of terrorists and protection of civil liberties, the revelations caused an uproar among his liberal supporters (and among libertarians on the right). He was forced to create a task force to undertake thorough review of the existing programs. The task force report prompted Obama to propose some modest changes in the programs but he also offered a vigorous defense of much of what the NSA was doing.

Obama's battles with congressional Republicans reached its peak in the early fall of 2013. Republicans sought to attach a provision to defund Obamacare to a short-term funding bill needed to keep the government operating. Obama and congressional Democrats stood firm. With the end of the fiscal year approaching, John Boehner, under pressure from the Tea Party rebels in his conference, tried one provision after another, hoping to force Obama to yield. Instead, the Republicans' ill-considered tactics ran the party over a cliff. On October 1, a partial shutdown of the government took effect.

The standoff lasted sixteen days. Republicans were deeply divided over the strategy that brought it about. Establishment Republicans blamed the Tea Party wing, and the likes of Senator Ted Cruz of Texas, who held a marathon talk session on the Senate floor to call for his party to not to give in to the White House demands. Shut out of museums and national parks, voters were enraged. Gallup and other organizations reported that public impressions of the Republican Party—hardly promising before this—had reached an all-time low.

This was Obama's lone victory of the year and it was quickly swallowed up by his biggest setback of all, the debacle of the rollout of the Affordable Care Act. October 1 marked the opening of the period in which people without insurance could begin to sign up for coverage under the new law, through state and federal exchanges. The federal Web site, the backbone of the system because so many Republican-led states had refused to establish their own exchanges, immediately broke down. The site was plagued by hundreds of glitches, major and minor, which forced administration officials to undertake an almost complete revamping of the site.

Other problems cropped up. Millions of Americans who had their own coverage were informed by insurance companies that those policies would be canceled. During the debate over the law as it was moving through Congress, Obama had said repeatedly, "If you like your health plan, you can keep your health plan." Politi-Fact would dub Obama's statement the "lie of the year" for 2013, an ignominious award that highlighted just how politically damaging the health care rollout became. Conservatives long had hated the law. Now Obama's own supporters turned on him. Senate Democrats nervous about reelection campaigns in 2014 railed against the White House in private meetings. Liberal elites took to the pages of the *New York Review* to castigate the president for the failure. Eventually the Web site began to function normally and many Americans who never had health insurance were able to sign up. White House advisers expressed confidence that public opinion would become more favorable as the law's benefits reached more and more people. But for months, the administration's efforts to combat negative stories about the law's impact had no effect on public attitudes about the new law.

Polls documented the extent to which Obama's image was suffering. Not only were his approval ratings the worst of his presidency, but also assessments of his leadership turned negative. Obama had long been buoyed by perceptions that he was likable, honest, a strong leader, and understood the problems of ordinary people. A *Washington Post–ABC News* poll in November 2013 showed that, for the first time, that a majority now had an unfavorable impression of the president; half said he was not honest; and a majority said he was not a good manager. Everything added up to make 2013 Obama's annus horribilis.

By early 2014, official Washington seemed to have all but given up on serious work for the year. Republicans decided to avoid another political calamity (and possible economic crisis) by allowing a vote to increase in the debt ceiling without conditions. Along with the earlier two-year deal on the budget, that acquiescence wiped fiscal issues from the agenda. Congress could continue to fund the government without brinksmanship. But there was little appetite to tackle entitlement reform, which at one time had been at the heart of the fractured negotiations between the president and House Speaker John Boehner and which Obama had said was one of his long-term priorities. In his fiscal 2015 budget, Obama even eliminated a proposal he had offered in earlier years aimed at strengthening the financial health of Social Security. It had been an olive branch to Republicans when there was hope of possible negotiations. By taking it back, the president showed he was now more interested in keeping his base happy than trying to entice Republicans to the fiscal bargaining table.

Immigration reform remained stuck. Early in 2014, House Republican leaders issued their principles for immigration reform. The next week, after a backlash from his conference, Boehner announced there was little likelihood of action on comprehensive reform in 2014 because his members did not trust the president to the law. Why they would trust Obama more in 2015 or 2016 was never explained. No one would quite say the issue was dead, but prospects for action remained dim. The Republican chairman of the Ways and Means Committee, Representative Dave Camp of Michigan, presented a blueprint for major tax reform—an issue that both the president and leading Republicans had said was long overdue. But there was no sign of willing partners ready to take it up.

All eyes in Washington turned to the 2014 midterm elections, and of course beyond them to the contest to succeed Obama. For both Republicans and Democrats, the future poses hard questions. Demographics and the shape of the electoral map give Democrats confidence that they could sustain their hold on the White House into another presidency. But history shows that it isn't easy for a party to win the White House in three consecutive elections. Republicans could envision scenarios that would make them an even bet or better to capture the White House in 2016, especially if there is public exhaustion with the Obama presidency—if they could unite their divided party and overcome the structural obstacles in their way.

Election 2012 exposed the GOP's weaknesses as a national party. Since that election, the intraparty divisions have only become more acute. Whatever consensus existed after Romney's defeat about a path forward has rapidly eroded. The Tea Party's role in shutting down the government triggered a backlash from the party's establishment wing. Hostility between the establishment and Tea Party wings intensified. Though united on some issues, Republicans nonetheless remain a party divided over style, tactics, and issues.

Nothing may be as important to the Republicans' future hopes as finding a way to attract a broader coalition of voters. In 2012, white voters cast nine of every ten of the votes Mitt Romney received at a time when white voters' share of the presidential electorate continued to tick downward. Obama won a smaller share of the white vote than any other victorious Democratic presidential candidate and still won a majority of the popular vote. Four of every ten Obama voters were minorities. The GOP's coalition—white, older, and male—is shrinking. Obama's coalition—women, minorities, young people, highly educated whites, and secular voters—represent most of the rising portions of the population. Teenagers who will enter the electorate in the future have grown up in a diverse and increasingly tolerant world. That has erased what once was a Republican advantage on social issues. Republican strategists know they have lost the political battle over same-sex marriage, but the party's base—Christian conservatives and advocates of traditional values—makes a sudden shift in policy impossible.

Virginia's gubernatorial race in 2013 highlighted the GOP's problems. The race pitted state attorney general Ken Cuccinelli, a favorite of the party's most conservative wing, against Terry McAuliffe, the former chairman of the Democratic National Committee. McAuliffe's campaign was successful in casting Cuccinelli as outside the mainstream and was able to reconstitute the same coalition that had helped Obama win Virginia twice. Democrats swept all three statewide offices. The victory signaled the continuing evolution of the commonwealth, which until Obama had not voted for a Democratic presidential nominee since 1964, and provided a painful post-2012 lesson for the GOP about its vulnerabilities.

Republicans have become a congressional party, capable of controlling the House and possibly the Senate, but challenged in trying to win national elections. Congressional leaders cannot solve the party's problems. Only a presidential nominee can do so. The Republicans face what could be a contentious nominating process as they select their next presidential nominee in 2016, pitting those who say no compromise on conservative principles and those who say the path to victory does not lie on the hard right. The question is whether the party will define the eventual nominee or the nominee redefines the party, as Bill Clinton did for the Democrats in 1992.

Republicans have no shortage of potentially capable candidates. But many have already struggled as they began to step onto the national stage. Marco Rubio, the Florida senator, embraced immigration reform and got hammered by the right. Ted Cruz rode the anti-Obamacare message to prominence and made himself a hero to many conservatives. But fellow GOP senators resent him. Can he go from leader of a faction to leader of a party? Chris Christie cruised to reelection in November 2013 and then saw his national prospects damaged after revelations that members of his staff had slowed traffic on the George Washington Bridge, apparently as political retribution. Rand Paul, the Kentucky senator, sought to make his brand of libertarianism more attractive than his father was able to do and showed some possibility for success. But his foreign policy views represent a dramatic break from GOP orthodoxy of many years. Paul has taken an anti-interventionist stance on military matters, at odds with the GOP's neoconservative wing. On the issue of government surveillance, he has come down strongly in favor of the protection of civil liberties. The list of other possible contenders to lead the party is lengthy: former Florida governor Jeb Bush; Louisiana governor Bobby Jindal; Wisconsin representative Paul Ryan; Wisconsin governor Scott Walker; Texas governor Rick Perry; former Pennsylvania senator Rick Santorum; former Arkansas governor Mike Huckabee; Ohio governor John Kasich—and others so far unnamed, all of whom have strengths they're touting and liabilities yet to be uncovered.

Democrats are rushing to embrace Hillary Rodham Clinton as their next standard-bearer. Other Democrats besides Clinton are certainly contemplating running, among them Vice President Biden. But Clinton begins as an overwhelming favorite, if she runs. Of course, at the start of the 2008 campaign, she was also the dominant front-runner. She lost not only because she ran up against a political phenomenon in Barack Obama but also because her campaign made critical mistakes and because she presided over a dysfunctional team of advisers. But at this point, there is no young Barack Obama on the horizon to challenge her the way he did.

Whoever runs for the Democratic nomination will be dealing with a party that, though more united than the Republicans, nonetheless has tensions between its establishment wing and a newly assertive progressive, populist wing, led by people like Massachusetts senator Elizabeth Warren and symbolized by the victory of New York mayor Bill de Blasio, who ran as an unabashed liberal. Over the past decade, Democrats have moved left, a fact made clear by any number of surveys. How powerful its populist wing is at this point is a matter of debate, just as there is disagreement over whether the policies that progressives favor can find favor with a national electorate.

The Pew Center's Andrew Kohut noted that Republicans are far more likely to be seen by the public as an extremist party, though he added that on many issues, liberal Democrats now are to the left of the rest of their party and of the country. Kohut cited several ways in which this is true. Liberals are to the left of the rest of the Democratic Party on social issues. Unlike much of the rest of the population, they disagree with the statement that "people can get ahead if the work hard." They care less about the budget deficit as a priority issue. On foreign policy issues, Kohut wrote, "a majority would find it acceptable if another country became as militarily powerful as the United States." He argued that this has been of little consequence during Obama's presidency, but questioned what will happen to the party as Democrats seek a presidential nominee in 2016. "In the shutdown era, Democrats have had a more moderate image nationwide than the tea-party-burdened GOP," he wrote. "But that image may be at risk if liberal Democrats set the pace for the party." One veteran of a previous Democratic administration predicted outright chaos in the party should Clinton not run.

The warfare over the direction of the party already had begun by early 2014. Populists expressed frustration with Obama and the failure of his administration to take on Wall Street more aggressively for its role in the 2008 economic collapse. Establishment and centrist Democrats said a sharp shift to the left could doom the next nominee. Populists said corporate interests and fundraisers had captured the party's soul, compromising the party's commitment to working people and wanted a hard-edged message aimed at the "1 percent." But Andrew Stern, the former president of the Service Employees International Union, warned Democrats against such a strategy. "I think it's really not helpful for the Democrats to turn this into an attack on the '1 percent,'" he told me in early 2014. "I don't think it's in the American spirit, or at least the Democratic Party's future spirit. As Republicans attack immigration, we attack rich people? If you learned anything from the president, selling hope is better than selling hate."

What is the future of elections in a divided America? The outlines already are evident, based on the 2012 campaign and subsequent events, and they do not offer immediate hope for a change in the polarized politics that have become the norm over the past decade. The elements include ever larger amounts of money poured into Super Pacs and used to attack or defend candidates, internal competition that threatens to push candidates farther to the left and right (especially in the Republican Party), a struggle by the national political parties for relevance beyond the role of data collection agency, and increasing difficulty for presidential candidates to chart their own course independent of these outside forces. The new architecture of politics has created something of a Wild West environment, with strategists flocking to the outside groups and with these committees even less accountable than candidates for the tone and conduct of their work.

The spending by outside groups during the 2014 midterm election signaled another escalation in their role in the free-spending days since the *Citizens United* decision by the Supreme Court in 2010. Republican groups in particular spent freely on television ads in volumes not seen before in midterm elections. Meanwhile, outside groups dedicated to the election of Hillary Clinton in 2016 were already formed and laying plans. These groups represented a soup-to-nuts array of political operations—one for recruiting a grassroots army, another designed to air television commercials on her behalf, another for the explicit purpose of defending her from GOP attacks and amassing opposition research against her prospective Republican rivals. There has never been anything of this magnitude and focus so far in advance of a presidential campaign.

Nothing is permanent in politics. For now the two parties seem locked into a system designed to enlarge the chasm between Red and Blue America. An alternative future can come from two places. One is from the candidates, the men and women who seek the presidency in 2016. What kind of campaigns will they run? Will they break with the patterns of today? Will they challenge their own parties' orthodoxies? Will they advance fresh policies in place of what Republicans and Democrats have been clinging to now for several decades? Is it possible today to campaign with the optimism and positive spirit that all candidates claim is the ideal but which few ever achieve? The danger for Republicans is that the power of its most conservative wing will pull all the candidates far to the right, as happened to Romney in 2012. The risk for Democrats is the assumption that embracing what has worked in the past two elections is what will be best for the country over the next decade. Running a comfortable and safe campaign—the instinct that long has guided Hillary Rodham Clinton—will not necessarily change the nature of America's broken politics.

The other place to look for a change is from the voters themselves. They decry the mess in Washington. An NBC–*Wall Street Journal* poll in March 2014 found that more than 80 percent of the country said they would be more likely to vote for a candidate who promised to work across party lines. But on Election Day, voters tend to divide into their predictable red and blue camps. They have shown reluctance to cast votes that truly send a signal to politicians that they want to see a change in behavior in Washington. At some point, voters may tire of what this behavior has produced and decide to punish one side and reward the other for the good of the country, rather than adhering to narrower partisan interests. Until then, the future of politics looks to be very much what we saw in Election 2012.

Acknowledgments

I owe debts and thanks for all the encouragement, assistance, and support during the two-plus years it took to produce this book. Authors are lucky to have one good editor. I was fortunate to have two. Jim Silberman of James H. Silberman Books was a guiding hand from start to finish on this book. Wendy Wolf at Viking brought her keen eye and good humor to every page. My agent, Philippa Brophy, was both counselor and friend. Special thanks to all three. Haynes Johnson, my coauthor on our book about the 2008 campaign, was an enthusiastic advocate of this project. Sadly, he died shortly before publication.

A handful of others deserve particular thanks. Aaron Blake, my colleague at the *Washington Post,* played an invaluable role. He conducted some interviews, researched specific issues, and read and reread the chapters. He improved the book immeasurably. Sam Adams, a Harvard student who became part of this project through the good graces of the Institute of Politics at Harvard's Kennedy School of Government, produced an invaluable timeline of events and supplied other research. Cynthia Colonna and Olwen Price listened to and transcribed hundreds of hours of recorded interviews. Lucy Shackelford, formerly of the *Post,* provided research material at the front end of the project. Pollster Peter Hart again provided insights into the electorate through the series of focus groups he conducted for the Annenberg Public Policy School at the University of Pennsylvania. The team at Viking who helped guide this book through to publication was invaluable: Margaret Riggs, Carolyn Coleburn, Nancy Sheppard, Roland Ottewell, Jane Cavolina, and Bruce Giffords.

I especially want to thank the candidates who generously made time during or after the campaign to share their experiences with me. It is not always enjoyable to be asked to explain why things didn't work out as planned, but they were good-natured and responsive to all my questions. This group includes former governor Mitt Romney, former governor Tim Pawlenty, former Speaker Newt Gingrich, Governor Rick Perry, and former governor Jon Huntsman Jr. Governor Chris Christie also was generous with his time for this project.

I owe thanks to many people inside all the campaigns. Senior officials in both the Obama and the Romney campaigns offered their insights both in real time and through post-November interviews. Officials in all the other Republican campaigns were helpful in describing the action from their vantage points. Many of these strategists show up by name in the book. Some others spoke only on the condition that they not be identified by name. No one in any of the campaigns will agree with all of the conclusions here, but I deeply appreciate what they did to help me see the campaign through their eyes.

The *Washington Post* has been my journalistic home for three decades. Chairman Don Graham is all any reporter could ask for in an ultimate leader. Publisher Katharine Weymouth encouraged me throughout this long project. Former executive editor Marcus Brauchli and former managing editor Liz Spayd were at the helm in the newsroom when I began the book, and I thank them for their encouragement. Martin Baron, the *Post*'s current executive editor, was gracious in allowing me time to finish the book. Other editors were instrumental in making this book a reality. Kevin Merida was national editor when I began and was appointed managing editor while I was writing it. He made the book possible in numerous ways, and I owe him special thanks. Steven Ginsberg guided the *Post*'s political coverage with creativity and a steady hand. Other editors to whom I owe thanks are Cameron Barr, Anne Kornblut, Terry Samuel, Barbara Vobejda, Tim Curran, and Scott Vance.

I have drawn on the work and friendship of a large group of people at the *Post* who were part of the political operation during the 2012 campaign. They are Karen Tumulty, who generously shared transcripts of interviews with some of the candidates and noncandidates, Phil Rucker, Amy Gardner, Scott Wilson, Ann Gerhart, David Nakamura, Peter Wallsten, Tom Hamburger, Roz Helderman, David Fahrenthold, Paul Kane, Ruth Marcus, Al Kamen, Emily Heil, Dana Milbank, Sandhya Somashekhar, Nia-Malika Henderson, Ed O'Keefe, Dan Eggen, Tim Farnam, Krissah Thompson, Lori Montgomery, Jerry Markon, Glenn Kessler, Ezra Klein, Robert Barnes, Joel Achenbach, Zach Goldfarb, Jason Horowitz, Felicia Sonmez, David Maraniss, Eli Saslow, Stephanie Mc-Crummen, Bill Turque, Melinda Henneberger, Alice Crites, Madonna Lebling, Carrie Camillo, Kathy Tolbert, Liz Ward, and Anne Bartlett.

Thanks also to the invaluable Fix team at the *Post,* led by the irrepressible Chris Cillizza, and including Aaron Blake, Rachel Weiner, and Sean Sullivan. Our polling team, led by Jon Cohen and including Peyton Craighill and Scott Clement, supplied me with a steady stream of data and interpretation. Our digital team did extraordinary work. They include Vince Bzdek, Ryan Kellett, Cory Haik, Ken Smith, Matt DeLong, Terri Rupar, and Natalie Jennings. I'm also indebted to members of the *Post*'s graphics and data team, Ted Mellnik,

Dan Keating, and Karen Yourish, as well as photographers Nikki Kahn and Melina Mara, who logged endless miles with Obama and Romney. Other *Post* friends to whom I owe thanks are Len Downie, Maralee Schwartz, and Bob Kaiser.

I am also indebted to friends and colleagues at other news organizations. Roger Simon, my pal for more than forty years, has been an inspiration and good counselor. Both he and his wife, Marcia Kramer, were supportive throughout this project. Both read and critiqued the manuscript. Ron Brownstein offered original insights all along the way, as he has been doing for two decades, and his helpful suggestions improved the book. Others whose work I have drawn on or whose company I've appreciated during days together on the road include: Jeff Zeleny, Adam Nagourney, Jim Rutenberg, Ashley Parker, Peter Baker, Gwen Ifill and the team at *Washington Week,* Chuck Todd and the gang at *The Daily Rundown,* Jonathan Martin, Betsy Fischer Martin, Lois Romano, Amy Walter, David Chalian, John Dickerson, Jackie Calmes, Ron Fournier, Jon Ward, Mark Leibovich and Steve Scully.

I thank Anne Kornblut, Phil Rucker, Haynes Johnson, Doug Balz, and Colette Rhoney, who read all or portions of the book, for their critiques and suggestions, all of which helped to improve the final product. Whatever errors remain in this book are mine and mine alone.

Most important to me are my family. John Balz, my son, understands both politics and journalism in ways I don't and has been a steadying hand. His wife, Erica Simmons, has brightened our lives as the newest member of the family. My brother Doug got me into journalism in the first place, and for that alone, no thanks are enough. Thanks also to his wife, Jane Scholz.

The biggest debt I owe is to Nancy, my wife of more than forty years, who seemed to know at every stage of this project whether I needed support, criticism, encouragement, or a gentle shove to stay on schedule. She was good-humored when I was sometimes not, and her love has been a source of sustenance for as long as we've been together.

Notes and Sources

As stated in the note to the reader, quotations in the narrative not otherwise identified are either from interviews with the author (almost all of them digitally recorded) or from events witnessed on the campaign trail. In reporting this book, I had access to countless transcripts of candidate debates, convention addresses, press conferences, speeches, and other events as described. I have tried to cite the time and place of those events in the narrative but for obvious space reasons do not list all of them here in the source notes.

BOOK ONE: THE PIVOT

23   **"As Obama approached the fourth year":** David Maraniss, *Barack Obama: The Story* (New York: Simon & Schuster, 2012), xxi.

24   **The *Washington Post*'s Scott Wilson:** Scott Wilson, "Obama, the Loner President," *Washington Post*, October 7, 2011, http://articles.washingtonpost.com/2011-10-07/opinions /35280751_1_president-obama-politics-obama-administration.

25   **One of the most thoughtful efforts:** James T. Kloppenberg, *Reading Obama: Dreams, Hope, and the American Political Tradition* (Princeton, NJ: Princeton University Press, 2011), Kindle edition, Loc 2 of 302.

29   **In their revealing biography:** Michael Kranish and Scott Helman, *The Real Romney* (New York: HarperCollins, 2011), 7.

30   **"he preferred eating only the tops":** Ibid., 5.

32   **"My son said that having Senator Kennedy":** Ibid., 276.

47   ***New York Times* columnist David Brooks:** David Brooks, "Convener in Chief," *New York Times*, June 27, 2011, http://www.nytimes.com/2011/06/28/opinion/28brooks.html?_r=0.

47   **That spring, an unnamed official:** Ryan Lizza, "The Consequentialist," *New Yorker*, May 2, 2011, http://www.newyorker.com/reporting/2011/05/02/110502fa_fact_lizza.

49   **"You'll remember this as the day":** Robert Draper, *Do Not Ask What Good We Do: Inside the U.S. House of Representatives* (New York: Free Press, 2012), Kindle edition, Loc 229 of 8039.

61   **Bill McInturff, one of the nation's:** Dan Balz, "Debt-Ceiling Debate's Negative Implications for 2012 Elections," *Washington Post*, August 31, 2011, http://articles.washingtonpost.com /2011-08-31/politics/35270526_1_president-obama-and-republicans-analysis-confidence.

62   **One article in particular:** Drew Westen, "What Happened to Obama?," *New York Times*, August 6, 2011, http://www.nytimes.com/2011/08/07/opinion/sunday/what-happened-to-obamas -passion.html?pagewanted=all&_r=0.

64   **"While many folks here are flattered":** "Welcome, Mr. President," *Dubuque Telegraph Herald*, August 16, 2011.

64   **On his second day:** Eileen Mozinski Schmidt, "Obama in Iowa," *Dubuque Telegraph Herald*, August 17, 2011.

64   **The *New York Times*' Mark Landler:** Mark Landler, "Far from Capital, Obama Still Finds Its Woes," *New York Times*, August 17, 2011, http://www.nytimes.com/2011/08/18/us/politics /18obama.html?_r=0.

64   **At his last stop:** Jeff Zeleny, "Obama, on Midwest Tour, Moves to Regain Mantle of Campaigner," *New York Times*, August 18, 2011, http://www.nytimes.com/2011/08/19/us/politics /19memo.html?_r=0.

66   **"It was distressing"**: "Oh, Grow Up," *New York Times*, September 1, 2011, http://www.ny times.com/2011/09/02/opinion/oh-grow-up.html?_r=0.

69   **"Mr. Boehner, Mr. McConnell"**: Jack Brammer and Kelsey Sheridan, "At Ohio River Bridge, Obama Calls Out McConnell, Boehner on Jobs," *Lexington Herald-Leader*, September 23, 2011, http://www.mcclatchydc.com/2011/09/23/125034/at-ohio-river-bridge-obama-calls.html.

70   **One blog, created by a pair:** *We Are the 99 Percent,* http://wearethe99percent.tumblr.com/.

70   ***Mother Jones* magazine:** Adam Weinstein, "'We Are the 99 Percent' Creators Revealed," motherjones.com, October 7, 2011, http://www.motherjones.com/politics/2011/10/we-are-the-99-percent-creators.

73   **"Obama has gone from a modest favorite":** Nate Silver, "Is Obama Toast? Handicapping the 2012 Election," *New York Times Magazine*, November 6, 2011, http://www.nytimes.com/2011/11/06/magazine/nate-silver-handicaps-2012-election.html?pagewanted=all&_r=0.

80   **Later that year:** Sasha Issenberg, "How President Obama's Campaign Used Big Data to Rally Individual Voters," *MIT Technology Review*, December 19, 2012, http://www.technologyreview.com/featuredstory/509026/how-obamas-team-used-big-data-to-rally-voters/.

83   **They consulted with:** Benedict Carey, "Academic 'Dream Team' Helped Obama's Effort," *New York Times*, November 12, 2012, http://www.nytimes.com/2012/11/13/health/dream-team-of-behavioral-scientists-advised-obama-campaign.html?pagewanted=all.

BOOK TWO: THE REPUBLICANS

87   **One clip showed Romney saying grace:** To view the video, go to http://www.gather.com/viewVideo.action?id=11821949021852363.

89   **"State auditors, county commissioners":** Nicholas Confessore and Ashley Parker, "Romney, Always Campaigning for Others . . . and for Himself," *New York Times*, November 5, 2011, http://www.nytimes.com/2011/11/06/us/politics/mitt-romney-campaigns-tirelessly-and-not-just-for-himself.html?pagewanted=all.

94   **"Romney had accomplished":** Ryan Lizza, "Romney's Dilemma," *New Yorker*, June, 6, 2011, http://www.newyorker.com/reporting/2011/06/06/110606fa_fact_lizza?currentPage=all.

96   **The morning of the speech:** Editorial, "Obama's Running Mate," *Wall Street Journal*, May 12, 2011, http://online.wsj.com/article/SB10001424052748703864204576317413439329644.html.

97   **The next morning:** Untitled Romney letter to the editor, *Wall Street Journal*, May 13, 2011, http://professional.wsj.com/article/SB10001424052748703730804576319660196107724.html?mod=WSJ_Opinion_AboveLEFTTop&mg=reno-wsj.

97   **"The likely Republican presidential candidate":** Editorial, "Romney's Daredevil Act," *Wall Street Journal*, May 13, 2011, http://online.wsj.com/article/SB1000142405274870386420457631931274376234.html.

100   **In the first year of Obama's presidency:** Sam Tanenhaus, *The Death of Conservatism* (New York: Random House, 2009), Kindle edition, Loc 4 of 127.

101   **"President Obama, are you listening?":** Video of CNBC's Rick Santelli, February 19, 2009, http://www.youtube.com/watch?v=bEZB4taSEoA.

101   **Some scholars saw it:** Alan Abramowitz, "Partisan Polarization and the Rise of the Tea Party Movement," prepared for the American Political Science Association Annual Meeting, September 2011.

101   **Others described it:** Gary Jacobson, "The President, the Tea Party, and Voting Behavior in 2010," prepared for the American Political Science Association Annual Meeting, September 2011.

102   **Still others noted:** Nicole C. Rae, "The Return of Conservative Populism: The Rise of the Tea Party and Its Impact on American Politics," prepared for the American Political Science Association Annual Meeting, September 2011.

103   **In the summer of 2012:** Dan Balz and Jon Cohen, "Big Gulf Between Parties, Divisions Within," *Washington Post*, August 18, 2012, http://articles.washingtonpost.com/2012-08-18/politics/35492941_1_democratic-party-fractious-coalitions-gop-coalition.

108   **In another case:** Andrew Ferguson, "The Boy from Yazoo City," *Weekly Standard* 16, no. 15 (December 27, 2010), http://www.weeklystandard.com/articles/boy-yazoo-city_523551.html.

110   **"I take a little umbrage":** Karen Tumulty interview with Mike Huckabee, transcript of interview shared with the author.

111   **"Instead of throwing red meat":** Karen Tumulty, "Does Mike Huckabee Still Want to Be President?," *Washington Post,* February 21, 2011, http://www.washingtonpost.com/wp-dyn/content/article/2011/02/20/AR2011022003760.html.

111   **She turned to Jason Recher:** To view the video, go to http://www.youtube.com/watch?v=eO5pzipR6uc.

112   **In the video, Palin said:** "Full Text of Sarah Palin's Statement," Politico.com, January 12, 2011, http://www.politico.com/news/stories/0111/47478.html.

115   **In January 2010, Daniels:** A fuller account of this meeting is contained in Tom Bevan and Carl Cannon's e-book *Election 2012: The Battle Begins* (New York: Crown, 2012), Kindle edition, Loc 1206 of 2342.

118   **Christie was born in Newark:** Almanac of American Politics, http://www.nationaljournal.com/almanac/member/1782.

119   **"He was indisputably":** Ibid.

120   **As talk of a candidacy continued:** Andy Barr, "Chris Christie: 'Zero Chance' for 2012 Bid," Politico.com, November 4, 2010, http://www.politico.com/news/stories/1110/44712.html.

128   **Former Minnesota senator David Durenberger:** Graydon Royce, "A Mix of Boyish Charm and Drive That Found a Purpose," *Minneapolis Star Tribune,* October 20, 2006.

129   **"Not because he was negative":** Ibid.

130   **On one occasion:** Brian Montopoli, "Sarah Palin, Michele Bachmann Rally Thousands in Minneapolis," CBSnews.com, April 7, 2010, http://www.cbsnews.com/8301-503544_162-20001959-503544.html.

131   **CNBC's Lawrence Kudlow:** Larry Kudlow, "Pawlenty 5 Percent Growth Vision," Town-hallFinance.com, http://finance.townhall.com/columnists/larrykudlow/2011/06/11/pawlenty_5_percent_growth_vision.

131   **Jack Welch, the former CEO:** Abby W. Schachter, "Pawlenty Boring? Not When He Envisions 5 Percent Growth," *New York Post,* June 10, 2011, http://www.nypost.com/p/blogs/capitol/pawlenty_boring_not_when_he_envisions_1Zmbl3s31XUfEk3JFijvdI.

136   **Veteran reporter Walter Shapiro:** Walter Shapiro, "The New Hampshire Debate: Michele Bachmann's Surprisingly Mature Performance," NewRepublic.com, June 14, 2011, http://www.tnr.com/article/politics/89944/new-hampshire-debate-michele-bachmann.

136   **"His job description is debate coach":** Amy Gardner, "The Candidate Whisperer: The Man Behind Michele Bachmann," *Washington Post,* September 21, 2011, http://articles.washingtonpost.com/2011-09-21/lifestyle/35274117_1_bachmann-team-michele-bachmann-debate-coach.

138   **The *Register*'s Jennifer Jacobs wrote:** Jennifer Jacobs, "Iowa Poll: Bachmann in Lead; Cain Third; Others Find Little Traction," *Des Moines Register,* June 25, 2011, http://caucuses.desmoinesregister.com/2011/06/25/iowa-poll-romney-bachmann-in-lead-cain-third-others-find-little-traction/.

143   **The *Dallas Morning News* reported:** "50 Things You Need to Know About Texas Gov. Rick Perry," *Dallas Morning News,* October 11, 2010, http://www.dallasnews.com/news/politics/state-politics/20101011-50-things-you-need-to-know-about-texas-gov.-rick-perry.ece.

144   **His mother made his clothes:** Mark Z. Barabak, "Rick Perry Has a History of Acrimony with George W. Bush," *Los Angeles Times,* June 30, 2011, http://articles.latimes.com/print/2011/jun/30/nation/la-na-0630-perry-bush-20110630.

144   **He was an Eagle Scout:** "50 Things You Need to Know About Texas Gov. Rick Perry."

156   **Jay Root of the *Texas Tribune*:** Jay Root, *Oops: A Diary from the 2012 Campaign Trail* (San Francisco: Byliner, 2012), Kindle edition, Loc 3051 of 3136.

161   **On the night of October 30:** Jonathan Martin, Maggie Haberman, Anna Palmer, and Kenneth P. Vogel, "Herman Cain Accused by Two Women of Inappropriate Behavior," Politico.com, October 30, 2011, http://www.politico.com/news/stories/1011/67194.html.

162 **Cain's lawyer appeared to contradict:** Brian Montopoli, "Herman Cain 'Reassessing' Candidacy After Affair Claim," CBSnews.com, November 29, 2011, http://www.cbsnews.com/8301-503544_162-57332967-503544/herman-cain-reassessing-candidacy-after-affair-claim/.

162 **Four days after White made her statement:** John DiStaso, "Cain: Wife Didn't Know About Friendship, 'Financial Assistance' to Ginger White," *New Hampshire Union Leader,* December 1, 2011, http://www.unionleader.com/article/20111201/NEWS0605/111209989.

166 **"We went through the two worst months":** Karen Tumulty, "Newt Gingrich: GOP's Consummate Survivor Is Back on His Feet," *Washington Post,* October 29, 2011, http://articles.washingtonpost.com/2011-10-29/politics/35277681_1_newt-gingrich-chick-fil-a-herman-cain.

169 **"I think he's making a big mistake":** Jonathan Martin, "Iowa Governor Terry Branstad to Mitt Romney: 'Iowans Don't Like to Be Ignored,'" Politico.com, November 16, 2011, http://www.politico.com/news/stories/1111/68489.html.

172 **Ten of those committees:** R. Sam Garrett, "Super PACs in Federal Elections: Overview and Issues for Congress," Congressional Research Service, October 6, 2011, http://op.bna.com/der.nsf/id/rtar-8n6pkq/$File/Super%20Pacs%20in%20Federal%20Elections.pdf.

173 **"This isn't a year-and-a-half campaign":** Richard A. Oppel Jr., "Paul's 'Ground Game,' in Place Since '08, Gives Him an Edge," *New York Times,* December 16, 2011, http://www.nytimes.com/2011/12/17/us/politics/ron-pauls-ground-game-gives-him-an-edge.html?pagewanted=all.

178 **Then came this paragraph:** "Romney Leads Paul in New Des Moines Register Iowa Poll; Santorum Surges," *Des Moines Register,* December 31, 2011, http://caucuses.desmoinesregister.com/2011/12/31/romney-leads-paul-in-new-des-moines-register-iowa-poll-santorum-surging/.

186 **"If he wants to counterbalance":** Nicholas Confessore and Eric Lipton, "A Big Check, and Gingrich Gets a Big Lift," *New York Times,* January 9, 2012, http://www.nytimes.com/2012/01/10/us/politics/sheldon-adelson-a-billionaire-gives-gingrich-a-big-lift.html?pagewanted=all&_r=0.

187 **The *New Yorker's* Steve Coll:** Steve Coll, "The Truth in 'King of Bain,'" *New Yorker* blog, January 19, 2012, http://www.newyorker.com/online/blogs/comment/2012/01/romney-king-of-bain.html?printable=true&currentPage=all.

190 **When a woman in the audience:** Jim Rutenberg and Ashley Parker, "As Attacks Heat Up, Romney's Lead Narrows in S.C.," *New York Times,* January 18, 2012, http://www.nytimes.com/2012/01/19/us/romneys-lead-narrows-in-south-carolina-as-negative-advertising-heats-up.html?pagewanted=all.

195 **Later, as he rode up the elevator:** Philip Rucker, "Which Romney Will Show Up After Defeat?," *Washington Post,* January 21, 2012, http://articles.washingtonpost.com/2012-01-21/politics/35441333_1_mitt-romney-enterprise-and-economic-freedom-guest-laundry-room.

195 **Gingrich, greeted with chants:** Jim Rutenberg, "Gingrich Wins South Carolina Primary, Upending G.O.P. Race," *New York Times,* January 21, 2012, http://www.nytimes.com/2012/01/22/us/politics/south-carolina-republican-primary.html?pagewanted=all&_r=0.

197 ***Politico's* Reid Epstein:** Reid J. Epstein, "Mitt Romney: Newt Gingrich Is a 'Failed Leader,' 'Disgrace,'" Politico.com, January 22, 2012, http://www.politico.com/news/stories/0112/71802.html.

211 **Those comments came:** "Excerpt from Santorum Interview," *USA Today,* April 23, 2003, http://usatoday30.usatoday.com/news/washington/2003-04-23-santorum-excerpt_x.htm.

222 **"We're giving the Democrats":** Joe Hallett and David Eggert, "Front-Runners Busy on Final Day Before Primary," *Columbus Dispatch,* March 6, 2012, http://www.dispatch.com/content/stories/local/2012/03/06/supershowdown-front-runners-busy-on-final-day.html.

227 **Republican pollster Bill McInturff:** Mark Murray, "NBC/WSJ Poll: Primary Season Takes 'Corrosive' Toll on GOP and Its Candidates, NBCNews.com, March 4, 2012, http://firstread.nbcnews.com/_news/2012/03/04/10578249-nbcwsj-poll-primary-season-takes-corrosive-toll-on-gop-and-its-candidates?lite.

232 **"The 160 pages and 59 proposals":** Editorial, "Mitt Romney's 59 Economic Flavors," *Wall Street Journal,* September 7, 2011, http://online.wsj.com/article/SB10001424053111904537404576554692126810066.html.

BOOK THREE: THE CHOICE

240 **The *Economist* magazine:** "An Intractable Problem Is Getting Worse," *Economist,* October 1, 2011.

242 **William Frey, one of the nation's:** William H. Frey, "The 2010 Census: America on the Cusp," *Millken Institute Review,* Second Quarter 2012, http://www.milkeninstitute.org/publications/review/2012_4/47-58MR54.pdf.

243 **Frey sketched out Romney's challenge:** William H. Frey, "Why Minorities Will Decide the 2012 Election," Brookings Institution, May 2012, http://www.brookings.edu/research/opinions/2012/05/01-race-elections-frey.

244 **Gary Jacobson of the University of California:** Gary Jacobson, "Barack Obama and the American Public: The First 18 Months," prepared for the American Political Science Association Annual Meeting, September 2010.

244 **In 1976, about a quarter:** Bill Bishop with Robert Cushing, *The Big Sort: Why the Clustering of Like-Minded America Is Tearing Us Apart* (New York: Houghton Mifflin/Mariner Books, 2009), 10, 305–6.

245 **A Pew Research Center study:** "Partisan Polarization Surges in Bush, Obama Years: Trends in American Values: 1987–2012," Pew Research Center, June 4, 2012, http://www.people-press.org/2012/06/04/partisan-polarization-surges-in-bush-obama-years/.

245 **The summer 2012 study:** Dan Balz and Jon Cohen, "Big Gulf Between Political Parties, Divisions Within," *Washington Post,* August 18, 2012, http://articles.washingtonpost.com/2012-08-18/politics/35492941_1_democratic-party-fractious-coalitions-gop-coalition.

248 **He urged everyone he knew:** Michael Luo, "99 Weeks Later, Jobless Have Only Desperation," *New York Times,* August 2, 2010, http://www.nytimes.com/2010/08/03/us/03unemployed.html?_r=0.

251 **Ed Rendell, the former governor:** Zeke Miller, "Is This Obama's Party?," Buzzfeed.com, May 22, 2012, http://www.buzzfeed.com/zekejmiller/is-this-obamas-party.

255 **On June 21, the *Washington Post*:** Tom Hamburger, "Romney's Bain Capital Invested in Companies That Moved Jobs Overseas," *Washington Post,* June 21, 2012, http://articles.washingtonpost.com/2012-06-21/politics/35460959_1_american-jobs-private-equity-firm-employment.

257 **In July a *Boston Globe* story:** Callum Borchers and Christopher Rowland, "Romney Stayed Longer at Bain," *Boston Globe,* July 12, 2012, http://www.boston.com/news/politics/articles/2012/07/12/government_documents_indicate_mitt_romney_continued_at_bain_after_date_when_he_says_he_left/?page=full.

257 **The next morning, Obama was interviewed:** "Obama: Romney Not Necessarily Qualified to Think About 'Economy as a Whole,'" CBSnews.com, July 13, 2012, http://www.cbsnews.com/8301-505267_162-57471664/obama-romney-not-necessarily-qualified-to-think-about-economy-as-a-whole/.

257 **Romney went on Fox News:** "Romney Calls 'Felony' Remark 'Beneath the Dignity' of Presidency, Urges Obama to 'Rein in' Team," FoxNews.com, July 13, 2012, http://www.foxnews.com/politics/2012/07/13/romney-calls-felony-remark-beneath-dignity-presidency-urges-obama-to-rein-in/.

262 **"The political science research":** John Sides, "Were Obama's Early Ads Really the Game Changer?," *FiveThirtyEight* blog, *New York Times,* December 29, 2012, http://fivethirtyeight.blogs.nytimes.com/2012/12/29/were-obamas-early-ads-really-the-game-changer/.

263 **Sherry Magner, a pharmacy clerk:** Philip Rucker, "As Romney, Ryan Campaign Across Wisconsin, 'Chemistry' and Talk of a Ticket," Washington Post, April 4, 2012, http://www.washingtonpost.com/politics/as-romney-and-ryan-campaign-across-wisconsin-chemistry-and-talk-of-a-ticket/2012/04/04/gIQAB4sCvS_story_1.html.

270 **The *New York Post*, citing sources:** Josh Margolin and Beth Defalco, "Christie Chose NJ over Mitt's VP Role Due to Fears That They'd Lose: Sources," New York Post, August 27, 2012, http://www.nypost.com/p/news/national/christie_had_veeping_doubts_b1gkN5io8CtDgcuiuEgMqL.

271 **In addition, then-representative Dave Rivera:** Chris Cillizza, "Could David Rivera Cost Marco Rubio the Vice Presidency?" *Washington Post,* May 1, 2012, http://www.washington

post.com/blogs/the-fix/post/could-david-rivera-keep-marco-rubio-from-the-vice-presidency/
2012/05/01/gIQAVYSauT_blog.html.

273 **A *Guardian* writer dubbed:** Rachel Shabi, "Mitt Romney's Insult-the-World Tour Excels in Picking on the Palestinians," *Guardian,* July 31, 2012, http://www.guardian.co.uk/commentisfree/2012/jul/31/mitt-romney-world-tour-palestinians.

274 **The *Weekly Standard* had put:** Stephen F. Hayes, "Man with a Plan: How Paul Ryan Became the Intellectual Leader of the Republican Party," *Weekly Standard* 17, no. 42 (July 23, 2012), http://www.weeklystandard.com/articles/man-plan_648570.html.

274 ***National Review*'s Rich Lowry:** Rich Lowry, "Don't Fear Paul Ryan," *New York Post,* August 9, 2012, http://www.nypost.com/p/news/opinion/opedcolumnists/don_fear_paul_ryan_ykQKQgfNTms4EZVtXr9FAJ.

284 **He learned that David liked fireworks:** Larry Bivins, "Vermont Couple Give Romney Testimonial at GOP Convention Tonight," *Burlington Free Press,* August 30, 2012, http://www.burlingtonfreepress.com/article/20120830/NEWS03/308300029/Vermont-couple-to-give-Romney-testimonial-at-GOP-convention-tonight.

294 **Within minutes of his posting:** David Corn, "The Story Behind the 47 Percent Video," MotherJones.com, December 31, 2012, http://www.motherjones.com/politics/2012/12/story-behind-47-video.

298 ***New York Times* columnist:** David Brooks, "Thurston Howell Romney," *New York Times,* September 17, 2012, http://www.nytimes.com/2012/09/18/opinion/brooks-thurston-howell-romney.html.

298 ***Wall Street Journal* columnist:** Peggy Noonan, "Time for an Intervention," *Wall Street Journal,* September 18, 2012, http://blogs.wsj.com/peggynoonan/2012/09/18/time-for-an-intervention/.

299 **Romney taped an interview:** "Romney: My Campaign Doesn't Need a Turnaround," transcript, CBSnews.com, September 21, 2012, http://www.cbsnews.com/8301-18560_162-57518137/romney-my-campaign-doesnt-need-a-turnaround/.

319 **A cartoon by Rob Rogers:** Rob Rogers, "Electoral Map," *Pittsburgh Post-Gazette,* October 23, 2012, http://blogs.post-gazette.com/opinion/rob-rogers-cartoons/35850-electoral-map.

321 **The writer Susan Orlean:** Matt Weiland and Sean Wilsey, eds., *State by State: A Panoramic Portrait of America* (New York: Ecco, 2008), 360.

321 **An analysis by the Bliss Institute:** "Basic Information on Ohio Politics #2: The 'Five Ohios,'" Bliss Institute, University of Akron, undated, http://www.uakron.edu/bliss/research/biop-2-the-five-ohios.dot.

328 **Taylor Havens told a *Denver Post* photographer:** The quote is taken from a video prepared by the *Denver Post.* To view video, go to: http://www.denverpost.com/ci_21839256/romney-ryan-rally-at-red-rocks.

333 **An analysis of Ohio voting statistics:** Brent Larkin, "Surge of Black Voters Wasn't Romney's Undoing," *Cleveland Plain Dealer,* March 9, 2013, http://www.cleveland.com/opinion/index.ssf/2013/03/surge_of_black_votes_wasnt_rom.html.

334 **The historical average had been:** Bill Bishop, "Finding the 'Flippers' in 2012 Vote," DailyYonder.com, January 1, 2013, http://www.dailyyonder.com/finding-flippers-2012-vote/2012/12/26/5560.

334 **Alan Abramowitz, a political scientist:** Alan Abramowitz, "The Emerging Democratic Presidential Majority: Lessons of Obama's Victory," prepared for the Southern Political Science Association Meeting, January 2013.

337 **And then they waited:** Glenn Thrush and Jonathan Martin, *The End of the Line,* Politico.com e-book (New York: Random House, 2012), 7.

EPILOGUE: INTO THE FUTURE

349 **America was still divided:** Alan Abramowitz, "The Emerging Democratic Presidential Majority: Lessons of Obama's Victory," prepared for the Southern Political Science Association Annual Meeting, January 2013.

349 **Conservatives dominated the Republican Party:** William Galston, "The 2012 Election: What Happened, What Changed, What It Means," Brookings Institution, January 4, 2013, http://www.brookings.edu/research/papers/2013/01/04-presidential-election-galston.

Index

The Battle for America
The Story of an Extraordinary Election

Dan Balz and Haynes Johnson

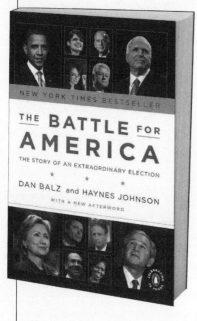

ISBN 978-0-14-311770-4

The election of 2008 shattered political barriers and ignited an extraordinary battle among some of the most formidable political rivals ever to seek the presidency. Named as one of the Best Books of the Year by the *Washington Post* and the *Los Angeles Times*, this gripping account of 2008's landmark election offers the first complete picture of the strategies—and singular personalities—that accompanied the 2008 candidates' first campaign forays through Obama's historic victory. Updated through 2009, *The Battle of America* is filled with insider details and captures the attention of everyone who witnessed it, as well as future generations who wished they had.

PENGUIN
BOOKS